No. 2811
$27.95

ADD A ROOM
A PRACTICAL GUIDE TO
EXPANDING YOUR HOME

PAUL BIANCHINA

TAB BOOKS Inc.
Blue Ridge Summit, PA 17214

For Rose—my critic, my friend,
my insightful editor, my patient inspiration

Notices

Fixall is a registered trademark of Dowman Products Inc.
Freon, Teflon, and Tyvek are registered trademarks of E.I. Du Pont de Nemours & Co.
Durabond is a registered trademark of Durabond Division of USG Industries, Inc.
Romex is a registered trademark of GK Technologies Inc.
Sheetrock is a registered trademark of U.S. Gypsum Co.
Styrofoam is a registered trademark of Dow Chemical USA.

FIRST EDITION
FIRST PRINTING

Copyright © 1987 by TAB BOOKS Inc.
Printed in the United States of America

Library of Congress Cataloging in Publication Data

Bianchina, Paul.
Add a room.

Includes index.
1. Dwellings—Remodeling. 2. House
construction. I. Title.
TH4816.B52 1987   643'.7   87-1954

ISBN 0-8306-1311-0
ISBN 0-8306-2811-8 (pbk.)

Questions regarding the content of this book
should be addressed to:

Reader Inquiry Branch
Editorial Department
TAB BOOKS Inc.
P.O. Box 40
Blue Ridge Summit, PA 17214

Contents

Acknowledgments

I wish to extend my deep appreciation to the following individuals, manufacturers, and organizations for their tremendous help in preparing this book. I am especially grateful to Rose Bianchina, for her patient and skillful editing, and to Mr. Jack Merry of the American Plywood Association and Ms. Judith A. London of Stanley Tools for all of the material they provided.

Andersen Corporation, Bayport, MN
Armstrong World Industries, Inc., Lancaster, PA
Asphalt Roofing Manufacturers Association, Rockville, MD
Brick Institute of America, Reston, VA
Cellulose Industry Standards Enforcement Program, Dayton, OH
Celotex Corporation, Tampa, FL
Channellock, Inc., Meadville, PA
David White Instruments, A Division of Realist, Inc., Menomonee Falls, WI
Dow Chemical USA, Midland, MI
Foundation of the Wall and Ceiling Industry, Washington, DC
Georgia-Pacific, Atlanta, GA
KC Metal Products, Inc., San Jose, CA
Manina, Steve, General Contractor, Manina Construction, Sacramento, CA
Masonite Corporation, Chicago, IL
Maze Nails, W.H. Maze Co., Peru, IL
National Concrete Masonry Association, Herndon, VA
National Electrical Manufacturers Association, Washington, DC
National Forest Products Association, Washington, DC
National Oak Flooring Association, Memphis, TN
National Paint & Coatings Association, Inc., Washington, DC
Nibco, Inc., Elkhart, IN
Owens-Corning Fiberglas Corporation, Toledo, OH
Red Cedar Shingle & Handsplit Shake Bureau, Bellevue, WA
Senco Products, Inc., Cincinnati, OH
Skil Corporation, Chicago, IL

Stanley Tools, Division of The Stanley Works, New Britain, CT

The Trane Company, Tyler, TX

United States Department of Agriculture, Forest Service, Forest Products Laboratory, Madison, WI

United States Gypsum Co., Baltimore, MD

Velux-America Inc., Greenwood, SC

Western Wood Products Association, Portland, OR

Wood Moulding & Millwork Producers Association, Portland, OR

Wood Truss Council of America, Glen Ellyn, IL

Wykes, R. Thomas, Energy Extension Agent, Oregon State University Energy Extension, Bend, OR

Introduction

Whether it's new bedrooms for a growing family, a sorely needed second bathroom, a bigger kitchen for a budding chef, or a place to put the new pool table, sooner or later every homeowner faces an important question: to move to a larger home or to expand the existing one. In some cases, a new home might be the only answer. For many, however, and for a wide variety of reasons, room additions make sense.

A recent United Press International article on remodeling observed that a $10,000 addition will increase the value of an $85,000 house to over $100,000—overnight. The return is immediate, beginning from the moment the last nail is driven. So, in terms of investment value, a room addition can easily be a better bet than stocks, bonds, or anything else you choose to do with your money. After all, where else can you double your investment in 30 to 60 days?

Investment, however, is only one of the many reasons to choose an addition over a move to a bigger house. Perhaps you don't want to move the children to a new neighborhood and a new school; perhaps the interest rate you have on your present house is more attractive than that on a new house, or your house is already paid for; maybe you can't find exactly what you want in another house; or maybe you just can't bring yourself to leave the apple tree you planted in the back yard, the one that's just now beginning to bear fruit. Whatever your reasons are, this book is here to help.

With this book, you'll walk through all the steps, from the first gleam of an idea to the very last nail. You'll learn how to ask yourself questions that will define your needs. You'll discover some planning options, and see what's right for you. You'll see how to turn the dreams and ideas into practical plans. Finally, whether you've been itching to swing a hammer yourself or plan to have a contractor do all the work, you'll learn how it's all put together, from the foundation to the roof.

If you've made the decision to expand, or even if you're still in the thinking stage and need a little extra push, this is the book for you. A little at a time, refining your ideas and your skills as you go, you'll achieve an addition that looks as though it's meant to be there. And that's the real goal of this book: to guide you in creating an attractive, logical expansion of your home's living space that will increase the value of your home and enhance your lifestyle for years to come!

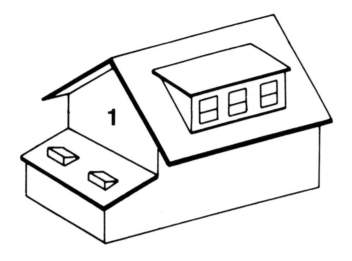

Evaluation and Planning

Every successful room addition project, like any remodeling, begins with good planning. Deciding what you want, what you need, how much you can afford—these and many other questions need to be answered before the first pencil line is drawn on the plans. In this chapter, you'll guide yourself through these important questions and answers, refining your needs and evaluating what's practical, both for you and for your home.

Begin by sitting down with some paper and a pencil. Ask yourself the following questions, then really take some time to evaluate the answers you've written down. Involve the entire family in this evaluation and decision-making process. It's fun, and it'll provide you with some valuable insight.

WHAT DO YOU NEED?

As basic as this seems, it's necessary to really question what you need out of a room addition. Your answers can eliminate costly, unneeded space while ensuring that your family's real needs are being met. Since you're considering adding space to your home, you probably already have specific needs in mind. Now is the time to write them down.

First, what exactly are your needs? Will this new space serve a growing family? If so, are you adding one or more bedrooms? Will you also need one or more additional bathrooms? Except for a kitchen, a bathroom is the costliest room to add to a house. The extensive plumbing requirements and the cost of all the fixtures make it an expensive room if it's not really needed. On the other hand, nothing is more inconvenient than a house without enough bathrooms, so if a new one is important, write it down.

Perhaps the addition will serve to accommodate a larger kitchen. As I mentioned earlier, a kitchen is the most expensive of all rooms to add, simply because of the amount of cabinetry and equipment it houses. If a new kitchen is your goal, you'll need to look closely at what you need. Are you looking for more counter space? If so, how much? Do you need room for specific work areas, such as a baking center? Do you have your eye on new appliances that require a large amount of space or special hookups, such as some of the commercial fixtures now finding their way into more and more residential kitchens?

Another popular reason for adding space is the desire for a family, game, or hobby room (Fig. 1-1). If this is your goal, there are several things to take into consideration. Will the room be serving a special purpose, such as housing a pool table, and therefore need to be a certain size? Will it contain a wet bar, cooking or refrigeration facilities, or other appliances or fixtures that require special spaces or connections? Will special provisions need to be made for stereo, television, computer, or other electronic hookups? What about a built-in desk, worktables, shelving, or other hobby or work areas—perhaps a darkroom, which requires a light-tight area with running water, or a painting studio that you'd like to flood with natural light?

Other add-on spaces with their own special requirements would be a garage, a workshop, or a combination of both. How many cars will need to be accommodated? What about an RV or boat? Will your shop require special electrical hookups for machinery, welding equipment, or an air compressor? How about storage for lumber or metal stock? Once again, work and assembly tables, space for painting, or other special use areas might be desirable. If the shop area is to be used for any sort of commercial enterprise, are there any city, county, or state restrictions that apply, or any special requirements for ventilation, sanitation, or fire safety that you need to include in your plans?

In these energy-conscious times, maybe you're thinking about a sunspace to help with your heating bills. Can you get the necessary solar orientation? What special ventilation needs must be met, both for getting heat to the house in winter and from the sunspace in summer? Will you need special window coverings or landscaping to shade the room in the summer?

In addition to the many considerations about the added space itself, have you considered whether it might be advantageous to do some other remodeling or repairs at the same time? Perhaps your home needs reroofing. You'll get a better price on the job if you have the contractors do it while they're roofing the addition. Maybe you need to add insulation, update your electrical wiring, replace some carpeting, or repaint. Whatever your home needs, it's wise to get it all done at once if possible. Prices will be lower; you save yourself some mess and inconvenience later; and if you're borrowing money to build the addition, the other work often can be covered under the same loan.

TAKE A LOOK AT YOUR LIFESTYLE

While the family's together and ideas are flying, take a moment to evaluate your lifestyle. This often overlooked consideration sometimes can make a big difference in getting the addition you really want and need.

For example, does your family entertain a lot? If the answer is yes, you might consider the need for extra kitchen facilities, such as a built-in barbecue, a wet bar, or a second sink. Maybe an expanded dining area would be helpful, or a kitchen eating area for the children to use when you entertain in the dining room. If you have a lot of out-of-town guests, a guest room with its own bath might be ideal. If you have or are adding a swimming pool or spa, adding a separate shower and dressing area can save a lot of wear and tear on the bathrooms in the house. Some other considerations for the avid entertainer might be outdoor lighting, backyard seating and table space, a gazebo, a patio enclosure, or a built-in video entertainment center.

Does your family have special hobbies? If so, you might plan your new space to accommodate a ham radio center, a complete computer room, your home wine-making operation, a painting or photography studio, a growing model railroad layout, a darkroom, or even a ceramic workshop complete with kiln. The possibilities are endless, and giving some thought to your hobbies when planning an addition can enhance your enjoyment of them tremendously.

Are there just one or two people in your home? If your home environment is especially important and your entertainment needs are few, consider a whole wall to house all of your audio and video

Fig. 1-1. Adding space can create the living room or family room you've always wanted (Courtesy of American Plywood Association).

3

equipment. In one convenient area, you can group your television, stereo, VCR, video games—the works! Add a couple of easy chairs and you've got an area made for relaxation. You might think about an expanded master bedroom suite, complete with a lavish bathroom. A home sauna, a steam room, a whirlpool spa—all this and much more might be just what you need to suit a predominantly stay-at-home lifestyle.

How about teenagers or perhaps small children? Specialized game and entertainment rooms for them and their friends might be well worth considering. This is also the time to take another look at your needs for an extra bathroom, an expanded kitchen, a practical laundry room, and even small, easily overlooked items like extra telephone, stereo, and television jacks.

Taking the time to study and honestly evaluate your lifestyle can go a long way toward making your expanded living space practical and enjoyable for everyone. Remember, at this early planning stage, no consideration is too small or unimportant.

EVALUATING YOUR EXISTING HOUSE

As your ideas and needs begin to become clearer, the next step is to determine what's realistic for your home. Some homes lend themselves quite naturally to extending out, while some, either because of space limitations or architectural design, are best served by extending up. Still other types of homes easily encompass both types of additions.

First among your questions and considerations at this point is what type of house you have. Is it a sprawling one-story ranch house that would look awkward with a second story? Is it a two story that could be added to on one or both levels? Do you think you have enough land around you to add out? (More on property line setbacks in Chapter 2.) Does your house have a particular architectural style, such as Tudor or Colonial, that must be accurately matched in order for the addition to blend in (Fig. 1-2)? Are there natural jogs in the home's contour or in the relationship between the floors that would lend themselves to being filled in with new rooms?

Now consider how the interior of your home is

laid out. Are there hallways that serve various rooms? What are the traffic patterns in the house; that is, how does traffic flow between various rooms and areas? How would the addition tie into the existing house to provide access to the new rooms? This is a very important aspect of your planning at this stage. The usefulness of the new space could be diminished greatly if access is awkward, such as a new guest room that can only be reached by going through another bedroom, or a dining room that doesn't have a direct connection to the kitchen.

You'll also want to consider the materials originally used in building your home. Can the siding and roofing be matched, or are they of a style, pattern, color, or material that's no longer available? Are there moldings or other trim that will need to be matched and are no longer available?

As mentioned earlier, take a close look at any repairs, major or minor, that will need to be done in conjunction with the addition. If you have an older home, major updating of the electrical system may be necessary to accommodate the addition (see Chapter 17). If your planned addition includes adding to your plumbing system, you'll need to consider the water pressure available to your house, and, if you're on a septic system, you'll need to determine if it can handle the increased capacity (see Chapter 16).

EVALUATING YOUR NEIGHBORHOOD

One aspect of adding on to your home that's too often ignored is the possibility of "overbuilding" for your neighborhood. Overbuilding occurs when the proposed value of the work being done would necessitate a selling price for the house that is way out of line for the area, virtually ensuring that you will lose money if and when you sell the house. Although the primary reason for adding on is to create needed space, a room addition is also an investment in your home. It pays to look realistically at the value of your home, the cost of the intended addition, and the potential for recovering that cost. You may not have all of the necessary figures at this point in your planning, but as soon as they're available to you, be sure you don't overlook this important financial evaluation.

Fig. 1-2. Careful planning is needed to ensure that the addition blends with the home's existing style, and becomes a part of it (Courtesy of American Plywood Association).

First, you'll want to determine the *fair market value* of your house. This is an approximation of what the home actually could be sold for today, given the cost of similar homes in your area that recently have been sold. (The fair market value might vary considerably from what your home is appraised at for tax purposes.) You may want to consult with a real estate agent who specializes in your area, or at least follow the real estate advertisements in the local newspaper for several weeks to determine the selling price of homes comparable to yours.

Next, you'll need an approximation of what the addition will cost. Add this cost to the fair market value of your home and you'll have a pretty good idea of what your home would have to sell for in order for you to realize a return on your investment.

Finally, look at the selling price of homes in your area that would be comparable to your house after the addition. If you feel that the estimated value of your house with the addition is roughly in line with values in your area, or would be in a relatively short time, then your plans are realistic and you are probably not overbuilding for your area.

EVALUATING YOURSELF

As part of your overall evaluation, it's important to be honest with yourself about your abilities and your weaknesses. This self-assessment will help you decide how much of the addition you realistically can undertake yourself.

Do you feel comfortable with the designing aspect of your addition? Can you put all the various pieces together and come up with rooms that both serve your needs and logically fit your home? Do you have any drafting skills that would allow you to prepare a set of plans?

When it comes to the actual construction of the addition, are you an avid do-it-yourselfer? Do you have most of the tools you need? Are there areas of expertise best subcontracted to others, such as plumbing or electrical wiring? If you decide to act as your own general contractor, will you be comfortable with the tasks of running the job, ordering materials, and hiring and scheduling any necessary subcontractors (Fig. 1-3)?

Another consideration at this point is how much time can you realistically devote to the project? For the typical room addition, a contractor working full time might require 4 to 8 weeks from start to finish. If you're only working nights and weekends on the project, it may take 6 months or longer. This may or may not make a difference to you, but it is worth considering.

By no means should the answers to these questions discourage you from doing as much of the addition as you can. You certainly can save money, sometimes a substantial amount, and you'll have the priceless feeling of pride in what you've accomplished. An honest look, however, can help you avoid taking on more than you can handle, and can help ensure the best possible finished product.

CHOOSING A DESIGNER OR ARCHITECT

If you decide to leave the design aspect of your addition to someone else, there are a few simple guidelines to follow when choosing a designer. First of all, be aware of the difference between an architect and a building designer. An architect typically has a much broader formal education in design and engineering, and is licensed by the state. Both architects and designers usually charge by the hour, and you will pay quite a bit more for an architect.

There are several types of designers, including those who specialize in kitchens and bathrooms, and those who deal mainly with interior design and decoration. For an addition, you typically will be using a building designer. Building designers work primarily with residential projects, both for new homes and remodeling. They are usually well versed in building codes, techniques, and materials, and can blend the creative with the practical.

If your remodeling project is fairly extensive, requiring a lot of structural design work and calculations, you probably would be better off with an architect. For most residential and light commercial additions, however, a building designer is usually the better choice. (See Fig. 1-4.)

The best way to choose a designer or an architect is through word of mouth. Knowing some-

Fig. 1-3. Acting as your own contractor usually involves coordinating a number of subcontractors and other people (Courtesy of Georgia-Pacific Corporation).

one who has used a particular person and was pleased with the results is about the best source you could ask for. Other avenues for obtaining names is through your city or county building department, from contractors or material suppliers, through a professional referral service, from the Better Business Bureau, or through the telephone Yellow Pages.

Initially, set up an informal meeting with the person at his office. Discuss your project in general, and find out if he has done similar work in the past. Some may specialize in areas other than what you have in mind, and might not be suitable for your project. Try to get to know the person, and see if you feel comfortable with him. You'll be working closely with him through what can, at times, be a difficult creative process, and you want someone who will listen to your ideas while offering his. This is your home and your addition, and you don't want to have to deal with someone who is trying to force you to accept his ideas. Finally, agree on a fee, either hourly or for the whole project, and be sure you know exactly what that price includes.

Once the designer or architect has been selected, he'll need to make at least one visit to your home. Provide him with all the information you've put together from your hours of evaluation, and be as specific as possible about exactly what you want. This will help ensure that you get what you want, and will avoid unnecessary hourly design costs. A number of options can be discussed, and then measurements of the house and lot will need to be taken.

Ask the designer to provide you with some

Fig. 1-4. The services of a designer might be helpful in achieving an addition that blends perfectly with the existing house (Courtesy of American Plywood Association).

sketches as soon as possible. You may be charged a little extra for the sketches, but it's better than paying for finished drawings that may not be exactly what you want. When you have agreed on all the design aspects, the designer will prepare a full set of finished drawings. Be sure and ask for at least four copies, which will give you enough for contractors and suppliers to bid from, and also some to submit with your building permit application.

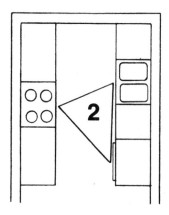

Preliminary Layouts

Having worked through the evaluations and questions of Chapter 1, you now should have a much clearer picture of what your addition will include. If you've decided to do your own design work, now is the time to begin getting specific.

UP OR OUT

As you begin the process of consolidating your ideas and finalizing the design, the obvious first decision is what part of the house to add on to. As mentioned in Chapter 1, your addition might extend out from the existing house or up from it, either adding to an existing second floor or creating an entire new one. It might even be a combination of both. Depending on the existing house and the intended addition, where and how to add on might be obvious. In other cases, both options might be open to you. Each has its own pros and cons, and you need to decide which one is best.

If you choose to extend out, the first consideration is space. Is there enough room for the intended addition? Most areas have specific setback requirements, which limit how close you can build to your property lines. These setbacks are typically 15 to 25 feet in front and back, and 5 to 10 feet on the sides, but they can vary widely among locales. Be sure you check with your local building department or planning commission to determine exactly what the setbacks are for your particular neighborhood.

When extending out, the addition will require a new foundation. You also will need to determine how the roof of the addition will intersect and tie in with the roof on the existing house. Connecting the siding at the point the walls intersect is another consideration.

If you decide to extend up, the floor of the addition is the biggest problem. If you are creating an entirely new second floor, you might encounter two problems. First of all, one-story and two-story houses utilize different sizes of foundations and footings, because of the greater amount of load that the foundation on a two-story house must be able to bear. If the existing foundation is undersized for a second story, it might be necessary to reinforce it. If this appears to be a problem for your addition, it's best to consult with the building officials or an engineer before you proceed with your plans.

The second problem is the size of the existing ceiling joists. In a one-story house, the ceiling joists need only be large enough to support the finish ceiling material that is attached to them. They usually are too small to handle the additional load imposed on them if they must act as floor joists for the second floor. This problem is usually easy to solve by adding new floor joists of the proper size next to the old ceiling joists. Consult Table 10-2 to get an idea of the joist sizes you'll need, and confirm them with the building department.

DECIDING ON SIZES

As your ideas and needs for specific rooms and areas become clearer, it's important to begin thinking in terms of sizes. Bear in mind that adding on a room that's too small to serve its intended use, now or in the future, isn't much better than not having the room at all. On the other hand, creating excessively large rooms is a financial drain for a number of reasons. The larger the addition, the more expensive the initial construction costs will be, and the more you will pay for heating and cooling, taxes and insurance, and even furnishings. Try to keep these two things in mind when considering room sizes, and attempt to strike a happy medium between an addition that's too small to be useful and one that's too large to be practical.

If you have a room that will house an object of a specific size, a pool table for example, you will have a good basis from which to determine the room's ultimate dimensions. (See Fig. 2-1.) Look at the actual size of the table, then consider how much room you'll need to have around it in order to play comfortably. Add space for other furnishings, and you'll be assured of a room that will serve its purpose adequately.

Other rooms also have minimum size requirements. A bathroom, for example, typically requires a wall of at least 5 feet in length to accommodate a bathtub. Toilets and bidets each require approximately 3 feet × 3 feet, and are usually set side by side for convenience in routing the plumbing. In planning a bathroom, it's usually best to ascertain what fixtures will be in the room and what their sizes are, and use those required spaces as a minimum. Additional room then can be allocated as space within the addition permits, helping you avoid a room that's too cramped.

A common mistake when planning the overall size of an addition is to simply add up the sizes of the rooms you want the addition to contain. This method overlooks two basic considerations that need to be planned for: storage space and access. Say, for example, that you have decided your new guest bedroom will be 12 feet × 12 feet, and that it will fit nicely next to your 12-×-16 game room. The bedroom will require a closet, perhaps 2 × 6. To take 2 feet off the length of the room might make the bedroom too small. Taking the necessary 2 feet out of the game room might interfere with that room's intended use. Simply placing the 2 feet between the rooms makes the entire addition larger, which affects the building costs, the appearance, perhaps even the maximum space you have available in the yard.

A similar problem might arise with access. The bedroom might be a perfect size, and you might have allowed for the closet, but will the room need to be served by a hallway? How much of the room must be set aside for doorways or perhaps a stairwell? These seemingly minor considerations can upset the best laid plans, and need to be kept in mind at this stage of the planning process.

KITCHEN PLANNING

The kitchen of today, far removed from its often ignored and unloved predecessors, has achieved new status as a family meeting place, casual entertaining center, and pleasant, comfortable place for meal planning and preparation. If a new kitchen is part of your addition, the planning becomes somewhat more complicated, and also a little more critical. Many of the planning considerations for a kitchen will affect how efficient it is, and it's very important that this room in particular be laid out correctly. You might even wish to consult with a designer who specializes in kitchens.

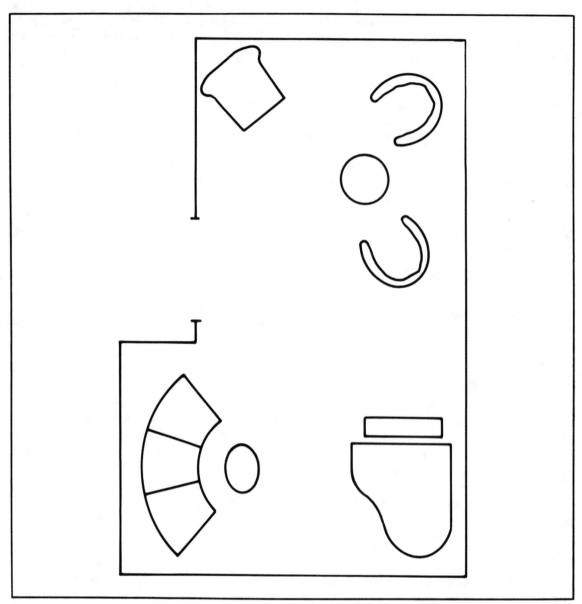

Fig. 2-1. Making a sketch to scale can help you be certain the room that you're designing is large enough for everything you want to put in it.

Once again, you need to really examine your lifestyle, and honestly assess what you need in a new kitchen. Are you a gourmet cook or an avid baker requiring special equipment? Do you entertain often? (Formal or casual?) Do you have a large collection of kitchenware? Do you stock up on food for future use? Do you need room for formal meals, or would a small eating counter be more practical? Is there more than one cook in the house? Does the family gather for meals, or does your house resemble a 24-hour cafeteria? Do you want a kitchen with everything packed neatly away out of sight, or do you want open shelves and hanging cookware to create a particular mood?

Now, what don't you like about your existing kitchen? Too small or poorly laid out? Not enough storage or counter space? Poor lighting or ventilation? Drab decorations? Do you need new or additional appliances? Make a list of everything you don't like, no matter how minor.

A typical kitchen requires about 100 to 160 square feet of floor space. Certain activity centers are basic to all kitchens, and understanding what they are is of prime importance to a good design.

The Refrigerator Center. Your refrigerator should be located separate from the range, dishwasher, or any other heat-producing appliance. It should have a minimum of 18 inches of counter space on the latch side of the door for setting groceries.

The Preparation Center. The area where food is prepared for cooking should contain 36 to 48 inches of counter space, near the sink or refrigerator if possible. The area should allow ample storage space for pans, bowls, and dry ingredients, and adequate electrical outlets should be provided.

The Cooking Center. The cooking center contains the cooktop and oven. If the oven is separate, it should be located near the cooktop. Allow a minimum of 24 inches of counter on one side and 12 inches on the other, and make sure one side is equipped with a permanent or portable heatproof surface for setting hot cookware. Provide ample storage for pots, utensils, spices, and canned goods. For safety, do not locate the cooktop near a window or at the very end of a counter.

The Cleanup Center. The cleanup area handles the cleaning and trimming of food, cleanup of kitchenware, and disposal of waste. In addition to the sink, it contains the garbage disposal, dishwasher, and possibly a trash compactor. Provide at least 30 to 36 inches of counter on each side of the sink, and storage for cleaning supplies and garbage pail. If you do not intend to install a dishwasher at this time, it is wise to make provisions for one in the future by planning on a 24-inch cabinet next to the sink, which later can be removed.

The Work Triangle. The work triangle is the relationship between the kitchen's three major work areas, and a proper triangle is essential for an efficient kitchen. (See Fig. 2-2.) The three legs of the triangle should total between 12 and 22 feet, combined as follows: refrigerator to sink, 4 to 7 feet; sink to cooktop, 4 to 6 feet; cooktop to refrigerator, 4 to 9 feet. The distance between any two centers should never be less than 4 feet.

With these activity centers in mind, the next design step is to fit them efficiently into one of the basic layouts (Fig. 2-2), which follow.

U-Shaped Layout. The U-shaped layout is considered by most designers to be the most desirable layout, if space permits. It allows an effective traffic flow and work triangle, and makes the most use out of a given space. It requires a minimum of 6 feet between the base cabinets and special corner cabinets, so it is usually the most expensive of all the layouts to construct.

L-Shaped Layout. The L-shaped layout still allows good traffic flow, but less of the kitchen area is put to practical use as compared to the U-shape. One leg of the L can be extended to create a room divider or eating/serving counter. Care must be taken in the placement of the cabinets to avoid a bad triangle, and the layout can be somewhat exhausting if either of the legs are too long.

Corridor Layout. This economical layout, having unconnected cabinet runs on two parallel walls, creates a good work triangle. One end of the corridor should be blocked off to prevent inefficient traffic flow. About 5 feet should be allowed between the cabinet runs, and some space is wasted at the blind end of the corridor.

One-Wall Layout. The one-wall layout is best for small spaces, usually opening on to another room. The sink should be located in the middle, and the total run of counter should not exceed 22 feet. A triangle is not possible, so the appliance layout is somewhat poor.

Island Layout. Used in conjunction with the U, L, or one-wall kitchen, a permanent or rolling island can add storage and counter space within the same square footage of area. The island often is

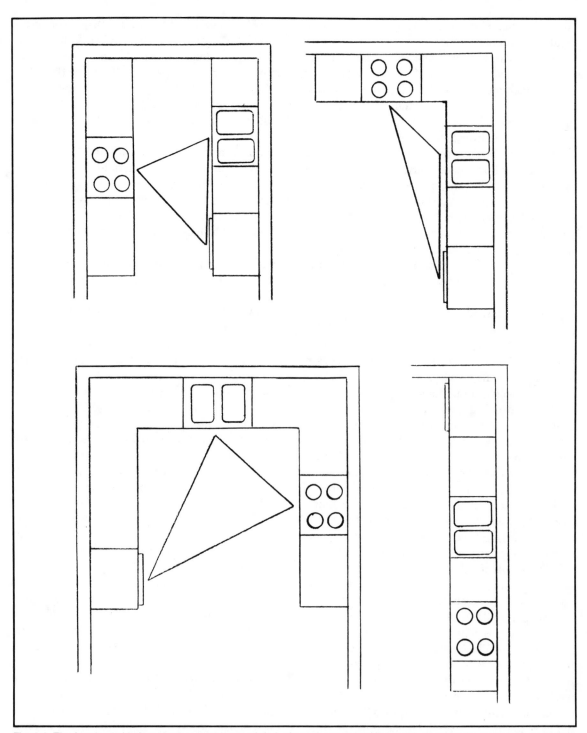

Fig. 2-2. The four basic kitchen shapes: corridor, top left; L-shaped, top right; U-shaped, bottom left; and one wall, bottom right. Note how the work triangle is figured in the first three designs.

used to house the sink or cooktop, thereby shortening the triangle.

PRELIMINARY SKETCHES

As room sizes begin to take shape, don't be afraid to get them down on paper. Make simple sketches of rooms, or parts of rooms, as you go. Try out various relationships between rooms, and consider how traffic patterns will develop, both within and between the rooms. Visualize window and door layouts, furniture arrangements, ceiling heights —anything and everything. The cheapest investment you can make in your addition is plenty of scratch paper. It's much easier to move a pencil line than it is to move a completed wall!

One simple method for arranging rooms on paper is to draw a series of circles, with each circle representing a specific room. The size of the circle should be in proportion to the size of the room, such as a small circle for a bathroom, a larger one for a bedroom, etc., and the circles should touch where the rooms would join. This is a quick way of getting something down on paper, and lets you compare and visualize a variety of room relationships and traffic patterns with a minimum of effort.

SKETCHING TO SCALE

When you are comfortable with the room sizes and layouts, the next step is to determine if they will "fit together." Quite often, although everything lays out quite neatly on your preliminary sketches, the relationship of the rooms in their actual sizes may create problems. You may find that the 12-foot bedroom you penciled in next to the 13-foot kitchen leaves a 1-foot jog in the wall that you can't remove!

Ideally, you'd like to lay out the rooms full size

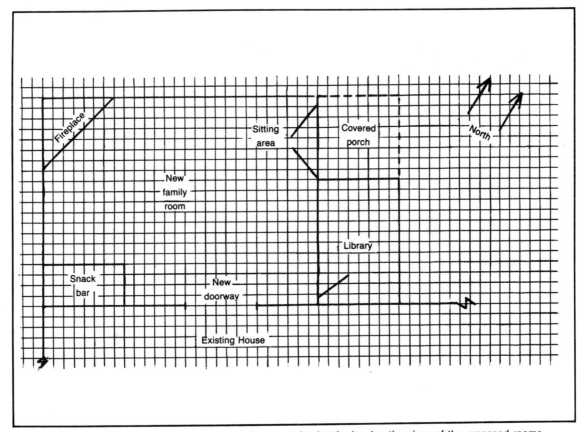

Fig. 2-3. You can use a piece of graph paper to draw a scale sketch showing the sizes of the proposed rooms.

and take a look at them. Since space considerations make this impractical, a scale drawing is the next best thing. All building plans are drawn to scale, making them accurate and easy to read, and enabling the actual dimensions and relationships of the rooms to be seen in true proportion.

Scale drawing is not at all difficult to understand. It is simply a matter of substituting one unit of measurement for another. Suppose you have a room that will be 12 feet wide by 14 feet long. Since drawing this room full size obviously is out of the question, a smaller unit of measurement is made to equal each foot in the size of the room. This smaller unit could be any size you wish, and is governed primarily by the size of the paper on which you are drawing. For architectural drawings such as these, common scales are 1/8 inch = 1 foot; 1/4 inch = 1 foot; and 1/2 inch = 1 foot.

For example, consider your 12-foot- × -14-foot room. If you choose a scale of 1/4 inch = 1 foot, then 1/4 inch on your drawing will equal 1 foot of actual size. (This size is referred to simply as *1/4-inch scale*, since the scale size is always equal to 1 foot.) Therefore, for the 12-foot wall of your room you would draw a line 3 inches long (1/4 inch × 12). The 14-foot wall would be drawn as 3 1/2 inches long (1/4 inch × 14). As long as you maintain the same scale for any one drawing, each of the room sizes you draw will be in correct proportion to each other.

At the sketching stage, the simplest way of making a scale drawing is to use graph paper. (See Fig. 2-3.) This type of paper is laid out in a grid of small squares. It can be purchased in a variety of grid sizes, such as 4 squares per inch, 8 per inch, 10 per inch, and 16 per inch.

If you are using a paper with 4 squares to the inch, each square will be 1/4 inch × 1/4 inch. Since this corresponds to the 1/4-inch scale described in the previous example, it's a simple matter of letting each square equal 1 foot of actual size. Counting off 12 squares in one direction and 14 squares in the perpendicular direction will allow you to quickly sketch out your 12- × -14-foot room. This procedure eliminates the need for repeated measurements, and allows you to quickly sketch out a variety of room layouts, window and door arrangements, even furniture placements.

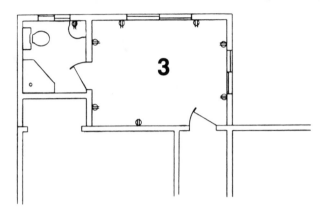

Preparing a Set of Plans

Before your project can move from planning to actual construction, your ideas need to be transformed into a working set of plans. These plans will be used by just about everyone associated with your addition, including the bank, the building department, contractors, and material suppliers. Therefore, your plans need to be accurate, readable, and along certain standard guidelines.

If you are working with a designer or an architect, he generally will supply you with a finished set of working drawings, usually in the form of blueprints. If you are doing your own design work, you can hire a draftsman to prepare the plans. The draftsman usually will need to make at least one visit to your house to take a series of measurements, after which he will provide you with a basic set of drawings based on your sketches. The alternative to these two courses of action is to prepare the plans yourself.

DRAFTING SUPPLIES

Before you can begin preparing your drawings, you will need some basic, inexpensive supplies to make the job easier and more accurate. Remember that a number of people might be working from these plans, so they need to be correct and well prepared. All of these supplies can be purchased from drafting supply companies, art stores, and some department and stationery stores. Some stores offer kits that contain all the basics, and often prove to be a good, low-cost way of outfitting yourself with everything you need to get started.

Drawing Board. Drawing boards normally are made of smoothly finished, kiln-dried softwoods, often with metal or hardwood edges to prevent wear. There are a variety of sizes available, both portable and in table form. For general use, a 20- × -26-inch or 23- × -31-inch board will work fine.

T Square and Triangles. The T square and triangles are the basic instruments used for accurately laying out lines. The T square may be wood, metal, or plastic, and should be purchased in a length that corresponds to the size of your drawing board. Triangles are most commonly made of plastic, and are available in two basic configurations: the 45, which gives you a 90-degree and a 45-degree surface, and the 30-60-90, which is used for 30-degree, 60-degree, and 90-degree angles. Both are available in several sizes, and the 8-inch and 10-inch types are about the most common.

Compass. The compass is used for drawing circles, arcs, and curves, and also for transferring measurements. The least expensive types have a steel point on the end of one leg, and an opening on the other leg into which a standard pencil can be inserted. The better compasses hold short pieces of interchangeable lead, and some also will adapt to hold a pen tip. Compasses come in all sizes and price ranges, but a 6- or 8-inch bow compass with interchangeable tips will handle all of your basic needs.

Architectural Scale. As discussed in the last chapter, your drawings will need to be prepared to an accurate scale. A real timesaver in making the necessary measurements is a type of ruler called an architectural scale. Usually triangular when viewed from the end, the architectural scale offers a different ruled edge on each face, ranging from 3/32 inch = 1 foot up to 3 inches = 1 foot.

Templates. If you do very much drawing, templates can speed the work while increasing the accuracy. They usually are made of a flexible plastic, and are available in literally hundreds of different designs. Two common types for architectural drawing are the circle template, which can be used in place of a compass for making circles and curves, and the architectural symbols template, which contains a number of universal symbols such as plumbing and electrical symbols, door swings, appliances, and much more. Architectural symbols templates come in several scales and need to be matched to the scale of the drawing you're preparing.

Pencils. There are a variety of pencil types available for drafting, depending on the intended use. Drafting pencils will produce cleaner lines than regular pencils, which will in turn reproduce better. Pencils are graded by the hardness of the lead, ranging from 6B, which is very soft and black,

through 5B, 4B, etc., to HB and F, which are medium grades, then to H, 2H, 3H, and up to 9H, the hardest. The B grades are soft and rather messy, and are used primarily for sketching, while the H grades are used for most instrument drafting. For starters, purchase an HB (semi-soft) for dark outlines and borders, an H (medium) for general work, and a 4H (semihard) for guidelines and lighter lines. Regular wood pencils in these lead types are the cheapest, but are hard to maintain a sharp point on, and, of course, get shorter with each sharpening until they are discarded. An alternative is the mechanical lead holder, a metal or plastic pencil that holds interchangeable leads. The leads are advanced by pushing a button, and are sharpened with a special sharpener, or by twirling the lead against a piece of very fine sandpaper.

Paper. Since you will need to reproduce the drawings, you will want to prepare them on tracing paper, which is the only kind of paper from which a blueprint can be made. Tracing paper is available in rolls, which can be cut to any desired size, or in standard size sheets ranging from 8 1/2 × 11 inches up to 17 × 22 inches.

DRAFTING SKILLS

You do not need to be a fully qualified draftsman in order to prepare an accurate, readable set of plans for your addition. All you need are the right tools, as just described, and some basic skills.

To begin, set your drawing board out in front of you on a table, with the long dimension horizontal. Set the head of the T square against the left edge if you are right-handed, or against the right edge if you're left-handed. This is the basic position for the T square, and by guiding the pencil against the upper edge of the T square's blade, you can draw horizontal straight lines that always will be parallel to each other.

Select a sheet of tracing paper that is large enough to accommodate your drawing in the scale in which you intend to draw it. Align the bottom edge of the paper with the top edge of the T square blade, which ensures that all the lines you draw will be parallel with the edge of the paper. Secure the paper to the board with drafting tape. Do not use masking or other types of tape, since they are hard to remove from the paper when the drawing is completed.

The T square is moved with the left hand along the left edge of the board (for right-handed people), leaving the right hand free for drawing. When you are using the T square, always be certain the head of the square is fully and firmly pressed against the board's edge. If you allow it to slip, your lines will not be truly horizontal, causing inaccuracies in the drawing that could be critical.

To use the triangle, place one edge against the top of the T square blade. As you can see, this allows you to draw perfectly vertical lines, perpendicular to the lines drawn by the T square. Depending on the type of triangle and its position, you also can draw angled lines at 30, 45, and 60 degrees.

To use the architectural scale, first select the scale you wish to use, for example 1/4 inch. Locate the edge of the architectural scale that is designated 1/4. Notice that there is a 0 at one end, followed by a series of marks, some of which are numbered. Each of the larger marks are equal to 1 scale foot, while the smaller marks are equal to 6 scale inches. On the other side of the 0 is a series of 12 smaller marks, each of which equals 1 scale inch. If you wish to draw a line representing 12 full-size feet, simply make a pencil mark at the 0 and another one at the 12. Connect the two marks, and you have accurately drawn a 12-foot line in 1/4-inch scale. If the actual size was 12 feet 9 inches, you would make a mark at the 12 on the foot side of 0, and a second mark at 9 on the inch side of 0. Connecting these two marks will give you 12 feet 9 inches.

When you are first laying out a drawing, use a fairly hard lead, such as 4H. This lead will leave light, thin lines that are easily erased as the drawing progresses. When the drawing is complete, darken in the lines by drawing over them with a softer lead, such as the HB or H. Keep the pencil points sharp to ensure lines of even thickness. A

little experimentation will quickly show you how everything works.

THE SET OF WORKING DRAWINGS

Certain drawings are necessary to make up a full working set that fully shows all the details of your project. These drawings are fairly universal, and can be read and understood by anyone who must deal with them. The actual number of drawings that make up a full set varies, depending on the complexity of the project. Following are descriptions of the basic drawings that are always necessary. A call to your local building department will tell you if any others are required.

Floor Plan

The floor plan (Fig. 3-1) is the main drawing of the set, and is the one that usually will be referred to most often during construction. It is drawn in two dimensions as though you were looking directly down on the addition, which is known as a *plan view*. Width and length are the two dimensions drawn; height is not shown. The floor plan shows the outside walls of the existing house, at least as far as they pertain to the addition. (If you're adding on to the back of the house, for example, it's not necessary to show the front walls of the existing house.) The floor plan also shows the interior and exterior walls of the addition; window locations; door locations and swings; stairwells; plumbing fixtures; stationary electrical appliances; cabinet locations; the size, direction, and spacing of ceiling joists; and any other similar details relevant to the new rooms.

The floor plan also includes most of the important dimensions, including the overall outside length and width; the distance from fixed points, usually a corner, to the center of interior walls; the sizes of windows and doors and the distance from a fixed point to the center of each; the interior sizes of each room; and any other important sizes and dimensions. You also can include general notes on this drawing, such as wall insulation levels, floor covering materials for each room area, etc. Use

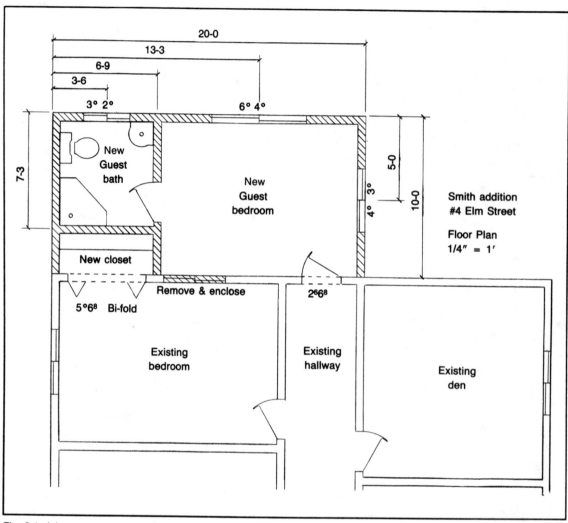

Fig. 3-1. A homeowner-prepared set of plans for an addition. The floor plan was drawn to 1/4-inch scale, and the bathroom was laid out with a template.

your own judgment, and include any general information you feel is not noted anywhere else in the set of drawings. Also, be sure to note in what scale the drawing was prepared.

Elevations

Elevations (Fig. 3-2) show what the outside walls, roof, windows, and doors of the addition will look like, and how they tie into the existing house. The drawings are again two-dimensional, this time showing width and height. They are drawn from the perspective of someone standing a short distance outside the addition and looking directly at each wall. Typically, one drawing is made for each major wall area of the addition, such as the north wall, the west wall, etc. Label each drawing as to its location on the actual job site, either by compass direction or by reference to it as the front elevation, rear elevation, or left or right side elevation.

The elevation drawings should provide a good visual look at the theoretical finished project, and

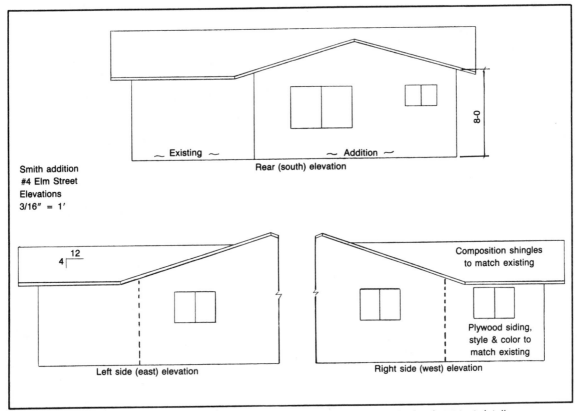

Smith addition
#4 Elm Street
Elevations
3/16″ = 1′

Rear (south) elevation

8-0

~ Existing ~   ~ Addition ~

12
4

Left side (east) elevation

Composition shingles
to match existing

Plywood siding,
style & color to
match existing

Right side (west) elevation

Fig. 3-2. Elevations, showing the look of the addition, the height of the walls, and other important details.

offer a valuable perspective on how the finished product will appear. This is a good time to make any changes in the pitch of the roof, the window layout, or other things that will make the finished appearance of the addition more pleasing. These drawings are often of major importance if the addition is being checked by your local planning commission, an architectural review board, or any kind of neighborhood standards committee.

In addition to the visual depiction of the addition, certain notes should be included on the elevation drawings. These include information on the type of siding; details of the roof-covering materials; wall heights and the heights of major features, such as deck railings, usually measured from the ground up; door and window types and materials; and any other exterior details such as paint colors, chimney heights, or masonry work. Again, include any in-

formation you feel is relevant, and make note of the drawings' scale.

Electrical Plan

The electrical plan (Fig. 3-3) shows the location of electrical outlets, switches, lights, and other wiring details. Standard electrical symbols are used to eliminate the need for a number of written notes. This drawing also should include the location of the electrical panel; any special use wiring, such as circuits for large tools or appliances; low-voltage wiring for intercoms or alarms; and telephone, stereo, television, and other electronic wiring.

For most standard residential wiring, it is not necessary to show the actual wiring runs. It is assumed, for example, that all the outlets in the addition will be divided into the proper number of

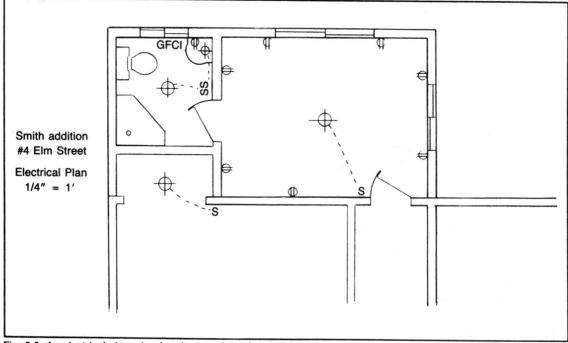

Fig. 3-3. An electrical plan, showing the complete electrical layout.

circuits—only their locations within each room are shown on the drawing. The exception is the wiring for lights and switches. It is common practice to use a dotted line to connect each switch shown on the drawing with the location of the light fixture it controls. Written notes are used as necessary to provide complete information.

The electrical plan is prepared in plan view just like the floor plan, showing the walls, windows, and doors, in addition to the electrical details. In many cases, electrical information can be placed directly on the drawing of the floor plan, as long as sufficient detail can be provided without cluttering the drawing. If the addition is to contain a large amount of wiring, or if a lot of extra information must be provided, it's best to make a separate drawing. If possible, prepare this drawing in the same scale as the floor plan.

Foundation Plan

The foundation plan (Fig. 3-4) is devoted entirely to details of the foundation. It should show stem wall locations; footing sizes and details; pier block locations; the size, direction, and spacing of girders and floor joists; slab details; and vent sizes and locations. The foundation plan is usually a simple plan view drawing, with individual details, such as a cross section of the footings, included as needed.

Plot Plan

In order for the building department and other agencies to determine if the addition meets their setback requirements, a plot plan (Fig. 3-5) is required. This drawing, depicting the area as viewed from above, shows the boundaries of the property; the size of the existing house and its location on the property; the size and location of the proposed addition; driveways and adjacent roads; other separate buildings on the property; parking areas, if needed; septic tank and drain field size and location; and any large trees, streams, ponds, or other major landscaping features.

Dimensioning is very important on this draw-

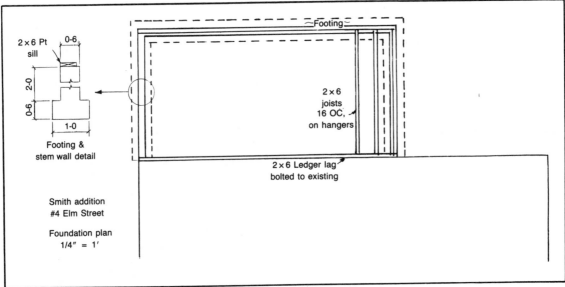

2 × 6 Pt sill

0-6

2-0

0-6

1-0

Footing & stem wall detail

Footing

2 × 6 joists 16 OC, on hangers

2 × 6 Ledger lag bolted to existing

Smith addition
#4 Elm Street

Foundation plan
1/4″ = 1′

Fig. 3-4. The foundation plan. Note the detail of the footing and stem wall.

ing. You should show the distance from the house to each adjacent property line, and the distance from the addition to adjacent property lines. You also will need to note how far the addition is from other buildings on the property, and its location relative to the septic system. A simple arrow or other mark should be included to indicate north.

Cross Section

Most building departments also require a cross section drawing, which depicts the building as though it were cut in half. The drawing perspective is the same as for the elevations, showing the width and height. Details to be included in the cross section are the method of framing, size and spacing of the wall studs, roof pitch, roof braces, amount of cornice, ceiling height, attic ventilation, bearing partitions, post and beams, foundation, finished grade, and any necessary excavations.

Roof Plan

The roof plan (Fig. 3-6) shows the ridge and valley lines of the addition roof, and how the addition will affect the roof lines of the existing house. This drawing is optional, and needs to be included only if the elevations do not show the roof lines clearly.

Detail Drawings

Additional drawings can be included as necessary to show important details, such as cabinet elevations, and construction and material details; perspectives, which show all or part of the project in three-dimensional form; unusual framing details, such as a cornice or bay; cross sections of special moldings or trim; or details of any built-ins.

LAYING OUT KITCHEN CABINETS

If your addition plans include a new or remodeled kitchen, now is a good time to consider the layout of the cabinets. The following guidelines are intended primarily for modular cabinets that are purchased individually, but they will help with the layout of custom cabinets also. Before you start, you'll need to obtain a copy of the manufacturer's specification catalog, which shows the sizes and accessories available.

Begin by making a scale drawing of the kitchen's floor plan. Work with as large a scale as possible, usually 1/2 inch to the foot. Make note of everything in the room that will affect the cabinets,

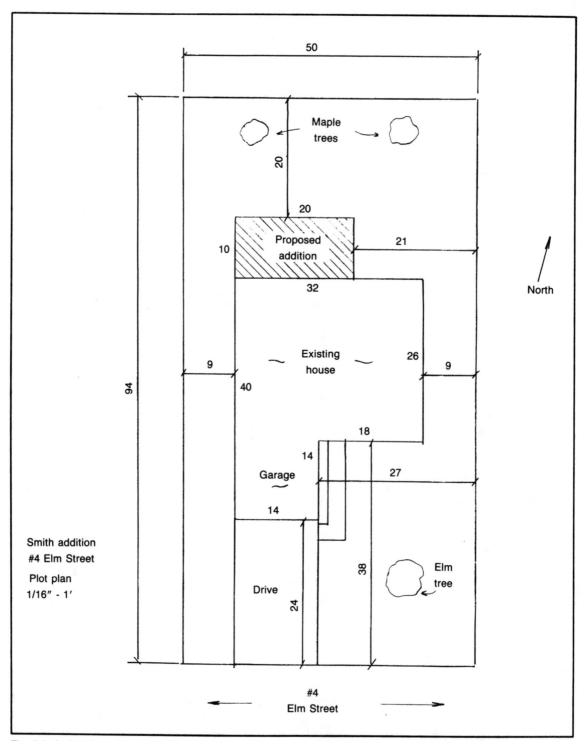

Fig. 3-5. A plot plan, showing the exact location of the house on the lot, as well as the proposed addition.

24

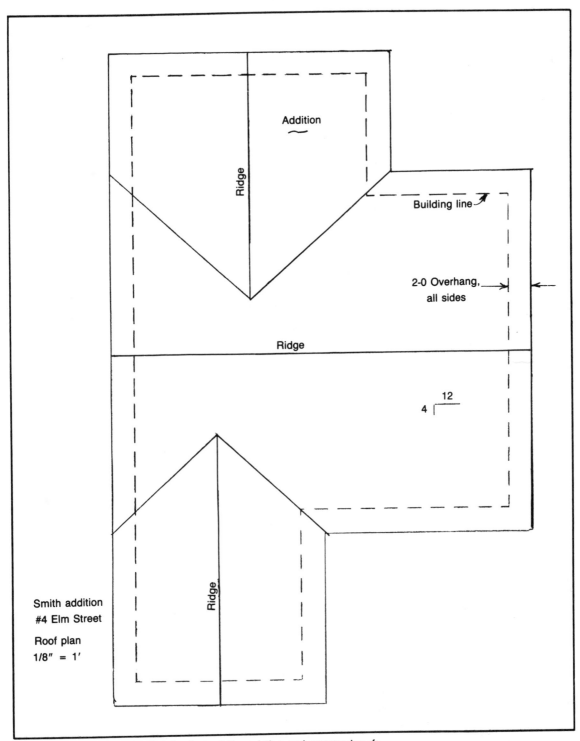

Fig. 3-6. The roof plan, showing the lines of the existing and proposed roofs.

Labels within figure:

Addition

Ridge

Building line

2-0 Overhang, all sides

Ridge

$4 \frac{12}{}$

Ridge

Smith addition
#4 Elm Street

Roof plan
1/8″ = 1′

including window and door sizes and locations, plumbing, and wall offsets. Also note all your dimensions on the drawing.

Now study the catalog. You'll notice three major product groupings, usually in the form of drawings: wall cabinets, base cabinets, and accessories and trim. After each cabinet, you'll see a series of numbers, which indicate the available sizes for that particular cabinet.

For wall cabinets, some manufacturers use numbers such as 1230, 1830, etc., indicating that the cabinet is available 12 inches wide × 30 inches high, 18 inches wide × 30 inches high, etc. Other companies will simply say "30-inch cabinet," indicating its height, then follow it with 12, 18, 24, and so on, indicating the available widths. Wall cabinets are offered in both 12- and 24-inch depths.

Base cabinets are offered in one standard height, usually 34 1/2 inches, with a choice of widths from 9 inches up to 48 inches or more. In addition to the base and wall cabinets, most manufacturers also offer oven and pantry cabinets, which are 24 inches deep, 84 or 96 inches high, and 12 to 36 inches wide. Some companies also offer island cabinets and special wall cabinets that enclose the range hood.

In the third group, accessories and trim, you'll find all the miscellaneous parts and optional add-ons you'll need to complete your installation. What's available will vary widely with the manufacturer, but you'll usually find wine racks, roll-out shelf kits, side and front panels for dishwashers and refrigerators, and moldings and fillers.

Begin laying out the various cabinets on your drawing, starting with the base cabinets. Start with the wall that houses the sink, since the sink is usually the one thing in the kitchen that cannot easily be relocated. Select a sink base cabinet, (a cabinet with no shelves), and center it where your sink will be. Work from the sink base to the nearest corner, using either a blind corner cabinet or an L-shaped lazy Susan cabinet in the corner.

Try the available corner, sink, and other base cabinets until you arrive at a combination that fits the available space. Note that blind corner cabinets usually will allow you 3 to 4 inches of "pull" away

from the corner to let you make up for odd room dimensions. The gap behind the cabinet is later hidden with the counter top. Lazy Susan cabinets do not have these allowances, so odd inches need to be made up by shifting the sink base to one side or the other, keeping the plumbing locations in mind, or by adding filler strips between the cabinets. Continue around the room, first locating the major features such as the oven, pantry, cooktop, and dishwasher and then filling in with applicable base cabinets.

Use the base cabinets as keys to the layout of the wall cabinets, maintaining a symmetry of appearance so that the room appears fairly balanced. Shorter cabinets, usually 12 or 15 inches high, are used over cooktops, refrigerators, and other areas that require more clearance, so be sure to make your selections accordingly. A proper layout may require several attempts at shifting the available sizes of cabinets around before you have a cohesive appearance.

Take a list of the individual cabinets and options you're ordering to your dealer, along with a copy of your drawing. He can help you double-check any possible oversights or problems, and can assist you in ordering moldings and other necessary trim pieces. Place your order, getting a firm commitment from the dealer on a delivery date. Orders normally need to be placed several weeks or more in advance.

BLUEPRINTS

During the process of constructing your room addition, several people will need copies of your plans. The building department will usually require two or three sets for review, and material suppliers and contractors will need to see copies also. Even your lender will require a set for his records. Therefore, you will need to have several copies of your plans, and the most accepted method of copying architectural drawings, especially large ones, is blueprinting.

In the blueprinting process, your original tracing is placed on a sheet of light-sensitive paper, then the two sheets are passed through a blueprinting machine. The machine exposes the sheets to intense light, causing the blueprint paper to fade to a light blue. Wherever the light was blocked by the lines on the tracing paper, the blueprint paper remains a much darker blue. The sheets are then developed in a chemical that fixes the colors. The result is a durable, easy-to-read copy. The process takes only a few minutes and is quite inexpensive.

Alterations cannot be made on a blueprint, since the lines cannot be erased. Also, additional blueprints cannot be made from a blueprint. If you need to make any changes, or if you require more copies, you will need to supply the blueprinter with your original tracings, so be sure you hang on to them.

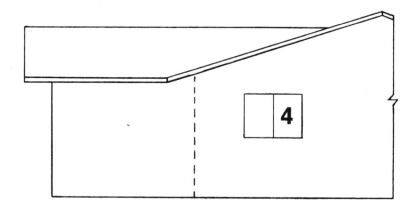

Estimating Materials and Costs

As the time draws closer to begin construction, you will need to deal with a little more paperwork. First, you will need to come up with an estimate of how much the addition will cost to complete. If you are hiring a general contractor to construct the addition, he will provide you with a written estimate of labor and material costs. If, however, you are doing all or part of the work yourself, you will need to do your own estimating. In addition to providing you with an estimate of the finished cost, estimating also will give you a material list, which you can use when dealing with suppliers.

THE BASICS OF ESTIMATING

The easiest form of estimating costs is by square footage. If, for example, you are building a 15- × -30-foot addition, simply multiply the length by the width to arrive at the square footage. In this case, you would be adding a total of 450 square feet. If the going rate in your area for contractor-built additions is $30.00 per square foot, the addition would cost approximately $13,500 to have built. If

you are doing all of the work yourself, you will save about 40 percent of this overall cost. The other 60 percent is about what the materials will cost. Therefore, the cost of the addition is now approximately $8,100. This is a fast and fairly accurate method for estimating the cost of a basic addition, and you usually can get the approximate going rate for a contractor's square-foot prices from your designer or your town's building department.

In most cases, however, you will want a more accurate figure to work with. When you're budgeting for the addition, or borrowing money for it, being $1,000 or $2,000 low in your estimate can cause a lot of problems. The only way to get a truly accurate idea of your costs is to break the addition down into its various stages, and estimate the cost for each. Again, if you are doing all the labor yourself, you need only concern yourself with material costs. If part of the work is being done by subcontractors, have them provide you with a written labor and material estimate for their portion, and add those figures to your estimated material costs for the portions you intend to do.

The following sections will help you with the basic estimating process for each stage. Every addition is different, and some have special requirements you won't find covered here, so you'll need to adjust your own estimates accordingly.

TERMS

First, you should acquaint yourself with the various terms used in estimating, and understand the simple mathematics behind them. The common abbreviation for each term is given in parentheses.

☐ *Each (ea)*: The most basic unit of estimating, *each* is the cost of one item, regardless of size. Examples include plumbing and electrical fixtures and components, appliances, and specialty hardware.

☐ *Sheet (sht)*: Similar to the each, some building materials are sold by the sheet, such as plywood and drywall. Most sheets are 4 feet × 8 feet, but you will need to verify the size for the particular product you are ordering.

☐ *Linear Foot (lf or lin ft)*: Equal to 1 foot of distance measured in a straight line, regardless of height or width. For example, a 10-foot-long 2 × 4 is 10 linear feet, as is a 10-foot-long piece of molding. Linear foot measurements are common for moldings, certain types of lumber, electrical wire, and pipe.

☐ *Square Foot (sf or sq ft)*: An area's width in feet times its length in feet. For example, an area 12 feet × 15 feet contains 180 square feet. Tile, screen, plastic, and wood veneers are common items sold by the square foot.

☐ *Square Yard (sy or sq yd)*: The length in yards times the width in yards. A 12-foot-×-15-foot area would be 4 yards × 5 yards, or 20 square yards. Since there are 9 square feet in a square yard, you also can determine the square yardage of an area by dividing the square footage by 9. Fabrics and many types of floor covering are measured in square yards.

☐ *Square (sq)*: Equal to 100 square feet. Most types of roofing products are sold by the square.

☐ *Cubic Yard (cy or cu yd)*: A measure of volume, equal to the length in yards times the width in yards times the height in yards. As an example, if a 12-foot-×-15-foot area were 9 feet high, or 4 × 5 × 3 yards, it would contain 60 cubic yards. Materials such as concrete, sand, and dirt are measured in cubic yards.

☐ *Board Foot (bf or bd ft)*: A common measurement for lumber is equal to an area 12 inches wide, 12 inches long, and 1 inch thick. To convert into board feet, multiply the board's thickness in inches by its width in inches by its length in feet, then divide by 12. For example, a 10-foot-long piece of 2 × 12 lumber would contain 20 board feet. (2 × 12 × 10 ÷ 12 = 20). See Appendix C.

☐ *M, C*: M stands for 1,000, and when it is placed in front of a unit designation, it indicates 1,000 of that unit. MBF would be 1,000 board feet, MLF would be 1,000 linear feet. A less commonly used letter is C, indicating 100.

A SAMPLE ESTIMATE

As mentioned earlier in this chapter, you will want to break the project down into various logical stages, and then estimate each one individually. Working from the ground up, you'll want to begin by estimating the cost of the foundation. You may wish to refer to later chapters of this book to be certain you understand what's involved in each stage, and to help you determine if that stage is something you'll be undertaking or having someone else do for you.

For purposes of example in the following estimates, assume that two rooms are being added to the back of an existing house. The total size of the addition is 20 feet × 10 feet, with 8-foot-high walls, and a gable roof with a 4-in-12 pitch and 2-foot overhangs.

Estimating the Foundation

First of all, are there any excavation costs? If your building site is level and you are hand digging the footing trenches, there is no cost involved here. If you need the services of an excavator or if you have to rent any equipment, list those costs.

Forms are next, and what you need is governed by how high and how long the forms need to be. For example, if you are building the forms out of 3/4-inch plywood and they will be 2 feet high, you will get two 8-foot-long strips of 2-foot-high plywood out of each 4- × -8 sheet, or enough to build 16 linear feet of forms. Add up the total linear footage you need (remember you need forms on both the inside and the outside of the stem wall), then divide by 16 to get the total number of sheets you need. In this case there are 40 linear feet of foundation, so you'll need 80 feet of forms. 80 ÷ 16 = 5 sheets of plywood. If plywood costs $12 per sheet, the total is $60.

If your soil conditions are such that footing forms are needed also, which are usually constructed from 2- × -6 lumber, include the material cost for these, too. Add in the cost of stakes and other miscellaneous materials, and you have your form costs.

The second step is estimating concrete. (See Fig. 3-4.) A 6-inch-high- × -12-inch-wide footing is 1/2 square foot, and a 6-inch-wide- × -24-inch-high stem wall is 1 square foot. Together, they equal 1 1/2 square feet. Since the foundation is three-dimensional, length must be considered also, so each linear foot of foundation would contain 1 1/2 cubic feet of concrete (1 linear foot times 1 1/2 square feet). Since concrete is ordered by the cubic yard, divide 1 1/2 by 27, which is the number of cubic feet in a cubic yard. This means that there is approximately .06 cubic yard of concrete in each linear foot of foundation. There are 40 linear feet of foundation, so 40 × .06 = 2.4, or approximately 2 1/2 cubic yards of concrete.

Multiply the number of cubic yards by the cost per cubic yard, and you have the total cost of the concrete. Add this cost to the cost of the forms, and you'll know how much the foundation will cost.

Estimating Framing Costs

Floor Costs. Again working from the ground up, begin by figuring your floor costs, starting with the joists. Suppose you intend to use 2 × 6s for floor joists on 16-inch centers. This addition will require

16 joists. (20 feet × 12 inches = 240 inches of length for the addition. 240 ÷ 16 = 15 joists, plus 1 to start.) Each joist needs to be 10 feet in length; 10 feet times 16 joists = 160 linear feet. You also will need 20 feet of lumber for the rim joist, and 20 feet for the ledger, giving you a grand total of 200 linear feet. If you are paying $0.35 per foot for 2 × 6, your material cost for the joists will be $70. You also will need to figure in 40 linear feet of pressure-treated lumber for the sill plates.

The subfloor is the next consideration. If you intend to use plywood, you'll need to determine the total square footage of floor you need to cover. A 10-foot- × -20-foot addition has 200 square feet of floor area (10 × 20). Since a sheet of 4- × -8 plywood covers 32 square feet (4 × 8), you'll need to divide 200 by 32 to arrive at 6.25, or 7 sheets of plywood. If plywood is $13 a sheet, your subfloor materials will cost $91.

Wall Costs. To estimate the cost of wall framing, perhaps the easiest method is to first determine the total number of linear feet of walls you have, both interior and exterior. (See Fig. 3-1.) If your wall studs will be on 16-inch centers, simply figure that you will need 1 stud per linear foot of wall. This allows enough extra lumber for trimmers, corners, cripples, and wall-framing needs. Then, multiply the total linear footage of wall by 3 to determine how many feet of lumber you need for the sole plate and two top plates.

For example, this addition has 57 linear feet of 8-foot-high walls, so you will need approximately 57 studs and 171 feet of plate (3 × 57). This would be a total of 456 linear feet of lumber for the studs (57 × 8), giving you a total of 627 linear feet of 2 × 4 (171 + 456). If you are paying $0.25 a linear foot for 2 × 4, your total material cost for studs and plates would be $166.75. Add in the cost of window and door headers, and you have the wall costs.

Ceiling Costs. Rafters and ceiling joists are calculated the same way as the floor joists. First determine the length of one rafter and one joist, then multiply these lengths by the number of each that you'll need. Multiply the total footage by the cost per foot to determine the total material cost. You also will need to include the ridge board, gable end framing, and lumber for the barge rafters and cornice framing.

Roof Costs. Working from your scale drawings (Fig. 3-6), measure along the slope of the roof from the ridge to the fascia. You will see that each side of the roof is approximately 12 1/2 feet long, including the overhangs. In the other direction, along the ridge, the roof is 12 feet wide with the overhang. By multiplying 12 1/2 by 12, you can determine that each side of the roof has an area of 150 square feet. Multiply by 2 for both sides, and you arrive at a total of 300 square feet of roof area.

You also will need to include the two triangular areas where the roofs intersect. Measuring off the roof plan (Fig. 3-6), you can determine that the two legs of the triangle are 9 and 11 feet. The formula for calculating the area of a triangle is $1/2 \times base \times height$, which in this case is $1/2 \times 9 \times 11$, or 49 1/2 square feet. There are two equal areas of intersection, totaling 99 square feet ($49 \ 1/2 \times 2$). The total area of the roof, therefore, is 399 square feet (300 + 99).

For the roof sheathing, plywood is a common choice. Divide the total area by the 32 square feet in a sheet of plywood, and the answer is 12.5. Therefore, you'll need 13 sheets of plywood to sheath the roof.

Shingles are sold by the square, which is 100 square feet. Since the roof is 399 square feet, you'll need 4 squares of shingles. You also will need extra shingles for the ridge and for a starter course, so figure on buying one additional bundle, which ranges from 1/3 of a square for composition shingles to 1/5 of a square for wood shakes. You'll also need felt paper under the shingles, which is usually sold in 3-square or 4-square rolls. Figure a waste and overlap allowance into the total length of the roll.

Include your cost for doors and windows in with your framing calculations. For this cost, you simply need to count the total number of each type of window and door you'll be using, and multiply by the cost of each.

Estimating Siding

For this addition, plywood siding is being used.

Since the walls are 8 feet in height, 9-foot-long sheets of siding will be needed to cover the walls and the floor framing. If you measure around the perimeter of the addition, you'll see that there are 40 feet of exterior wall to be covered. Each sheet of plywood is 4 feet wide, so 10 sheets will be needed for the walls (40 ÷ 4).

In addition to the walls, the gable end must be covered. Since the gable end forms a triangle, use the formula for calculating the area of a triangle to determine exactly how much area you need to cover. From the drawings, you can determine that the gable end is approximately 3 1/2 feet high, and is 20 feet wide at the base. Applying the formula, you arrive at an answer of 35 square feet ($1/2 \times 20 \times 3 \ 1/2$). This is just over one 4-×-8 sheet of siding, but because of the waste from the angled cuts, 3 sheets probably will be needed. For this addition, therefore, you will need 10 sheets of 4-foot-×-9-foot siding, and 3 sheets of 4-foot-×-8-foot siding.

These types of simple square footage calculations can be used regardless of what type of wood siding you are using. If you are using brick, stucco, or other types of masonry, use the square-foot figures to determine the quantity of these materials also. Finally, use these numbers to determine your needs for exterior paint or stain.

Estimating Electrical, Plumbing, and Heating Needs

Electrical Costs. Estimating your costs for electrical supplies is pretty straightforward. It is primarily a matter of counting the number of 110-volt receptacles shown on your plan (Fig. 3-3), then multiplying this number by the combined cost of a receptacle, box, and cover plate. Repeat the process for all of the 220-volt receptacles, all of the switches, and all of the lights that require a fixture box.

Electrical wire is sold by the foot, or in boxes of 100 or 250 feet, so next you'll want to calculate the total feet of wire needed, and multiply by the cost per foot. Different wire types will have different per-foot prices, so separate your figures into how much of each wire type you'll need. If you are adding new circuits, add in the cost of new circuit breakers and any conduit or other fittings necessary to enter the panel box.

The rest of the electrical material costs are based on *each* prices. Add up the individual cost of each light fixture you need, along with appliances, fans, room heaters, etc. Adding an additional 10 percent to the electrical total should cover all of your miscellaneous needs, such as staples, fittings, wire nuts, and waste.

Plumbing Costs. Accurately estimating plumbing costs is a little more tedious. Begin by dividing the plumbing into two separate systems: hot and cold water lines; and drain, waste, and vent (DWV) lines. Study the plans to determine where each water and waste line will originate, such as at a sink, toilet, etc. You'll also need to take a close look at the house to determine where each line will tie into the existing house plumbing.

Beginning with the water lines, make a sketch on paper of where each line begins and where it goes. Follow it all the way to where it ties into another line, noting the approximate footage of each run, any changes of direction, and the size of pipe you'll be using. Do this for each water line, both hot and cold. Add up the footages for the pipe, and multiply the total by the cost per foot of each pipe size. For the elbows, tees, and other fittings, it's easiest to just get an average cost per fitting and multiply it by the total number of fittings needed, regardless of size. For example, if most 1/2-inch fittings are $0.60 and most 3/4-inch fittings are $0.80, and you have a total of 40 fittings, multiply 40 by an average per-fitting cost of $0.70, to arrive at an approximate cost of $28 for fittings.

Repeat the procedure for the DWV lines, beginning with a separate sketch. Figure up the number of fittings and the total footages for the different sizes of pipe, and multiply them by their respective costs. Add the water and DWV estimates together and, depending on how accurate you think your takeoffs were, add in another 10 percent to 25 percent to cover any unforeseen needs that always seem to arise. This total should give you a fairly accurate cost for your rough plumbing materials.

Most of the finished plumbing is figured on the basis of individual needs. Add up the cost for sinks, toilets, bathtubs, and other kitchen and bath fixtures, along with the related needs of each fixture, such as faucets and shutoff valves. Other special needs, such as a new water heater, also are added in at this time. It's important that you take the time to visualize as many of your material needs as possible in order to avoid underestimating.

Heating Costs. Finally, you'll need to ascertain your needs for heating, cooling, and ventilation materials. If you are adding to an existing heating or cooling system, you'll need to figure up the lengths of the duct runs, then multiply the total by the cost per foot. Remember to add in any necessary fittings. If you're adding exhaust fans or any type of combustion appliances, you'll need to determine the ventilation requirements of each, and add in these costs also. If you are adding an entirely new heating and/or cooling system, your dealer will supply you with the costs for the unit and any related accessories.

INTERIOR COSTS

Using some of the examples given, calculate the total square footage of four areas: the inside surface of all exterior walls, both surfaces of all new interior walls, the surface of the ceiling, and the surface of the floor. These four figures, separately and together, will be used several times in calculating your material costs for finishing off the interior of your addition.

Insulation. You will usually be using three different types of insulation for the ceiling, floor, and exterior walls. Since insulation is sold by the square foot, determine the cost of each type and multiply it by the total square footage of each area.

Drywall. If you are applying drywall to the entire interior, add up the square footages of the ceiling and all of the interior and exterior walls. Divide the total by 32 to determine the number of 4- × -8 sheets you'll need. In some areas it may be advantageous to use 4- × -12 sheets, so divide by 48 for these areas. Add in approximately 15 percent for waste, then multiply by the cost per sheet. Allow an additional 20 percent to cover nails, tape, and joint cement.

Wall Coverings. A wide variety of wall coverings are available to finish off the interior drywall, and most are sold by the square foot. Use your ceiling and wall calculations to determine how much paint, wallpaper, or other materials each area will require. You might need to consult with your supplier to determine how much waste allowance to include for materials like wallpaper, where the waste created by pattern matching can be substantial.

Floor Coverings. Most floor coverings are sold by the square yard, with the exception of wood and ceramic tile, which are sold by the square foot. To calculate your needs for any material sold by the square yard, divide the floor area's square footage by 9. Multiply the result by the cost per square yard to determine the total material cost. Don't forget to include any miscellaneous material needs, such as carpet padding and adhesives, and include a waste allowance of 5 percent to 15 percent.

OTHER COSTS

Most of the other costs associated with the addition need to be figured in one at a time, depending on the individual needs and the cost of each item. A few of the costs you might need to be aware of include: permit fees; disposal of old materials and other debris removed or accumulated during construction; concrete flatwork not associated with the foundation; gutters, flashings, and other sheet-metal work; hardware, such as hinges, doorknobs, etc.; cabinets and counter tops; and rental equipment.

Another consideration is waste. As mentioned in a few of the previous calculations, a waste allowance must be figured in for some materials. In addition to those noted earlier in this chapter, allow approximately an extra 10 percent of the cost for foundation concrete, plaster, carpet, linoleum, rough lumber, and electrical wire. Allow 5 percent for concrete flatwork, plumbing pipe, conduit, and floor tile. Allow anywhere from 10 percent to 30

percent for tongue-and-groove or other matched lumber.

MATERIAL BIDS

A good way to save some calculation time, and hopefully some money, is to shop for competitive material bids. Many companies will give you exact bids for the total cost of any materials they supply you. They also can be quite helpful in pointing out necessary extras you might have overlooked, or in helping you eliminate unneeded materials.

During the process of performing all of the calculations and material takeoffs described in this chapter, keep track of exactly what materials you need, including the quantities, sizes, and grades. Organize like materials, such as lumber and plywood, plumbing supplies, doors, windows, and other similar groups, and write out your needs in a clear, readable manner. Take each relevant list to at least two suppliers, and ask for a material bid based on your takeoffs. Be sure they give you a breakdown of how they arrived at their bid, not just a total. In this way, you can compare prices between suppliers more accurately. Be as thorough and complete as possible in specifying what sizes and grades of material you want, to be certain that each company is bidding the same thing. Allow them a few days to do the bidding.

In addition to price, compare other services each company offers. Will they deliver your materials, and is there a charge? Are the items you need in stock, or will they need to be ordered? What's the return policy for unused materials in new condition? Is the staff helpful and knowledgeable? Are any discounts offered for quantity purchases?

All of these considerations will help you arrive at the best materials for the best price. Remember, too, that price is not always the only consideration. Service also should weigh on your decision. If you find that you like one company over another, even though it is higher priced, don't be afraid to show the staff their competitor's bid. In many cases, they will discount their prices to be somewhere near the other company's.

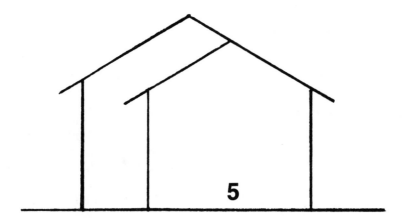

5

Financing, Variances, and Permits

As the time draws closer for beginning construction, there are a few more preliminaries, all of them equally important, that must be considered. Building an addition is much more than just driving nails, and with this chapter the last of the paperwork will be finished up.

FINANCING

If you haven't already done so, now is the time to deal with one important question: how will you pay for this project? No matter how small or simple the addition, the costs can mount up quickly. It's better to be well prepared at this stage than to run out of money before the project is finished.

Out-of-Pocket Financing

The first and most obvious method for paying for the addition is simply referred to as *out of pocket*. For those with the means, or the patience, footing the bill for the project out of your own liquid funds offers several advantages. For one, when the proj-

ect is done, it's done. You don't have loan payments, and no encumbrance has been placed against the property or any other form of collateral. It also saves you the hassle of securing financing, which can be time consuming and frustrating.

You need to be certain before you start that you actually do have enough money to pay for the project, without cutting unnecessarily into the personal finances you have budgeted for everyday expenses. Remember that when the bills come in for materials or contractor services, you open yourself up to serious legal action, perhaps even foreclosure proceedings against your home, if you don't have the money available to pay them. The other potential problem is coming up short and being forced to leave the project half finished until additional money becomes available.

Private-Party Financing

If your personal finances are not such that the out-of-pocket approach is feasible, your only other avenue is to borrow the money. There are any number of ways to borrow money, but following are some of the basics. The simplest way is to borrow from personal sources. This approach eliminates the paperwork of dealing with a bank, and may give you the advantage of a lower interest rate.

Remember to treat any such dealings completely as a business proposition. To protect both yourself and the party you're borrowing from, you need to put all the arrangements in writing. Agree on the rate of interest, the amount of time you have to repay the money, and the terms under which the payments will be made. Each of you need to sign the agreement and keep a copy for your records. Remember that friends and relatives have legal recourse against your property, just as does a lending institution.

Bank Financing

The method chosen by most people is financing through a lending institution, usually either a bank, savings and loan, or mortgage or finance company. As you would with any other major purchase, shop around for the best interest rate before applying for the loan. Check with your own bank first; if you're a regular customer, the bank may provide you with better rates or services. Also, don't be afraid to negotiate for a better interest rate than what the bank is offering you. Remember that banks make their money from the interest they collect on loans. If they're at all interested in your business, they may very well be willing to give you a better rate than the one they advertise. Typically, you'll also get a much better interest rate on loans made through banks or savings and loans than you will on one made through a finance company.

When you've chosen the lending institution you'd like to deal with, be prepared for some paperwork. During the initial consultation with the loan officer, he will explain the general terms of the company's loan program, and provide you with a loan application. You'll also probably be asked to agree to having a credit check run, for which you may be charged a small, nonrefundable fee.

Complete the application at home, and be sure you accurately provide all the information requested. When you return the application, you also

will need to provide the loan officer with several other items. Be as professional, thorough, and confident as possible in your dealings with the loan officer. The better impression you make, and the better you understand and present your proposal, the more likely you are to obtain the loan. You should be prepared to present:

☐ *An Exact Dollar Amount.* Be certain you know exactly what you need to borrow, and that you've allowed enough to complete the project. It may prove difficult to go back and ask for more money later.

☐ *A Set of Plans.* Provide a set of plans for the use of the loan officers. They will want to review your project to see exactly what it is you intend to do, and that the amount of money you're asking to borrow is in line with what they feel the project should cost. Your plans should be complete at this time, and in addition to all the drawings mentioned in Chapter 3, they should include a legal description of the property. This description can be found in the papers you received when you first purchased your home, or from the assessor's office in the county where the property is located.

☐ *A Contractor's Estimate.* If you are doing the work yourself, explain this fact to the loan officer. It wouldn't hurt to have a few typewritten paragraphs detailing your qualifications to undertake the work. Many banks recently have become leery of lending money to an owner/builder. Looking at it from the bank's point of view, your house is often the only collateral it has for the loan. If you default on your loan, the bank would have to foreclose on the house, then sell it to recover its money. Foreclosing on a house with a half-finished addition, or one that was poorly built, is not at all in the bank's best interest, so the loan officers want to be sure that whoever undertakes the project is capable of completing it, and completing it correctly.

☐ *A Material Breakdown and Cost Estimate.* Type up a list of the materials that will go into the project, including sizes, quantities, grades, and brand names and models, if applicable. Include exact estimates from material suppliers if you have any, and also bids from any subcontractors you'll be using. Use the bank's forms if provided.

☐ *Collateral*. Collateral usually takes the form of a second deed of trust on your house. As mentioned previously, collateral gives the bank the right to take your property, through a series of legal foreclosure proceedings, should you default on the payments.

☐ *An Appraisal Fee*. Before granting a loan, the bank will need to know the current market value of your home. To ascertain it, the bank will send an appraiser, usually from an outside company but sometimes a bank officer, to visit your property and make the necessary evaluation. You will be required to pay any fees associated with this appraisal.

If all goes well, you'll receive a loan approval in several days, and you'll be asked to visit the bank to sign all the papers. Be certain you read and fully understand everything you're signing. If you have any questions, ask them before you sign!

When all the papers have been signed, you will receive the money in the form of a cashier's check. If you are building the addition yourself, it pays to open a separate checking account with this money. Doing so allows you to keep the loan separate from your normal household money, and makes it much easier to keep track of all the project's expenses. Much of the money you invest in the addition may be tax deductible if and when you ever sell the home.

If you are having a contractor perform all or most of the work, the bank usually will stipulate that it will make the money available in two-party checks issued jointly to you and the contractor. These payments are issued in draws as various stages of the work are completed, rather than as a check for the entire amount when the loan is approved. This procedure enables the bank to better control its financial involvement in the project in the event that something goes wrong and the addi-

tion is never completed. If the addition is a large one, the bank might insist on its own inspections at each stage of the work before a check is issued.

ZONING

The areas within a community are broken up into zones, each of which have specific purposes and restrictions. A store or office building, for example, cannot be built in an area that is zoned for residential use only. Multifamily dwellings such as an apartment building, even though considered a residential building, cannot be constructed in an area having a single-family residential zoning.

It's rare that the addition you are planning would be subject to zoning restrictions. It can happen, though, so it pays to check. The addition of a shop, for example, might violate a residential zoning area if you intend to service paying customers or park commercial equipment. The addition of an apartment that has separate cooking facilities is another example, even if it's only to be used as a guest house. Since it has the potential for being rented out as a self-contained dwelling, it might not be an acceptable addition in a neighborhood that's zoned for single-family residences only.

As a precaution, find out what the zoning is for your neighborhood. Then, if you have any question about whether your planned addition might violate a zoning ordinance, take your plans to the county planning commission and check with them.

VARIANCES

As discussed in Chapter 2, specific setback ordinances apply to any building, or an addition to that building, that is constructed within a given neighborhood. Also, as just mentioned, certain zoning restrictions apply. These restrictions are for the good of everyone, helping to guarantee that each new building becomes an asset to the neighborhood, not an eyesore. At times, however, the construction of an addition might require that these restrictions be exceeded. In those cases, it is necessary to request a *variance*. A variance is simply legal permission for your building to vary from the accepted standards.

Setback Variances

A variance from setback restrictions is probably the most common type. Some older homes were built when no setback rules were in effect for their neighborhood. When judged by today's rules, these homes might be too close to the neighboring property line. If you intend to construct an addition that follows the existing walls of such a house, your addition will violate the setback restrictions. In this type of situation, it's necessary to request an exception from these restrictions to avoid having to jog the addition in from the existing house. (See Fig. 5-1.)

Height Variance

Most neighborhoods restrict the height of residences to two stories. If you intend to construct a third story on your house which requires raising the roof to a new height (Fig. 5-2), you'll need to request a variance. If you are converting an existing second-story attic into living space, and the height of the existing roof will not be affected, these restrictions usually do not apply. However, it pays to double-check with the planning commission just to be sure.

Height restrictions are being watched much more closely these days, primarily because of the advent of solar access laws. With the growing popularity of active and passive solar systems in residential construction, these laws are intended to guarantee that your neighbor's access to sunlight is not blocked by the height or positioning of your building.

Zoning Variance

In some cases, such as the example of the apartment addition cited previously, a zoning variance might be necessary. These variances occasionally are granted if the intended use of the addition does not seriously violate the neighborhood standards set by a particular zoning. Zoning variances usually require a full hearing of the county planning commission, and are more difficult and time-consuming to obtain than simple setback variances.

Variance Applications

An application for a variance needs to be made at the offices of the planning commission in the city or county where the house is located. If possible, try to plan your addition in such a way that setbacks and other restrictions do not present a problem. If you feel a variance is necessary, make your application early. Variances are usually time-consuming affairs, requiring from 2 weeks to 1 month or more to complete, and the fees associated with them sometimes can be substantial.

You'll need to complete the forms provided to you by the planning commission. You will be asked for a legal description of your property, a description of the addition, a plot plan showing the loca-

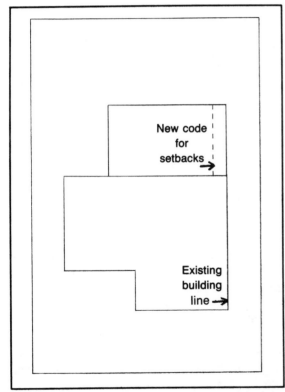

Fig. 5-1. A setback variance is sometimes necessary to allow the addition to line up with the existing house, even though the setback rules have changed since the house was first built. In this way, you avoid having an unsightly jog in the wall (dotted line) where the addition meets the house.

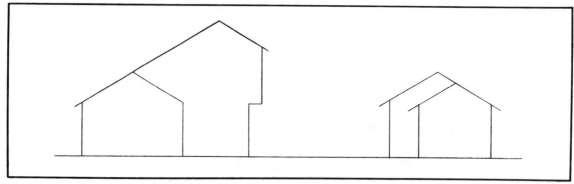

Fig. 5-2. Height variances are sometimes necessary when you are adding upward.

tion of the house and the proposed addition, and a set of plans. You will be asked to pay a fee at the time the variance application is made, and all or a large part of it is nonrefundable if the variance is denied.

In addition to the forms and other paperwork, you usually will be asked to present a map showing the owner and location of each of the properties within a certain distance around your house. In addition, you will be required to visit each of those neighbors, explain your intended project, and have them sign a statement saying that they have no objection to its construction.

Requesting a variance is no guarantee that it will be granted. It depends on the strictness of the ordinances in your area, the type of addition being constructed, and the cooperation of your neighbors. The better you present your case, and the more convincing you are as to why the need for a variance cannot be avoided, the better your chances of success.

BUILDING PERMITS

Any project requiring alterations to the structure, electrical wiring, or plumbing system of your home almost certainly will require a building permit. As with the zoning, height, and setback restrictions, building permits serve an important and necessary function. They are intended to promote safety in construction, and to avoid potential life-threatening hazards such as faulty wiring and poor framing. Al-

though they admittedly can be a nuisance at times, they are by no means something that should be avoided. They are there for your protection.

The building permit process is the last step before actual construction begins. By this point, you should have your plans completed, your financing arranged, and any necessary variances approved. If you're having a general contractor do the work, he should have been selected. In this case, it is his responsibility to take out the permits. If you're doing the work, you'll need to take out the permits yourself. Check with the building department to see if any major subcontractors you might be using, such as plumbers or electricians, can operate under your permit or will be required to obtain their own.

You will need to visit the offices of your city or county building department to apply for a building permit. As with the other agencies you've had to deal with, you will be required to fill out an application describing the addition and giving its estimated value. You will need the legal description of the property, and at least two sets of plans. A fee will be charged at the time you apply for the permit, and is based on the size and estimated value of the addition.

Your plans will be checked by the department to be sure they are in keeping with current codes. Changes might be required, and they will be noted on the plans for future reference both by you and the building inspector. When the plans are approved, they will be stamped as official copies. One of the sets will be returned to you along with a permit card, and the other will remain on file at the building department. Depending on the complexity of the plans and the backlog at the building department, the entire process might take from 1 day to 2 weeks or more.

Post the permit card and the stamped set of plans on the job site where they are visible and accessible to the inspector. Provide a plastic covering or other weather protection to keep all of the paperwork safe and dry. During the course of construction, you will need to call the building department and request inspections of the work in progress. An inspector will visit the job and check the work, and you must receive his approval before you move on to the next stage. Any violations he finds will be noted on a corrections card, and you will be required to correct them and have them reinspected before you proceed.

Excavation, Form, and Setback Inspections

Excavation, form, and setback inspections are the first set of inspections, and the inspector will be double-checking setback requirements and other possible zoning violations. Footing and stem wall forms will be checked, as will any plumbing or electrical work that will be underground or contained within the concrete. These inspections need to be completed before any concrete is poured.

Underfloor Inspections

Before the subfloor is installed, some inspectors require a site visit to check the floor framing to be certain it's properly constructed. Plumbing, wiring, and heating ducts that will be covered by the floor also are checked at this time. Not all areas require an underfloor inspection.

Rough Inspections

During the rough inspection, the inspector has a number of things to check. Underfloor framing, wiring, plumbing, and mechanical systems will be inspected, if they were not already checked during the underfloor inspection. You will need to have the subfloor installed, all of the walls completed, including the siding, the ceiling and roof framing in place, and the roof sheathing and roofing installed. Woodstoves and fireplaces need to be in, as does the heating and cooling system. The inspector also will be looking at the rough plumbing and electrical wiring. Do not install any insulation or otherwise cover the insides of the walls until this inspection has been completed successfully.

Insulation and Drywall Inspections

Requirements for the insulation and drywall inspections vary from place to place, and may not be necessary in your area. If an insulation inspection is required, the inspector will be checking that the insulation levels in the walls, ceiling, and floor meet the current codes, and that the material is securely installed. Dams used to prevent the insulation from contacting heat-producing fixtures such as exhaust fans, flues, and ceiling heat lamps also will be checked. Have this inspection done before you apply the drywall.

If a drywall inspection is required, the inspector will check that the panels are securely nailed and that fireproof and/or waterproof plasterboard was used where required. The lath base for a plaster finish also will be inspected.

Do not tape the drywall or apply the plaster until the insulation and drywall inspections are done.

Final Inspection

Before the addition can be occupied, the inspector will make the final inspections. Building, electrical, plumbing, and mechanical systems all will be checked. Among the items he'll inspect will be proper electrical grounding, proper operation of heating and cooling equipment, compliance with fire regulations around woodstoves and fireplaces, plumbing systems and electrical appliances, and the overall quality of the structure. Once this inspection is completed, retain the permit card for your records.

If you have any questions about what inspections are required or what they entail, check with your building department before requesting a site visit. You also can check with the reference department of your local library for copies of *The Uniform Building Code, The National Electrical Code,* and *The Uniform Plumbing Code*. Although a little hard for the nonprofessional to decipher, these books provide valuable information on what codes apply to your project, and will give you some idea of what the inspector will be checking.

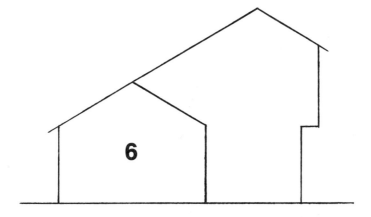

6

Selecting a Contractor

If, after due consideration, you have decided to hire a contractor to perform all or part of the labor, you're faced with the problem of who to hire. The selection of the right contractor and a thorough understanding of your rights and obligations under the contract you sign are essential. Choosing the wrong person can quickly take all of the joy out of your long-awaited addition.

GENERAL CONTRACTORS

If you intend to have all or almost all of the work done by someone else, your best bet is to use a *general contractor.* General contractors are usually skilled in several different building trades, and are well versed in estimating, scheduling, and material ordering. It is their job to oversee an entire project from start to finish, rather than doing only one phase of a job, as a specialty contractor would.

Normally, the general contractor is brought into the picture at the point when the plans have been completed and the project is ready for bids. In some instances, he can even prepare the plans himself, or arrange for them to be drawn up based on your specifications. When the plans are done, he will review them and provide you with a complete estimate of all labor and materials involved. It is his responsibility to take out all the necessary permits, order the material deliveries, and schedule each subcontractor on and off the job in the proper sequence, and at the proper time. He will arrange for all necessary inspections, and take care of any required corrections.

General contractors also are known as *prime contractors,* in that they are the ones who contract directly with the homeowner. They in turn hire and pay the subcontractors, and are responsible for their work. Typically, the homeowner has no dealings whatsoever with the subcontractors. When you hire a general contractor, you are in essence turning the construction phase of your project over to him—subject, of course, to the agreed-on specifications and your own input as the job progresses.

SUBCONTRACTORS

Subcontractors, also known as *specialty contractors,* limit themselves to being highly skilled in only one or perhaps two aspects of the construction process. Plumbers, electricians, painters, tile setters—these are all examples of subcontractors who specialize in one particular field. As mentioned earlier, if you have decided on a general contractor, he will arrange for each subcontractor as needed.

If, however, you are doing most of the work yourself, you may only have need for one or two specialty contractors to perform those phases of the project with which you're not comfortable. In this case, each individual will contract directly with you, and you will oversee his work to be sure it's done to your satisfaction. If you decide to hire the subcontractors yourself, use the same selection and contract procedures as outlined in the following sections for hiring a general contractor.

OWNER/BUILDERS

As a homeowner, you have the right to act in the unofficial capacity of general contractor—securing your own permits, hiring your own subcontractors, etc. This is what is meant by the term *owner/builder.* Although it is possible to save a little money by acting in this capacity, if you're not familiar with construction, it is very seldom worth it. As an owner/builder, you, not your subcontractors, assume overall control of the project. You become responsible for scheduling, which is not as easy as it might seem. If you schedule the wrong people at the wrong time, you could impact the quality of the finished product, and also might be responsible for paying for any lost time or ruined materials that result from your error.

In addition to scheduling, your responsibilities include plans, permits, and engineering reports; bank and building inspections; specification of materials and arrangements for delivery; overall project liability and quality control; and a host of other problems. If your project is large and requires the use of three or more different trades (plumbing, electrical, framing, plasterboard, roofing, etc.), and if you do not intend to do any of the work your-self, your best bet is to leave the project in the hands of a competent general contractor.

FINDING A CONTRACTOR

During the process of evaluation, planning, and layouts, you have established exactly what it is you need to have done. You now need to decide what contractor you want to do the work. Although the vast majority of contractors are both honest and competent, it is always best to enter the selection process with a "buyer beware" attitude. A few simple precautions will help ensure a smooth job.

Contractor Referrals

There are a number of ways of finding appropriate contractors for the job you have in mind, the best being a recommendation from a satisfied customer. Check with friends and relatives who have had work done recently, or stop by and talk with other homeowners in your area where you have seen work in progress. Even if you don't personally know them, you'll find that most people are more than willing to talk about their own remodeling projects.

Another good source of contractor referrals is your local lumberyard, plumbing and electrical store, or other construction supplier. These stores often keep lists of reputable contractors with whom they're familiar. Since their recommendations will reflect on their own businesses, these lists are usually quite reliable. Other sources include the state contractor's board, the Better Business Bureau, and local consumer groups.

Bid Solicitation

Shop around as you would for any major purchase, soliciting bids from at least three qualified contractors. Although getting three bids might seem a bit time-consuming, it is one of your best assurances of getting the right contractor at a fair price.

When you are dealing with the contractors that will be bidding your job, be sure to provide each with as much information as possible, and be sure that the information is the same for each. If, during the course of the bidding process, some of your plans should change, be sure that all the bidders are apprised of the changes. Be certain to discuss any work you wish to do on the project yourself, and see how it will fit in with each contractor's scheduling. Bidding between contractors is a competitive and exacting task, and seeing that each has the same information and opportunities will make it easier to compare and evaluate all of the proposals.

Make it a point to obtain and verify each contractor's state license number. Every state has laws that regulate the activities of contractors, and dealing with an unlicensed one can turn into a legal and financial headache. A quick call to the state contractor's licensing board will verify if the number is valid, active, and in good standing. Also obtain and verify each person's business address and telephone number.

Ask each contractor for a list of recent jobs, and arrange to see some of them. Ask the previous customers if they were pleased with the work. Was it done on schedule? How well did the contractor accept changes during construction? (This is important, because there's always bound to be changes.) Were any problems easily resolved? Were the contractor's employees, and the employees of any subcontractors, courteous and efficient?

Finally, ask each contractor for a list of business and bank references, and check a few of them out. Although all of these precautions might seem excessive, they're not; they're just common sense. Most reputable contractors keep this information on hand and are used to providing it when asked. If a contractor is not willing to provide the information, look elsewhere.

When all of the bids are in, compare them carefully. Did each person bid the same work, using the same quality of materials? How did previous customers rate them? Are they willing to work with you if you wish to do some of the work yourself? Did you feel comfortable with them? Beware of bids that are substantially higher or lower than the others. If a bid is extremely low, the bidder might have overlooked something. If it's way too high, he might have included extras you don't really need. Evaluate all the facts, and make your decision accordingly.

THE CONTRACT

Before work begins, you will be asked to sign a contract (Fig. 6-1), which protects both you and your contractor. Most contractors use a simple, plain English contract which is easily understood without the advice of an attorney. Once again, common sense and simple precautions should be used. The important thing is to get all the main details in writing. Assume nothing. Remember that this contract binds you as well as your contractor, and as such it should clearly state your final agreement.

Your contract should list as many specific construction details as are reasonable, bearing in mind that during the actual construction process the contractor must be allowed some latitude to build as he feels is best. If you have trust and confidence in your contractor, this shouldn't be a problem.

If possible, the contract should include the sizes, types, and grades of materials, and the brands and model numbers of appliances and fixtures. Any work you wish to do yourself should be specified, along with an agreement of the amount of time you'll be allowed to complete your portion without interrupting the contractor's schedule. Some contractors include a clause stating that they are not responsible for any work you perform or any materials you supply, including any adverse effect that work or those materials might have on the work they're performing.

Drawings of the proposed work, whether prepared by you, your contractor, or a designer or architect, should be included with the contract and designated a part of it. These drawings should include such things as electrical and plumbing locations, window and door locations, and room sizes.

Contract Items

Any contract you enter into with a contractor should contain several basic items, for your protection as well as his. These items include the following:

TIMBERLINE CONSTRUCTION
Sacramento, CA 95819
Contractor's Lic. No. 326242
PROPOSAL AND CONTRACT

TO: _____ at _____

_____
(address & zip)

Dear_____

TIMBERLINE CONSTRUCTION proposes to furnish all materials and perform all labor necessary to complete the following:
Room addition approximately 14-6 × 19-6, as per attached specifications.

_____
_____
_____
_____
_____

(All further materials and labor not specified above shall be further set forth in attachments to this contract)

All of the above work (and any work set forth in attachments, if applicable), shall be completed in a substantial and workman-like manner according to standard practices for the total sum of $7,800.00 (Seven thousand eight hundred & 00/1000 Dollars) Payment shall be made according to the following schedule:

Amount	Due
20% $ 1,560.00	Down Payment
20% $ 1,560.00	Upon completion of foundation
20% $ 1,560.00	Upon completion of framing
20% $ 1,560.00	Upon completion of drywall
20% $ 1,560.00	Upon completion of job

Note: (Amount and schedule of payments shall be set forth specifically setting forth the amount of each payment as a sum in dollars and cents)

The approximate date when the work herein described shall commence shall be May 17, 1983, and the approximate date the work shall be substantially completed shall be June 17, 1983.

The entire amount of the contract price shall be paid no later than __10__ days after completion.

Proposal and Contact

Any alteration or deviation from the specifications set forth in this proposal and contract involving extra cost of material or labor will be only executed upon written orders for same, and will become an extra charge over and above the sums set forth in this agreement. All agreements must be in writing.

Dated: May 13, 1983   Respectfully submitted,

TIMBERLINE CONSTRUCTION

By_____
Paul Bianchina, Owner

Fig. 6-1. A typical construction contract. This one is quite straightforward and easy to understand.

☐ The contractor's name, business address, and license number.

☐ The total cost of the job.

☐ A payment schedule, which clearly shows the amount of each payment and when it is due. The schedule should include the amount of any down payment, and the terms, if any, under which the final payment will be released. If you have a home-improvement loan from a bank, the bank might wish to make its own inspections and issue payments directly to the contractor. If so, be certain the details are spelled out in the contract and understood.

☐ The date the work will commence and the date it will be substantially completed. If you don't understand what constitutes *commencement* and *substantial completion,* ask your contractor for clarification.

☐ The signature of the contractor or his authorized agent, and the date signed.

☐ A place for your signature, the date you sign, and the specific terms under which you accept the contract proposal.

Be certain that you read and understand everything contained in the contract, that it contains no blank spaces, and that you get a copy that is exactly like the original. If the contract is quite involved and contains things that you don't understand and that your contractor can't explain to your satisfaction, you might wish to consult an attorney. Remember that you will be responsible for attorney's fees, but in some cases it might be worth it.

Bonding

In almost all states, a contractor must have a bond posted with the state contractor's board, usually for $5,000 to $10,000. In the event that a contractor defaults on a contract, the state, after a hearing, might award you the bond. In order to be bonded, a contractor must show a certain amount of net worth and a history of financial responsibility. This is another good reason for using only licensed contractors.

Although this bond might be awarded by the state, it does not insure that your job will be completed. If added protection is desired, you can request that your contractor supply you with a completion or performance bond for the amount of your job. This type of bond insures that if the contractor is unable to finish the job for any reason, money will be available from the bonding company for you to complete the job properly. The drawback to this type of bond is that it's expensive, anywhere from 2 percent to 5 percent of the value of the job, and you will have to bear the cost.

Under most circumstances, careful control of the payments made to the contractor by you or by the bank is enough protection, but if you desire the additional security of a bond, ask for it. Be certain that your contractor is advised of it in advance so that he can include the cost in his bid, and see that details of the bond appear in the contract.

BEFORE CONSTRUCTION

Before construction begins, sit down with the contractor and get an idea of what sequence of steps the job will entail. In this way, you will have a better understanding of what inconveniences to expect, such as periods without water or electricity, and what rooms or areas of your home will be disturbed. Clean out affected rooms as much as possible (this is your responsibility), and close off other rooms to keep them clean. If the work involves the kitchen, set up temporary cooking facilities elsewhere, such as a hot plate or microwave oven in a spare bedroom. Agree on a place where materials can be stacked, as well as where job-site debris can be accumulated. Anything you can do to prepare your home and your family for the upcoming project will be a big help to both you and your contractor.

If your job requires a building permit, it should be on the job before the work starts. The permit will help ensure you that the building department has seen and approved your proposal before it gets underway. Bear in mind also that if the building inspectors find any dangerous conditions in your home during their routine inspections of the new work, such as unsafe wiring, you might be required to make repairs, even if the unsafe items have nothing to do with the new work in progress. The cost of repairing these items will be in addition to your original contract.

Start a job file of any papers relating to your job. This file should include a copy of your contract, plans, and change orders; bills, invoices, and canceled checks; preliminary lien notices and lien releases; correspondence and notes relating to your contractor; a list of subcontractors and what jobs they performed; and, if possible, a list of major material suppliers and what they supplied.

DURING CONSTRUCTION

As construction progresses, you might find items you wish to change from your original plan. There's nothing wrong with changes, and most contractors will take them in stride. The two things to remember about changes are to make them as early as possible so as not to cause costly delays in the schedule, and to get them in writing. As with the original contract, this step protects both you and the contractor, and saves a lot of misunderstanding.

If you plan to do any of the work yourself, and it was clearly agreed upon in the contract, be sure that you are ready at the appropriate time, and that you complete your portion promptly and correctly, without causing unnecessary delays for the contractor.

No job ever seems to run its course without some delays, however minor. Bad weather, late shipments, back-ordered materials, sick employees—all these things can plague a contractor during the course of a job. Take these things into consideration and be reasonable about them, even extending the date of completion if necessary. Your understanding of the problems a contractor faces on a job will help the entire project to run more smoothly.

Try your best to have the payments ready on time. The contractor depends on each payment to pay his employees, subcontractors, and material suppliers for the work they've done on your job up to that point, and your prompt payment helps avoid unnecessary delays and bad feelings.

AFTER CONSTRUCTION

When the job is complete and the final inspections have been passed, you might wish to make a walk-through inspection of the job with the contractor.

INFORMATION NOTICE TO OWNERS ABOUT CONSTRUCTION LIENS

OREGON LAW REQUIRES YOUR CONTRACTOR TO GIVE YOU THIS NOTICE if your contract price exceeds $1,000. The purpose of this notice is to explain the basics of the construction lien law and to help you protect yourself.

IF YOUR CONTRACTOR FAILS TO PAY SUBCONTRACTORS, MATERIAL SUPPLIERS OR LABORERS OR NEGLECTS TO MAKE OTHER LEGALLY REQUIRED PAYMENTS, THOSE PEOPLE WHO ARE OWED MONEY CAN LOOK TO YOUR PROPERTY FOR PAYMENT, EVEN IF YOU HAVE PAID YOUR CONTRACTOR IN FULL. THIS IS TRUE IF YOU:

HAVE HIRED a contractor to build a new home;

ARE BUYING a newly-built home;

ARE REMODELING or improving your property.

Under Oregon's laws, those who work on your property or provide materials and are not paid have a right to enforce their claim for payment against your property. This claim is known as a construction lien.

Persons who supply materials or labor ordered by your contractor are permitted by law to file a lien only if they have sent to you a Notice of the Right to Lien.

If you enter into a contract to buy a newly-built home or a partly-built home, you may not receive a Notice of the Right to Lien. Be aware that a lien may be claimed even though you have not received notice. You may want to ask your contractor or title insurance company about an ALTA title insurance policy based upon the receipt of lien waivers.

You have final responsibility for seeing that all bills are paid even if you have paid your contractor in full.

If you receive a Notice of the Right to Lien, take the Notice seriously. Let your contractor know you have received the Notice. Find out what arrangements are being made to pay the sender of the Notice.

WAYS TO PROTECT YOURSELF

- If you are dealing with a lending institution, ask your loan officer what precautions the institution takes when disbursing mortgage money to your contractor to verify that subcontractors and material suppliers are being paid.

- If you are paying your contractor directly, request a current statement of labor or materials provided to your property from each party that has sent you a Notice of the Right to Lien. You should make this request in writing and send it by certified mail. The party sending this Notice is required by law to respond to your request within 15 days from the date your letter is received.

- Make your check payable jointly. Name the contractor and the subcontractor or supplier as payees.

- Ask your contractor for a lien waiver from each party who has sent you a Notice of the Right to Lien.

- Consider using the services of an escrow agent to protect your interests. Find out whether your escrow agent will protect you against liens when disbursing payments. If you are interested in this alternative, consult your attorney.

When in doubt or if you need more details, consult an attorney. When and how to pay your contractor is a decision to which you should give serious thought.

By signing this notice you are indicating that you have received this notice, have read it and understand it. Your signature does not, in any way, give your contractor or those who provide materials, labor or services any additional rights to place a lien on your property.

Job Site Address: _____

This notice was furnished by: _____ This notice was received by: _____

_____ _____
Contractor   Property Owner

_____ _____ _____
Builders Board   Date   Date
Registration Number

If you find yourself in a "pay twice" situation, help **may** be available to you through the Builders Board. You may be able to file a claim with that agency.

For more details about the assistance available through the Builders Board, you may write to: **Builders Board, Department of Commerce, 403 Labor and Industries Building, Salem, Oregon 97310-0180.**

The material in this notice is not intended to be a complete analysis of the law (ORS Chapters 87 and 701). For more detailed information, contact your attorney.

WHITE COPY — CONTRACTOR   YELLOW COPY — PROPERTY OWNER

Fig. 6-2. Be sure your contractor gives you a notice regarding construction liens if such a notice is required in your state.

```
┌─────────────────────────────────────────────────────────────┐
│                 NOTICE OF THE RIGHT TO LIEN                  │
│       WARNING:  READ THIS NOTICE.  PROTECT YOURSELF FROM PAYING │
│       ANY CONTRACTOR OR SUPPLIER FOR THE SAME SERVICE.       │
│                                                             │
│                 Date of Mailing: _____          │
│                                                             │
│   TO:   _____    │
│         _____    │
│         _____    │
│                                                             │
│         THIS IS TO INFORM YOU that: _____     │
│   _____  │
│   has begun to provide (description of materials) _____  │
│   _____  │
│   _____  │
│   _____  │
│   _____  │
│                                                             │
│   ordered by _____  │
│   _____  │
│   for  improvements  to  property  you  own.  The  property  is │
│   located at: _____  │
│   _____  │
│                                                             │
│       A  lien  may  be  claimed  for  all  materials,  labor  and │
│   services  furnished  after  a  date  that  is  eight  days  not │
│   including  Saturdays,  Sundays  and  other  holidays  as  defined  in │
│   ORS 187.010 before this notice was mailed to you.         │
│                                                             │
│       Even  if  you  or  your  mortgage  lender  have  made  full │
│   payment  to  the  contractor  who  ordered  these  materials  or │
│   services,  your  property  may  still  be  subject  to  a  lien  unless │
│   the supplier providing this notice is paid.               │
│                                                             │
│       THIS  IS  NOT  A  LIEN.  It  is  a  notice  sent  to  you  for  your │
│   protection  in  compliance  with  the  construction  lien  laws  of │
│   the State of Oregon.                                      │
│                                                             │
│       This notice has been sent to you by:                  │
│                                                             │
│   Name:    _____  │
│   Address: _____  │
│            _____  │
│   Telephone:_____  │
│                                                             │
│       IF  YOU  HAVE  ANY  QUESTIONS  ABOUT  THIS  NOTICE,  FEEL  FREE │
│   TO CALL US.                                               │
│                                                             │
│             SEE OVER FOR IMPORTANT INFORMATION              │
└─────────────────────────────────────────────────────────────┘
```

Fig. 6-3. A typical preliminary lien notice from a subcontractor.

NOTICE TO MORTGAGEE OR BENEFICIARY UNDER TRUST DEED
OF DELIVERY OF MATERIAL AND SUPPLIES

TO ....

....

    This is to advise you, the owner of record of a mortgage or a beneficiary in a trust deed, on either the said land or improvements thereon, that the undersigned is delivering materials and supplies upon the order of

....

....

for use in the construction of an improvement located upon the following

described site in .... County, Oregon:

....

....

....

....

also known as .... Oregon.
STREET ADDRESS IF KNOWN

    You are further notified that a lien may be claimed for all such materials and supplies so delivered, after a date that is 8 days, not including Saturdays, Sundays and other holidays, as defined in ORS 187.010 before this notice is delivered to you in person or mailed to you by registered or certified mail and that payment by the owner or lender to the contractor does not remove the right of the undersigned furnishing such materials or supplies to claim a lien against the above described property unless the undersigned is in fact paid. No further notice to you of this or any subsequent delivery is necessary.

....
NAME

....
ADDRESS

Delivered to you by registered or certified mail	When delivered in person:
	Receipt of above notice is acknowledged.
at ...., Oregon	
on ...., 19........	Dated: ...., 19........
....	....
....	....
	MORTGAGEE—BENEFICIARY UNDER TRUST DEED

ORS 87.025(3) provides: (3) No lien for materials or supplies shall have priority over any recorded mortgage *or trust deed* on either the land or *improvement* unless the person furnishing *the* material or supplies, not later than 8 days, not including Saturdays, Sundays or other holidays as defined in ORS 187.010, after the date of delivery of material or supplies for which a lien may be claimed, delivers to the *mortgagee*, a notice in the form required by ORS 87.023 or substantially the same information as said Form.

FORM No. 1160A © 1983
Stevens-Ness Law Pub. Co.
Portland, OR 97204   OA

NOTE: THIS FORM TO BE USED ONLY FOR CONSTRUCTION COMMENCED AFTER OCTOBER 14, 1983.

Fig. 6-4. A typical preliminary lien notice from a material supplier.

Make a list of those things that were not completed to your satisfaction, and have your contractor take care of them.

A contractor's livelihood depends on word-of-mouth advertising, so if you're satisfied with the work, offer to be a reference for him in the future.

IF PROBLEMS OCCUR

If problems should occur during or after the job, sit down with the contractor and make every effort to resolve them. Most problems are the result of simple misunderstandings, and talking them out is usually all it takes. If the problem still can't be worked out, most state contractors' boards have an arbitration department that might be able to help. Arbitration, however, like any legal action, takes time, so make every effort to resolve the problem yourselves before seeking any outside help.

Most states have ruled that a contractor must warranty the job for a period of 12 months after completion against any problems that might occur, in addition to any separate warranties offered by the manufacturers of specific pieces of equipment. Completion is generally considered to be the date of final payment or the date of occupancy of the new work, whichever is first. If problems occur during that 12-month period, call your contractor back out for the necessary repairs.

CONSTRUCTION LIENS

The laws of most states provide that anyone who furnishes labor or materials can file a *construction lien,* also called a *mechanic's lien,* against your home if he is not paid. In extreme cases, such a lien could result in the legal forced sale of your home to satisfy these debts. Even if you have paid your contractor in good faith, these liens still can be filed against you if the contractor fails to pay his subcontractors or suppliers.

Many states require that an information notice about construction liens be provided to you by the contractor at the time you sign your contract. (See Fig. 6-2.) Be sure you receive a copy of this notice. Soon after your job gets underway, you may receive preliminary lien notices in the mail from subcontractors and suppliers (Figs. 6-3 and 6-4). This does not mean that a lien has been filed. It is simply to notify you that your contractor has made purchases or been supplied with labor in connection with your job, and that these people have the right to file a lien in the event of nonpayment.

The laws concerning licensing, bonding, and regulating contractors, construction liens, and other subjects dealing with the construction industry vary among states. Before you start any project involving a contract, write or call the contractor's board in your state for more information.

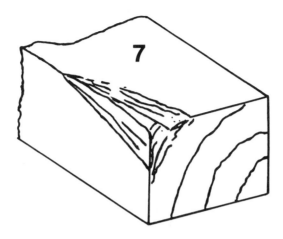

Lumber, Nails, and Tools

Before any actual construction begins, it's important to know something about some of the materials you'll be using, in particular lumber and nails. The selection process can at times be confusing, given the wide selection of materials available at most lumberyards. Having a basic knowledge of how lumber is graded and what grades are best for each application can help ensure a successful framing job. It also helps you avoid paying extra for a better grade of lumber than you actually need.

With nails, the selection is equally confusing. There is quite a variety of sizes, types, and head styles of nails, each with a specific application. It's a good idea to familiarize yourself with the main types, since choosing the proper nail for the job at hand is an important consideration.

LUMBER

You will often hear the terms *hardwood* and *softwood,* which might be a bit confusing. The terms do not refer to the wood's actual hardness or soft-

ness, but rather to the type of tree from which it comes. Softwoods come from a group of trees known as *conifers,* meaning that they bear cones. Softwood trees are usually needle bearing and evergreen, and include such common species as fir, pine, cedar, redwood, hemlock, and cypress. (See Table 7-1.)

Hardwood trees are *deciduous,* meaning that they seasonally lose their leaves. Common hardwood species include maple, oak, walnut, birch, and cherry.

The actual species of lumber used in framing varies in different parts of the country. In most Western and Midwestern states, for example, softwood lumber such as fir, hemlock, and pine are all quite common; however, high transportation costs might make some of these species unavailable or prohibitively expensive in the East. It is best to be guided in your selection of framing lumber by what is readily available in your area, and by the recommendations of a reputable lumberyard.

Table 7-1. Common Softwood Grades and Their Uses.

WOOD	TOP GRADE, BEST APPEARANCE, FEW IF ANY DEFECTS.	SLIGHT DEFECTS, OKAY FOR MOST EXPOSED WORK.	GENERAL USE FOR FRAMING, OUTDOOR USE.	MANY DEFECTS, GOOD FOR SOME ROUGH USAGES.
Redwood	Clear All Heart Clear	Select Heart Select	Constr. Heart Construction	Merchantable
Red Cedar	C and Better Finish	C Finish	Select Merchant. Construction	Standard
Douglas Fir	C and Better Finish	C Finish	Construction	Standard
Pine	C and Better 1 and 2 Clear Supreme	C Select Choice	Quality D Select	1-3 Dimension 1-5 Common Utility

Lumber Grades

Lumber grading again varies according to region, species, and the rules and standards of each particular grading association. (See Appendix B.) In general, you will find lumber divided into three wide groups.

Yard Lumber. *Yard lumber* is the group most widely found in lumberyards, and is the most common for framing applications. Certain standard sizes are commonly available regardless of species. Lumber in this category is appropriate for joists, plates, studs, and most other framing members.

Structural Lumber. *Structural lumber* indicates lumber graded specifically for strength, and is sometimes specified by an engineer for certain high-load applications. The term *structural* or the abbreviation *struc* is typically included in the grade stamp on the lumber.

Factory and Shop Lumber. *Factory and shop lumber* is intended solely for remanufacturing applications, and is used in the construction of doors, moldings, trim, and similar applications.

Grade Stamps

As wood is milled from logs into finished lumber, each piece is inspected by an experienced lumber grader, who is certified under the rules and standards of the governing association for that species and region. These graders separate the lumber into appropriate categories, then stamp each piece with a mark known as a *grade stamp*. A grade stamp, like the label on a can of food, tells you ex-

actly what you need to know about a particular piece of wood.

Grade stamps vary, but each usually contains the following information: the association that graded the lumber, the mill that produced the lumber, the actual grade designation, the lumber species, and the moisture content of the wood at the time it was surfaced. Ask your lumber dealer for an explanation of the grade stamps used in your area. They are your assurance that you're getting the right lumber for a particular application. They also offer some assistance in avoiding defects (Fig. 7-1).

Dimension Lumber

Most framing lumber falls within the classification of dimension lumber. Although it's again important to point out that these grades and standards vary, dimension lumber is commonly broken into four categories:

Light Framing. Light framing lumber is 2 to 4 inches thick and 2 to 4 inches wide. Light framing lumber is intended for general framing use, and should not be used where high strength is essential. The grades, from highest to lowest, are Construction, Standard, Utility, and Economy. Only Construction or Standard grades should be used for framing, and the two are often grouped together and specified simply as "Standard and Better." Utility grades are suitable for blocking, bracing, and other similar uses.

Studs. Studs are lumber that is 2 to 4 inches

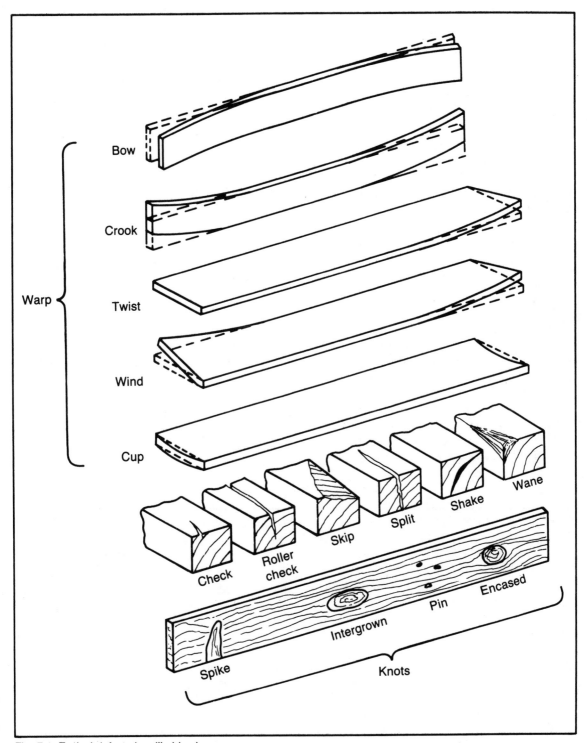

Fig. 7-1. Typical defects in milled lumber.

Bow

Crook

Twist

Warp

Wind

Cup

Check

Roller check

Skip

Split

Shake

Wane

Spike

Intergrown

Pin

Encased

Knots

thick and 2 to 4 inches wide. Studs are available in two grades: Stud and Economy Stud. This category is actually a sub-category to Light Framing, and is limited to boards that are 10 feet or less in length.

Structural Light Framing. Structural light framing is used where greater strength is required. Sizes range from 2 to 4 inches thick and 2 to 4 inches wide. The grades are Select Structural, No. 1, No. 2, No. 3, and Economy.

Structural Joists and Planks. Structural joists and planks include lumber that is 2 to 4 inches thick and 6 inches wide or wider. Like Structural Light Framing, the grades are Select Structural, No. 1, No. 2, No. 3, and Economy. Lumber from this group is used for joists, headers, rafters, and general framing. The most common framing grades are No. 1 and No. 2.

Moisture Content

Another important consideration in lumber selection is its moisture content. When a tree is first cut, a large portion of its weight, in some cases up to one-half, is moisture. As this moisture leaves the wood, the cells shrink, which affects the wood's size. In order for wood to be milled into usable lumber, its moisture content must be reduced to a level where further drying will only marginally affect its surfaced dimensions.

Lumber is dried, or *seasoned,* in one of two ways. *Stack drying,* also called *air drying,* is accomplished by stacking the lumber outside with small sticks between each layer, then allowing the lumber to dry over a long period of time through natural air circulation.

Kiln drying, a superior but more costly method, uses large ovens, called *kilns,* to dry the wood. Temperature, humidity, and air circulation within the kiln are all carefully controlled, producing lumber of a more uniform size and moisture content, with fewer defects.

Lumber used in framing should never exceed 19 percent moisture content, and 15 percent is preferable. On most grade stamps, you will see one of the following designations, referring to the lumber's moisture content at the time of surfacing:

☐ *MC 15.* A moisture content of 15 percent maximum.
☐ *S-DRY.* 19 percent maximum moisture content.
☐ *S-GRN.* Over 19 percent moisture content, meaning the lumber is *green,* or unseasoned.

Nominal and Actual Size

Lumber is almost always described and ordered by its *nominal size,* which is the rough-cut size of the board before final milling. In almost all grades of lumber, a board's nominal size is different from its actual size. For example, a board classified as a 2 × 4 is actually 1 1/2 inches × 3 1/2 inches (dry). These actual sizes are now fairly universal, and you will quickly get used to the difference in what you specify and what you receive.

Another common size specification, primarily for hardwoods, is by 1/4 inches. A board specified as 4/4 is four 1/4 inches thick, or one inch. A 6/4 board is 1 1/2 inches; an 8/4 board is 2 inches, etc.

NAILS

Nails are specified by their size, shank type, head type, point type, and coating. Every type, with the exception of a few special-purpose nails like gutter spikes, are sold by the pound. The number of nails per pound will, of course, vary with the nail's size. Most types of nails are also sold in 50-pound boxes, which is a convenient and money-saving way to purchase those types of nails you'll use for a lot of the construction.

Nail size is specified by the word *penny,* such as a 16-penny nail. This designation originally was the cost in pennies per 100 nails of a given size, but is now an indicator of a nail's length. (See Fig. 7-2.) Penny is abbreviated by a lowercase letter *d,* such as *16d.*

Common Types

☐ *Common Nails.* The most popular type of nail for general carpentry and framing. It has a large-diameter shank and good shear strength,

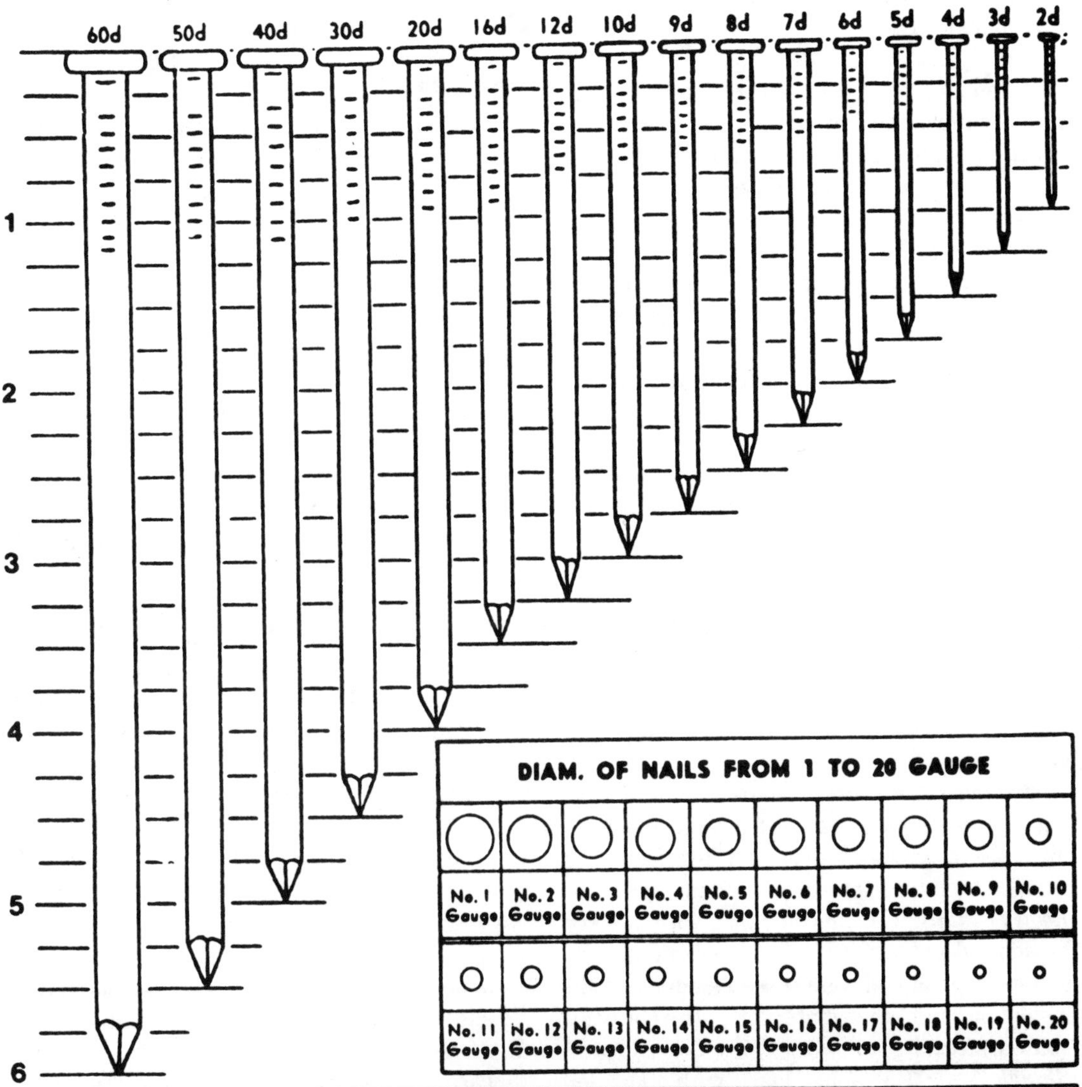
60d
50d
40d
30d
20d
16d
12d
10d
9d
8d
7d
6d
5d
4d
3d
2d
1
2
3
4
5
6
DIAM. OF NAILS FROM 1 TO 20 GAUGE
No. 1 Gauge
No. 2 Gauge
No. 3 Gauge
No. 4 Gauge
No. 5 Gauge
No. 6 Gauge
No. 7 Gauge
No. 8 Gauge
No. 9 Gauge
No. 10 Gauge
No. 11 Gauge
No. 12 Gauge
No. 13 Gauge
No. 14 Gauge
No. 15 Gauge
No. 16 Gauge
No. 17 Gauge
No. 18 Gauge
No. 19 Gauge
No. 20 Gauge

COMMON NAILS REFERENCE TABLE

SIZE	LENGTH AND GAUGE	DIAMETER HEAD	APPROX. NO. TO POUND	SIZE	LENGTH AND GAUGE	DIAMETER HEAD	APPROX. NO TO POUND
2d	1 inch..........No. 15	11/64	845	10d	3 inch..........No. 9	5/16	65
3d	1 1/4 inch..........No. 14	13/64	540	12d	3 1/4 inch..........No. 9	5/16	60
4d	1 1/2 inch.........No. 12 1/2	1/4	290	16d	3 1/2 inch..........No. 8	11/32	45
5d	1 3/4 inch..........No. 12 1/2	1/4	250	20d	4 inch..........No. 6	13/32	30
6d	2 inch..........No. 11 1/2	17/64	165	30d	4 1/2 inch..........No. 5	7/16	20
7d	2 1/4 inch ....No. 11 1/2	17/64	150	40d	5 inch..........No. 4	15/32	17
8d	2 1/2 inch..........No. 10 1/4	9/32	100	50d	5 1/2 inch..........No. 3	1/2	13
9d	2 3/4 inch..........No. 10 1/4	9/32	90	60d	6 inch..........No. 2	17/32	10

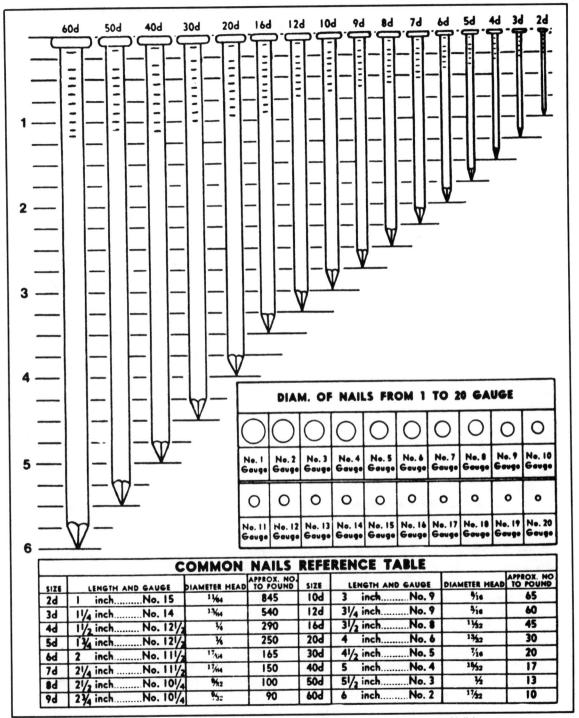

Fig. 7-2. The lengths, gauges, and quantity per pound of common nails (Courtesy of Maze Nails).

and is available in a wide selection of sizes, styles, and finishes.

☐ *Box Nails.* Lighter and with a smaller diameter than common nails, with less tendency to split the wood; used in framing applications where shear strength is not a consideration, as for nailing subfloors, and in many types of assembly work.

☐ *Concrete Nails.* Made of tempered steel in round, square, and fluted shank styles; used primarily for fastening wood members to concrete and masonry.

☐ *Finishing Nails.* Designed for finish and trim applications, finish nails have a small, slightly rounded head and are designed to be driven below the surface so the resulting hole can be filled and finished.

☐ *Casing nails.* Similar to finishing nails in style and application, but with a tapered head and a heavier shank.

☐ *Drywall Nails.* Ring-shank or cement-coated nails; designed specifically for installing drywall sheets. Most drywall nails have a slightly cupped head, which makes them easier to conceal with joint compound.

☐ *Joist Hanger Nails.* Short, hardened nails having a large-diameter, barbed shank and very high shear strength; designed for fastening wooden members into timber connectors.

☐ *Roofing Nails.* Galvanized nails with a very broad head and a barbed shank; designed for installing asphalt and composition shingles, rigid insulation, and other materials with relatively soft surfaces.

☐ *Shingle Nails.* Galvanized nails with a slender shank and a relatively small head; used to install wood shingles and shakes.

☐ *Siding Nails.* Galvanized nails, usually with a slender, barbed or ring shank; designed specifically for installing wood siding.

☐ *Washer Nails.* Any of a variety of nails having a washer, commonly of rubber, plastic, vinyl, or lead, located beneath the head. The washer flattens out under the head as the nail is driven, providing a weathertight seal over the nail hole.

They are commonly used with plastic and metal roofing, and in similar applications.

Finishes

Nails quite often are coated with various materials to improve their weather resistance, holding strength, and driving ease. Some of the more common coatings follow.

☐ *Bright-Finished.* A bright, uncoated steel finish; used where corrosion resistance is not required.

☐ *Galvanized.* A thick, somewhat rough coating applied to a nail to increase its corrosion resistance. Zinc chips are sprinkled over steel nails in a drum, then the drum is rotated in a furnace to melt the zinc over the nails. In common usage, *galvanized* is often used to describe a nail that has been zinc-coated using any of a variety of methods.

☐ *Hot-Dipped Galvanized.* Nails that have been dipped into a vat of molten zinc for corrosion resistance. The resulting coating is thick and uniform, and is considered by many to be the most effective galvanizing process. The nails can be dipped a second time for additional protection, and then commonly are referred to as *double-dipped.*

☐ *Electroplating.* A corrosion-resistant coating applied by immersing the nails in an electrolytic solution. A shiny film of zinc then is deposited on the nail by an electrical current from zinc anodes. The resulting coating is relatively thin and best suited for indoor applications.

☐ *Mechanical Plating.* Cold nails are rotated in a barrel with zinc dust and small glass pellets. The pellets hammer the zinc into the nails, which are then immersed in a chromate rinse, giving them their characteristic gold or greenish color.

☐ *Blued.* Nails that are sterilized by heat until an oxidation coating is formed, offering good temporary rust protection for interior applications.

☐ *Cement-Coated.* A semipermanent resin coating designed to give the nail greater holding power.

☐ *Colored.* Small-diameter finishing nails with a dyed, painted, or anodized finish, available in a variety of colors; mainly used with prefinished paneling and moldings to eliminate the need for countersinking and finishing.

☐ *Quench-Hardened.* Nails that have been heated, quenched, and tempered to increase their resistance to bending; often used when nailing into hardwoods and concrete.

☐ *Vinyl-Coated.* Nails that have a thin coating of vinyl resin, usually green in color, to provide easier driving and some pullout resistance; used primarily for framing applications.

TIMBER CONNECTORS

For many framing applications, particularly remodeling, timber connectors have become quite commonplace in recent years. There is a growing selection of special-purpose connectors for a variety of applications. (See Fig. 7-3.) Having some knowledge of the more common ones and what

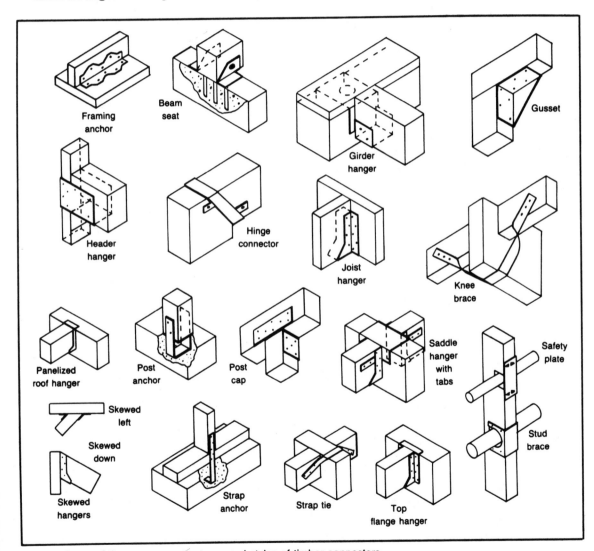

Fig. 7-3. Some of the more common types and styles of timber connectors.

their uses are can be very helpful, since timber connectors can provide increased strength while saving time and labor at many stages of the framing process.

As well as stocking some of the more common types of timber connectors, most lumberyards have catalogs of special-purpose hangers in stock sizes, which they can usually order for you quite quickly. Most timber connector manufacturers also will make up custom hangers for you at a reasonable cost. This is worth remembering for some of the odd framing and transition situations when you can't devise any other way of making an important connection.

Common Types

- [ ] *Anchors and Clips.* Any of a variety of connectors used to tie and reinforce the joint between two wooden members. They might be used between a rafter and the top plate, between a stud and the sole plate, or in hundreds of other wood-to-wood areas.
- [ ] *Beam Seat.* Used to connect a wooden beam directly to concrete, eliminating the need to form a beam pocket in the concrete. It has metal prongs, which are embedded in the concrete, and a U-shaped plate, which receives the beam.
- [ ] *Girder Hanger.* In certain applications, such as a dropped floor, you need to have the floor girders level with the foundation stem wall rather than resting on it. The girder hanger sits over the top of the stem wall and under the sill plate, providing a pocket into which to set the girder.
- [ ] *Gusset.* An L-shaped bracket with a 45-degree reinforcing web; used to add support where two members meet at right angles, such as a post and a beam.
- [ ] *Header Hanger.* Some types of energy-efficient framing emphasize the elimination of extra lumber, and the header hanger can help. Attached to the king stud, it carries the weight of a window or door header, eliminating the need for the trimmers.
- [ ] *Hinge Connectors.* Available in a variety of sizes,

and used to splice and support two beams of different heights.
- [ ] *Joist Hanger.* A U-shaped connector used to connect horizontal members at right angles. Common uses are attaching floor joists to a girder or ledger, or ceiling joists to a beam.
- [ ] *Knee Brace.* A U-shaped connector that spans the underside of a beam for additional stability and a more positive connection between the beam and adjacent purlins or joists.
- [ ] *Panelized Roof Hanger.* A small, top flange hanger for use with prefabricated roof panels, primarily in commercial building.
- [ ] *Post Anchor.* Any of a variety of connectors having a prong or leg, which is embedded in concrete, and a seat, which receives the post. Post anchors raise the post above the concrete, keeping water away from the wood and prolonging its life.
- [ ] *Post Caps.* Used at the other end of the post, these connectors form a positive connection between the post and the beam or other member it supports.
- [ ] *Saddle Hanger.* Essentially a double joist hanger, the saddle hanger is hung over the top of the supporting member and receives a joist from each side.
- [ ] *Skewed.* Joist or saddle hangers that angle down or to the side; used to connect members at angles other than 90 degrees.
- [ ] *Strap Anchor.* A hooked strap which is embedded in concrete; used as a tie between the concrete and framing.
- [ ] *Strap Tie.* Similar to a knee brace, this connector goes over the top of a beam to tie it to the adjacent purlins.
- [ ] *Stud Braces and Safety Plates.* Metal plates used to reinforce studs that have been cut out for pipes, and to protect pipes and wires from being punctured by nails.
- [ ] *Top Flange Hanger.* A type of joist hanger having a 90-degree flange at the top. It is secured to the top as well as the sides of the supporting member for additional strength.

Timber connectors should be installed using an

adequate number of special hardened steel joist hanger nails, or with bolts. Check with your building inspector for specific restrictions that might apply to certain applications.

TOOLS

No advice is more valuable than the old saying "The right tool for the right job." Having the proper tools for a specific project can make the work safer, faster, and much more enjoyable.

Before you begin work on your addition, you should take a moment to assess the tools you have available and their condition. It might be necessary to purchase some of the more basic items in order to round out your tool box, and perhaps add a few more specialized tools as the need arises. Many of the more expensive, special-purpose tools that you'll only need once or twice can be rented much more cost effectively than buying them.

Buying Tools

When you are purchasing tools, always buy the best you can afford. You'll get tools that are more accurate and easier to use, and that will prove a very wise investment in years to come. The initial cost will be somewhat higher than tools on the "bargain rack," but good tools, properly cared for, will last a lifetime. In fact, some manufacturers offer lifetime guarantees on their hand tools; if you break one in normal use, no matter how long you've owned it, you'll get a replacement free.

When you are shopping for tools, don't use price as an absolute indicator of quality. Look closely at the tool's construction. It should feel sturdy, with solid, well-joined metal parts. Movable parts should operate freely and smoothly. Adjustments, if any, should be easy to make, and then should lock firmly in place. Electric tools should have either a grounded (three prong) plug or a double insulated case, and also be UL approved. Finally, and perhaps most important, a tool needs to feel right in your hands.

The Basic Tool Kit

The following list is composed of the tools most carpenters consider to be the basics. They will meet most of your tool requirements for the addition. Check over the list and compare it to your own tool box, then add any tools you feel you're likely to need. Getting this procedure out of the way before construction begins will save you the frustration of needing a tool on the job site and not having it available. Above all, don't try to substitute by using a tool for a purpose other than the one for which it was designed. It never works quite right and often can be dangerous.

Hammer. A 16-ounce hammer with a curved claw is about the best for all-around use. The handle can be wood, fiberglass, or steel, whichever feels best. The striking face should be crowned (slightly rounded over) to prevent dangerous chipping around the edges. You might wish to add a 10- or 12-ounce hammer for finish work, and a heavier framing hammer for rough work. Framing hammers have a longer handle for a more powerful swing, and range in weight from 20 to 32 ounces. Don't buy one that's too heavy for you, since constant use can be quite tiring.

Handsaw. You should have a handsaw that is at least 20 inches long, preferably 26 inches, with 10 teeth per inch. The handle should be solid wood, and well attached to the blade. Although it's not really a basic tool, most people immediately add an electric circular saw, which, on a project as large as a room addition, is almost a necessity. Select a solid, commercial-duty model for long life and accurate adjustments. Most carpenters use a saw with a 7 1/4-inch blade.

Screwdrivers. Four basic sizes will handle most projects: 1/4 × 4 (or 6) and 5/16 × 8 slotted (sizes refer to blade width and blade length), and a #2 and #3 Phillips head. Adding a 3/16 × 4 slotted and a #1 Phillips will help. Blades should be quality alloyed steel, well attached to heads of wood or contoured, high-impact plastic. A good feel is very important.

Adjustable Wrench. Two adjustable wrenches will cover most nut and bolt sizes: a 6-inch one for small jobs and a 10- or 12-inch one for general use. Look for high-quality steel and an easily adjustable head with little play.

Pliers. The basic is the 6- or 8-inch slip-joint

plier, preferably with a wire-cutting slot. If possible, add a pair of adjustable pliers, about 12 or 13 inches long. Look for an interlocking, slotted adjustment on the handle, not just a nut in a series of interconnected holes.

Measuring Tape. What you buy is a matter of preference. For general use, most carpenters use a retractable steel tape with a locking blade. It should be at least 16 feet long, preferably 25 feet. You might consider adding a 50- or 100-foot retractable tape also, which can be a big help in layout work.

Utility Knife. Get one with a steel handle and retractable, interchangeable blades. Purchase a name brand that you know will always have replacement blades available.

Level. A 24-inch level is about the most versatile, with at least one vial each for level and plumb. Machined aluminum levels work well, as do metal-trimmed wood. Look for sturdy, solid construction.

Clamps. You'll want at least one pair of C-clamps with solid metal bodies, not the type that is made from two metal pieces stamped together. A good, all-around size is 4 inches, and you can buy larger and smaller sizes as you need them.

Square. A metal combination square will handle most marking jobs, acting as a square for both 45 and 90 degrees. Look for solid-steel construction in both head and blade, with a solid-locking knob. You also should have a steel framing square, which is essential for roof and stair layout, and for many other uses.

Drill. With the proliferation of good-quality, low-cost electric drills on the market, one definitely belongs in the basic tool kit. You can get by with a 1/4-inch chuck, but a 3/8-inch one is much more versatile. Useful options include reverse and variable speed. Add a starter set of quality twist drills, and also a set of wood-boring bits. Other drill accessories are usually quite inexpensive, and can be added as you need them.

Miscellaneous Small Tools. Round out your basic tool kit with at least two nail sets (1/16 inch and 1/8 inch), a 1- to 2-inch putty knife with a flexible blade, a 2-inch rigid blade scraper, and

two pry bars—a small one for moldings, and a large one for general tearout work. It's also useful to have a plastic container of screws in various sizes, and one with a variety of nails.

Toolbox. Finally, you need a place to keep everything, both for convenience and to protect the tools. A good metal toolbox with fairly deep storage will handle just about everything, or you can make a nice wooden one, custom designed for your needs. A lift-out top tray is a desirable option, making it easy to keep track of small tools and have them handy where you're working.

RENTAL TOOLS

Good tools are expensive, especially if you only intend to use them once, and cheap tools usually aren't worth buying. An alternative is to simply rent the tool you need, especially if you'll only be needing it once or twice. You'll have the use of the tool for a fraction of what it would cost you to buy it, and you're assured that it's a tool of professional quality.

The following list will give you some idea of what equipment is available and what its purpose is. Half-day rates are available on most items, at about 75 percent of the cost for a full day. You also can rent most tools by the weekend, week, or month at reduced rates.

Builder's Equipment

Air Compressors. Air compressors are used for powering nail guns, painting equipment, or a variety of other uses. Accessories, such as a nail gun, are extra, as are the nails you use. You'll usually be given a whole box of nails, then be charged for what you've used out of the box when you return it.

Builder's Level. This is a tripod-mounted instrument for establishing level lines. You also can rent a level transit, for plumb as well as level lines.

Drills. Rental yards have a variety of drills, including 3/8- and 1/2-inch general-purpose models, right-angle drills for confined areas, and roto-hammers, which combine drilling with hammering for making holes in concrete. Bits are extra.

Gas-Powered Generators. Gas-powered generators are used to provide remote electrical power.

House Jacks. A house jack is used for general lifting and leveling, available in both screw and hydraulic models.

Ladders. There is a variety of ladders from which to choose, including extension ladders in lengths ranging from 16 to 40 feet, and step ladders, ranging from 6 to 16 feet. Ladder accessories such as ladder jacks and scaffold planks are also available.

Miter Saw. These saws are available in both hand and electrically operated models.

Powder-Activated Gun. A 22-caliber gun is used to fire special nails or threaded studs into concrete. Shells and nails are extra.

Reciprocating Saw. Commonly called a Sawzall, after the most widely known brand name, this is a truly handy tool for remodeling, capable of cutting a variety of materials.

Router. A router is used for routing wood or for trimming plastic laminates. Bits are extra.

Drywall Jack. A drywall jack is a very handy device that allows one person to lift a full sheet of drywall or plywood into position on a ceiling. Some types also can be used for walls.

Table and Circular Saws. These saws are available in sizes and blade types to handle all your cutting needs. Blades are extra.

Welder. Welders are available in gas or electric models.

Concrete and Masonry Work

Brick Saw. This tool is a small, table-mounted electric saw used to cut bricks, concrete blocks, ceramic tile, and some types of stone. Most types use a small pump to circulate cooling water over the blade.

Concrete Saw. A concrete saw is a water-cooled, gas-powered unit for cutting concrete slabs.

Cut-Off Saw. This saw is a portable gas- or electric-powered unit for cutting blocks, stone, brick, and some metal.

Cement Mixer. Gas or electric mixers for concrete or mortar are available.

Trowel Machine. A gas-operated power troweler is used for finishing concrete slabs.

Vibrator. An electrically operated, vibrating cable is inserted into wet concrete to encourage the necessary packing action that helps prevent voids.

Excavating

Compacter. A compacter is used for settling and compacting loose dirt.

Demolition Hammer. A demolition hammer is used in breaking up concrete, rock, asphalt, etc. It might be either air operated, for use with a compressor, or electric.

Loader. A loader is a small, gas-powered tractor for moving dirt, gravel, etc. A trailer is usually included in the price for transporting the machine to the site, or the rental yard can deliver it for you.

Trencher. A gas-powered trencher is used for digging trenches, footings, etc.

Flooring

Carpet Laying Tools. These tools include power stretchers and knee kickers for stretching the carpet, electric-seaming irons for making seams, and electrically powered staplers for some types of carpet installations.

Floor Polisher. Interchangeable heads on this tool permit cleaning, waxing, wax stripping, or polishing.

Floor Sanders. These tools are used for sanding down hardwood floors after installation, or prior to refinishing. They are electrically operated and are available in large drum types, for the main floor area, and edgers, for finishing off the areas against the wall.

Linoleum Roller. This tool is used for rolling the bubbles out of linoleum.

Tile Cutters. This hand-operated tool is used for cutting ceramic or asphalt tile.

Painting and Decorating

Acoustic Sprayer. An acoustic sprayer is used for blowing decorative, sound-absorbing acoustic material onto ceilings.

Airless Paint Sprayer. An airless paint sprayer is a clean, easy method for spraying most types of house paints without the use of compressed air.

Banjo. This device is used for taping drywall joints.

Compressed-Air Paint Sprayer. This sprayer is a compressor and paint-gun combination, used for spraying lacquer and certain types of paint.

Electric Paint Remover. This flat, electrically heated tool softens paint, simplifying its removal from wood.

Pressure Washer. This gas- or electric-powered unit is used for high-pressure washing prior to painting or for general cleaning.

Sand Blaster. A sand blaster is used for heavy cleaning and paint removal.

Wallpaper Steamer. This tank and hose assembly turns water into steam to soften old wallpaper and simplify its removal.

Plumbing

Pipe Cutters. Various types of pipe cutters are available for cutting galvanized, copper, and cast-iron pipe.

Propane Equipment. You can rent a soldering torch for soldering copper pipe, or a melting furnace for melting the lead used in older types of cast-iron pipe assembly.

Pipe Threaders. Pipe threaders are used to cut external threads on steel pipe.

Snakes. These hand- or power-operated units are used to clear clogs in toilets or sewer lines.

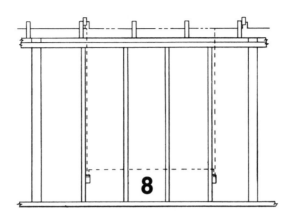

Transitions and Demolition

Perhaps the most unique aspect of building a room addition is the need to remove a portion of the existing home in order to tie the old and new sections together, all the while making the new section look like it has always been there.

The amount of demolition work and the number of transition areas will vary widely among room additions. Some might only require the removal of a little siding, while others might necessitate removing walls, plumbing, and electrical wiring. All the demolition might occur at the start of the job, or recur in different areas as the addition progresses. For that reason, this chapter has been placed before the actual construction chapters. It will offer a good introduction to some of the problems that might lie ahead, and will equip you better to prepare for them as they occur.

DEMOLITION SAFETY

The first and foremost rule of demolition, no matter how minor the task, is safety! Never take a demolition operation for granted, and always be completely prepared for the job at hand.

The following safety precautions always should be followed, both for your personal safety and so as not to undermine the structural integrity of the building:

☐ Always know exactly what it is you're about to remove. Check to see what's behind it, below it, and what it might support.

☐ Never assume that a structural member you're about to remove doesn't support anything.

☐ When you are removing framing that is near electrical wiring, shut off the electricity, even if you're not actually removing the wiring. Do the same for any plumbing or gas lines.

☐ When you are removing electrical wiring, shut the circuit breaker or remove the fuse controlling the circuit you're working on, then post a note on the electrical panel warning others not to turn it back on.

☐ When you are working on plumbing and gas lines, shut off the water and gas, respectively.

□ Use only the proper tools; never improvise. If you don't have the right tool, buy or rent it.

□ When you are doing demolition work, wear heavy clothing, including gloves and heavy boots.

□ Always wear eye protection. When there is a danger of anything falling from above, also wear a hard hat.

RECYCLING MATERIALS

In many instances, it might be to your advantage to reuse some of the materials you are removing. If you have an older home, for example, much of what you tear out might be difficult to match, or in some cases might even be valuable. Be especially careful in removing anything that might be of use. Even if you don't intend to reuse it, you might be able to sell it. Many cities have used building material outlets that will buy what you have, or you can try an advertisement in the local paper.

Wood Moldings

Some of the items most often saved during demolition work are wood moldings and trim. Reusing these moldings can save you money over having to purchase them new, and you might not always be able to match older patterns. Look carefully at any moldings you need to remove, and decide if they can be reused in the new addition.

If a molding has been painted several times, its joints might be obscured. Also, the paint acts as a binder to keep the molding stuck to the wall or other surface, which can damage the molding when you try to remove it. To begin, use a utility knife or single-edge razor blade and cut through the paint at the joints. Also cut along the seam where the molding joins the wall or other surface. Work slowly, and be careful not to gouge into the molding or wall.

Using a small, flat wrecking bar, work the molding away from the wall, starting at one of the joints. Pry the molding up slowly, a few inches at a time. You will find it easiest if you place the bar near each nail that fastens the molding.

When the molding has been removed, do not try to drive the nails back through the front. This will cause the head to push up the surrounding wood, often splintering it. Instead, use a pair of end cutters and work from the back. Grip the nail near where it protrudes through the back of the molding, and with a rolling motion of the curved head on the end cutters, pull the nail through the molding from front to back.

These same procedures can be used for removing siding, paneling, trim, hardwood flooring, and other wooden components of the house.

Windows and Doors

The techniques for removing windows will vary depending on the type and style of window. In general, depending on whether the window has a wood or metal frame, one of three methods was used when it was installed. Reversing the installation methods, therefore, will work to remove just about any window you encounter.

Most wood windows are installed in one of two ways. Operable windows are built similar to doors, and the sash is set in a frame to make up a one-piece unit. The window unit is placed in the wall opening, shimmed as necessary to make it plumb and level, then fastened by driving finish nails through the window frame into the wall framing. The joint between the window frame and the wall opening then is covered with a molding.

To remove this type of window, first remove the moldings. Then, using a hacksaw blade or a reciprocating saw equipped with a metal cutting blade, cut between the window frame and the wall opening. This procedure will sever the nails, and allow you to remove the entire window unit.

Fixed windows often have the glass held in the frame with small moldings, so simply removing the moldings will enable you to remove the glass. Wear gloves, and handle the glass edges carefully. Once the glass is out, use the same method employed for operable windows to cut the nails and remove the frame. Discard the glass in a safe place rather than reuse it.

The third installation method applies primarily to metal-frame windows, which usually have an installation flange around the outside of the frame.

Nails or screws are driven through the flange to secure the window to the outside of the wall framing, then the flange is covered with trim. Your first step is to remove the trim and expose the flange. Then, working with a flat pry bar, get behind the flange and carefully pry it away from the wall. As the flange begins to come loose, work your bar or a pair of end cutters between the nail head and the flange, and pull the nails.

Doors are removed pretty much like operable wood windows. Drive the hinge pins out and remove the door, then remove the door casings. It is then simply a matter of cutting between the door jambs and the wall opening to sever the nails and remove the door frame in one piece.

Other Building Components

Among the other components of the building that are worth saving is just about anything that is bolted or screwed down, and is therefore easy to remove in an undamaged condition. The list includes electrical appliances and fixtures; bathroom and kitchen fixtures such as sinks, faucets, and toilets; and cabinets and preformed counter tops. Study the item to be removed carefully, determining as accurately as possible how it was originally installed, then reverse that procedure. Follow the safety tips outlined previously, and again, be certain you know what you're removing and what it supports before you take it out.

With the exception of carpeting and hardwood flooring, most floor covering cannot be removed in any usable form. Linoleum, floor tile, and most types of ceramic tile are applied with adhesives that are strong enough to bond them to the floor for the life of the flooring, making them virtually impossible to pry up in good condition.

To remove wall-to-wall carpeting, it's necessary to separate it into workable pieces, usually room size. You will almost always find seams in doorways between rooms. Using a straightedge as a guide, slit through the seam with a utility or carpet knife. Starting from the seam, grip the carpet firmly and work your way around the room, pulling the carpet up from the tack strip, which is located around the room's perimeter. Once the

carpeting is loose, lay it back out and then roll it up, binding it with twine to keep it rolled. If the carpet is to be reused or sold, rolling it up is preferable to folding it because rolling it prevents the backing from becoming creased. For large rooms, cut the carpet up along the original seams so that the pieces will be easier to handle.

REMOVAL OF A BEARING WALL

The one aspect of demolition that causes the greatest amount of concern for most people is the removal of a weight-bearing wall. Improper removal can be very dangerous to the person doing the work, and can also seriously damage the structure of the house. When properly planned for and executed, however, this phase of the demolition should cause you no more problems or be any more dangerous than any other tear-out operation.

The bearing-wall removal operation consists of four phases: determination of the load on the wall, erection of temporary bracing, removal of the wall, and transference of the wall's load. Each phase will be dealt with separately in the sections that follow.

Determination of Load

Every house has two types of walls: *weight-bearing walls*, which carries a load in addition to the weight of the wall itself, such as a ceiling joist resting on the wall's top plate; and *nonweight-bearing walls*, also called *curtain* or *partition walls*, which only carry their own weight. Before removing a wall, it is first necessary to determine if it is weight bearing, and if so, what load it carries.

For a one-story house, or for walls on the upper floor of a multistory house, the best way to tell if a wall is weight bearing is to look in the attic. Locate the top of the upper plate of the wall you're checking (you might have to move some insulation), and study it carefully. Are ceiling joists spliced across the top of it? Do the rafters have vertical or diagonal bracing extending down onto the wall plates? Does the wall support any other weight, such as a roof air conditioner or solar panels? These are all obvious indications that a wall is weight bearing.

In addition to loads that are clearly visible, certain assumptions must be made for those walls that cannot be checked. All exterior walls, for example, always are considered to be weight bearing. In all but a few cases, they carry the weight of the roof structure. Also, since it's usually impossible to verify, assume that every wall on the lower floors of a multistory house is weight bearing. In most instances, these walls will carry the weight of the floor joists for the floor above them. Finally, always treat a wall as being weight bearing unless you can positively verify that it isn't.

Temporary Bracing

Before work can begin on removal of the wall, it's necessary to erect a framework of temporary bracing to support the wall's load. If you're removing an interior wall, begin by cutting four 2 × 4s to the same length as the length of the wall you intend to remove. For an exterior wall, only cut two boards. Nail one to the ceiling on each side of the wall, about 2 feet out from the wall and parallel to it. Nail the other two to the floor directly under each of the ceiling boards, forming a temporary top and bottom plate. Measure the distance between the two boards, and cut 2 × 4s 1/8 inch longer than that measurement. Wedge them in between the plates about every 2 1/2 feet, and toenail them to the plates to be sure they aren't inadvertently knocked loose.

Removal of the Wall

With the wall's load now supported by the two temporary walls, demolition can begin. Measure out along the ceiling 18 inches from the wall at each end, and make a mark on the ceiling. Snap a chalk line across these two marks, then cut the drywall or plaster along the line and remove it back to the wall. Repeat for the ceiling on the other side of the wall. This procedure forms a clean area in the ceiling that is easier to patch once the wall has been removed. (See Fig. 8-1.)

Strip all the drywall, plaster, or siding off the wall itself. On drywalled areas, use a utility knife to cut through the joint tape on the corners to avoid tearing off the paper face on the adjacent sheets. Always work slowly, cutting back the materials neatly as you proceed. Remove all debris immediately and pile it where it won't be in the way of subsequent operations.

Now that the wall is stripped, study it carefully to determine any potential problems with its removal. If there is plumbing or electrical wiring in the wall, remove or reroute it as described later in this chapter.

Remove the wall studs one at a time, watching carefully to see that the temporary bracing is carrying the weight of the wall's load. If you intend to reuse the studs, the easiest way to remove them is with a reciprocating saw. Fit the saw with a metal-cutting blade, then cut carefully between the bottom of the stud and the plate, cutting the nails that hold the stud in place. Pull the stud off the plate at an angle, then pull it sharply downward to take it off the nails in the top plate. The alternative is to simply saw through the stud anywhere along its

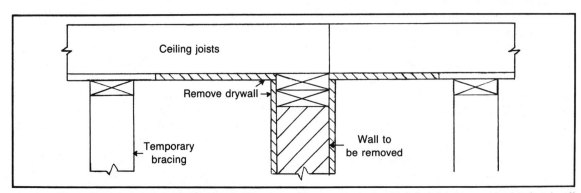

Fig. 8-1. The stages of removing a bearing wall. First, erect temporary supports (left & right) then mark, cut, & strip off the drywall from the ceiling & wall (shaded areas).

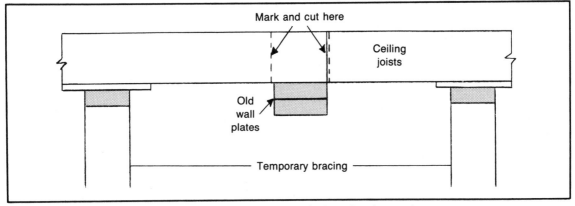

Fig. 8-2. Second, cut the joists (dotted lines), leaving a space for inserting the new beam.

length, then pull the two halves off the nails in the top and bottom plates and discard the boards. When all of the studs have been removed, pull up the bottom plate also. Bend over any protruding nails before you discard the board.

If ceiling or upper floor joists are resting on the top plate, they need to be cut back. Using a square, mark a vertical line on each of the ceiling joists, 1/16 inch out from the top plates on each side of the wall (Fig. 8-2). Next, remove the two top plates. Using a sharp handsaw or a reciprocating saw, cut along the lines and remove the ends of the ceiling joists. Work from below to avoid putting any strain on the joists and their temporary supports.

Permanent Transfer of the Wall Load

The last step in this procedure is to transfer the load that had been on the wall to new, permanent supports. To transfer the load, you will usually insert a beam into the opening in the ceiling where

the wall had been, then attach the cut joists to the beam (Fig. 8-3). This procedure will work in the majority of cases, but be sure to follow any recommendations that your designer or building officials have made for your specific circumstances.

Measure the distance between the top plates of the two adjacent walls, outside to outside, and cut a beam to this length. Check with your building inspector for recommendations on beam size. Remember that the opening you have formed in the ceiling by cutting back the joists along the old top plate is intended to fit the width of a 3 1/2-inch beam (a 4 × 8, 4 × 10, etc.) If a thicker beam is required for your opening, cut the joists back accordingly.

Lift one end of the beam up through the gap between the joists and rest it on the adjacent wall plate. Lift the other end through the gap and slide it toward you, centering the beam so it rests fully on both plates. Toenail the beam to both of the plates (Fig. 8-4).

Slide an appropriate size joist hanger under

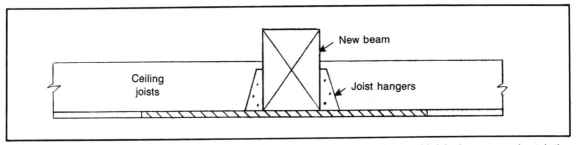

Fig. 8-3. Finally, insert the new beam (center), transfer the cut joists onto the beam with joist hangers, and patch the drywall (shaded area).

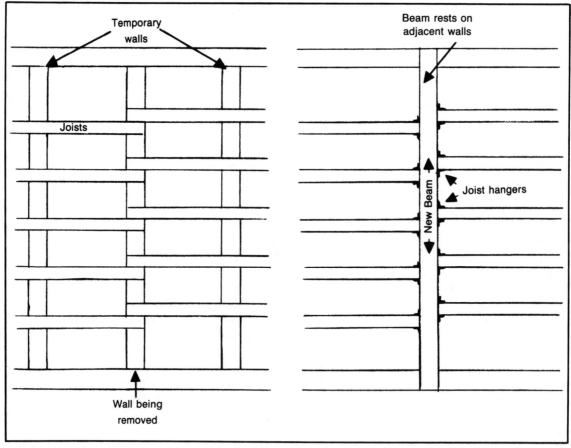

Fig. 8-4. The view from above, showing how the joists overlapping on the top plates are supported, cut, and transferred onto the new beam.

each joist end, and nail it to the beam with approved joist hanger nails. Be certain the bottom of the hanger does not extend past the bottom of the beam, which will cause problems with the drywall or plaster is patched back in. The joist hangers transfer the load, in this case the joists, onto the new beam (Fig. 8-5).

The advantage to this procedure is that all of the reworking of the beam and joists is done above the ceiling line. When the ceiling material is patched back in, a smooth, uninterrupted line between the new room and the existing room is possible, with no visible supports to mar the transition.

Finally, gently remove the temporary supports and allow the joists to settle down into the hangers, then nail through the hangers into the joists. Watch

for any sags or other signs of undue stress as the temporary bracing is removed.

Although placing the framing out of sight above the ceiling will always give the best finished appearance and avoid an "added on" look, it might not always be possible. An alternative is to use a beam below the ceiling line (Fig. 8-6). After you have erected the temporary braces as just outlined, completely remove the wall. Replace the wall framing with an appropriately sized beam, supporting it either with framing that is contained within the cross walls (Fig. 8-7), or with exposed posts that can be covered later. If you are using exposed posts, they must be attached to solid framing within the wall so that they cannot become dislodged from under the beam.

Fig. 8-5. Rafters attached to a new joist after removal of an outside wall.

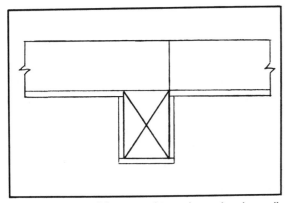

Fig. 8-6. A dropped beam used to replace a bearing wall.

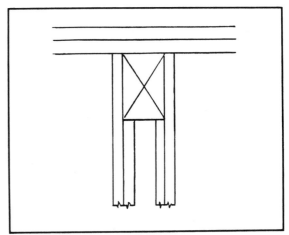

Fig. 8-7. Framing a pocket inside the wall to support the ends of a dropped beam.

REMOVING ELECTRICAL COMPONENTS

Locate and disconnect the electrical service supplying the circuit you're going to be working on. This step should be done in advance of any work, including removal of drywall. Don't assume that the circuit identification makings on the electrical panel are correct; once you've shut the circuit breaker or removed the fuse for that circuit, test the outlet or fixture you're removing to be sure it's off. Finally, place a strip of tape over the circuit breaker or the open fuse socket to indicate that it's not to be used, and place a note on the panel warning others that work is in progress.

If you are removing a wall containing outlets in the middle of a circuit, it's necessary to route around these outlets in order for the other outlets downline on the circuit to continue to function. (See Fig. 8-8.)

Routing Around Outlets

Once the wall has been stripped of drywall or plaster, the electrical cables will be visible. Trace how the cables enter the outlet box you wish to remove, and then see where they go when they leave it. Follow the cables back in each direction to a point in the attic, or under the floor if they come up that way, where they are out of the way of the wall being removed. Cut each cable at those points.

Attach a junction box to a convenient joist near

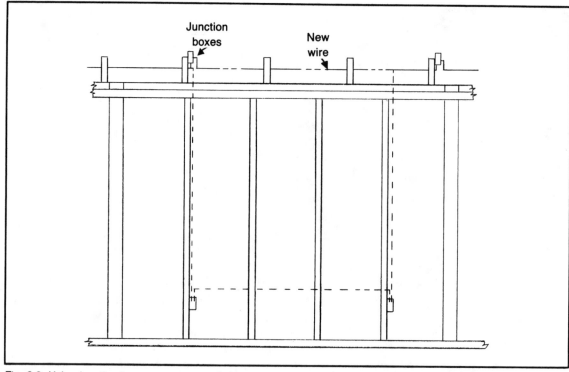

Fig. 8-8. Using junction boxes, reroute an existing run of wiring serving two receptacles (dotted line).

each cut cable, again making sure it is out of the way of the wall being removed. Feed each cut cable into its respective junction box, and strip the ends of the wires. All that remains is to run a new piece of cable between the two junction boxes. Color match the wires and connect them with wire nuts, making certain you splice the ground wires also. Secure a blank cover over each junction box to protect the splices, and label the cover as to the circuit you've spliced.

In some instances, you might find an outlet in a wall at the end of the circuit run, which is indicated by having only one cable entering the box. If at all possible, trace this cable back to the box from which it originated, and disconnect it there. If this can't be done, cut the cable and place the cut end in a junction box as just described. Cap the ends with wire nuts, and place a blank cover on the box. Label the cover with the origin of the wires. Never leave a live electrical cable loose in the attic or under the floor, even if the ends are capped.

Moving a switch is done in essentially the same manner as moving the outlet. First, trace the switch cable back to the fixture it serves and disconnect it. Install an electrical box at the new switch location, then simply run a new cable from the existing fixture to the new switch box.

Moving a 220-Volt Outlet

If the wall you're removing contains a 220-volt outlet, such as one for a clothes dryer or other appliance, you either can move it or disconnect it. If you're going to move the outlet to a location closer to the service panel, you can use the same cable. Simply route it to the new location, feed it into a box, cut off the excess, and attach the appropriate receptacle.

If the circuit is being removed, or if it's being extended to a new location farther from the service panel, the run must be traced back to the panel and disconnected there. You should never splice a

220-volt cable. Since this type of cable contains three wires (two hot and one neutral), it's possible for someone to mistake it for a cable carrying two individual 110-volt circuits. Improper splicing into the 220-volt connection could be quite dangerous.

Disconnecting at the Panel

To disconnect the circuit at the panel, first shut off the main circuit breaker to disconnect the home's supply of electricity, then carefully remove the panel cover. Remember that the wires coming into the main breaker from the electric meter are still live, so work carefully. Locate the correct circuit breaker, and disconnect the two wires attached to it. Disconnect the ground and neutral wires from the neutral bar, and remove the cable from the panel.

If you are running a new circuit of the same amperage, bring the new cable into the panel and secure it to the existing breaker. If the circuit is being eliminated, remove the circuit breaker also. Be sure to close off the open slot in the panel cover to prevent accidental contact with the wires inside the panel. Special plates are available from most electrical supply companies for this purpose.

The most difficult tear-out situation to handle occurs when the wall you wish to remove contains the service panel itself. In this instance, the service drop feeding the panel needs to be disconnected by your utility company, then each of the circuits must be spliced or rerun. It is strongly suggested that this operation be left to the skills of a qualified electrician.

REMOVING PLUMBING AND GAS LINES

If a plumbing line is present in the wall, it needs to be traced back to a joint and disconnected, then rerouted if necessary. Locate the main water shut-off valve for the house and close it. Next, trace the pipe to the fixture it serves and disconnect it there. Working back from this fixture, disconnect and remove the pipe until you reach a point that is out of the way of the wall being removed. If you are working with threaded steel pipe, you'll need to unscrew each individual length of pipe and each fit-

ting in order to remove it. Copper and plastic pipe can simply be cut wherever you wish and then removed. If the pipe is cast iron, you'll need to rent a special cutter in order to cut it.

When you have removed the pipe back to a point that's clear of the wall, you can simply cap it with an appropriate fitting if you don't intend to reuse it. If you need to run the pipe back to the fixture it once served, connect it to the fitting you've worked back to and reroute a new pipe run as necessary. (See Fig. 8-9.)

Gas lines are removed in the same manner as threaded-steel water pipe, after the gas supply has been shut off at the meter. Black pipe, or pipe with a yellow wrapping, is used for gas lines to distinguish them from the galvanized (silver) pipe used for water (Fig. 8-10). When you are replacing gas line fittings or sections of pipe, always use black pipe, or cover it with a code-approved yellow wrapping.

When you have finished rerouting or capping the gas line, be sure to check all the connections for leaks. To do so, you'll need to disconnect the meter from the main gas line that enters the house. Attach a pressure gauge, which can be rented at a rental yard or plumbing-supply company, to the end of the gas line. Connect a bicycle tire pump to the inlet on the pressure gauge, then pressurize the line with air to about 10 pounds per square inch (PSI). Spray each connection with a solution of water mixed with a little dishwashing soap. If the solution bubbles around a connection, you have a leak. Tighten the fitting, repressurize the line, and test it again. Repeat this procedure until all of the connections test out okay.

After the testing, remove the pressure gauge and reconnect the meter. Turn the gas supply back on and check the meter connections also. If you detect any smell of gas, or if you have any doubts about the procedures involved in dealing with a gas line, be sure to consult with a plumber or your gas company.

SCHEDULING DEMOLITION

In most cases, demolition work is best left until the last possible moment in order to help avoid weather

Fig. 8-9. Temporarily rerouting the lines serving a water heater until the new enclosure for it is completed.

Fig. 8-10. New gas lines under an addition. The gas meter will be moved to a new location outside the addition's foundation.

and security problems. The addition should be completely framed, roofed, and enclosed with siding, and the exterior windows and doors should be installed before the walls connecting the addition with the existing house are removed.

Try to work in stages as much as possible, again only doing demolition work when it's absolutely necessary. For example, it might be necessary to remove a small section of siding at the base of the wall in order to align the new foundation with the old one (Fig. 8-11), or perhaps some drywall needs to come down to line up the new ceiling joists. Even if the entire wall is coming down eventually, only remove what's necessary to accomplish the task you are working on at the moment.

WEATHER AND SECURITY PRECAUTIONS

When you are cutting into an existing roof (Fig. 8-12), always have tarps or plastic sheeting available, even in the middle of summer. The house is extremely vulnerable when any section of roofing

Fig. 8-11. A minimum of siding and sheathing is torn out to align a new foundation with the old one.

Fig. 8-12. Cutting into the existing house requires weather and security precautions.

is off, and a sudden unexpected rain storm can cause a considerable amount of interior damage. To a lesser degree, the same considerations apply when you remove windows, exterior doors, or sections of siding. Always plan ahead when you are doing any demolition work, and be prepared for the worst.

In addition to weather considerations, security and safety are always factors when you are cutting into a home's roof or walls. (See Fig. 8-13.) You'll need to have some scrap plywood handy whenever you open up a section of the house that is not otherwise enclosed. Work from the inside, and attach the plywood over the opening with long nails or screws. Keep any boarded up areas well lit at night, even with portable lights rigged up with an extension cord. If you must leave the house for an extended period of time, alert your neighbors or the police to keep an eye on any vulnerable areas.

As demolition of the interconnecting walls proceeds, isolate the addition from the rest of the house as much as possible. Use 4 or 6 mil plastic sheeting and masking tape to seal off doorways, and keep furniture covered to protect it from dust. Always seal off the furnace's return air grill whenever the furnace is not in use, and close the heat registers in any room near the demolition work. This procedure prevents the furnace from sucking up dust and circulating it throughout the house. Remember to change the furnace filter when the demolition is

Fig. 8-13. Flashing barricades, which can be rented inexpensively, provide safety and security around a new foundation.

complete and the debris has been cleaned up.

LIVING WITH A PARTIAL HOUSE

One of the inescapable facts of building almost any addition is the disruption of the normal household routine. Water is shut off at inconvenient times; the electricity is off at odd moments; entire rooms may be unusable for weeks at a time. The only solution is patience and good planning.

Think ahead whenever you are shutting off any of the home's utilities. Try to have all the necessary parts and tools on hand to complete the job you're working on, and allow yourself plenty of time. Don't shut off the electricity for a rewiring project with only an hour of daylight left, or try to replumb the bathroom when guests are coming for dinner that evening. Sometimes even the simplest of projects can go awry.

If a room or section of a room is going to be lost during construction, prepare for it well in ad-

vance, whether you're doing the work or a contractor is. Alert the family to the construction schedule, and clear out the room in advance. This procedure saves a lot of confusion and disorganization, and protects the room's contents from possible damage. An empty room is also much easier and safer to work in, and speeds up the entire construction process.

If you must do without a bathroom during any stage of construction, be certain you provide adequate facilities for your family's use. Always keep one bathroom in operation if at all possible. If you must do without all of the bathrooms, arrange for the rental of a portable toilet, and see if a neighbor will allow you to use his shower. Another alternative is to stay in a local motel until the bathrooms are back in operation.

No room is harder to do without than the kitchen. The loss of food storage and preparation facilities, dishes and utensils, and the family gathering place is usually quite disrupting. You'll need to select a room away from the construction and set up a temporary kitchen. First, box up any appliances, dishes, glassware, and other kitchen items that you don't actually need, and store them. Place sturdy wooden or cardboard boxes along one wall of the room for use as temporary storage for dishes, as well as food that doesn't require refrigeration. Move the refrigerator into the room if possible, or set it up in the garage or other out-of-the-way location.

Set up a small table to act as a counter top for food preparation. Keep your meals as simple as possible, and plan them around food that can be prepared easily on a hot plate or in a microwave oven. Dishes will need to be cleaned in the laundry sink, bathtub, or outside in a dishpan, so consider using paper plates and disposable plastic glasses and cutlery to keep your washing needs to a minimum.

Remember: plan ahead and plan for the worst. The entire project will run much more smoothly and with a lot less confusion and frustration.

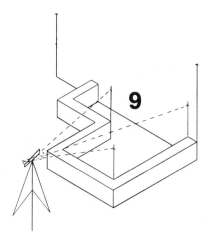

Foundations

The first step in the actual construction of an addition is the foundation. This structure, normally of concrete, is the base upon which all subsequent construction will rest. If your addition will have a crawl space or basement under it, the foundation consists of two parts: the footings, and the stem walls or basement walls. If the addition is to be constructed on a concrete slab, then only footings are involved. Although it will be covered in this chapter, the slab is actually part of the floor system and technically not part of the foundation.

The foundation is probably the single most important aspect of your addition in terms of getting it right the first time. It needs to be absolutely square and level in order to ensure that the rest of the addition will follow suit. If the foundation is poured wrong, you'll fight the rest of the construction all the way through.

that is wide enough to carry it. Footing sizes will vary depending on soil conditions, but for residential construction the footing is typically twice as wide as the foundation wall. The footing's thickness usually varies from 6 inches to 8 inches, depending on how many stories it must support. Your local building department will have specifications for footing sizes in your area.

In addition to supporting the foundation walls, separate footings are used to carry the weight of heavy, concentrated loads, such as a fireplace or hot tub. The size and design of special-purpose footings such as these will vary widely, depending on soil conditions, the depth of the frost line, and the total amount of weight they will need to support. In most cases, your designer or the building department can help you with the exact size, but in some cases it might be necessary to consult an engineer.

FOOTINGS

The purpose of the footing is to spread the downward weight of the addition over an area of ground

FOUNDATION WALLS

The foundation wall rests directly on top of the footing (Fig. 9-1) and usually is constructed of poured

Fig. 9-1. A footing and a stem wall. This stem wall will tie into another one being poured later, so rebar was provided to reinforce the connection. Note the metal form plate on the footing.

concrete or concrete blocks. It can be poured continuously with the footing, or poured separately after the footing has set. If the addition is to have a basement, the basement walls will rest directly on the footings and will act as the foundation walls also.

In houses having a crawl space, the foundation walls are relatively low, usually 18 to 24 inches. Depending on the number of stories it must support, it might be anywhere from 6 to 10 inches wide. Foundation walls such as these are commonly referred to as *stem walls*. They provide a solid, weight-bearing enclosure for the crawl space, and form the transition between the foundation and the first of the floor framing.

CONCRETE SLABS

Some houses, particularly in recent years, have been constructed on concrete slabs. If you are adding onto a house with a slab floor, or if you wish the addition to be at a lower level than the floor of the existing crawl-space house, a slab floor is a good choice. It offers the advantages of low cost and faster construction time, since no floor framing is needed. The disadvantages of a concrete slab are that it is rather cold and hard underfoot, and it offers no access to underfloor plumbing, wiring, and ducts in the event modifications or repairs are necessary.

As with the stem wall, the edges of the concrete slab need to rest on concrete footings, in order to evenly distribute the weight of the walls. Most residential slabs are *monolithic*, meaning they are poured at the same time as the footings. (See Fig. 9-2.) After a period of curing, the slab is ready to be framed on, and the smooth, hard surface forms a good underlayment for the finish floor covering, without the need for additional underlayments.

LAYING OUT THE FOUNDATION

Begin by clearing the ground where the addition

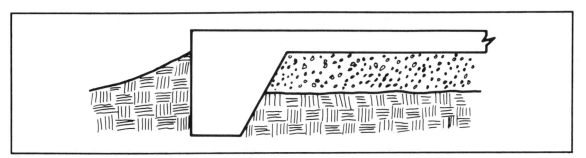

Fig. 9-2. A typical monolithic concrete slab on grade.

is to be constructed. Trees and shrubbery need to be removed, and grass or weeds should be cleared back about 2 feet in all directions from the intended addition. Rake the area clean and relatively level.

The lines of the addition are laid out first, and should correspond to the addition's finished outside size. (See Fig. 9-3.) Starting against the existing house, mark the exact point where you wish the addition to intersect the house wall. Measure along the house the length of the addition, and make a second mark. About 6 inches above ground level, drive a nail into the wall at each of these two marks. Finally, measure along the wall 6 feet from each of the original marks, and make a second mark.

Measure out from the house to the points where the addition's outside corners will be. Drive a stake at each of these points, and make a pencil mark on top of the stake at the exact distance from the house where the back wall of the addition will be. Make a saw kerf in the stakes at the pencil lines, then stretch a string between the two stakes. This string is the location of the addition's back outside wall, and should be exactly parallel to the wall of the house.

Attach a string to one of the nails you drove into the house wall, and stretch it out beyond the string you just installed. While one person holds the string tight, make a pencil mark on the string 8 feet out from the house. Now, measure the distance between the 6-foot mark you made on the house and the 8-foot mark on the string. If the diagonal distance between these two marks is 10 feet, then the

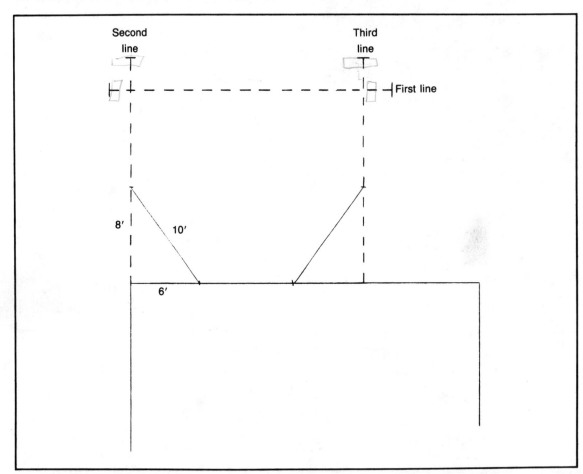

Fig. 9-3. Laying out the outside walls of an addition, using strings, stakes, and the 3:4:5 method.

string is square to the house wall. If it isn't, have the person holding the string move to left or right until the measurement is correct. Drive a stake at this point. Recheck your 10-foot measurement from house to string, and make a pencil mark at the exact point where the string crosses the stake. Make a saw kerf at this point, and secure the string to the stake. Repeat this procedure for the other side of the addition.

This type of measurement is based on the Pythagorean theorem of geometry, which in the building trades is commonly referred to as the 3:4:5. (See Fig. 9-4.) Simply stated, it means that if the base of a triangle is three units long (the units can be feet, inches, yards, etc.) and the height is four units long and the hypotenuse (the diagonal side) is five units long, then the corner of the triangle opposite the hypotenuse is exactly 90 degrees. In laying out the string, you formed a triangle with the house as the base, the string as the height, and the measurement between the two marks as the hypotenuse. Since the theorem will work in any multiple of 3:4:5, when you laid out 6:8:10 the corner of your layout was square. This is an extremely useful trick to remember, and it will come in handy time and time again at all phases of your addition. Remember to be accurate in making the marks, and use the longest measurement possible—6, 8, and 10 feet is more accurate than 3, 4, and 5 feet.

If your addition is to have any jogs in it, continue with the strings in the same manner until all

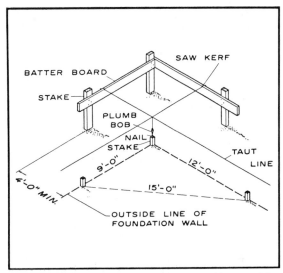

Fig. 9-5. Batter boards erected at the outside corner of the foundation lines.

of the outside walls have been laid out. Recheck all of the 3:4:5 measurements you made, and check that all the outside dimensions of the addition are correct as shown on the plans. As a final check, measure the diagonal distance between the corners of any square or rectangular areas. If the area is properly laid out, the diagonals will be equal.

To mark the building lines so they aren't disturbed during the excavation process, batter boards are used in place of the strings. (See Fig. 9-5.) About 4 feet outside each of the addition's corners, drive three 2 × 4s into the ground. Nail two 1 × 6s across the stakes at a height slightly higher than what the finished foundation will be. Stretch new strings parallel with the first strings you laid out, using a plumb bob at the corners as a check. Secure the strings to saw kerfs made in the cross boards, then remove the original strings and stakes. You now have the outside of the foundation accurately marked out.

EXCAVATION

The amount of excavation needed for a particular foundation varies with the soil conditions and the depth of the crawl space. In very rocky conditions,

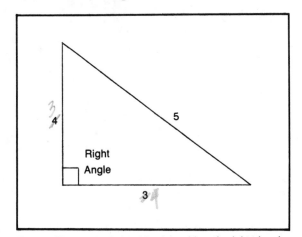

Fig. 9-4. The 3:4:5 relationship of the sides of a right triangle.

footings often are formed directly on top of the rock, with little or no excavation necessary or even possible. In sandy conditions, it might be necessary to take the footing trenches down quite far until firm soil is reached.

The Lay of the Land

In all cases, the footing trenches need to be deep enough so that the footings are below the *frost line*. As moisture in the soil freezes each winter, it can cause the ground to heave upward. Likewise, a sinking motion often occurs in the spring when the ground thaws. The frost line is the point below the soil where the earth is relatively safe from these movements, and varies depending on the climate conditions in different areas. Bear in mind also that the footings must rest on undisturbed soil.

If the building site for the addition is level, you can simply lay out the batter boards and begin the footing excavation. If your site is on a slope, two options are possible. For low to medium slopes, the soil can be removed to a point where the site is level for the foundation. On steep slopes, it will be necessary to step the foundation one or more times, then frame up from the foundation to make the floor level.

If a large amount of excavating needs to be done, it is best to employ a professional excavator. In order to properly prepare the site, enough soil needs to be removed to make the area level, but care must be taken not to remove too much. Because the foundation cannot rest on disturbed soil, you cannot fill the areas where you have over excavated. The only answer is to extend the height of the foundation walls, which is a costly solution.

Footing Trenches

Following the specifications on the foundation plan, begin removing soil to create a trench for the footings to sit in. Remember that the strings you laid out represent the outside of the building, which are in line with the outside of the stem wall. The footing trench will need to extend out past these lines to a point equal to half the stem wall's thickness.

In areas with solid soil, the building department might allow you to pour concrete directly into the footing trench, without using footing forms. If so, excavate the trenches to the exact size and depth needed for the footings. Use a square-point shovel to cut straight, vertical sides, and remove all loose dirt from the trench.

If soil conditions are such that footing forms will be needed, excavate about 6 to 12 inches beyond the footing line to allow for the forms to be erected. Check the bottom of your footing trenches periodically with a level placed on a long, straight board to be sure the trenches are staying relatively level. Final, exact leveling will be done with the forms.

CONCRETE

Concrete is actually a mixture of four materials: cement, typically portland cement (named for its resemblance to an English limestone); coarse aggregate, which is any of a variety of rocks in different sizes, depending on the intended application; fine aggregate, usually sand; and water. The ratio of these materials varies with the concrete's intended usage. One part cement to two parts sand to four parts rock is about the most common. Other materials also might be added under special circumstances to make the concrete lighter, stronger, or faster drying.

Concrete is measured and ordered by the cubic yard (typically referred to simply as a *yard*), or by a fraction thereof. As discussed in Chapter 4, 1 cubic yard is the equivalent of an area 1 yard (3 feet) wide by 1 yard long by 1 yard high, and contains 27 cubic feet. To estimate your needs, measure the length, width, and thickness in feet of the area you intend to cover, then divide by 27.

There are actually four ways to get concrete to the job site. For small jobs, such as making repairs, setting posts, or pouring a small step or walkway, it can be purchased in dry form in bags. The bags weigh 90 pounds each, and contain a predetermined ratio of cement, sand, and small gravel. Once water is added, one bag will yield 2/3 cubic foot of concrete, so you would need about 41 bags to equal 1 cubic yard. On a price per cubic yard basis, this is the most expensive way to purchase concrete, but for small jobs it's by far the easiest and most convenient.

For larger jobs, dry materials for making concrete can be purchased in bulk. Outlets that carry sand, rock, and gravel usually will carry a concrete mix, which is simply premixed sand and medium to large rock. This mix is sold by the cubic yard also, and you can pick it up yourself with a pickup truck, or it can be delivered to your house. The portland cement is purchased in bags, and is mixed with water and the sand/rock mix to form concrete. A cement mixer, which you can rent, is the best way to mix the materials, and you have the advantage of only mixing what you need as you need it.

A much more convenient way of purchasing concrete for larger jobs is to buy it already mixed and ready for use. For jobs requiring up to 1 yard, some concrete outlets will provide you with a cart that can be towed behind your car or truck. A small hydraulic jack on the back of the cart will tip it up to allow the wet concrete to flow out a chute and into your wheelbarrow, or directly into your forms.

The other method of purchasing concrete is by truck, delivered directly to your site. Most trucks can handle about 7 yards at a time, and will mix the concrete to your specifications before leaving the yard. Purchasing ready-mixed concrete assures you of a mixture that is correctly proportioned for your application, and that is thoroughly mixed. It saves you any guesswork about the ratios of materials, and also spares you the tiresome task of hand mixing.

Unlike dry mixes, where you can mix only what you need at the moment, ready-mixed concrete obviously must be used immediately and completely. This means you must be certain that you have completely prepared your site, that all necessary forms are in place and fully secured, that you have all of the necessary tools ready and waiting, that you have enough people to help you place the concrete before it hardens, and that you have ordered the correct amount.

Most concrete companies will charge you extra for standing time if their truck and driver must wait while you finish your site preparations. You'll also have to pay for all the concrete you order, even if it's more then you need for your job. You also might be faced with the need to get rid of the excess in the event your driver can't take it on to his next job, so it definitely pays to plan carefully before you order a delivery.

FOOTING FORMS

After the excavation is complete, forms will need to be erected to contain the concrete during the pouring operation. If your job requires footing forms, they will be the first to be built. There are three things to bear in mind about foundation forms of any type: they must be level, square, and securely braced. Remember that a poorly placed foundation will create a host of other problems as the construction proceeds.

Leveling

If your foundation area is small, a spirit level might be enough to accurately level the forms. Select a good-quality level at least 48 inches in length for best results. Longer levels are also available, and will work even better for longer runs.

On larger foundations, a builder's level (Fig. 9-6) is highly recommended. One can be rented for a moderate cost at most rental yards. This level is a tripod-mounted instrument with two main parts: a telescope, through which the object to be leveled is sighted, and a leveling vial. The leveling vial acts like the bubble in a spirit level, but is more accurate. Once the tripod has been set up outside the line of the addition's foundation, three or four leveling screws on the base of the instrument enable you to perfectly center the bubble in the vial, establishing a level line of sight through the telescope. The telescope then can be rotated on its base without disturbing its level.

Builders' levels are used in conjunction with a leveling rod, which is a straight pole precisely marked in graduations of feet and inches. While one person holds the leveling rod on the form, a second person sights through the telescope and focuses on the rod (Fig. 9-7). Crosshairs inside the telescope

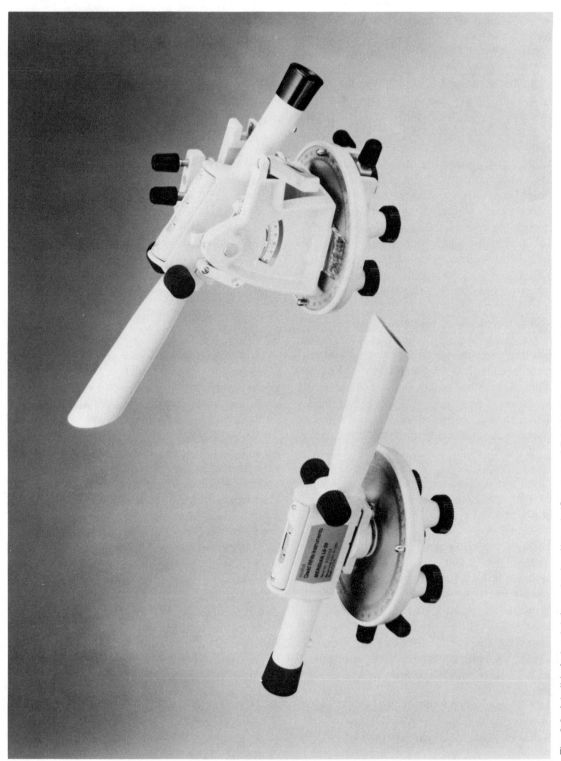

Fig. 9-6. A builder's level, left, and a level/transit (Courtesy of David White Instruments).

Fig. 9-7. Using a builder's level on a tripod to sight a leveling rod. Note the square sighting target near the center of the rod (Courtesy of David White Instruments).

allow you to accurately judge where your line of sight is hitting the rod. By moving the leveling rod to another point on the form and resighting it through the telescope, you can tell if this point on the form is high or low, relative to the first sighting you took.

Since the telescope has been accurately leveled on its base, the line of sight viewed through the instrument's telescope will always be level also, with no deviations. No matter where on the site you place the leveling rod, the sighting you take through the telescope will always be exact.

To use the builder's level, erect the tripod in a stable area outside the lines of the addition, at a

point where it can be swung around to sight all points on the foundation. Level the instrument accurately using the screws on the base.

Start at one point on the footing or stem-wall form that is easy to establish. This point, called the *control point*, is usually where the addition meets the existing house, since it's important that the floor levels match up. Have someone hold the leveling rod at this point while you sight it through the telescope. Most leveling rods have a small disk, called the *target*, that slides up and down the rod for use as a reference marker. Have the person holding the rod slide the target up or down until you have it exactly centered in the telescope. If no target is available, mark the rod with a bright grease pencil or simply record the number of the mark on a piece of scratch paper.

Next, by simply moving the rod to other points on the form and taking additional sightings (Fig. 9-8), you can easily determine if those points are high or low relative to the control point, and can adjust the height of the forms accordingly. When you have leveled the entire form, it's a good precaution to start back at the control point and resight all the forms to be certain nothing has moved.

If you are using a level/transit, you also can easily establish vertical lines. (See Figs. 9-6 and 9-9.)

Building the Forms

Select straight, solid lumber for the footing forms, ripped to the same depth as the depth of the footings. For a 6-inch-deep footing, for example, you might wish to rip a 1 × 8 or 2 × 8 down to 6 inches, or use 3/4-inch plywood similarly ripped to size.

Working out from the house, begin by erecting the outside form. Use a plumb bob to take sightings off the strings on the batter boards, and measure out from these sightings the proper distance to establish the location of the form board. Drive a stake behind the board every 2 to 3 feet,

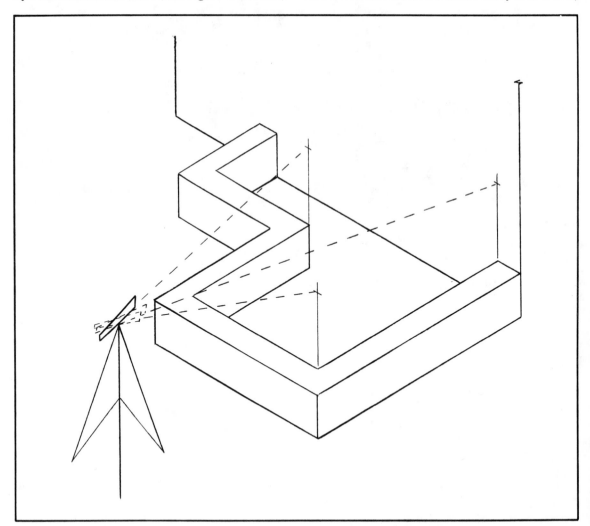

Fig. 9-8. Using a builder's level and a leveling rod to sight and compare the height at various points around a foundation.

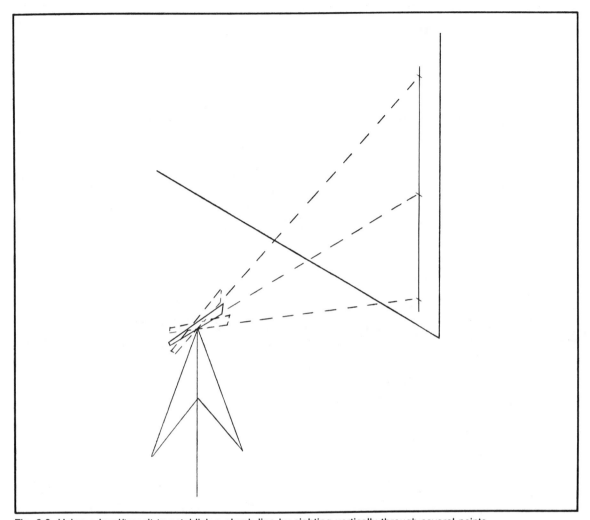

Fig. 9-9. Using a level/transit to establish a plumb line by sighting vertically through several points.

using your spirit level or builder's level to be certain the forms are remaining true.

Duplex nails are used to secure the stakes to the forms. These nails have two heads, one behind the other, so that when the nail is driven in to the first head, a second head remains exposed. This allows for easy removal of the nail when the forms are disassembled. Remember to nail through the stake into the form, not the other way around.

Continue around the footing trench in this manner, securing and leveling the form boards as you go. Securely nail the boards together at the corners, again using duplex nails driven in from the outside.

Use the 3:4:5 method described previously to be certain the corners are square.

When the outside forms are in place, erect the inside forms in the same manner. Use precut spacers nailed across the tops of the forms to maintain the correct distance between the forms, ensuring a consistent width for the footings. (See Fig. 9-10.) Check the inside forms for level, and also level across the forms to be certain the inside and outside form boards are at the same level.

POURING THE FOOTINGS

If possible, arrange to have the concrete truck back

Fig. 9-10. Footing forms. Note the stakes and spacers.

up to the area where the foundation is being constructed. Using the truck's chute, the concrete then can be placed directly into the forms with a minimum of extra labor. If the truck cannot get close enough or if you are hand mixing your own concrete, you will need to bring the concrete to the site in wheelbarrows. For best results, use a heavy wheelbarrow having a large capacity. They can be rented if necessary.

Pour or shovel the wet concrete into the forms. As you work, tamp the concrete down with a shovel to be sure it is worked evenly into the forms with no voids. Tap the outsides of the forms with a hammer to help the concrete settle and to avoid hollows on the finished edges.

Lay a 2 × 4 across the forms, starting at one end. With one person on each side, slide the board back and forth across the forms, scraping off the

excess concrete as you work your way to the other end of the forms. This process, called *screeding*, acts to level and settle the wet mix, pushing the aggregate down and bringing a layer of cement and water to the surface, making the concrete easier to finish.

Finish off the concrete with a wooden trowel, called a *float*, to provide a level but slightly rough surface, which will bond well with concrete poured in the wall forms. To create a positive bond between the footing and the foundation wall, steel reinforcing bars, or *rebar*, can be inserted in the footings, or a keyway can be created by embedding a strip of 1- × -2 lumber in the wet concrete. Remove the board after the concrete has set.

FOUNDATION WALL FORMS

After you allow the footings to cure for about 48

hours, you can erect the foundation wall forms. Replace the strings on the batter boards, and use them as guides for laying out the form boards. Take sightings off the strings with a plumb bob in several places and mark the top of the footings, then snap a chalk line across the marks to show the line the forms will follow. Mark off the width of the foundation wall on each footing, and snap a second chalk line to show where the inside form will be.

Because of the height of the stem walls, plywood is a good choice for the forms. Rip each sheet as needed, bearing in mind that the stem wall should be high enough to provide at least 18 inches of clearance between the soil and the bottom of the joists. Coat the inside surface of the plywood with used motor oil to help prevent it from sticking to the concrete, and to allow for easier removal of the forms.

Following the chalk lines on the footings, begin erecting the plywood panels. The panels may be secured to the footings using wooden cleats, or with special metal ties that support the bottom of the form while automatically establishing the spacing. (See Fig. 9-11.) The ties or cleats can be secured to the footing using special hardened concrete nails (Fig. 9-12). Erect the outside forms first, then do the inside panels. As with the footing forms, carefully square all the corners, then secure them with duplex nails.

As the forms are erected, drive a long stake into the ground diagonally from the top of the form, spacing them 2 to 3 feet apart. These stakes, called *back stakes*, brace the top of the forms to prevent them from spreading when the concrete is placed. Use wooden spacers or metal ties to maintain the correct spacing between the tops of the forms. (See

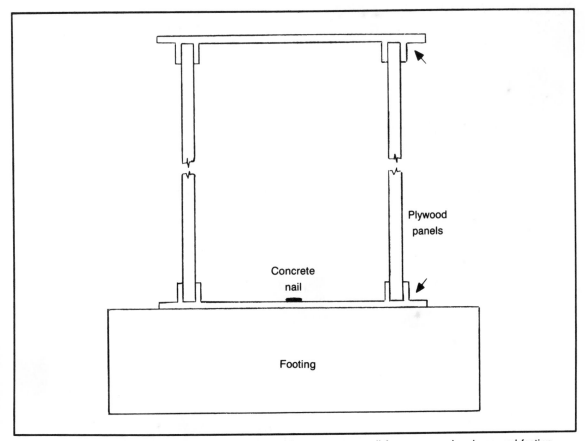

Fig. 9-11. Prefabricated plates (arrows) used to space and support stem-wall forms on an already poured footing.

Fig. 9-12. The footing after pouring. The inside form has been removed.

Fig. 9-13.) After all the forms are in place, check them carefully to be certain they are level, square, and well secured.

If access to the crawl space is to be provided through the stem wall, block off an area of the forms to create an opening where no concrete will be poured. Access holes should be no smaller than 18 × 24 inches, and should have a removable door. Several types of manufactured crawl-space door and frame units are available, and offer the easiest solution to a sturdy, operable access.

POURING THE WALLS

Place the concrete in the forms as described for the footings, pouring to a height of about half the forms. Carefully watch for spreading of the forms as you pour, and quickly add more stakes if necessary. When you have filled the entire run of forms half full, return to where you started and fill the forms to the top.

Carefully pack and tamp the concrete into place to prevent voids. If the wall forms are quite deep, you can rent a *vibrator*. This tool consists of a small motor that powers a vibrating rod at the end of a long cable. The rod is pushed down into the wet concrete at regular intervals, where it vibrates the concrete into a more liquid state that helps it to flow into the forms more evenly. Be careful not to allow the vibrator to operate in one spot for too long.

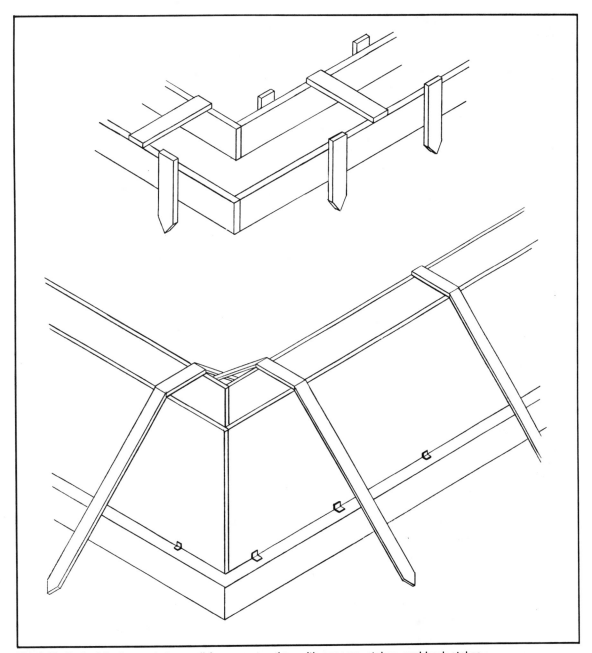

Fig. 9-13. Typical footing and stem-wall form construction, with spacers, stakes, and back stakes.

As the forms are filled, screed off the top. Add wet concrete as needed during the screeding process to fill in any voids. Use a steel trowel to smoothly finish off the concrete as it hardens. A smooth surface on top of the foundation wall sim-plifies the floor framing, which comes later.

CONCRETE BLOCK WALLS

After you have poured the concrete footings, you might wish to use concrete blocks for the foundation walls instead of poured concrete. This choice eliminates the need for constructing forms and pouring concrete, but is very labor intensive, particularly for the nonprofessional.

Concrete blocks come in certain standard shapes and sizes, and are designated by their nominal size, which makes an allowance for mortar joints. For example, the common block for foundation work is usually designated as being 8 inches wide × 8 inches high × 16 inches long. The actual size is 7 5/8 × 7 5/8 × 15 5/8. A 3/8-inch allowance is always made for the mortar joint.

Rebar must be installed in the footing when it is first poured, and the size and number you need will be specified by the building department. Wherever the hollow area in a concrete block coincides with the rebar, that hollow is filled solid with concrete, thus forming a positive tie between the footing and the block wall. Lay the blocks in a common bond, so that each subsequent course overlaps the joints in the course below it. Anchor bolts are set in the hollows of the top course of blocks, and those hollows also are filled solid. (See Fig. 9-14.)

POURING CONCRETE SLABS

As discussed previously, concrete slabs offer an alternative to conventional crawl-space construction, and might be desirable in certain instances. Depending on the details of your addition, two types of slabs are commonly used: floating and monolithic. The floating slab uses a conventional footing with a short stem wall (Fig. 9-15). The concrete slab is then poured within the enclosure formed by the stem walls, but is not tied into them. Somewhat more common is the monolithic slab, which is poured at the same time as the footings.

After the footings are dug and all underfloor wiring, plumbing, and heat ducts are installed, the ground where the slab is to be poured is compacted. Next, a layer of sand or gravel is poured and leveled. A good idea is to then place rigid foam insulation on top of the gravel in order to insulate the finished slab. Use an insulation specifically designed for below-grade applications, and cover it with 6-mil plastic sheeting before you pour the slab.

The concrete slab, usually 3 to 4 inches thick, is then poured directly on the insulation (or directly on the gravel if no insulation is used). A thick wire mesh, usually in 6-inch squares, is embedded in the concrete before or during the pour to reinforce the slab (Fig. 9-16). Anchor bolts are set in the wet concrete around the perimeter as needed (Fig. 9-17). The concrete is screeded off in sections, then smoothed with a float. As the slab hardens, steel trowels, either hand or machine operated, are used to finish off the slab to a hard, smooth surface.

Because of the large amount of concrete that needs to be worked in a relatively short period of time, several people are needed to pour and finish a slab floor. The slab floor, therefore, is probably one area of your addition that's best left to a professional.

ANCHOR BOLTS

Anchor bolts, also called *foundation bolts*, provide an easy means of transition between the foundation wall or slab and the sill plate, which is the first piece of floor framing. (See Fig. 9-18.) Anchor bolts are typically 1/2 inch in diameter and 10 inches long, with the end bent at a right angle. They should be placed no more than 6 feet apart, and within 12 inches of the end of each piece of sill plate. It might be necessary to lay out the sill plates on paper first in order to know exactly where the bolts need to be placed.

While the concrete is still soft, push the bolt into it with the bent end down. The bolt should enter the concrete at least 7 inches, and should be centered on the width of the foundation wall. Take care to prevent wet concrete from coating the bolt's threads, and use your trowel to smooth the concrete around each bolt after you have placed it.

VENTILATION

Moisture can enter the crawl space area from the soil and from the house, and if it is not removed, it can cause serious damage to wood members. For this reason, it is necessary to provide underfloor ventilation, which rids the crawl space of unwanted moisture.

A variety of prefabricated vents are available,

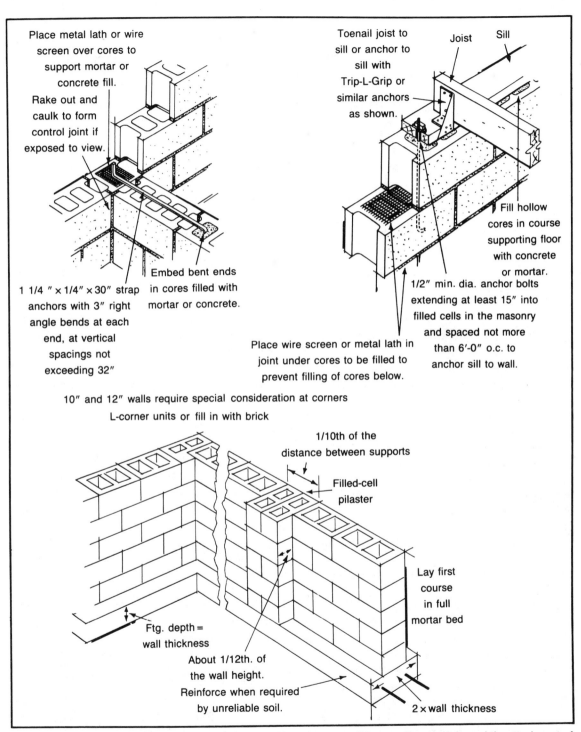

Place metal lath or wire screen over cores to support mortar or concrete fill.

Rake out and caulk to form control joint if exposed to view.

1 1/4 " × 1/4" × 30" strap anchors with 3" right angle bends at each end, at vertical spacings not exceeding 32"

Embed bent ends in cores filled with mortar or concrete.

Toenail joist to sill or anchor to sill with Trip-L-Grip or similar anchors as shown.

Joist   Sill

Fill hollow cores in course supporting floor with concrete or mortar.

1/2" min. dia. anchor bolts extending at least 15" into filled cells in the masonry and spaced not more than 6'-0" o.c. to anchor sill to wall.

Place wire screen or metal lath in joint under cores to be filled to prevent filling of cores below.

10" and 12" walls require special consideration at corners L-corner units or fill in with brick

1/10th of the distance between supports

Filled-cell pilaster

Lay first course in full mortar bed

Ftg. depth = wall thickness

About 1/12th. of the wall height. Reinforce when required by unreliable soil.

2 × wall thickness

Fig. 9-14. A typical concrete block foundation. Note the details of the wall intersection, top left, and the attachment of the sill plate, top right (Courtesy of National Concrete Masonry Association).

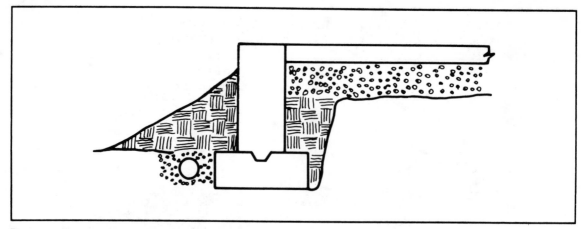

Fig. 9-15. A typical floating concrete slab, with footing and stem wall.

any of which will work fine for airing out the crawl space. Some types are meant to be cut into the rim joist, and so are installed at the time the floor is framed. Other types need to be installed in the stem wall itself (Fig. 9-19), and should be taken into consideration before the concrete is poured. It's best to discuss your plans with your material supplier, and ask for his recommendation on which type is best for your addition.

Vents are designated by size, which refers to their overall outside dimensions, and by net free area (NFA). A certain portion of every vent is screened to allow air to pass through it, and a certain portion is solid to support the screen. The NFA designation tells you exactly how much of the vent's total area is actually screen, and is usually stamped on the frame of the vent.

Most building codes recommend a minimum of 1 1/2 square feet of NFA for each 25 linear feet of exterior wall no matter which type of vent you use. Another way of calculating ventilation needs is to figure 1 square foot of NFA for every 300 square feet of floor area for homes with dry soil in the crawl space, or 1 square foot per 150 square feet for homes with damp soil in the crawl space. Position the vents near the corners of the stem walls first, then equally space around the rest of the perimeter until the necessary amount of NFA is achieved. Vents always should be placed to allow a good cross flow of ventilation through the crawl space (Fig. 9-20).

In colder climates, closable foundation vents are available, and are highly recommended to keep the crawl space warmer and reduce the risk of frozen water pipes. Some types have a lever-operated shutter to close off the screened portion, while others have precut foam blocks to seal the vent openings. Close the vents at the onset of cold weather, then open them when the danger of freezing has passed in order to allow the crawl space to ventilate and dry out.

VAPOR BARRIERS

In addition to underfloor ventilation, vapor barriers are now required by code in many areas. Most vapor barriers are formed from sheets of 6-mil black plastic (1 mil = 1/1,000 inch). The plastic is simply laid out on the ground, with sheets overlapping by at least 12 inches. Lap the plastic 6 inches up the stem walls also, but do not allow it to contact wood members. Whether or not you are required by code to install a vapor barrier, it is a very good, inexpensive precaution against accumulating unwanted underfloor moisture.

PERMANENT WOOD FOUNDATIONS

An alternative to the poured concrete or concrete-block foundation is the permanent wood foundation (PWF), a system developed by the wood-products industry and approved for use by all major model

Fig. 9-16. A monolithic slab, with vapor barrier and reinforcing wire, ready for pouring (Courtesy of Georgia-Pacific Corporation).

Fig. 9-17. The slab and anchor bolts after pouring (Courtesy of Georgia-Pacific Corporation).

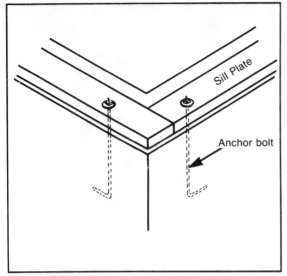

Fig. 9-18. Anchor bolts used for connecting the sill plate to the foundation (Courtesy of National Forest Products Association).

building codes. The system uses preservative-treated plywood and lumber foundation walls, supported by crushed rock, gravel, or poured concrete footings. Wood foundations are constructed like framed walls, thus eliminating the need for a concrete contractor and making the installation of a solid, square foundation more within the capabilities of most experienced do-it-yourselfers. The system can be used both for crawl spaces and basements.

Another distinct advantage to the PWF system is that it can be insulated easily—a real plus when you are constructing a heated basement. Blanket insulation is placed in the wall cavities, then the walls are drywalled and finished exactly like above-grade walls. Furring strips and special concrete fasteners thus are eliminated.

Materials

The plywood recommended for the PWF system is exterior type, sheathing grade. In addition, all lumber and plywood used in the foundation must be pressure preservative treated in accordance with the American Wood Preservers Bureau (AWPB) standard AWPB-FDN. Lumber that has been cut or drilled needs to have these areas treated with

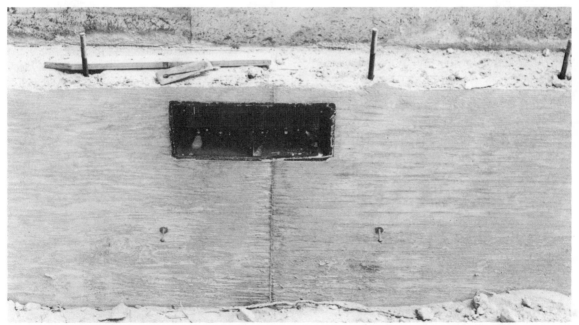

Fig. 9-19. A prefabricated, prescreened plastic foundation vent, set in a poured concrete stem wall. This type of vent can be closed off in the winter with precut foam blocks.

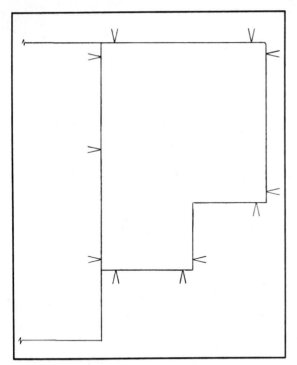

Fig. 9-20. Vent locations around an addition foundation. If possible, openings also should be made in the existing foundation, left, for best circulation.

additional copper naphthanate preservative until the wood will not absorb any more.

The footings and backfill should be of crushed stone, gravel, or coarse sand. Crushed stone should be a maximum of 1/2 inch in diameter; gravel, a maximum of 3/4 inch. Sand needs to be a minimum of 1/6 inch. Be certain the material is clean and free of silt, clay, and organic material. Conventional poured concrete footings also may be used.

The fasteners used in assembling the foundation walls must be corrosion resistant. Stainless steel nails or staples should be used for attaching below-grade plywood to the wall studs, while hot-dipped galvanized nails can be used above grade and for all lumber-to-lumber connections.

PWF Construction Sequence

After roughly laying out the area for the addition, remove the topsoil and excavate the site for the foundation footings and basement floor. A mini-mum layer of 4 inches of rock, sand, or gravel is recommended under concrete slab basement floors. The width and thickness of gravel under the footings is dependent on the width of the footing plate. After you level the gravel, accurately stake out the lines of the addition.

Next, place a treated wood footing plate, usually a 2 × 8 or 2 × 10, on the gravel and level it. The foundation sections are built with single 2 × top and bottom plates connected to foundation studs, usually 2 × 6s or 2 × 8s. For a full basement, they are usually built in 8- × -8-foot sections for easy handling without mechanical equipment. The sections can be built at the site and tipped up into place, or prefabricated in a plant and delivered to the site ready for installation, just as roof trusses are.

Following the layout lines, erect and brace the first corner section. Then stand additional sections one at a time and connect them to the previous ones. For basement walls, the joints between the sections should be caulked. This step is not necessary for crawl spaces. As you erect the sections, check them for plumb and level, and then brace them. Small stakes driven along the outside of the footing plates keep the sections from shifting during assembly.

When all of the sections are in place, check the entire assembly again for square, plumb, and level, then install the second overlapping top plate. For basement floors, you can pour a concrete slab over 6-mil polyethylene placed directly on the gravel, or you can construct a wood floor with preservative-treated 2 × sleepers, joists, and plywood. After the basement floor is finished, install and fasten the floor joists and subfloor to the top of the foundation wall to provide lateral bracing. Finally, install a moisture barrier of 6-mil polyethylene sheeting up to the level of the backfill, and backfill the area around the foundation.

For complete construction information on the PWF system, contact:

American Plywood Association
P.O. Box 11700
Tacoma, Washington 98411

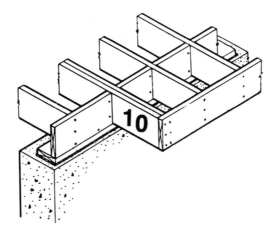

Floor Framing

For those additions that are not being constructed on a concrete slab, the construction sequence following the foundation is the framing of the floor supports and the floor itself. There are two basic types of framing systems for residential construction: *balloon framing* and *platform framing*. In balloon framing (Fig. 10-1), the wall studs extend full length from the foundation to the roof, even in two-story houses, and the floor joists are suspended on ledgers that are set in between the studs. This framing method was popular in some areas of the country in years past, but has a number of inherent problems that have led to a decline in use. Little if any balloon framing is practiced today, having been replaced by platform framing. If your home was constructed using balloon framing, a platform-framed addition is easily adapted to the existing framing.

PLATFORM FRAMING

Platform framing (Fig. 10-2) is the method em-

ployed in virtually all residential construction today, and is an easy method to learn and apply to room additions, even for the novice framer. It consists of three separate, interconnected framing stages.

The first stage is the floor, which is framed directly on the foundation stem walls and includes all the underfloor framing and the subfloor. The floor forms a platform upon which all subsequent framing is done, and gives rise to this framing method's name. In the case of a concrete-slab floor, the slab serves as the platform, and the floor-framing stage is eliminated.

The second framing stage is the walls, both interior and exterior, which are covered in detail in Chapter 11. After completion of all the wall framing, the third and final stage is the ceiling and roof structure (see Chapter 12).

Taken separately, the three stages are considerably easier to understand and complete. Also, the addition of framing follows a logical sequence in which each section of framing rests upon and is tied into the section before it.

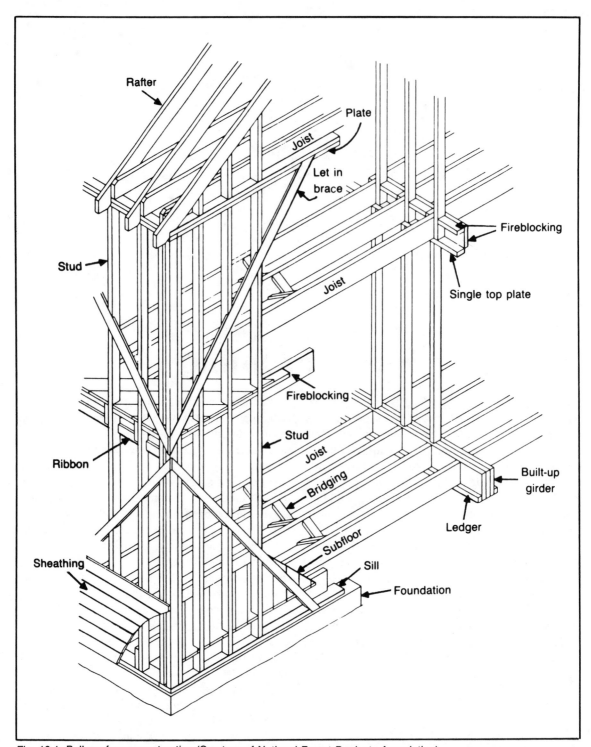

Fig. 10-1. Balloon frame construction (Courtesy of National Forest Products Association).

98

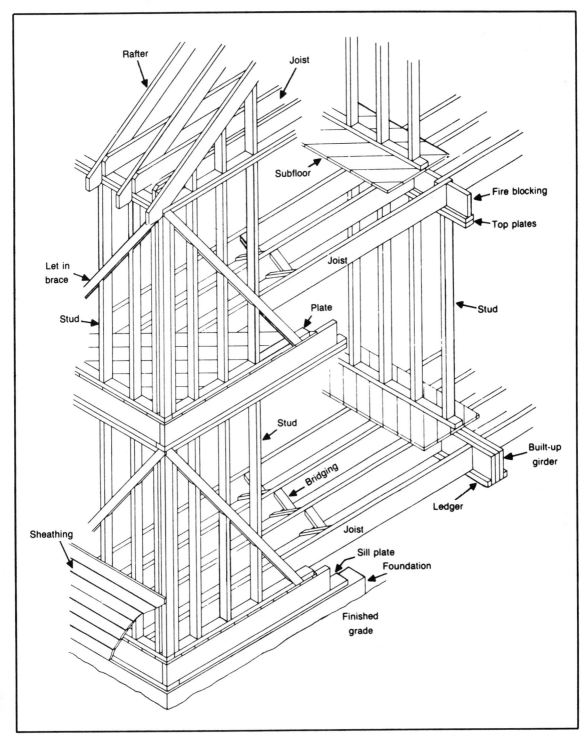

Fig. 10-2. Platform frame construction (Courtesy of National Forest Products Association).

UNDERFLOOR FRAMING

The underfloor framing consists of a carefully designed system of posts, girders, and joists that provide a firm base for the floor. The underfloor framing must carry the building's own weight, which is referred to as *dead load*, plus the building's *live load*, which is the weight of the occupants and furnishings. This load must be distributed equally over the entire floor area, with adequate support for any intended load placed at any floor location.

It is usually easiest to match your floor-framing method and materials to those used on the original building. This method makes it easier to align the foundation heights, and might simplify the tie in between the two floors. Whatever framing method you choose, you must decide on it in advance so that the stem walls can be constructed to the appropriate height.

Sill Plate

The first framing members installed under the floor are the sill plates, also called *sills* or *mudsills* (Fig. 10-3). They are usually 2- x -6 or 2- x -8 lumber, as specified on the plans. They are attached directly to the foundation, and serve as a transition between the concrete of the foundation and the subsequent wooden framing. Because the sill plate is in direct contact with the foundation, it is subject to the moisture that is present in the concrete. For this reason, it must be of a material that is water- and rot-resistant.

The most common choice today for sill plates is pressure-treated lumber. The pressure-treating process involves punching a series of small holes into milled lumber, and forcing one of a variety of wood-preservative chemicals through the holes deep into the wood. This process, unlike dipping or soaking, ensures that the entire interior of the board is uniformly treated, making it virtually impervious to rot. Pressure-treated lumber is also a very good choice for posts and other structural members that come into contact with concrete or earth, or that are subjected to constant weathering.

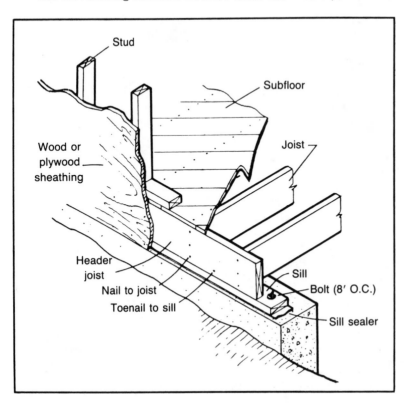

Fig. 10-3. Attachment of the sill plate. Note the use of a sill sealer under the plate.

Other choices for the sill plate include redwood, cedar, and other naturally rot-resistant woods. Check with your building department to see which lumber species are accepted for use in your area.

Before you install the sill plates, you'll need to determine if they will be set flush with the outside of the stem wall or if they'll be held back to allow for the installation of sheathing. This detail will be specified on your plans if you had them professionally prepared. You can make the determination yourself by thinking ahead to how you'll be installing your siding.

Remove the nuts from the anchor bolts and set them aside. Starting at one corner, set a section of sill plate on the foundation and abut it against the anchor bolts. Placing a square against each side of the first bolt, mark the bolt's location on the board. Repeat this procedure for each bolt. Next measure from the outside of the stem wall to the center of the bolt at each location, then transfer this measurement to the sill plate to give you the exact location of each bolt. Be sure to allow for the setback of the sill plate, if any, when you transfer the measurements.

Drill a hole at each marked location on the plate. Select a bit size that is about 1/4 inch larger in diameter than the diameter of the bolt, to allow some movement in the plate for ease of alignment. Apply a sill sealer to the top of the stem wall, set the plate over the bolts, and loosely secure it with the nuts and washers. Cut each subsequent section of sill plate to length and repeat the marking and drilling procedure until you have installed the entire run of plates. If necessary, shim under the sill plates to bring them level. Check that the corners are square and the boards are correctly aligned with respect to the stem wall, then securely tighten all the nuts.

Sill Sealers and Termite Shields

To prevent leakage of cold air under the sill plate, which can work its way into the house, sill sealers are commonly used under the plate. These sealers can be in the form of caulking, or you can use one of the many commercially manufactured sheets of foam or fiberglass that are made just for this application. Sill sealers are simple and inexpensive to install when the sill plates are laid down, and can add greatly to the energy efficiency of the addition.

If you live in an area where termites are a problem, you might wish to consider installing a termite shield. Made of galvanized sheet metal, the termite shield is installed under the sill plate so that it overlaps the stem wall on both sides. Angle the sheet metal down so that any termites coming up the stemwall cannot make their way out and around the shield. Similar shields should be placed on pipes, ducts, or other areas that might provide a path for termite entry into the house.

POST-AND-BEAM CONSTRUCTION

Also called *pier-and-beam, pier-and-post*, and a number of other names, post-and-beam framing is one method of constructing underfloor framing (Fig. 10-4). With this method, a series of beams, called *girders*, are placed on 4-foot centers from wall to wall, usually parallel with the shorter dimension of the foundation. The ends of the girders rest either on the sill plate or in beam pockets that were cast into the stem walls when they were poured. The girders then are supported approximately every 5 feet by 4- x -4 posts, which in turn rest on concrete piers. (See Table 10-1.) The piers may be precast and set on undisturbed soil, or cast in place in excavated holes or directly on the ground.

This framing method uses a minimum of materials and therefore assembles fairly quickly. It requires thicker subflooring than joist framing, and is a little more difficult to insulate. Post-and-beam construction is used only on the first floor of a building. Floor joists are necessary for each subsequent floor.

If post-and-beam construction is being used, the pier layout will be indicated on the foundation plan. Note the size and depth of the piers, and whether they are to be poured in holes in the ground or on the surface of the ground, or whether precast piers are to be used. The piers can be poured or placed now, or you can arrange to have them done at the same time the foundation is poured.

Measure in 4 feet from the outside edge of the

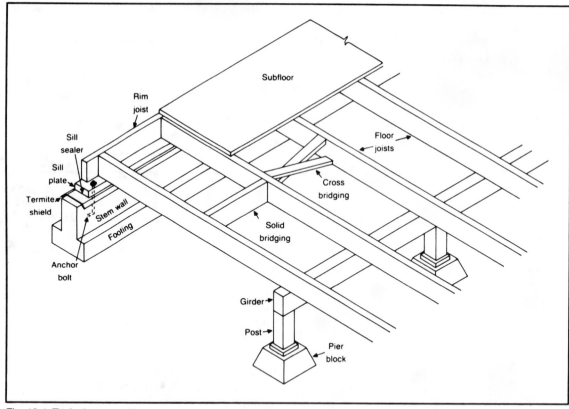

Fig. 10-4. Typical post- and beam-construction. In areas where termites are a problem, a sheet-metal shield can be placed under the sill plate.

foundation to locate the center of the first run, which should fall directly over the run of piers. Mark the center of the first girder, then all subse-

Table 10-1. The Amount of Floor Area That Can Be Supported by Piers of Various Sizes.

FLOOR AREA	MINIMUM PIER SIZE
16 square feet	12 × 12 inches
20 square feet	14 × 14 inches
24 square feet	15 × 15 inches
28 square feet	16 × 16 inches
32 square feet	17 × 17 inches
36 square feet	18 × 18 inches
40 square feet	19 × 19 inches
44 square feet	20 × 20 inches
48 square feet	21 × 21 inches
52 square feet	22 × 22 inches
56 square feet	22 × 22 inches
60 square feet	23 × 23 inches

quent girders, on the sill plates. Stretch a string tightly between the marks so that it is lying directly on the sill plates. This string indicates the bottom of the girder, and is used in determining the length of the supporting posts.

Carefully measure from the top of each pier to the string, and cut a post to this length. Some building codes require that a waterproof barrier be placed between the post and the pier, or that pressure-treated posts be used. A scrap of asphalt roofing shingle is a common choice to rest the post on, and its thickness must be taken into consideration when you are measuring for the post length.

If the girders will not reach from sill to sill in one piece, cut the first girder so that the splice will be centered over one of the posts. Continue the girder run until you reach the other sill plate, being certain you splice each piece over a supporting post. Toenail the ends of the girders to the sill plates and to the posts. Nail a 2-foot piece of 1-×-6 or 2-×-6 lumber to the sides of the girders over each splice to lock them together. When all of the girders are in place, use additional lengths of 4 × 6 to block in between the ends.

FLOOR JOISTS

The use of floor joists for underfloor framing is the other common method of floor construction (Fig. 10-5). Joist size depends on the length of the area the joist needs to span, and on the spacing between the joists. Common joist spacings are 12, 16, and 24 inches on center. Joist size information will be included on your plans, or the building department will have available a span table, which will show you the size and spacing necessary to span a given area. (See Table 10-2.)

Joists usually are laid out parallel to the shortest dimension of the floor in order to minimize the span. If the span is still too great to be handled by a joist in one piece, girders, posts, and piers are used as described previously, to provide a support over which the joists can be spliced.

Framing begins with the rim joist, which is laid on top of the sill plate perpendicular to the run of the other joists. Working from one end of the rim joist, lay out and mark the location of each joist according to the spacing you've selected. Begin installing the joists one at a time, checking each to see if there is any up or down warp along the edge. This warp, called a *crown*, should always be placed up so that the weight of the floor load will push it down. The load will tend to worsen the crown if it is installed in the down position.

Nail through the rim joist into each joist using three 16d nails. Overlapping splices should be secured by nailing through the two boards with 16d nails. Butt splices are joined using a wooden splice plate, secured with 8d nails for 1-inch lumber or 16d nails for 2-inch lumber. In either case, toenail the spliced boards down into the supporting girder.

In order to stiffen the joists over long spans, bridging is often necessary. There are two types of bridging: solid and cross. *Solid bridging* consists of solid blocks of lumber of the same dimension as the joists. The blocks are cut to fit between the joists (Fig. 10-6) and are secured using 16d nails driven into the blocks through the sides of the joists. Staggering the bridging makes nailing considerably easier.

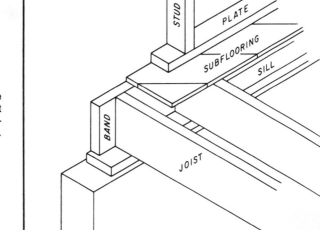

Fig. 10-5. Floor joists resting on the sill plate. Note the rim or band joist around the outside (Courtesy of National Forest Products Association).

Table 10-2. A Typical Span Table for Sizing Floor Joists.

	MAXIMUM SPAN	
	With Plaster or Drywall Below[1]	Without Plaster or Drywall Below[2]
2 × 6 at 16 inches OC	9′ – 6″	10′ – 0″
2 × 8 at 16 inches OC	12′ – 6″	13′ – 6″
2 × 10 at 16 inches OC	15′ – 6″	16′ – 6″
2 × 12 at 16 inches OC	18′ – 0″	20′ – 0″

[1]Second-floor joists that also will support ceiling finish material.
[2]First-floor joists.

Cross bridging is installed between the joists in the form of an **X**, extending from the inside top of one joist to the inside bottom of the adjacent joist, and vice versa (Fig. 10-7). Cross bridging can be hand-cut from 1-×-2 or 1-×-3 stock and secured to the joists with 8d nails. An alternative is prefabricated bridging, which is manufactured to the proper length to fit a given joist size on a given center. Teeth on the upper end of the metal bridging are driven into the top of the joist, then the angled bottom is driven into the joist bottom.

Bridging should be installed wherever the joists are spliced, and then should be placed approximately every 8 to 10 feet, or as specified by the building department. Either type of bridging can use up a lot of lumber, so remember to take that into consideration when you are estimating and ordering.

LEDGERS

A common situation that arises in the framing of a room addition floor is the need to extend directly

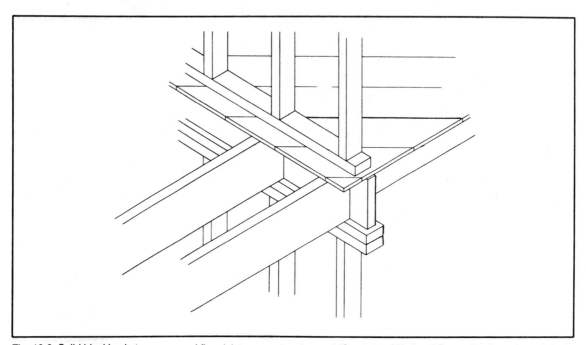

Fig. 10-6. Solid blocking between second floor joists over a bearing wall (Courtesy of National Forest Products Association).

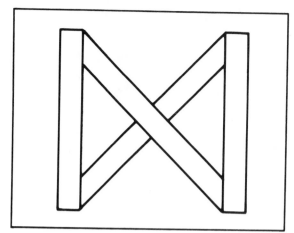

Fig. 10-7. Attaching cross bridging between second-floor joists.

off the existing house. This extension is accomplished through the use of a ledger, which is secured directly to the home's existing floor framing (Fig. 10-8).

The ledger should be of the same height as the

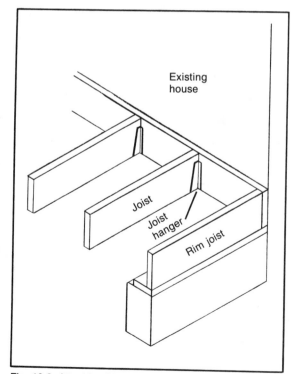

Fig. 10-8. Attaching joists to a ledger using joist hangers.

girders or joists that make up the new floor framing. After the sill plates are installed, rest one end of the ledger on the sill at the outside wall. Carefully align it with the existing floor, allowing for the thickness of the new subfloor. This step is extremely important to ensure that the two floors will be at the same level. Nail through the ledger into the existing floor framing with 16d nails. For long spans or for floors that will carry a substantial load, it might be necessary to bolt the ledger in place with lag bolts.

If the ledger cannot span the two outside walls of the addition in one piece, make butt splices as necessary. Reinforce each splice with a wooden plate that extends at least 1 foot beyond the joint in each direction. After the ledger is in place, extend the joists off it using prefabricated joist hangers.

SPECIAL FLOOR-FRAMING SITUATIONS

In some instances, the layout of the addition might require special framing in addition to the simple joist or girder layout. Care must be taken that these situations are well thought out and planned for during the framing operation to provide the proper support.

Openings

One of the most common floor-framing situations are openings, such as for a crawl-space access or a stairwell between floors. (See Fig. 10-9.) First, install the joists that will form the sides of the opening. These two joists, called *trimmers*, run parallel to the direction of the other joists.

Next, install a cross piece, called a *header*, between the trimmers at each end of the opening. Then extend short joists, called *tail joists*, off the headers to complete the framing. If only one joist space is being spanned by the opening, this framing will be sufficient. For larger openings, it is necessary to double both the trimmers and the headers to provide adequate support. Remember to allow for this second piece of lumber when you are initially framing the opening, so that the opening will be the correct size when all of the boards are in place.

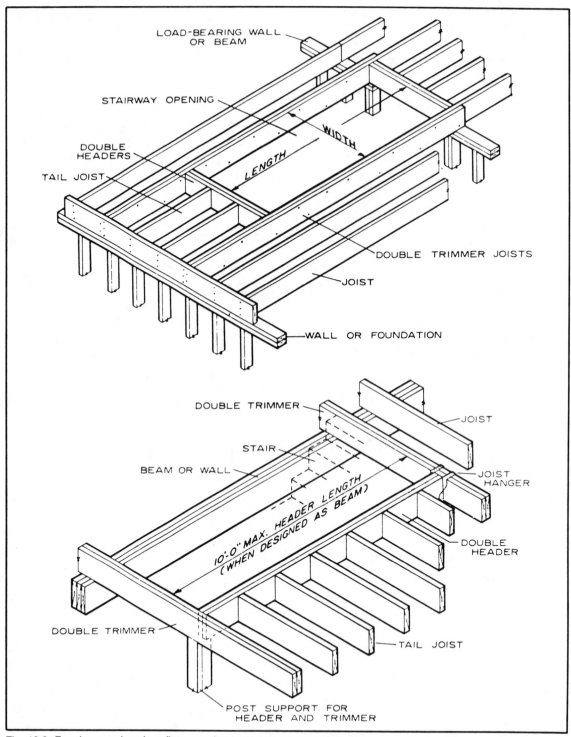

LOAD-BEARING WALL
OR BEAM

STAIRWAY OPENING

WIDTH

LENGTH

DOUBLE
HEADERS

TAIL JOIST

DOUBLE TRIMMER JOISTS

JOIST

WALL OR FOUNDATION

DOUBLE TRIMMER

JOIST

STAIR

BEAM OR WALL

JOIST
HANGER

10'-0" MAX. HEADER LENGTH
(WHEN DESIGNED AS BEAM)

DOUBLE
HEADER

DOUBLE TRIMMER

TAIL JOIST

POST SUPPORT FOR
HEADER AND TRIMMER

Fig. 10-9. Framing openings in a floor, running both with the joists, top, and across the joists.

106

Extensions

Another common framing situation arises when one section of the floor is to extend out past the foundation or lower story of the house, as in the case of a bay window. (See Fig. 10-10.)

If the extension occurs in the same direction as the run of the joists or girders, it is simply necessary to extend the joists out past the foundation or wall the necessary distance. Then secure another rim joist to the ends of the joists, and place solid blocking between the joists at the line of the foundation or wall.

For extensions that run perpendicular to the joists, a cantilever must be framed. In this situation, the joists supporting the extension need to extend in at least twice the distance that they

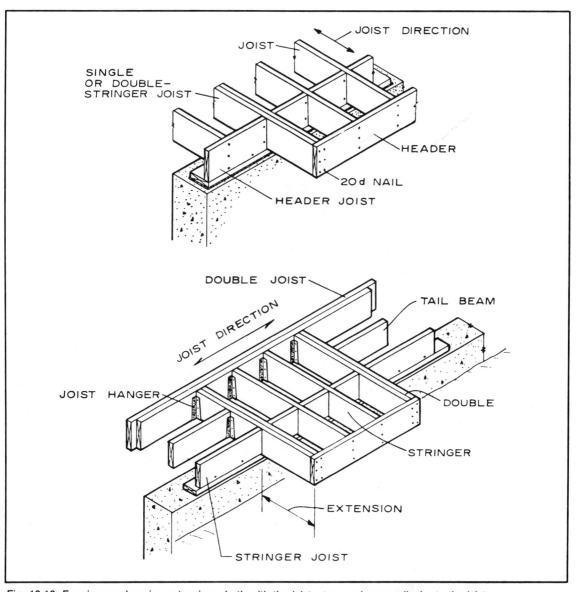

Fig. 10-10. Framing overhanging extensions, both with the joists, top, and perpendicular to the joists.

overhang outside. Double the joists at the outside of the extension in order to provide an adequate bearing surface for the walls, and also double the regular joist where the extension joists intersect it. Framing anchors commonly are used to reinforce the connection at this point. Another alternative is to use joist hangers installed upside down. Remember that the downward force being exerted on the extension will try to move the other end of the joists up, so the joist hangers in the upside-down position will provide the most support.

Dropped Floors

In some instances it might be necessary to have one portion of the floor lower than the surrounding area. This situation might occur when two finish-flooring materials of substantially different heights will intersect (Fig. 10-11), or it might be a desired architectural feature, as in the case of a sunken living room.

If the dropped area comprises a large portion of the floor area, it might be necessary to step the foundation down. This is an important consideration in the early planning stages, since the drop obviously must be built into the foundation when it is first poured.

Another method is to use joists that have a smaller height than the surrounding joists (Fig. 10-12). This method will work only if the lowered area is small enough that the shorter joists are adequate for the span. Consult a span table to determine the smallest joist you can safely use for the intended span. It might be necessary to decrease the spacing between the joists in order to gain adequate support out of smaller lumber.

Fig. 10-11. Using joists of different heights to form a dropped floor area. The area at left will receive a concrete slab for storage mass in a sunspace, bringing the two floors even.

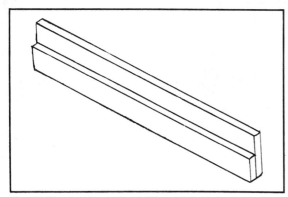

Fig. 10-12. Attaching joists of different heights to drop a floor.

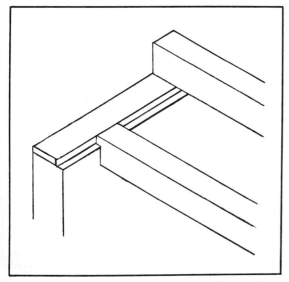

Fig. 10-13. Using a beam pocket to drop a floor girder to a lower level.

For post-and-beam construction, using a beam pocket in the foundation will enable the girders in one area to be set lower. (See Fig. 10-13.)

FLOOR TRUSSES

A relatively new development in floor framing is the use of the floor truss. Because of its greatly increased load-bearing capabilities, a floor truss can span much greater areas than conventional joists or girders. This can be a real advantage in some cases, particularly when you are framing a second-story floor. Using the floor truss usually enables you to span the entire distance between outside walls, thus eliminating the need for supports on the first floor and giving you more flexibility in how you position your walls. Because floor trusses are more expensive than conventional framing methods, they usually are used only when their greater span is absolutely necessary.

There are basically two ways that floor trusses are constructed. One type uses a solid top and bottom plate, connected by an open webbing of steel braces. This construction offers the additional advantage of providing numerous openings through which wiring, plumbing, and ducts can be passed.

The other type of truss uses a solid web of plywood between the plates. Be sure to consult with the manufacturer for the proper location within the web for drilling any holes, since this affects the strength of the truss.

Floor trusses are manufactured for given spans and loads, and must be carefully engineered at the factory to ensure adequate strength for the intended application. Ask for a copy of the engineering calculations when you are getting estimates on the trusses, and include the calculations with your plans when you apply for your building permit.

SUBFLOORING

The last step in constructing the floor platform is the installation of the subfloor. Subfloor materials and thicknesses vary widely with the intended application, and must be matched to the size and type of floor framing that supports it.

For post-and-beam framing, there are two subflooring options. Because of the greater distance that the subfloor must span, it needs to be thicker than the subflooring used over floor joists. One common choice is 2- × -6 tongue-and-groove lumber, usually a #2 or #3 grade. The boards are applied perpendicular to the run of the girders, starting with the grooved side against the existing house. Work out from the house one board at a time, interlocking the groove of one board with the tongue of the board preceding it. All splices must be made over a girder, and should be staggered so that they don't all fall on the same support. Secure the boards with two 16d nails in each girder.

109

Fig. 10-14. Installing plywood subflooring (Courtesy of Senco Products, Inc.).

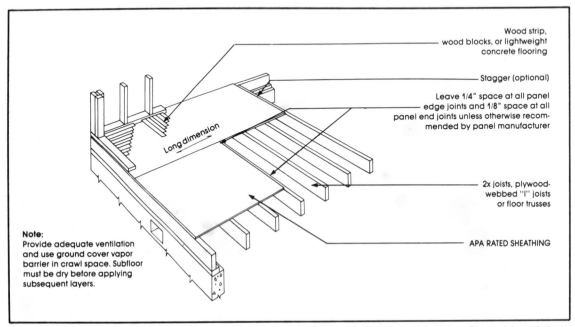

Wood strip, wood blocks, or lightweight concrete flooring

Stagger (optional)

Leave 1/4" space at all panel edge joints and 1/8" space at all panel end joints unless otherwise recommended by panel manufacturer

Long dimension

2x joists, plywood-webbed "I" joists or floor trusses

APA RATED SHEATHING

Note:
Provide adequate ventilation and use ground cover vapor barrier in crawl space. Subfloor must be dry before applying subsequent layers.

Fig. 10-15. Recommended details for installing plywood subflooring over joists (Courtesy of American Plywood Association).

Panel Recommendations for APA Glued Floor System[a]

Joist Spacing (in.)	Flooring Type	APA Panel Grade and Span Rating	Possible Thickness (in.)
16	Carpet and Pad	STURD-I-FLOOR 16 oc	19/32, 5/8, 21/32
	Separate Underlayment or Structural Finish Flooring	RATED SHEATHING 24/16, 32/16, 40/20, 48/24	7/16, 15/32, 1/2, 19/32, 5/8, 23/32, 3/4
19.2	Carpet and Pad	STURD-I-FLOOR 20 oc	19/32, 5/8, 23/32, 3/4
	Separate Underlayment or Structural Finish Flooring	RATED SHEATHING 40/20, 48/24	9/16, 19/32, 5/8 23/32, 3/4
24	Carpet and Pad	STURD-I-FLOOR 24 oc	11/16, 23/32, 3/4, 7/8, 1
	Separate Underlayment or Structural Finish Flooring	RATED SHEATHING 48/24	23/32, 3/4
32 or 48	Carpet and Pad	STURD-I-FLOOR 48 oc (2-4-1)	1-1/8

(a) For panel recommendations under ceramic tile, refer to Table 12.

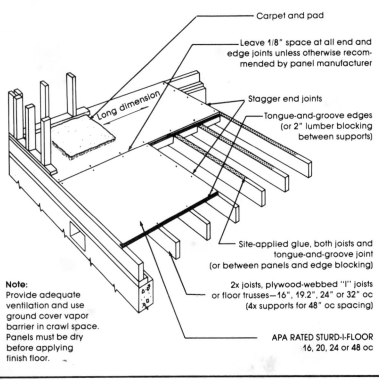

Carpet and pad

Leave 1/8" space at all end and edge joints unless otherwise recommended by panel manufacturer

Stagger end joints

Tongue-and-groove edges (or 2" lumber blocking between supports)

Site-applied glue, both joists and tongue-and-groove joint (or between panels and edge blocking)

2x joists, plywood-webbed "I" joists or floor trusses—16", 19.2", 24" or 32" oc (4x supports for 48" oc spacing)

APA RATED STURD-I-FLOOR 16, 20, 24 or 48 oc

Long dimension

Note:
Provide adequate ventilation and use ground cover vapor barrier in crawl space. Panels must be dry before applying finish floor.

Fig. 10-16. Gluing the subfloor makes for a sturdier floor system and eliminates squeaks (Courtesy of American Plywood Association).

If you have difficulty getting the boards to pull together, cut a small block of tongue and groove and fit it over the tongue of the board on which you're working. This gives you something to hammer against without damaging the tongue of the board being installed. Another helpful method is to drive a chisel into the girder directly in front of the board, then pull back on it to provide leverage against the board.

The other subflooring option is 1 1/8-inch

tongue-and-groove plywood. Install the sheets so the long dimension is perpendicular to the run of the girders, and the joints fall over a support. Secure the panels with 12d or 16d nails (Fig. 10-14).

Plywood panels such as these are more expensive and a little more awkward to handle than tongue-and-groove lumber, but they offer the advantages of faster installation, better prevention of air infiltration from the crawl space, and a smoother, more uniform surface for the installation of the finish flooring.

Plywood is also the common choice over floor joists. (See Fig. 10-15.) The thickness will depend on the spacing between the joists, but 3/4 inch is about the most common. The installation procedure is the same as for the 1 1/8-inch panels, except that 8d nails commonly are used.

Other choices for subflooring materials over floor joists include individual tongue-and-groove, or *shiplap*, boards, although material costs and increased installation time have pretty much made these a thing of the past.

To ensure a "no-squeak" floor, apply a bead of construction adhesive to the top of each joist or girder before installing the subfloor material. (See Fig. 10-16.) The adhesive creates a solid bond between the subfloor and the framing, and greatly increases the holding power of the nails.

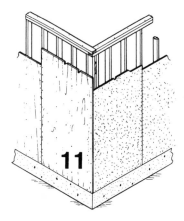

Wall Framing

In platform framing, the walls typically are framed while they are laying on the subfloor, then are stood up, moved into position, and secured. This procedure is the same for slab floors or floors over a crawl space, and it offers another real advantage over balloon framing. With balloon framing, sill plates are first secured to the foundation, then the wall studs are erected one at a time, extending full length to the roof.

PLATFORM WALL FRAMING

If you are adding on to a house that was constructed using the balloon framing method, or any method of framing other than platform framing, you still can adapt platform framing to it easily. Once the foundation has been poured at the correct level and the underfloor framing and subfloor have been constructed, the only other real framing considerations are building the walls to the correct height and matching up the roof framing. As mentioned in Chapter 10, platform framing will be the only method described.

THE COMPONENTS OF A WALL

Each wall you construct is actually an independent structure, several of which are joined together to form the addition. There are seven basic components of a wall structure, and each wall will contain most or all of them (Fig. 11-1).

☐ *Sole Plate.* Also called the *bottom plate,* the lowest horizontal member of the wall, to which the bottoms of the studs are attached.
☐ *Top Plates.* Usually doubled, the upper horizontal members of the wall.
☐ *Studs.* The main vertical components of the wall, which act to carry the downward load of the roof structure, and which provide the framework for the application of interior and exterior finish materials.
☐ *Headers.* Horizontal beams that carry a load across an opening; used over doors, windows, and other openings in the wall.
☐ *Trimmers.* Shorter studs used to support a header.

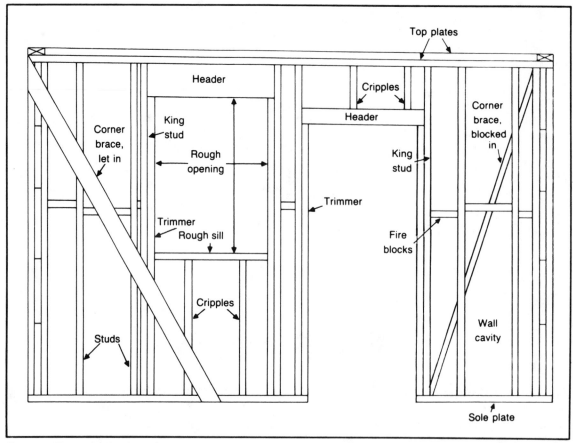

Fig. 11-1. The major framing components of a wall.

☐ *Sill.* The lower horizontal member of an opening, such as for a window.

☐ *Cripples.* Short vertical members used to fill above and below an opening, and in any area where a full-length stud is not used.

FRAMING LUMBER SIZES

For many years, 2 × 4s have been the overwhelming choice for wall studs and plates. However, as energy conservation becomes a bigger concern for many people, 2- × -6 walls are growing in popularity. (See Fig. 11-2.) In fact, the building codes in some areas now require 2- × -6 walls in new residential construction. The reason is quite simple: a 6-inch-deep wall will accommodate a thicker layer of insulation, a total of R-19, than a 4-inch-deep

wall, which can carry a total of only R-11.

In most cases, 2- × -6 walls cannot be used for additions to a house that was originally framed with 2 × 4s, since either the inside or the outside surfaces of the walls will not line up. If your addition is such that the new walls are not a direct extension of the old walls, as in a second-story addition, 2- × -6 construction is well worth considering. There is a higher initial cost for both the lumber and the insulation, but this cost will be offset in the future by utility savings. Also, most building departments will allow 24-inch spacing between the studs when you are framing with 2 × 6s, so you have a direct savings in lumber and labor.

Another framing consideration is ceiling height. In almost every instance, you will need to frame your new walls to match the height of the old walls

Fig. 11-2. Insulation space created through the use of a two-stud corner. Note the 2- × -6 wall construction.

in order for the ceilings to align. Time and labor savers worth considering are precut studs, provided they are the right height for your addition. While there are a couple of different precut stud lengths, one of the most popular is 92 1/4 inches. When this stud length is combined with 2-inch lumber (1 1/2 inches actual size) for the bottom plate and two top plates, the total wall height is 96 3/4 inches. With 1/2-inch drywall on the ceiling, you can use standard 8-foot sheets of drywall or paneling on the walls with 1/4 inch of play, which is later covered by the baseboards.

You will need to decide whether to use precut studs or to cut your own to the required length, and whether they will be 2 × 4 or 2 × 6, and then order your materials accordingly.

WALL-FRAMING TECHNIQUES

In order to accurately lay out the wall prior to fram-

ing, several items need to be established first, including the type of corners and intersections being used, the stud spacing, and the rough-opening sizes for windows, doors, and other wall openings.

Stud Spacing

By far the most common spacing for wall studs is 16 inches on center (OC), meaning that the distance from the center of one stud to the center of the next one is 16 inches. As just mentioned, 24 OC framing is just now starting to become popular when combined with 2- × -6 studs.

Openings

When you are framing the walls, you will need to know the exact size of any openings, such as for doors or windows. At the framing stage, this is known as a *rough opening,* since it needs to be large enough for the finished door or window unit to fit into it.

Rough-opening sizes sometimes are listed on the plans. If they aren't, you'll need to request them from your supplier before framing begins. As a general rule of thumb, rough openings for doors are framed 2 inches over in both directions. For example, if you're using a 3-0 6-8 door, the rough opening size would be 3 feet 2 inches wide and 6 feet 10 inches high. This extra space in the opening allows room for the door jambs and any shimming that is needed to plumb the door frame. What's left of the opening then is covered by trim.

Window openings often are framed to the actual size being used. A 4-0 3-0 window, therefore, would require a 4-foot-wide- × -3-foot-high rough opening. The manufacturer makes the necessary size adjustment when the window is built, usually making the actual window frame 1/4 inch smaller in each direction. If you're unsure at all about what the rough opening should be, find out before framing begins. A mistake in the rough opening size is extremely hard to correct later on.

Corners and Intersections

Wall corners can be framed using three studs, which has been common for years, or using two studs. (See Fig. 11-2.) Two-stud corners are gaining in popularity, since they allow for insulation to be placed in the corner of the wall behind the framing, which the three-stud corner doesn't. (See Fig. 11-3.) Two-stud corners are also easier to frame and require less lumber. The corner studs usually are nailed up first using 16d nails, then framed into the wall as it's being assembled.

There are also two ways to frame the area where one wall intersects another wall (Fig. 11-4). The traditional method has been to assemble three studs, nailing two of the studs to the edges of the third, center stud. This method provides a solid point of attachment for the intersecting wall, and also provides a nailing surface on each side of the wall for the attachment of the interior finish. Intersections of this type are preassembled and inserted into the wall at the exact location of each cross wall.

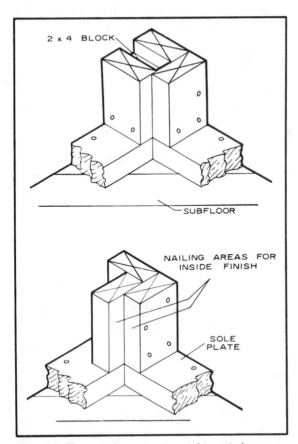

Fig. 11-3. Three-stud corners, top, and two stud corners.

An easier method is to simply frame the first wall with the studs on regular centers, then block between two studs wherever an intersection is needed (Fig. 11-5). This method allows for faster framing, less lumber, and more flexibility in the exact alignment of the cross wall. Six-inch-wide lumber, either 1-inch or 2-inch, is used to provide a backing for the wall finish, or drywall clips can be used. Another advantage to this type of intersection is that it can be insulated; the other type cannot be.

LAYING OUT THE WALL

Wall framing begins by making a full-size layout of the stud and opening locations directly on the top and bottom plates. Use a combination square to mark a line at the location of each vertical member in the wall. This line will help you be certain the stud is placed exactly at a right angle to the edge of the plate when the wall is being assembled. Then mark a letter next to the line to indicate on which side of the line the member is to be placed. Most carpenters use an **X** to indicate the location of a stud, a **T** for a trimmer location, and a **C** for a cripple. Remember that correct placement of the stud next to the line is essential in maintaining the correct stud spacing.

Begin by cutting the bottom plate and one top plate to the desired length and laying them out side by side (Fig. 11-6). Starting at one end, measure out 1 1/2 inches and make a mark, then draw a line across the face of both plates, perpendicular to the edge. Mark an **X** between the end of the plate and this line, to indicate the first stud in the wall. From the line, measure over 3 1/2 inches (5 1/2 inches if you're using 2-x-6 studs), and make a mark. This is the location of the second stud in the two-stud corner.

Measuring from the end of the plate, make a mark at 15 1/4 inches. This will be the edge of the first regular stud in the wall. Draw a pencil line at this mark, then place an **X** on the side of the line away from the end from which you measured. According to this measurement, the distance from the end of the plate to the center of the first stud will be 16 inches. From this first stud line, measure off

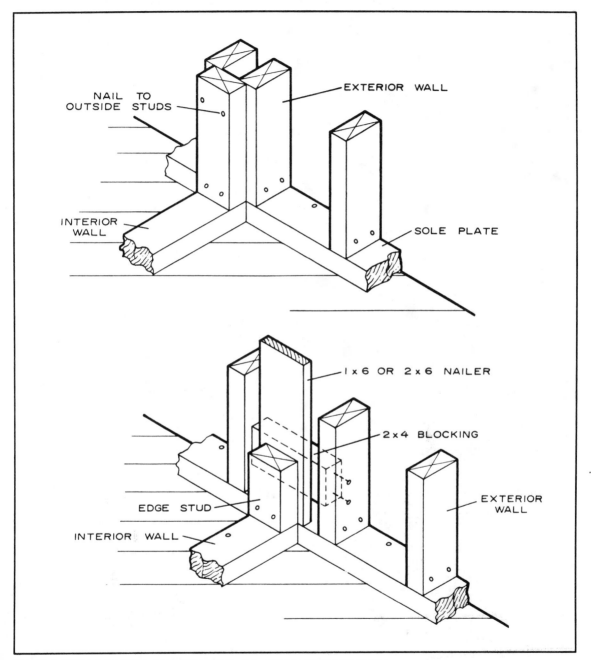

Fig. 11-4. Wall intersections using three studs, top, and two studs with blocks.

16 inches and mark another line and an X. Continue in this manner, measuring 16 inches between lines, until you come to an opening. Remember that only the first measurement is 15 1/4 inches, to establish the center location of the first stud, then it's 16 inches between lines from there on out. (These measurements are for studs being placed 16 inches OC. For 24 OC spacing, make the first mark at 23

Fig. 11-5. Insulation space created behind the intersecting wall through the use of a two-stud intersection.

1/4 inches, then 24 inches apart after that.)

Openings usually are noted on plans by the distance from the end of the wall to the center of the opening. After you have measured off the center location of the opening, you will need to measure back one-half of the rough-opening width to locate where the opening starts. From this point, measure back another 1 1/2 inches and mark a line and a **T** to show where the trimmer is located, then go back another 1 1/2 inches and mark a line and an **X** for the stud location. Finally, measure out the total rough-opening width from the inside of the trimmer, and mark another **T** and **X** for the locations of the stud and trimmer at the other side of the opening.

After you have laid out the opening, you will need to go back to the first regular stud before the opening (not the stud next to the trimmer). From there, continue your regular spacing marks across the width of the opening location, only mark them with a **C** instead of an **X**. These marks indicate the locations of the cripples, which will be placed below the sill of the opening and above the header. In the case of a door, only the top plate is marked for the cripples above the header.

From the location of the last cripple, continue with your 16-inch measurements so that the spacing of the regular studs resumes. Continue on in this manner until the entire bottom and first top plate are laid out. Although this procedure might seem confusing at first, the logic of it quickly becomes apparent in practice, since it's imperative that the stud locations continue in an even spacing, despite being interrupted by the locations of the openings. Lay out, assemble, and stand all of the outside walls before you begin on the partition walls.

ASSEMBLING THE WALL

Place the two plates on edge, marks facing each

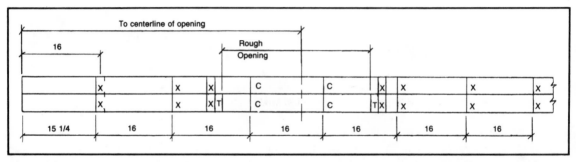

Fig. 11-6. Wall plate layout. Note that the edge of the first stud is placed 15 1/4 inches from the end so that all the studs will be spaced 16 inches apart from center to center.

other, with enough distance between them to allow the studs to be set in place. Place a corner assembly at the end, then set all of the regular, full-length studs in place. Be certain each stud is on the correct side of the line. If two or more plates are being joined to make up the full length of the wall, the splice must fall over a stud.

Next it is necessary to assemble the studs and trimmers that will make up each side of the openings. Using the dimensions given on the plans or a scale to measure the dimensions directly from the drawings, determine the height of each window. Subtract 1 1/2 inches from this height to allow for the thickness of the bottom plate, and cut two trimmers to this length. Nail each trimmer to a stud with 16d nails, then set them in place as indicated by the X and T on the plates.

Nail through the bottom plate into each stud with two 16d nails. Use the line on the plate to check that the stud is being assembled perpendicular to the edge of the plate and has not been twisted. Repeat the procedure for the top plate.

Headers are sized for the opening they will span, using an approved span table. (See Table 11-1.) You can make the headers out of two pieces of 2-inch lumber, placed flush with the outside edges of the wall with a space between them, or you can make them from one solid piece of 4-inch lumber. If desired, you also can use an oversized header that fills the entire area between the top of the trimmer and the plate, thus eliminating the need for cripples above the opening. Cut each header to length and install it between the studs on each side of the opening, so that the bottom of the header is resting on the trimmers. Nail through the studs into the ends of the header to secure it.

For window openings, install the sill next. Measure down from the bottom of the header the correct rough-opening height. Cut the sill to length and install it between the trimmers. Double-check the width and height of the rough opening at this point to be sure it's correct. Finally, cut and install the cripples below the sill and above the header (Fig. 11-7). The bottom plate is left in place across all door openings, and is cut out later, after the walls are standing.

Standing the Wall

When you are raising the wall sections into place, use enough people to comfortably lift the section and keep it under control. Have nails and extra lumber close by for temporary bracing.

Grasp the wall at the top plate and raise it until it is fully upright and resting on the bottom plate. Push or carry it until the bottom plate is in the correct location along the edge of the subfloor, then nail down through the plates into the floor. Do not nail through the plates in the door openings.

For the side walls that attach to the existing house, care must be taken with the alignment so that the finished wall surfaces will be flush. You will need to know what material will be used for both the siding and sheathing, if any, on the new walls, and make a determination at this point as to how they will align with the existing walls. Refer to the detailed explanation in the *Sheathing* section at the end of this chapter.

With one or more people steadying the wall, install temporary diagonal braces between the floor

Table 11-1. A Typical Span Table for Window and Door Headers.

LUMBER SIZE, ON EDGE	MAXIMUM SPAN	
Two 2 × 4, or one 4 × 4	Up to 4′	– 0″ openings
Two 2 × 6, or one 4 × 6	4′ – 0″ to 6′	– 0″ openings
Two 2 × 8, or one 4 × 8	6′ – 0″ to 8′	– 0″ openings
Two 2 × 10, or one 4 × 10	8′ – 0″ to 10′	– 0″ openings
Two 2 × 12, or one 4 × 12	10′ – 0″ to 12 ′	– 0″ openings

Note: Headers for openings over 12′ – 0″ require a beam that is sized for the intended load.

Fig. 11-7. A completely framed opening, with solid header, trimmers, sill, and cripples.

and the top of the wall (Fig. 11-8). Check the outside of the wall with a level as the braces are installed to be certain it is plumb. As each outside wall is added, nail the corners together.

Permanent Bracing

To prevent side to side movement in the wall, called *racking,* permanent bracing must be installed. If the walls are to be sheathed with plywood or covered with plywood siding, these panels will provide the necessary bracing (Fig. 11-9). In this case, 1 × 4s usually are nailed diagonally to the inside of the wall to hold it plumb until the sheathing or siding is installed. If you are using a nonstructural insulated sheathing, you can install plywood of the same thickness as the sheathing on the corners to serve as permanent bracing.

For unsheathed walls being covered with vertical or horizontal siding boards, or with stucco or other masonry, diagonal bracing must be installed in the wall itself. There are several ways this step can be accomplished. The easiest way is through

Fig. 11-8. Temporary bracing used to hold the wall plumb during framing.

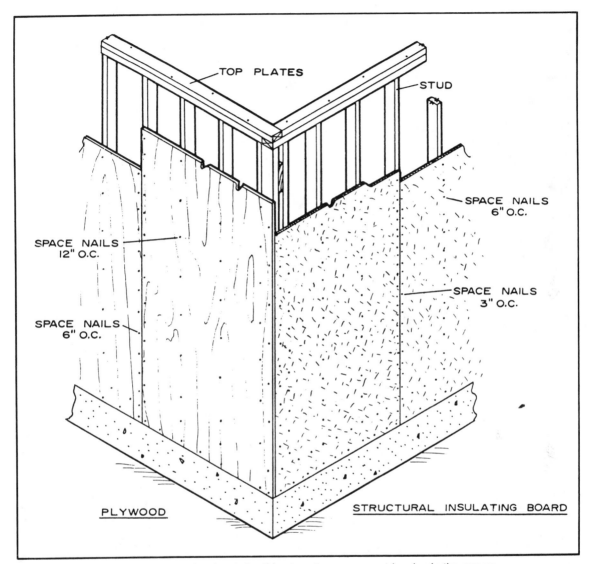

Fig. 11-9. Plywood panels used with insulated sheathing to act as permanent bracing in the corners.

the use of a perforated metal strap, specially manufactured for this application. Nail through one of the holes in the strap at the top plate on the outside of the wall, then extend the strap down at approximately 45 degrees. Use a level to plumb the wall, then nail the strap to each stud that it crosses.

Wooden braces, placed so that they don't interfere with the exterior wall covering, also can be used. They either can be let in or blocked in. For *let-in braces,* first plumb the wall and temporarily tack a 1 × 4 to the outside of the studs at approximately a 45-degree angle. Use a pencil and mark each stud where the board crosses it, both at the top and the bottom, then remove the board. Set the depth on a portable circular saw to 3/4 inch, which is the thickness of the brace. Cut along the inside of each line, then make several passes with the saw in the area between the lines. Use a chisel to clear out the excess wood, forming a diagonal notch in the outside face of each stud. Replumb the wall,

121

install the 1 × 4 in the notches, and nail it to each stud with two 8d nails.

Blocked-in braces are individual pieces of wood with ends cut on an angle, nailed between each stud. For this method of bracing, draw two parallel diagonal lines on the outside face of the studs, 1 1/2 inches apart. Using the lines as a guide, measure and cut blocks of wood to fit between each stud. Secure the blocks in place by driving two 8d nails into the studs at each end.

PARTITION WALLS

Partition walls are the interior walls that partition the inside area of the addition into individual rooms. If you are using roof trusses, none of the partition walls are bearing walls, since trusses bear only on the exterior walls. In this case, the roof structure and exterior siding are often completed to make the addition weatherproof before the interior walls are assembled.

Partition walls are constructed the way the exterior walls were, beginning with a plate layout and proceeding through the assembly of the studs, trimmers, and cripples. Referring to the plans, estab-

lish the location of each partition wall and mark it on the floor with a chalk line. This line helps ensure that the walls are installed straight, and that they're square to the outside walls. Assemble and install major interior walls first, then the cross walls.

Doubling the Top Plates

After all of the walls are standing, including the short walls that form the closets and smaller interior spaces, add the second top plate. Install these plates in such a way that they overlap the first top plate of each intersecting wall, locking the two walls together. (See Fig. 11-10.)

Blocking

As the final step in the wall-framing stage of the addition, take a moment to consider where blocking might be needed. A prefabricated shower stall or bathtub often requires blocking around its perimeter for support, or to provide a point of attachment.

Cabinets, towel bars, shelving, fixtures, curtain

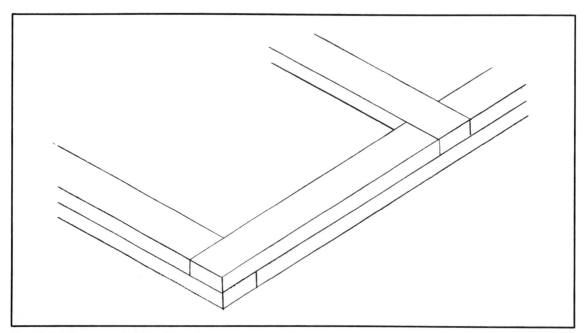

Fig. 11-10. Proper overlapping of top plates at corners and intersections.

APA Panel Wall Sheathing Under Stucco
(APA RATED SHEATHING panels continuous over two or more spans.)

Panel Type	Minimum Nominal Panel Thickness (in.)	No. of Plies (where applicable)	Minimum Span Rating	Maximum Stud Spacing (in.)	
				Vertical Application[a]	Horizontal Application[a][b]
Veneer-Faced	3/8	3	16/0 or Wall—16 oc	—	16
	15/32	3 or 4	24/0 or Wall—24 oc	—	24
		5		16	24
	19/32	4	40/20	16	24
		5		24[c]	24
Other Panels	3/8	—	24/0 or Wall—16 oc	—	16
	7/16	—	24/0 or Wall—24 oc	16	24

(a) Long panel dimension parallel to studs (vertical), or across studs (horizontal).

(b) For best performance use blocking or plywood cleat at horizontal joint. Blocking required for braced wall sections or shear wall applications.

(c) APA STRUCTURAL I RATED SHEATHING only.

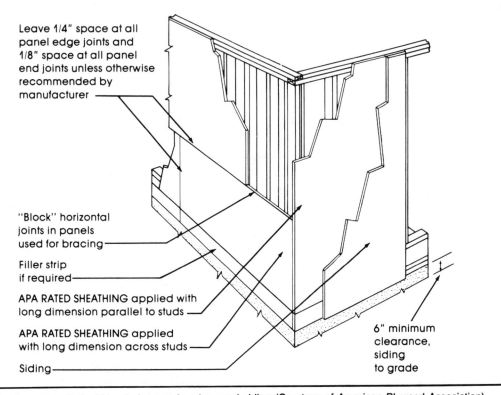

Leave 1/4" space at all panel edge joints and 1/8" space at all panel end joints unless otherwise recommended by manufacturer

"Block" horizontal joints in panels used for bracing

Filler strip if required

APA RATED SHEATHING applied with long dimension parallel to studs

APA RATED SHEATHING applied with long dimension across studs

Siding

6" minimum clearance, siding to grade

Fig. 11-11. Plywood wall sheathing being used under wood siding (Courtesy of American Plywood Association).

rods—all these items and many others might require some additional support within the wall. Installing the blocking now will make the later installation of these items much easier.

SHEATHING

Many types of siding require the installation of sheathing before the finish siding material is put in place. Sheathing usually is installed at the time the wall framing is completed. Most types of masonry and individual board siding will require sheathing for structural support and backing, and as a nailing surface. Plywood siding, or other siding types in solid sheets, usually do not require sheathing. You'll need to rely on an examination of the existing siding and also the advice of the building department to determine if sheathing is necessary.

In today's construction, plywood has almost completely replaced individual boards as sheathing material (Fig. 11-11). Ease and speed of installation, as well as greatly enhanced structural support, make plywood a logical choice. Since good appearance is not necessary, lower grades such as C-D-X are most commonly used, with 1/2 inch being about the minimum thickness. Be certain that, no matter what grade and thickness you use, the plywood is rated for exterior use.

One common problem is matching new sheathing to what's existing. Older houses often used 3/4-inch surfaced boards, or even rough boards measuring a full 1 inch in thickness. Sheathing an entire addition with 3/4-inch plywood or, since plywood is not available in 1-inch thickness, two layers of 1/2-inch can add unnecessarily to the cost of the building. Remember that the goal you're trying to achieve is a wall surface that aligns with the old wall, and there are a number of ways of accomplishing this alignment. Matching the exact thickness of the old sheathing is not always necessary.

If you are extending out a wall where a jog or interior partition makes alignment of the interior walls unnecessary (Fig. 11-12), the new wall framing can be set to whatever sheathing thickness you wish. For example, suppose the existing house is sided with 3/4-inch boards over 3/4-inch sheathing.

Fig. 11-12. An addition wall intersecting the existing house without the need to align it with an existing interior wall.

If you intend to side with 3/4-inch boards over 1/2-inch sheathing, then your wall framing should be set in 1 1/4 inches from the face of the existing wall, rather than a full 1 1/2 inches.

If the new walls are a direct continuation of the old walls (Fig. 11-13), making alignment of both the interior and exterior surfaces necessary, one solution is to stick with a minimum sheathing thickness on the exterior, then shim the interior walls as necessary. In the previous example, where a 1/4-inch difference between the overall thickness of walls exists, placing strips of 1/4-inch plywood or other material on the interior faces of the studs still will allow alignment of the interior finished walls. This method saves both time and money over sheathing with full sheets of a thicker material.

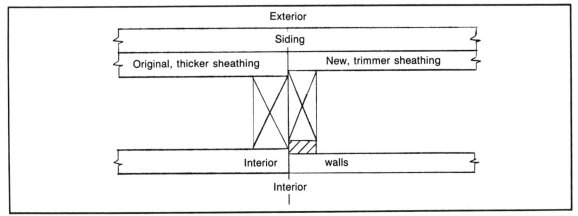

Fig. 11-13. Using shims (shaded area) on the interior face of wall studs to align the interior surfaces, correcting a jog in the wall created when the outside wall surfaces were aligned.

Remember also that it's not necessary to sheath the entire addition with the same thickness of material. If only one wall requires a facing of 3/4-inch material in order to align it with the old wall, the rest of the addition can be sheathed in 1/2-inch material.

Wall sheathing is applied in much the same manner as roof sheathing, except that it is usually applied over the framing vertically instead of horizontally. Begin installing the sheets from the same corner where your stud layout began, so that the sheets will fall over the center of a stud without cutting. Nail the sheathing directly to the studs with 6d or 8d nails. You can make cutouts for windows, doors, and other openings as you install each sheet, or you can cut them out later with a reciprocating saw.

In addition to plywood, other materials may be used for sheathing in various applications. Individual boards, OSB sheets, or any of the various insulated sheathing panels also may be used. Even with these materials, it's common to use a sheet of plywood of the same thickness as the sheathing material at each corner, in order to provide good lateral support and hold the structure plumb during the rest of the building process.

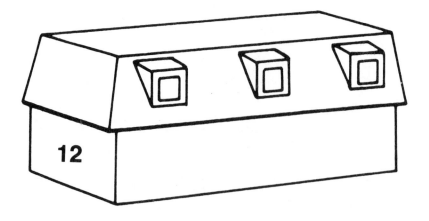

Ceiling and Roof Framing

Probably the most difficult part of framing a house is framing the roof. Calculation of the angles, determination of rafter lengths, design of the cornices—all these aspects of the roof frame require careful thought and execution. This is even more true with room additions because the addition roof must be so constructed as to intersect and blend with the lines of the existing roof.

All roof framing is based on the geometric formula for right triangles, called the Pythagorean theorem (Fig. 12-1). The formula is $A^2 + B^2 = C^2$, where A is one leg of the triangle, B is the other leg, and C is the sloping side opposite the right angle, called the *hypotenuse*. If you imagine looking at a cross section of a roof, you'll see that A is the horizontal distance from the outside of the wall to the center of the ridge, B is the vertical distance from the top of the wall to the center of the ridge, and C is the roof.

ROOF TYPES

There are a number of different roof shapes and designs used in residential construction, and sometimes a combination of two or more might be employed on the same house. (See Fig. 12-2.) The appropriate choice of roof type for an addition is usually dictated by the existing design, although in some cases a different roof type will blend very nicely with the architecture of the existing building.

Most roof types are a variation of the following basic configurations:

☐ *Gable.* Perhaps the most commonly used of all the roof types, gable roofs have two sloping surfaces extending down to two sides from a central ridge. Gable ends, which are extensions of the wall surface, make up the other two ends.
☐ *Hip.* Another popular roof style, hip roofs slope in all four directions.
☐ *Flat.* Technically, a flat roof is one having no slope at all. However, in actual practice flat roofs have a slight slope to allow for water drainage. Slopes of up to 1 in 12 (1/12) usually are considered flat roofs.

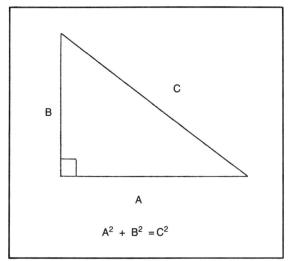

$$A^2 + B^2 = C^2$$

Fig. 12-1. The Pythagorean theorem as used in roof framing.

□ *Dutch Hip.* The Dutch hip is a combination of the gable and hip styles, in which a slight hip is added to the two gable ends for architectural interest and to provide an overhang on all four sides.

□ *Shed.* Shed roofs slope in one direction only, and are the easiest of all roof types to construct. When attached to the side of a building, this type of roof is also commonly referred to as a *lean-to.*

□ *Gambrel.* The traditional "barn" roof, gambrels are identified by their double-sloping roof lines. The upper slope is relatively flat, usually about 2/12 or 3/12, while the lower slopes are steeper, often 12/12 or greater. Gambrel roofs offer good interior headroom on the upper story, and are often used with dormers.

□ *Mansard.* Similar to both the hip and the gambrel, mansard roofs have a double slope, with the upper slope being almost completely flat and the lower slopes being almost vertical. Mansard roofs offer the greatest amount of interior headroom when they are used to enclose a second story.

□ *Butterfly.* The opposite of a gable roof, butterfly roofs slope down from the walls to a lower central valley. This type of roof is rarely seen in residential construction.

ROOF-FRAMING TERMINOLOGY

There are a number of terms associated with roof framing that should be understood before beginning (Figs. 12-3 and 12-4). This knowledge will make the layout and construction of the roof easier, and will enable you to make framing decisions based on your particular roof.

□ *Ridge.* The highest horizontal member of the roof frame, to which one end of all the full-length rafters are attached.

□ *Rafters.* There are three types of full-length rafters that make up a roof frame, depending on what type of roof you're constructing. *Common rafters* extend diagonally from the ridge to the plate. *Valley rafters*, found only where two roofs intersect, extend from the ridge to the inside corners of the intersection between two walls. *Hip rafters*, found only on a hip roof, extend from the end of the ridge to the outside corners of the walls.

□ *Jack Rafters.* Shorter rafters that do not go all the way from ridge to plate. There are three types: *hip jacks*, which connect the hip rafter to the plate; *valley jacks*, which extend between the ridge and the valley rafter; and *cripple jacks*, which connect a hip rafter with a valley rafter.

□ *Rafter Length.* The total length of a rafter, measured diagonally from the centerline of the ridge to the outside of the plate. Rafter length does not include any overhangs.

□ *Overhang.* The total distance, measured horizontally, that the roof extends out past the walls.

□ *Rafter Tail.* That portion of the rafter extending out past the walls to form the overhang.

□ *Span.* The total width of the building, from the outside of one wall plate to the outside of the opposite wall plate.

□ *Run.* The horizontal distance from the outside of the wall plate to the center of the ridge, equal to one-half the span.

□ *Rise.* The vertical distance from the top of the wall plates to the center of the ridge.

□ *Unit Rise and Run.* The angle of the roof is expressed as a ratio between one unit of *run*, which is always 12 inches, and one unit of *rise*,

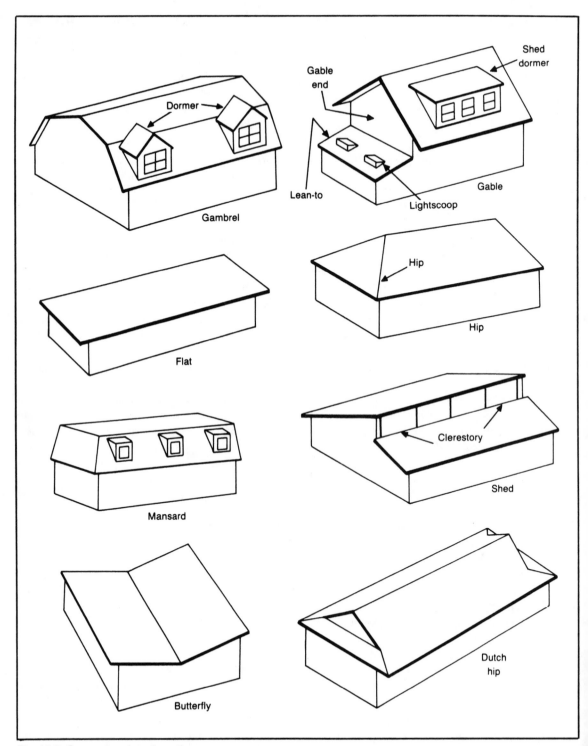

Fig. 12-2. Common roof configurations.

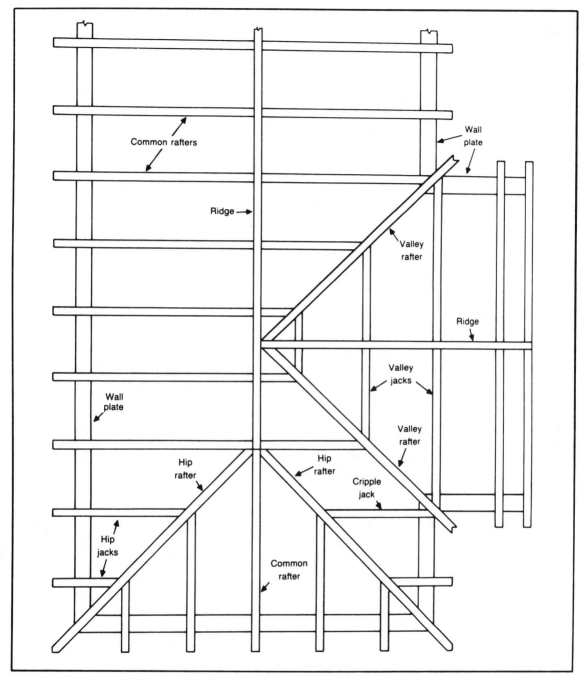

Fig. 12-3. The different types of rafters and their locations.

which is how much the roof rises within those 12 inches of run. For example, a 4/12 roof would rise 4 inches vertically for each 12 inches it extends out horizontally.

☐ *Slope.* The ratio between the unit rise and the unit run. Slope is commonly designated by sim-

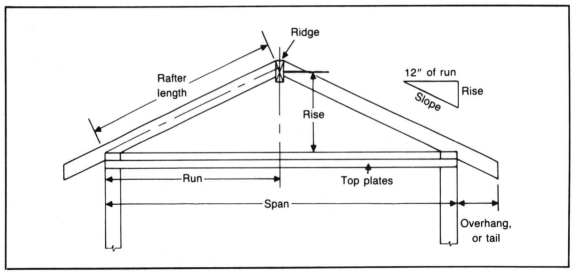

Fig. 12-4. Rise, run, and other dimensions used in calculating a roof layout.

ply referring to that ratio, as a 4/12 roof, a 6/12 roof, etc.

☐ *Bird's-Mouth.* A notch cut in the bottom side of a rafter so that it will sit down over the wall plate. The bird's-mouth consists of two cuts; the *seat cut*, which is horizontal, and the *plumb cut*, which is vertical. (See Fig. 12-5.)

☐ *Plumb Cut.* An angled cut on the end of a rafter that will be vertical when the rafter is installed in its diagonal position. Plumb cuts are necessary where the rafter meets the ridge, and are also commonly used at the end of the rafter so that the fascia will be vertical.

☐ *Level Cut.* An angled cut that will be horizontal when the rafter is in position. Level cuts are used at certain intersections, at the top of the bird's-mouth, and at the ends of the tails for certain types of cornice construction. Also referred to as a seat cut.

☐ *Cornice.* The section of the roof that overhangs the side wall. Cornice design and construction varies widely, and should be made up to match or complement the cornices on the existing house.

TOOLS

For the most part, the tools used in cutting and con-

structing a roof are the same as those used in the rest of the framing. A circular saw is virtually a must, since the precision of the angled and beveled cuts are hard to do accurately with a handsaw. A radial arm saw, if available, will speed the cutting and increase the accuracy even further.

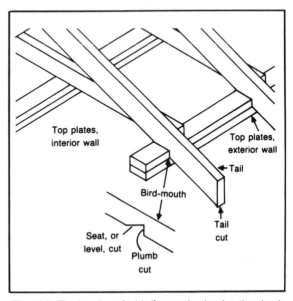

Fig. 12-5. The location of a bird's-mouth, showing the plumb and seat cuts. This cutout allows the rafter to seat down on the plate.

130

One tool that is virtually indispensable for roof framing is the framing square, also called a *rafter square*. It consists of a one-piece, L-shaped frame. The shorter side of the frame, 16 inches long, is called the *tongue*, and the longer side, 24 inches long, is the body. The square is ruled on the face side in 1/8-inch and 1/16-inch measurements, and on the back side in 1/10-inch and 1/12-inch measurements. In addition, it is printed or stamped with rafter-length tables and other useful information.

The design and information on a square is essentially the same for all manufacturers. Look for a square that is made from high-quality, sturdy materials, and that has the numbers and tables stamped into the face, not merely printed or painted on. An instruction booklet explaining the use of the square and the tables will accompany the better quality ones. It will be well worth your time to familiarize yourself with it.

In addition to the square, other marking and measuring tools are quite helpful in cutting a roof. A particularly handy one is the adjustable T square, which has a blade that pivots and locks at various angles. Plumb-cut angles for various common, hip, and valley rafters are cut into the blade, making determination of the proper cutting angle and repetitive marking quite simple. Another is the sliding T bevel, used for duplicating angles.

DETERMINING EXISTING SLOPE

When you are framing the roof for a room addition, it's important to know what the slope of the existing roof is. If you have a copy of the original house plans, check to see if the slope is noted. If it isn't, you can take scale measurements off the drawing to determine the slope.

If the drawings aren't available, you will need to take measurements off the actual roof. There are a number of ways you can do this procedure. If the existing house has a fairly accessible attic, you often can take your measurements there. Using a framing square, place the 24-inch mark on the body against the underside of a common rafter (Fig. 12-6). Holding a level on the body to be certain it's perfectly horizontal, read the number on the tongue where it meets the rafter. Because you are mea-

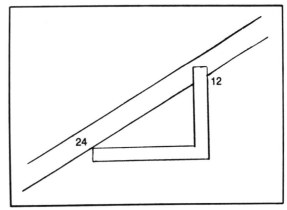

Fig. 12-6. Determining the slope of an existing roof from inside the attic using a framing square.

suring to the 24-inch mark on the body, you have doubled the unit run. Therefore you must divide the rise number on the tongue by 2 to determine the unit rise. For example, with the square held level and at 24, the 12 on the tongue is adjacent to the rafter. This would be a 12/24, or 6/12, slope.

If the attic is not readily accessible or the slope is too low to place the square on the rafter without striking the sheathing, take the measurements on the roof using two levels (Fig. 12-8). Place the end of a 24-inch level against the roof and hold it so it's level. Place a second level against the other end of the first level, and hold it so it's plumb. Have a second person measure from the bottom of the horizontal level to the roof, using the vertical level as a

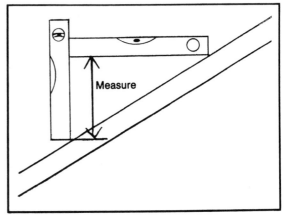

Fig. 12-7. Determining the slope of a roof from above using two levels.

guide. Once again, because the level is 24 inches long, the measurement must be divided by 2 to determine the actual unit rise.

CEILING JOISTS

Framing begins with the layout and installation of the ceiling joists. The ceiling joists act to tie the outside walls together and ensure that they are parallel to each other. They also serve as a stable working platform from which the roof can be framed. (See Fig. 12-8.)

Once again, a span table is necessary as a reference for selecting the size of the ceiling joists. (See

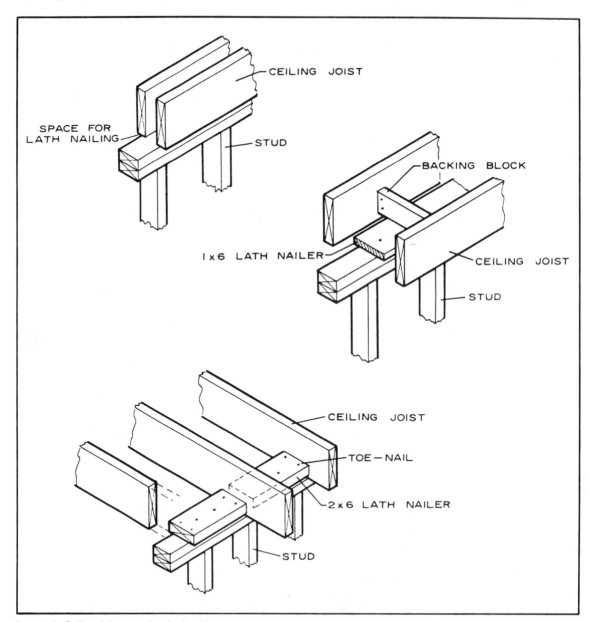

Fig. 12-8. Ceiling joists running both with and across the wall framing.

Table 12-1.) Joist size is directly dependent on the length of the area they must span. In some cases, the joists will need to be spliced over interior partition walls in order to reduce their overall span (Fig. 12-9). Those partition walls then become load bearing, and any openings in the walls must have correctly sized headers.

Ceiling joists are installed parallel with the shortest dimension of the building, again to reduce the span. In some instances, the joists in one section of the house might run at right angles to joists in another section, depending on how the bearing partitions are laid out. If necessary, a beam can be run between the plates, then the joists can be extended out from the side walls in each direction and attached to the beam with joist hangers. This method reduces the overall distance the joists must span while eliminating the need for a partition wall. If you had your plans professionally prepared, all these details will be worked out in advance and included, along with joist size and spacing.

Ceiling Joist Layout

After the spacing and direction of the joists have been determined, layout proceeds as it did for the floor joists or wall studs. If the joist spacing is 16 inches OC, measure in from one end of the wall 15 1/4 inches, as was done for the wall studs. This measurement locates the first rafter so that the spacing to the center is correct. From there, simply lay out the joists every 16 inches.

Table 12-1. A Typical Span Table for Determining the Size of Ceiling Joists.

16 INCHES OC		24 INCHES OC	
Lumber Size	Maximum Span	Lumber Size	Maximum Span
2 x 4	10' – 6"	2 x 4	9' – 0"
2 x 6	16' – 0"	2 x 6	14' – 0"
2 x 8	21' – 6"	2 x 8	19' – 0"
2 x 10	25' – 0"	2 x 10	21' – 2"

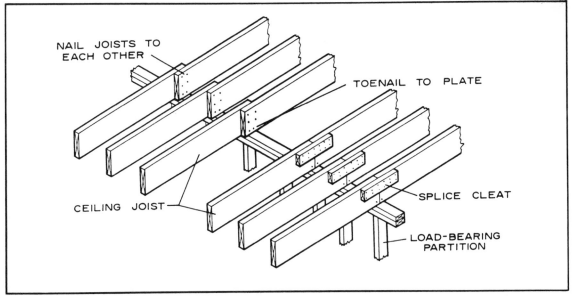

Fig. 12-9. Splicing ceiling joists over a bearing wall to reduce their span.

Fig. 12-10. Short tail joists, left, used with a hip roof to span the area between the first regular joist and the wall.

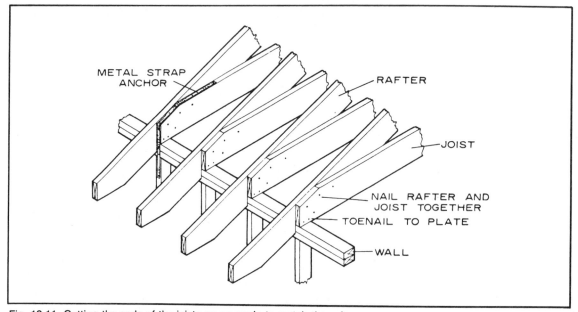

Fig. 12-11. Cutting the ends of the joists on an angle to match the rafters.

134

With a hip roof, the first ceiling joist sometimes must be eliminated if its height will interfere with the rafters. In this case, set the edge of the first joist at 31 1/4 inches (15 1/4 + 16), then continue on 16-inch spacing from there. After the rafters are in place, short tail joists (Fig. 12-10) are extended out perpendicular to this first joist to span the distance between it and the plate.

Installing the Joists

As with the floor joists, select straight lumber and check to see if it has a crown. Mark each crowned board with an arrow as a reminder during installation to put the crown up. Cut the joists to length.

Before you install the joists, you will need to taper each end that will rest on the plates so that it will not extend above the level of the rafters and interfere with the roof sheathing. (See Fig. 12-11.) You will need to first determine approximately how high the rafter will be at the plate. Mark this measurement on the end of the joist, measuring up from the bottom. Using a framing square, hold the body of the square at this mark. Pivot the square until both the unit run—the 12-inch mark on the body—and the appropriate unit rise number on the tongue are at the top edge of the joist. Mark a pencil line along the top of the body of the square to indicate where the joist should be cut. If desired, you can make these cuts after the joists and rafters are in place, using the angle of the rafter as a guide.

Lift one end of the joist and prop it against the top plate of one wall, then set a ladder at the opposite wall. Lift the other end of the joist and carry it up the ladder with you, pulling it toward you until it rests equally on both plates. The ends of the joists must be flush with the outside edge of the plates. Since all of the joists are cut to the same length, if they are not flush with the outside of the walls, the walls are leaning in or out. To correct this situation, place temporary diagonal bracing against the walls. Secure the joists by toenailing them into the plates.

Openings

Openings in the ceiling, such as for a stairwell, are framed exactly like those in the floor. Place double trimmer joists on each side of the opening, and doubled headers at each end. Shorter tail joists finish the frame by extending out from the headers in each direction. Smaller openings, such as those for an attic access hatch, can be framed by simply boxing in between the joists with single headers.

DETERMINING RAFTER SIZE

The size of the material that will be used for the rafters is determined from the span table. (See Table 12-2.) Rafter size is based on the slope of the roof (Table 12-3), the length of the rafter, and the spacing between the rafters. (See Appendix D.)

To determine the length of the common rafters, apply the Pythagorean theorem. These calculations can be done very quickly on any calculator equipped with a square root key.

Example No. 1

Run of the roof is 15 feet, slope is 4/12.

$$\text{Unit Rise} \times \text{Total Run} = \text{Total Rise}$$
$$4 \times 15 = 60 \text{ inches}$$
$$60 \text{ inches} \div 12 = 5 \text{ feet total rise}$$

Apply the formula $A^2 + B^2 = C^2$
$$A^2 = 15^2 = 225$$
$$B^2 = 5^2 = 25$$
$$225 + 25 = 250$$
$$\sqrt{250} = 15.81$$

Total rafter length is 15.81 feet

It is now necessary to convert 15.81 feet into feet, inches, and fractions of an inch so that the length can be accurately laid out on the board.

Convert .81 foot into inches

$$.81 \times 12 = 9.72 \text{ inches}$$

A simple method of converting the decimal into a fraction is to multiply the decimal by the accuracy of the fraction to which you wish it converted. In any framing, 1/8 inch is usually considered accurate enough, since there are disparities in the lumber and the practicalities of job-site applications.

Table 12-2. A Typical Span Table for Determining the Size of the Rafters Based on the Slope of the Roof.

	SPAN WITH SLOPE MORE THAN 4 IN 12	SPAN WITH SLOPE LESS THAN 4 IN 12
2 × 4 at 24 inches OC	7' – 6"	6' – 6"
2 × 6 at 24 inches OC	12' – 6"	12' – 0"
2 × 8 at 24 inches OC	17' – 0"	15' – 6"
2 × 10 at 24 inches OC	21' – 0"	19' – 6"

Convert .72 inch into eighths inch

$$.72 \times 8 = 5.76 \text{ (round off to 6)}$$
$$.72 \text{ inch} = 6/8 \text{ or } 3/4 \text{ inch}$$

Each common rafter in Example No. 1 is 15 feet, 9 3/4 inches long.

Example No. 2

Run of the roof is 19 feet 5 inches; slope is 6/12.

$$19 \text{ feet } 5 \text{ inches} = 19.42 \text{ feet}$$

(Divide 5 by 12 to convert to a decimal)

$$19.42 \times 6 = 116.5 \text{ inches total rise}$$

$$116.5 \text{ inches} = 9.7 \text{ feet } (116.5 \div 12)$$
$$19.42^2 = 377.14$$
$$9.7^2 = 94.09$$
$$377.14 + 94.09 = 471.23$$
$$\sqrt{471.23} = 21.71 \text{ feet}$$
$$.71 \text{ feet} \times 12 = 8.52 \text{ inches}$$
$$.52 \times 8 = 4.16 \text{ (round off to 4)}$$
$$.52 \text{ inch} = 4/8 \text{ or } 1/2 \text{ inch}$$

Each common rafter in Example No. 2 is 21 feet 8 1/2 inches long.

When you are ordering the lumber for the

Table 12-3. The Degrees of Slope for Various Rise and Run Combinations.

RISE PER 12" OF RUN	DEGREES OF SLOPE	RISE PER 12" OF RUN	DEGREES OF SLOPE
1/2"	2 1/2	12 1/2"	46 1/4
1"	4 1/2	13"	47 1/4
1 1/2"	7	13 1/2"	48 1/2
2"	9 1/2	14"	49 1/2
2 1/2"	11 3/4	14 1/2"	50 1/2
3"	14	15"	51 1/2
3 1/2	16 1/4	15 1/2"	52 1/4
4"	18 1/2	16"	53 1/4
4 1/2"	20 1/2	16 1/2"	54
5"	22 1/2	17"	54 3/4
5 1/2	24 1/2	17 1/2"	55 1/2
6"	26 1/2	18"	56 1/4
6 1/2"	28 1/4	18 1/2"	57
7"	30 1/4	19"	57 3/4
7 1/2"	32	19 1/2 "	58 1/2
8"	33 3/4	20"	59
8 1/2	35 1/4	20 1/2"	59 3/4
9"	37	21"	60 1/4
9 1/2"	38 1/2	21 1/2"	61
10"	40	22"	61 1/2
10 1/2"	41 1/4	22 1/2"	62
11"	42 1/2	23"	62 1/2
11 1/2	43 3/4	23 1/2"	63
12"	45	24"	63 1/2

rafters, be sure to add in the length of the overhangs as well as a waste allowance for the plumb cuts at each end of the rafter to determine the total length of the boards you'll need.

Estimating Rafter Length with the Framing Square

A quick method of estimating how long the rafters will be is to use the 1/12-inch scale on the back of the framing square. This scale is fine for estimating, but lacks the accuracy necessary for actually cutting the rafter.

Lay out the square on a board, with the back side up. Let each of the 1/12 marks equal 1 inch, and each of the 1-inch marks equal 1 foot. Align the tongue with the edge of board next to the number representing total rise, which in the case of Example No. 1 is 5. Align the body on the edge of the board next to the total run, which is 15. Mark the edge of the board at these two points. Now, use the 1/12 scale on the square to measure the distance between the two points. You will arrive at approximately 15 feet 10 inches.

As was done with the wall plates before the wall was assembled, the placement of the rafters must be marked out on top of the plates. This layout varies somewhat, depending on the type of roof your home has and on the rafter spacing. (See Fig. 12-12.)

Laying Out a Gable Roof

The layout of gable roofs is very straightforward. The first rafter is placed directly at the end of the wall, then each subsequent rafter is laid out according to the chosen spacing. Continue with the layout along the top of the plate until you reach the intersection with the existing house, making a pencil line and an **X** on the appropriate side of it, as was done during the wall layout. The last rafter sits at the end of the wall, regardless of the spacing between it and the rafter preceding it.

Remember to subtract one-half the thickness of the rafter from the first layout, making it 15 1/4 inches in from the end for 16-inch spacing, or 23 1/4 inches in for 24-inch spacing. Since 4- × -8-foot

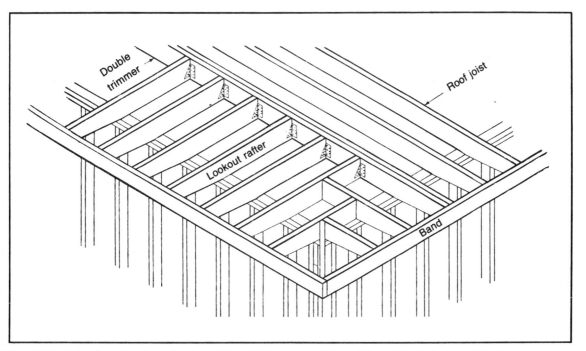

Fig. 12-12. Rafter layout and spacing for a flat roof (Courtesy of National Forest Products Association).

sheets of plywood are the overwhelming choice for roof sheathing, it's critical that the spacing of the rafters start off correctly and remain consistent, so that the joints between the panels will fall over the center of a rafter.

Laying Out a Hip Roof

The three common rafters at the end of a hip roof make two squares of equal size when viewed from above. The initial layout begins by dividing the total span of the building in half. Mark this dimension on the end wall, which indicates the location of the center of the one common rafter on that wall. Measure in this same distance from the end wall along each of the side walls, and mark the plates. This is the location of the center of each of the first two common rafters on the side walls.

Starting at the point you marked on the end wall, lay out the other rafters in each direction from there. From the point where the first two common rafters on the side walls will sit, lay out on both walls in each direction.

CUTTING COMMON RAFTERS

Common rafters are the first rafters to be cut and assembled on the roof. The first rafter must be accurately laid out and cut, then it can be used as a pattern for the cutting of all other common rafters of the same size.

Select a straight, solid piece for the pattern rafter, and lay it out across two sawhorses. Place the framing square on the board so that the unit rise on the tongue is against the board's top edge, as is the unit run on the body of the square. On Example No. 1, these points would be the 4 on the tongue and, as always, the 12 on the body. Mark a pencil line along the outside edge of the tongue to indicate the centerline of the ridge.

Measure off 15 feet 9 3/4 inches from this point, and repeat the procedure with the square, drawing a line to indicate the outside wall of the building. Form the bird's-mouth by using the square to draw a line perpendicular to the outside wall line. This line should be positioned so that it is approximately as wide as the wall plates.

Measure out from the bird's-mouth and lay off the length of the overhang. Return to the top end of the board and subtract one-half the thickness of the ridge, then draw another line with the square parallel to the first.

The pattern rafter is now ready for cutting. Cut along the second plumb line at the top end of the board, and along the line at the overhang. Finally, cut out the bird's-mouth. If you are cutting with a circular saw, cut only as far as the intersection of the pencil lines, then finish the cut with a handsaw. Cutting past the lines will weaken the rafter at its point of bearing on the wall.

ERECTING THE RIDGE
FOR INTERSECTING ROOFS

Setting the ridge board for an addition is slightly different than setting one for a totally new building, because of its intersection with the existing roof. The easiest way to set the ridge is to first attach some temporary supports to the ceiling joists to clamp the ridge to (Fig. 12-13). You might find it easier and safer to lay some boards or plywood across the joists to serve as a platform for standing and working.

Measure along the new ceiling joist closest to the existing house and mark the exact center of the span. Measure over from this mark one-half the thickness of the board being used for the ridge. Select a straight 2 × 4, and nail or clamp it vertically to the rafter along this second mark. Use a level to be certain the board is plumb. Repeat this procedure and stand another 2 × 4 at the last joist and at as many intermediate joists as you feel are necessary to support the ridge board.

Using the total rise figures calculated earlier, determine how high the bottom of the ridge will be, and mark this point on each of the upright supports. Clamp a block of wood to each upright to support the ridge.

Cut the ridge board to length, using a board that is one size wider than the rafters. For example, if the rafters are being cut from 2-×-6 lumber, use a 2 × 8 for the ridge. If the ridge is to be made up of two or more pieces, they must be spliced where a pair of rafters are in order to provide ade-

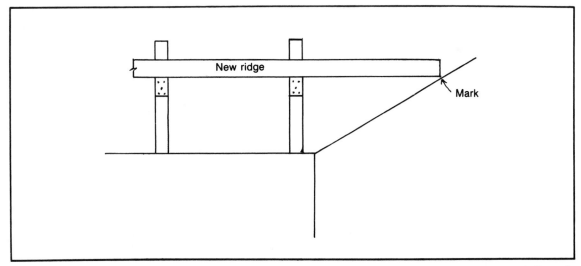

Fig. 12-13. Temporarily erecting the new ridge on blocks to determine the new roof's point of intersection with the existing roof.

quate support. Cut an angle on one end to match the slope of the existing roof.

With the help of at least one other person, lift the ridge board and set it on the blocks. Carefully slide it along the blocks until it intersects the existing roof, and mark the intersection. Set the ridge back down on the ceiling joists.

Use a chalk line and snap a line between the intersection and the point where the addition meets the existing house (Fig. 12-14). Repeat on both sides. Using the line as a guide, tear off the old roofing in a strip approximately 2 feet wide. Replace the ridge board, clamping it securely to the uprights and nailing to the roof sheathing at the intersection. Check it to be sure it's level, and adjust it as necessary by moving the clamps.

BUILDING A GABLE ROOF

Referring to the rafter layout marks on the plates,

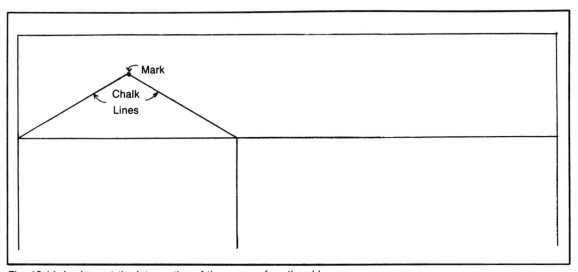

Fig. 12-14. Laying out the intersection of the new roof on the old one.

mark the ridge where each rafter will join to it. Stand the common rafters up on each side of the building where they can be reached easily.

Lift the rafter closest to the existing house into place and have someone hold it against the ridge. The plumb cut on the end of the rafter should meet the ridge; the top of the rafter should be even with the top of the ridge; and the bird's-mouth should drop into place over the plate (Fig. 12-15). Toenail the rafter to the plate, then nail through the ridge into the other end. Lift the second rafter and nail it into position.

Move down about five rafter spaces and repeat the procedure. Continue in this manner until you reach the end of the addition, and stand the two gable end studs. By this point the ridge is self-supporting, and the temporary uprights can be removed.

Fill in with the rest of the rafters until all are in place. Check the roof as you go to be certain it's plumb and that the ridge is remaining straight.

Shed roofs are constructed in the same man-ner, but the intersection with the existing roof or wall takes the place of the ridge. (See Figs. 12-16 and 12-17.)

Framing the Intersection

Measure along the ridge from the last common rafter and lay out the spacing for the jack rafters until you reach the intersection. Each jack rafter will have a plumb cut at one end where it meets the ridge, and a seat cut at the other end where it sits on the old roof. In addition, the seat cut will be beveled to match the slope of the existing roof.

Snap new chalk lines from the point where the ridge intersects the roof to the point where the wall plates meet the house. These lines will form the angle of the valley formed by the two intersecting roofs.

You can determine the length of the jack rafters by referring to the tables printed on the face of the framing square. Refer to the line on the square marked *diff in length of jacks 16 inch centers* (or the

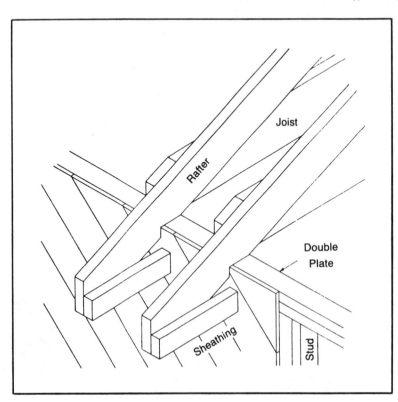

Fig. 12-15. Attaching the common rafters to the plate (Courtesy of National Forest Products Association).

Fig. 12-16. Erecting common rafters for a shed roof on a second-story addition.

Fig. 12-17. To reduce the span, the rafters have been split over a bearing wall, and then will extend out and intersect the existing roof.

next table down, *diff in length of jacks 24 inch centers* if your rafters are on 24-inch centers). Look under the number on the outer edge of the body of the square that corresponds to the unit rise of your roof. Read down to the line on the table, and you will see a number. That number is the amount by which each succeeding jack rafter will be reduced.

Start by laying out the length of a common rafter, marking the location of the ridge cut and the bird's-mouth. From the layout, subtract the measurement found on the rafter square table to determine the length of the jack rafter.

Reading the fifth line down on the tables, you will see *side cut of jacks use*. Again looking under the unit rise number, find the appropriate number from the table. Turn the rafter on its side, and hold the square against the edge of the board so that this number on the tongue is against the edge of the board, as is the 12 on the body. This will give you the angle of the bevel.

Using a circular saw, set the appropriate angle and cut along the seat cut mark you made earlier. Reset the saw for a straight cut and cut the plumb cut at the other end. Test-fit the jack rafter to see that it meets the ridge and the chalk line, and that it is parallel with the last common rafter. If it isn't, make any necessary adjustments and cut a new one. When the cut is correct, cut a second one for the other side. Continue cutting the jack rafters, reducing the length of each pair, until you reach the intersection. Secure the jacks by nailing them to the ridge and toenailing them to the roof sheathing.

Extending an Existing Gable Roof

If you are adding to an existing gable roof, the framing is considerably simplified by the elimination of any intersections. The main consideration is that the two roofs align exactly with each other, so that the transition between them is unnoticeable.

If the gable end to which you are adding has an overhang, extending the roof is easiest if the overhang framing is removed. New common rafters thus can join directly to the existing framing, and the framing and standing of the walls will be easier.

Once the walls and ceiling joists are in place,

framing proceeds as for any gable roof. Connect the ridge board to the end of the existing ridge, and support it on temporary uprights as described under *Erecting the Ridge for Intersecting Roofs*. The first two common rafters should be installed directly against the last two existing rafters, and the tops of the new rafters should be exactly flush with the tops of the existing ones. By placing the first rafters directly against the old ones, you are assured of an exact transition between the roofs, and adequate support for the end of the ridge is provided. Continue out from the house with the rest of the rafters until you reach the new gable end.

Gable End Framing

After all of the rafters are in place, gable end framing must be added. Since the gable end is actually an extension of the wall below it, the framing is essentially the same. Begin by finding the center point of the wall, directly below the ridge. Measure out the stud spacing distance from each side of the mark, and continue the regular stud spacing in each direction from there. An alternative is to simply extend the line of the wall studs straight up, and place the gable end studs directly above the wall studs.

Hold a piece of stud lumber upright on the top plate at one of the marks next to the center. Place a level against it to be certain it's plumb. With a sharp pencil, draw a line along both the top and the underside of the gable end rafter where it crosses the stud. (See Fig. 12-18.)

Cut the stud off straight at the lower end of the angled upper pencil mark. Set the depth of a circular saw to 1 1/2 inches, then cut along the lower line. From the end of the stud, cut along a line that is 1 1/2 inches in from the face of the stud. The resulting cuts will form a notch with an angled bottom.

Toenail the stud to the top plate at the layout mark, then nail through the back of the notch into the gable end rafter. Continue with these studs in both directions. Then, if you were measuring out from center, place a stud in the middle, directly under the ridge.

If a vent is to be placed in the gable end, box

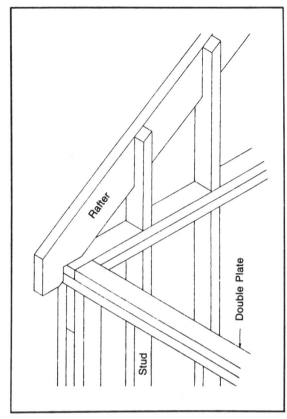

Fig. 12-18. Gable end framing (Courtesy of National Forest Products Association).

in an opening between the studs as necessary.

Gable End Overhangs

If it suits the architectural style of the house, an overhang at the gable end is always a good idea. It offers good weather protection for the upper parts of the wall, and eliminates the chance of wind-driven rain working its way behind the top of the siding.

Planning for an overhang should be decided on at the time the ridge is set. The ridge board should overhang the gable end wall by an amount equal to the width of the overhang minus the thickness of the rafter material.

The overhang is formed from horizontal supports, called *lookouts*, that are attached to the last regular rafters. (See Fig. 12-19.) Two more rafters,

called *barge* or *fly rafters*, are attached to the look-outs. These boards should be carefully chosen for appearance, and are usually one size wider than the stock used for the main rafters.

The 2-×-4 lookouts normally are placed 4 feet OC, measuring up from the fascia so that they fall in line with the 4-foot sheets of plywood used for the sheathing. Measure to the center of each lookout and mark this spot on both the gable end rafter and the next rafter in. From this mark, measure out 1 3/4 inches in each direction to make up the width of a 2 × 4.

With a circular saw set at a depth of 1 1/2 inches, cut through the top of the gable end rafter on the two marks, then at several places between the marks. Use a chisel or the claw end of a hammer to clear out a notch in the rafter. Do not cut the next rafter in.

Cut the lookouts to length so that they will reach from the inside of the second rafter to the inside of the barge rafter. Set them in the notches, then nail down into the gable end rafter and also through the second rafter into the end of the lookout.

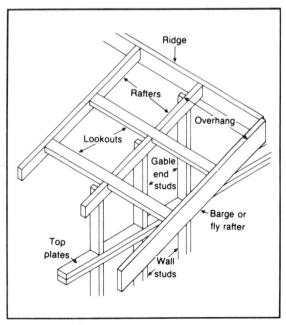

Fig. 12-19. The framing used to construct a gable end overhang.

Fig. 12-20. The intersection of the barge rafter and the fascia. Note how the bottom corner of the barge rafter has been trimmed to make it the same height as the fascia board. This will be a closed cornice, and both boards have been dadoed to receive a plywood soffit panel.

Cut the barge rafters to the same length as the common rafters, with a plumb cut at the top and the appropriate cut at the bottom. With one person holding the barge rafter at the ridge and another at the outside wall, nail the barge rafters to the lookouts.

Once all of the roof and barge rafters are in place, you can add the fascia board. Fascias are normally made from 2-inch lumber, one size wider than the width of the rafters. Some types of cornices require slotted or other specially prepared fascia boards. (See Fig. 12-20.) Refer to the fascia drawings on the plans for details and specifications.

Install the fascia directly to the ends of the rafters, using two 16d galvanized nails. Joints in the fascia should fall over a rafter, and should be scarfed for best appearance.

BUILDING A HIP ROOF

Hip roof frames employ the same common rafters as on a gable roof, with the addition of hip rafters and hip jacks (Fig. 12-21). After the common rafters are in place and following the hip roof layout done earlier, cut the ridge off flush with the outside of the last common rafters. Then install one additional

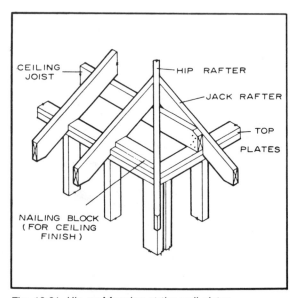

Fig. 12-21. Hip roof framing at the wall plates.

144

common rafter from the end of the ridge to the center of the end wall.

Since the last three common rafters (Fig. 12-22) form two squares when viewed from below, the hip rafters, which extend from the end of the ridge to the corner of the wall, are actually diagonals of those squares. Using the Pythagorean theorem, you can easily calculate the length of the hip rafter. *A* is the distance from the common rafter in the center of the end wall to the outside of the wall, and *B* is the length of the common rafter. *C*, which is calculated, is the length of the hip rafter.

Lay out the hip rafter as was done for the common rafters, using the length just calculated. Because the hip rafter is a diagonal of a square, the ends will be cut at 45 degrees to the other rafters. Just as the calculated length of the common rafters was reduced by half the thickness of the ridge, the hip rafter is reduced by half the thickness of the ridge measured on a 45-degree angle. With the saw blade set at 45 degrees, make a plumb cut on the end of the rafter from both sides, forming a point. (See Fig. 12-23.) Cut a bird's-mouth at the other end.

The hip jacks are similar to the valley jacks cut earlier for the intersection. At the lower end, the bird's-mouth, tail length, and plumb cut are the same as for a common rafter. At the upper end where the jack meets the hip rafter, make a beveled plumb cut.

After you have marked the tail and bird's-mouth cuts on the board, lay out the length as for a common rafter. Determine the common difference in length from the rafter tables on the square, as you did for the valley jacks. Subtract this difference from the length of the rafter, and also subtract half the 45-degree thickness of the hip rafter.

As with the other jacks, the angle of the cut can be determined from the fifth table on the framing square. Mark a plumb cut and, with the saw set at the appropriate angle, cut the top end of the rafter. Each subsequent rafter is reduced by the same common difference, providing that the spacing layout on the plate is consistent.

DORMERS

Dormers are cut into the roof on the top story of a house to provide additional headroom, and to allow windows to be placed vertically in a sloped ceiling. They allow the ceiling and roof structure to be brought lower over the walls for reduced overall height of the building, for conservation of siding materials, and for architectural appeal.

Fig. 12-22. Hip roof framing at the ridge. Note how the three common rafters (arrows) form two equally sized squares.

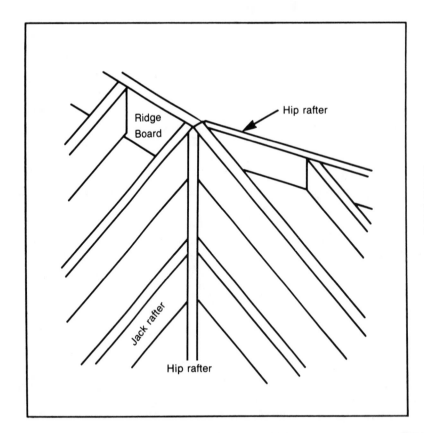

Ridge
Board

Hip rafter

Jack rafter

Hip rafter

Fig. 12-23. Detail of the plumb cut, made on two 45-degree angles, used where the hip rafters meet the common rafters at the ridge (Courtesy of National Forest Products Association).

Dormers might be quite small and used only for ventilation, or they can run the entire length of the house. Shed dormers (Fig. 12-24) are larger and easier to construct than conventional dormers, and typically house several windows, or even doors to upstairs balconies.

To begin dormer construction, frame an opening in the roof. The framing is similar to the openings in floors or ceilings. Doubled rafters run along the opening on both sides, and the ridge and plate can be used as a boundary at each end, or doubled headers can be placed at either or both ends.

After you frame the opening, construct the dormer like a miniature house. Erect the wall framing first, with headered rough openings for windows. Then construct the roof to tie in with the surrounding house roof, utilizing either a gable (Fig. 12-25), hip, or shed configuration. The ceiling within the dormer usually follows the underside of the dormer rafters, but you can easily frame the ceiling flat, if desired.

ROOF TRUSSES

A very popular alternative to all of the layout and cutting involved in constructing a roof is the use of prefabricated roof trusses. A truss is constructed in such a way that it forms a series of triangles (Fig. 12-26), and as such is quite structurally rigid. It can span the distance between the outside walls with no additional support, eliminating the need for weight-bearing interior partition walls and allowing greater freedom in the layout of the interior.

The truss consists of one or two upper members, the *top chords*, which form the roof lines. Lower chords, which can be horizontal or angled as desired, act in place of the ceiling joists to support the finish ceiling material.

Although trusses can be handmade at the site, a number of engineering calculations are required for them to be properly weight bearing and self supporting. The members are assembled in special adjustable racks to ensure uniformity, and are

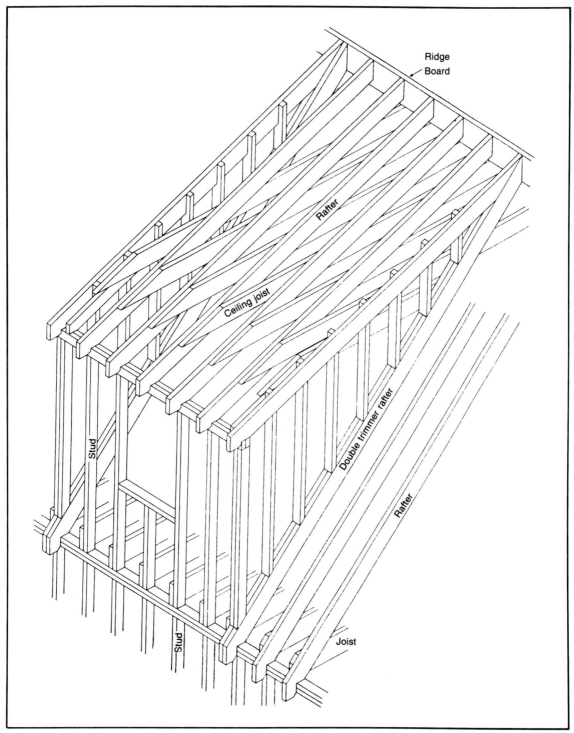

Fig. 12-24. Framing details for a shed dormer (Courtesy of National Forest Products Association).

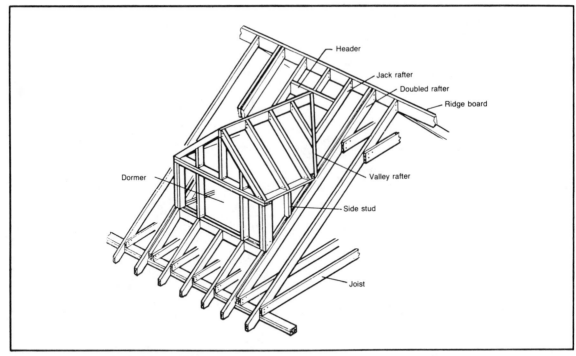

Fig. 12-25. Framing details for a gable dormer.

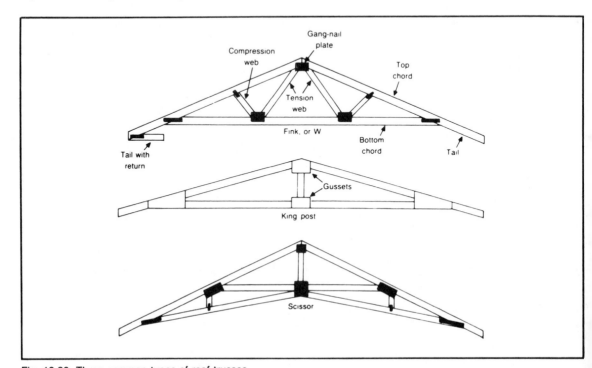

Fig. 12-26. Three common types of roof trusses.

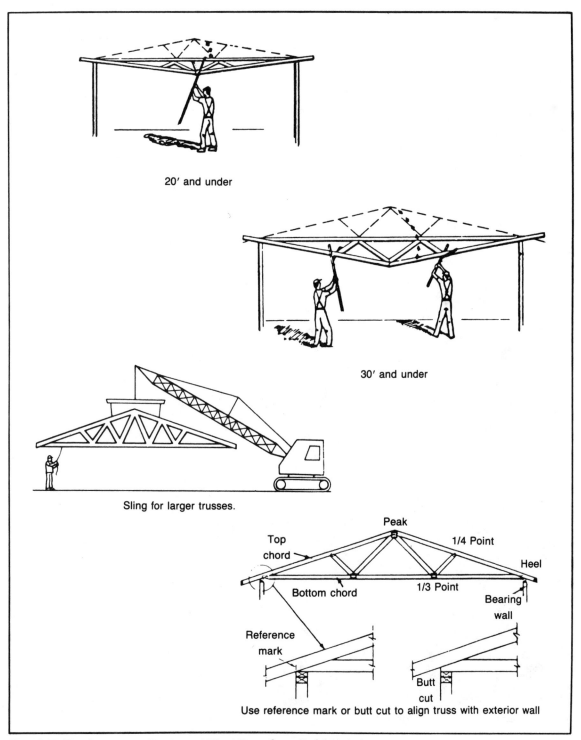

20' and under

30' and under

Sling for larger trusses.

Peak

Top chord

1/4 Point

Heel

Bottom chord

1/3 Point

Bearing wall

Reference mark

Butt cut

Use reference mark or butt cut to align truss with exterior wall

Fig. 12-27. Erecting trusses (Courtesy of Wood Truss Council of America).

Fig. 12-28. An open-beam ceiling used in a family room addition (Courtesy of Masonite Corporation).

connected with special steel plates applied under tremendous pressure. For these reasons, they are best left to a truss company to engineer and construct. The cost is quite reasonable, and you will be provided with an engineering certificate to submit with your plans for the permit.

To order trusses, you will need to know several things, all of which the truss company should be able to take from your plans. The total span from outside to outside must be provided, along with the slope of the roof, the size of the overhangs, and the desired configuration of the ceiling. Trusses take several days to several weeks to prepare, depending on their complexity and the backlog at the truss company. Order them at about the time the floor framing is being done to ensure they will be ready when you need them.

Each truss takes the place of one pair of common rafters and one ceiling joist. For a gable roof, order a gable truss for each gable end. Gable trusses

are constructed with vertical studding instead of the intermediate diagonal chords, making it easier to apply the siding. For hip roofs and intersections, some truss companies can supply precut hip and valley rafters and jacks, or you can cut your own as described previously.

Install the trusses as soon as you have completed and braced the exterior walls. You can erect the interior walls either before or after the trusses are set, but they are much easier to stand if you erect them first. Trusses are usually set 24 inches OC, and you should have the plates marked before the trusses are delivered.

Arrange with the truss company for plate top delivery, which is well worth any additional cost that might be involved. A truck equipped with a small crane will deliver them to the site, then set them in a bundle on top of the wall plates. Cut the banding and separate the trusses.

Begin with the gable end truss or, for a hip roof,

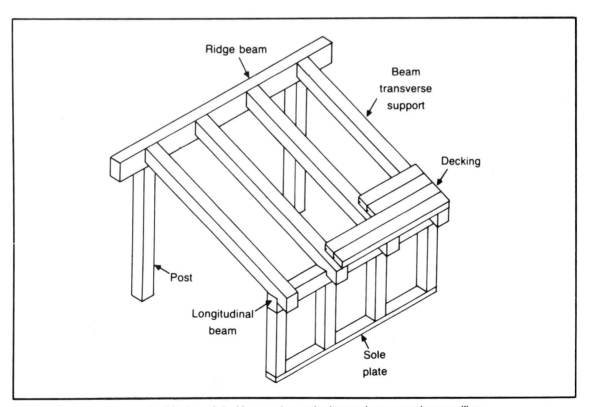

Fig. 12-29. Appearance-grade, 2-inch roof decking used over the beams in an open-beam ceiling.

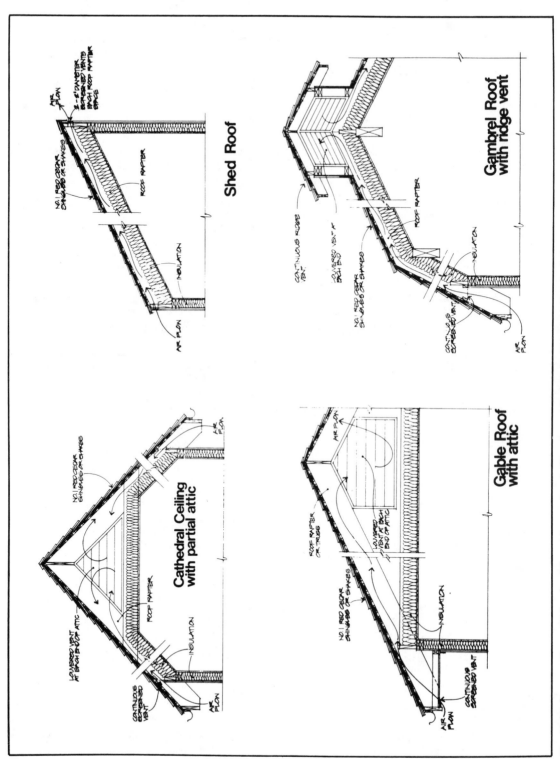

Fig. 12-30. Proper attic ventilation for different types of roofs (Courtesy of Red Cedar Shingle & Handsplit Shake Bureau).

with the last common truss before the hip. Using two people, set the truss on the plate marks and toenail it down to the plates (Fig. 12-27). Special framing anchors also may be used, if desired. Place a long diagonal brace from the truss to the ground, or to any other solid spot, and brace the truss in a plumb position.

Continue placing the trusses according to the spacing on the plates. Measure the distance between the trusses at the top, and nail a temporary board across them to hold them at the correct spacing until the sheathing is set. A 2 × 4 or 2 × 6 is usually nailed across the top of the bottom chords to keep the spacing consistent, and to provide a walkway between the trusses.

OPEN-BEAM CEILINGS

A popular architectural feature in some styles of

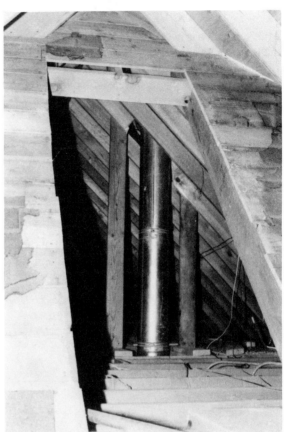

Fig. 12-32. Framing an opening in the existing roof to allow access and ventilation in the addition attic.

Fig. 12-31. The opening formed at the top of a gable roof to receive a continuous ridge vent.

homes is the open-beam ceiling (Fig. 12-28). In this type of construction, large beams are used in place of the rafters, and are left exposed to the inside of the house. The beams are placed on wider centers than rafters, usually 4 feet OC. There are no ceiling joists, and the roof structure is sheathed with 2-inch tongue-and-groove lumber that is selected for its appearance (Fig. 12-29).

This type of roof is constructed in the same manner as a gable roof, with the same lengths, plumb cuts, bird's-mouths, and other construction details. A fairly massive ridge beam is used in place of the normal ridge, and its thickness must be compensated for in calculating the length of the rafter beams. Because of the length of the spans and the need for good appearance, only No. 1 grade lumber should be used in this application.

ATTIC VENTILATION

Attic ventilation is necessary to allow moisture from the house to be exhausted to the outside. (See Fig. 12-30.) Allowed to collect in the attic, this moisture will do serious damage to the wooden framing members. Properly installed, attic ventilation has the added benefit of removing hot air from the attic during the summer, which helps keep the house cooler.

A simple formula for calculating ventilation requirements is 1 square foot of net free area of ventilation for each 300 square feet of ceiling area. Thus, for a 1,500-square-foot house, 5 square feet of ventilation would be required.

The vents should be placed so that half of them are low on the roof, typically in the soffits, and half are high, as close to the ridge as possible. Through the natural rising of warm air, this placement will allow cool air to be drawn in through the low vents while hot air is exhausted out of the high vents. A number of different vents are available, including screened soffit vents, vents for the gable end, roof top vents, and continuous ridge vents (Fig. 12-31).

Take a moment to calculate how much ventilation is required for the existing house and the addition combined, then see how much already exists. During construction of the addition, add extra vents as needed to be certain the entire attic area is sufficiently ventilated. You also should install an access between the existing attic and the addition attic, usually by cutting through the old roof sheathing and boxing in between two rafters. (See Fig. 12-32.) This feature allows easy access to the new attic, and provides a better cross flow of ventilation.

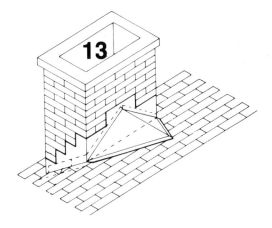

Roofing

There are a wide variety of roofing materials on the market today, and several considerations must go into choosing the right one for your addition. If you want to match the existing roofing, then this is the most obvious consideration. You will of necessity be limited to choosing the same roofing that's on the existing roof.

A major remodeling project like a room addition also might be a good time to consider reroofing the entire house if it needs it. This solution eliminates problems with matching the roofing and making clean transitions, ensures that all the roofing will age at the same rate, and gives the entire project a finished look. In addition, if a contractor is doing the work, it's usually cheaper to have the entire roof done while he's on the job than it is to have him come back later to reroof.

EVALUATING THE EXISTING ROOF

Now is the time to take a good look at the existing roof and decide if reroofing is necessary. Begin the inspection by looking closely at the ceilings to see if there are any water stains. Since water will tend to run down the rafters to the lowest point of the roof, no matter where the leak originated, pay particular attention to the areas where the ceiling intersects the outside walls.

Although water stains usually indicate a roof leak, it could also be that a flashing or skylight is leaking, or perhaps one or two shingles are missing. They do not immediately signal the need for a new roof.

If water stains are present, go up in the attic and use a bright light to examine the rafters. Look for dark streaks along the sides of the wood, especially in the areas where the ceiling stain was noticed. Try to trace any stains up the rafter and pinpoint their entry point. Use a tape measure to take measurements from the point of entry to any objects that will be readily identifiable on the roof, such as a chimney, vent pipe, or roof vent. Also, measure down from the ridge, and up and over from the outside walls.

A close inspection of the roof itself is next. Begin with a look at the roof in general, paying particular attention to such obvious signs of deterioration as missing shingles. If the roof has been covered with composition shingles or roll roofing, which looks the same only it is in large sheets instead of individual shingles, check if the shingles have begun to curl up at the edges. Another indicator of wear is the condition of the mineral granules that cover the shingles. If a considerable amount of them are gone, showing large portions of the black part of the shingle, chances are a new roof is needed.

For wood shingles and shakes, look for large cracks in the wood, and for loose shingles where the nails have begun to work loose. Look at the hip and ridge shingles for signs of deterioration. Signs of mildew growth on wood shingles and shakes is another sign of trouble, and one that also indicates a serious lack of attic ventilation.

Built-up roofing, commonly used on flat roofs, should be checked for signs of cracking, particularly around the edges and where flashings are embedded. If gravel or mineral surfacing was used on the top layer, it should be checked as the composition shingles were for obvious signs of loose and missing material.

Check the areas under overhanging trees for signs of wear. Low branches often will scrape over the roof during windy periods, wearing down the roofing. Trim back any branches where this kind of scraping action is apparent.

Now transfer your attic measurements to the roof and look for signs of where the water stains on the rafters might have originated. Check around pipe and vent flashings, around roof jacks, and along the perimeter of the chimney. Examine the flashings around skylights, and check the skylights themselves. This procedure will help you determine if the problem stems from a roof that needs redoing, or if the leak is a localized one.

Another good indicator is the age of the house itself, or the time that has elapsed since the last reroofing. Most composition shingle and built-up roofs have a life expectancy of about 20 to 25 years. Wood shingles are about the same, and wood shakes can last anywhere from 25 to 35 years, or even longer in some areas. Metal and tile roofing, kept in good repair, should last the life of the house. If the roof is approaching the end of its life expectancy, and if one or more of the problems just described above is readily apparent, reroofing is well worth considering.

ROOFING MATERIALS

Each roofing material has its own advantages and disadvantages, and some can be used only on certain types of roofs. Weigh the pros and cons of each before making a decision. (See Figs. 13-1 and 13-2.)

Composition Roofing

Composition roofing is made up of a thick layer of felt or fiberglass matt, impregnated and coated with asphalt. Mineral granules in a variety of colors are embedded in the asphalt, increasing the wear resistance and providing architectural appeal.

Composition roofing is available in two basic forms: rolls and shingles. Roll roofing is available in 36-inch-wide rolls, usually in 36-foot lengths. Shingles are available in a variety of shapes and sizes, with three-tab shingles being the most common. These shingles are 36 to 39 inches long and 12 inches wide. Most composition shingles are manufactured with a strip of asphalt adhesive on the back. As the shingle warms in the sun after installation, the strip affixes the top shingle to the one below it for greater wind resistance.

Applications. Composition shingles are applied over a solid roof deck such as plywood, and are limited to roof slopes of 4 1/2 and above. They have a weather exposure of 4 to 6 inches, depending on the style, and are usually packaged in 1/4- or 1/3-square bundles. Weight varies from under 200 pounds to almost 400 pounds per square.

Roll roofing also is applied over a solid deck and, depending on the amount of overlap, can be used on roofs as flat as 1/12. Weather exposure varies from 16 inches for the low-slope, double-coverage type, to 34 inches for most other types. Double-coverage rolls cover 1/2 square; all others cover 1 square. Weight varies from 75 to 90 pounds per roll, depending on the type.

Typical Asphalt Shingles								
PRODUCT	Configuration	Per Square		Size		Exposure	Underwriters Laboratories Listing
		Approximate Shipping Weight	Shingles	Bundles	Width	Length		
Self-sealing random-tab strip shingle 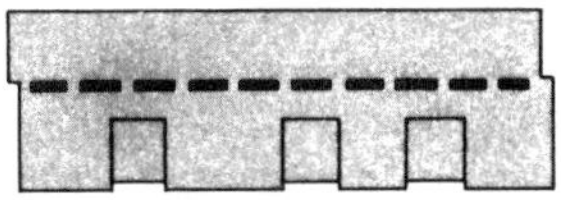 Multi-thickness	Various edge, surface texture and application treatments	240# to 360#	64 to 90	3, 4 or 5	11½" to 14"	36" to 40"	4" to 6"	A or C - Many wind resistant
Self-sealing random-tab strip shingle 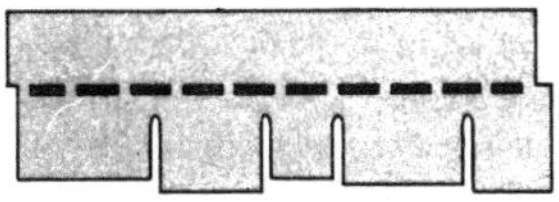 Single-thickness	Various edge, surface texture and application treatments	240# to 300#	65 to 80	3 or 4	12" to 13¼"	36" to 40"	5" to 5⅝"	A or C - Many wind resistant
Self-sealing square-tab strip shingle 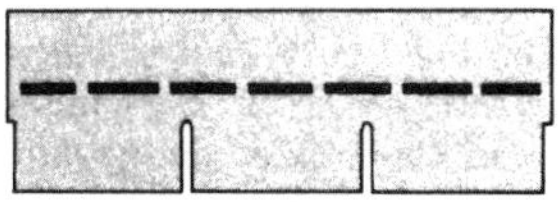 Three-tab	Two-tab or Four-tab	215# to 325#	65 to 80	3 or 4	12" to 13¼"	36" to 40"	5" to 5⅝"	A or C - All wind resistant
	Three-tab	215# to 300#	65 to 80	3 or 4	12" to 13¼"	36" to 40"	5" to 5⅝"	
Self-sealing square-tab strip shingle 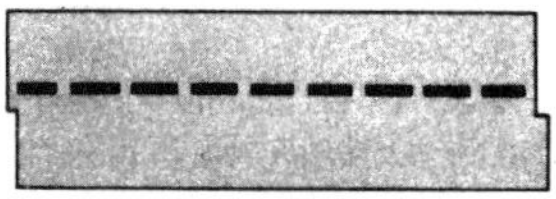 No-cutout	Various edge and surface texture treatments	215# to 290#	65 to 81	3 or 4	12" to 13¼"	36" to 40"	5" to 5⅝"	A or C - All wind resistant
Individual interlocking shingle 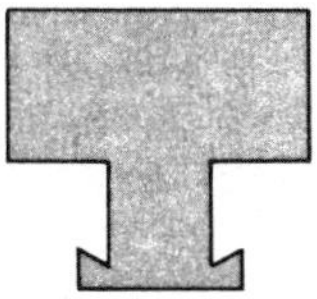 Basic design	Several design variations	180# to 250#	72 to 120	3 or 4	18" to 22¼"	20" to 22½"	—	A or C - Many wind resistant

Fig. 13-1. Typical asphalt shingles and roll roofing (Courtesy of Asphalt Roofing Manufacturers Association).

Typical Asphalt Rolls

PRODUCT	Approximate Shipping Weight		Squares Per Package	Length	Width	Selvage	Exposure	Underwriters Laboratories Listing*
	Per Roll	Per Square						
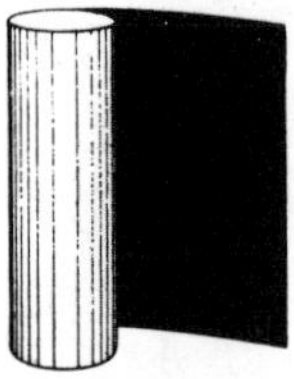 Mineral surface roll	75# to 90#	75# to 90#	1	36' to 38'	36"	2" to 4"	32" to 34"	C
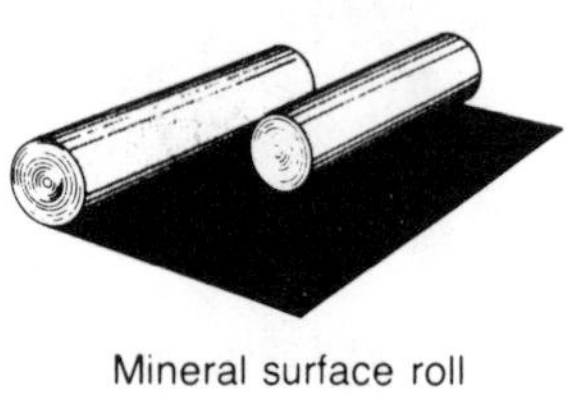 Mineral surface roll (double coverage)	55# to 70#	110# to 140#	½	36'	36"	19"	17"	C
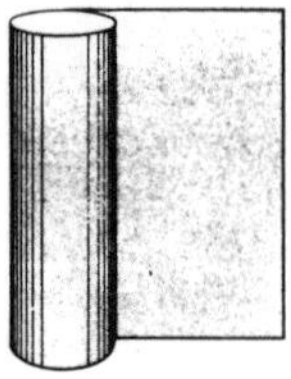 Smooth surface roll	50# to 86#	40# to 65#	1 to 2	36' to 72'	36"	2"	34"	None
 Saturated felt (non-perforated)	45# to 60#	11# to 30#	2 to 4	72' to 144'	36"	2" to 19"	17" to 34"	None

*UL rating at time of publication. Reference should be made to individual manufacturer's product at time of purchase.

Fig. 13-1. (Continued from page 157.)

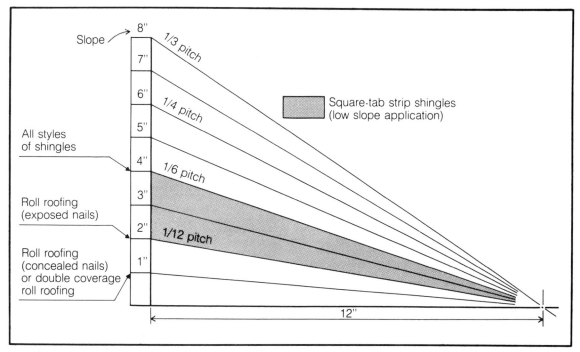

Fig. 13-2. Minimum slope requirements for various types of roofing (Courtesy of Asphalt Roofing Manufacturers Association).

Advantages. Composition shingles are less expensive than most other types of roofing materials, and are relatively easy for the do-it-yourselfer to install. A variety of colors and patterns are available, including double-thickness and random-cut shingles that imitate the appearance of wood. Roll roofing is perhaps the cheapest and fastest of all the roofing materials to install. All composition roofing offers good to excellent fire protection, and most types are very wind resistant.

Disadvantages. Composition roofing has a shorter life expectancy than most other types of roofing. Most types of shingles lack the richness and texture of wood, and roll roofing has no architectural appeal whatsoever.

Wood

Wood shingles and shakes usually are manufactured from cedar, but cypress or redwood are occasionally used. The wood is yellowish or reddish in tone when it is first applied, weathering to a moderate gray after several years. Wood shingles are produced by sawing, leaving a uniform taper

and width. Shakes are hand split, providing less uniformity and more surface texture, and are longer and thicker than shingles. Shingles are rated as No. 1, a clear and premium grade; No. 2, a slightly lower grade; No. 3, an economy grade used primarily for outbuildings; and No. 4, used only for undercourses. Shakes are No. 1 only.

Applications. Wood shingles and shakes are installed over a solid deck or spaced sheathing boards, and are limited to roofs of 4/12 slope or greater. Shingles range from 16 to 24 inches in length, depending on type, with weather exposures of 5 to 7 1/2 inches. They are packaged four bundles to a square, and weigh approximately 150 to 200 pounds per square.

Advantages. Wood has long been one of the most popular roof-covering materials because of its warm, natural appearance. It complements virtually any type of architecture, and is moderately priced. Installation is fairly easy for do-it-yourselfers. In many cases, wood shakes can be applied directly over old wood or composition shingles, eliminating the need to tear off the old roofing.

Disadvantages. Probably the biggest disadvantage to wood is its total absence of fire resistance. Some insurance companies might charge more to insure a house with a wood roof if it's located some distance from a fire department. The cost per square is higher than for composition shingles, particularly where the wood is not native to the area. Labor costs are also higher. More work is required for a proper installation than with composition shingles, which might be a problem for some do-it-yourselfers.

Metal

Metal roofing has been around a long time, but is only now beginning to enjoy an increase in popularity. The most common metals are aluminum and galvanized steel, although other metals are used. Sheet-metal roofing is available in large sheets, either corrugated or in stamped patterns resembling wood shakes or individual tiles. Individual metal tiles are also available, although they might be hard to find. Aluminum is manufactured primarily in strips that are stamped to look like wood shakes. Both are available in several different colors, and the sheet metal also can be purchased unpainted.

Application. Sheet metal can be applied over a solid deck or spaced sheathing, and can be used on slopes down to 3/12. Aluminum shingles should be installed only over a solid deck, and on slopes down to 4/12. The exposure, packaging, and weight vary with the manufacturer, but the panels are relatively light when compared with other types of roofing.

Advantages. Metal roofs are light and completely fireproof. Properly installed, they are virtually indestructible and should last the life of the structure. The newer styles offer some degree of architectural appeal, and are now available in several popular colors that are factory applied for durability. Snow will slide off them quite readily, which can be a real advantage in some areas of the country.

Disadvantages. This type of roof is usually fairly expensive when compared to other types, and most kinds are fairly difficult for the untrained do-it-yourselfer to install, especially if the roof layout is at all complex. Some kinds also require special tools. They are difficult to walk on, and also are difficult to cut should the need ever arise. Some people also complain that they are unusually noisy during rain or hail storms.

Tile

Tile roofing, like metal, has been introduced in new styles and colors in recent years, and is gaining in popularity. Most tile roofing is made from shale or shale mixtures, which is then formed in molds and burned. Most types are left unglazed. Color is added before the burning; therefore it is uniform and baked into the entire tile.

Application. Tiles may be installed over a solid deck or over spaced sheathing, although the second application varies with the type of tile. They should be installed only on roofs with a 4/12 slope or greater. Exposure is approximately the same as for composition shingles. Weight varies with the tile size and type, but all are quite heavy. Some types weigh as much as 800 pounds per square.

Advantages. There are two big advantages to a tile roof: they are completely fireproof, and they are so long-lasting that they usually will outlast the building itself. A tile roof, properly installed, is truly a lifetime roof. With the many styles and colors now available, tile roofs are compatible with virtually any architectural style, and they provide additional richness to many costlier homes.

Disadvantages. Tile roofs also have two big disadvantages: cost and weight. They are considerably more expensive than other types of roofing, and the use of trained roofers for a proper installation is a virtual necessity. Because of their extremely high weight, modifications to the roof structure are sometimes necessary. Trusses can be designed to carry the load for new construction, but existing roof structures might require bracing or the addition of extra rafters. Like metal, they are hard to walk on and rather difficult to cut through, and sealing flashing is sometimes a problem.

ROOF SHEATHING

Before the roofing materials are applied, the roof

frame must be sheathed. There are two types of sheathing: solid and spaced, which is also called *open* or *skip sheathing.* Spaced sheathing is usually done with 1-×-4 lumber spaced the width of one board apart. The boards are attached using two 8d nails in each rafter. Spaced sheathing can be used only with certain types of roofing materials, and the spacing of the boards should be coordinated with the kind of roofing being used. Check with the manufacturer or supplier for his recommendations.

Although individual boards can be used for solid sheathing, plywood and other sheet materials now are used almost exclusively. (See Fig. 13-3.) Plywood is considerably faster and cheaper to install, and it acts to stiffen the entire roof structure. The common plywood grade choice for all areas of the roof that cannot be seen from underneath is **C-D-X**, meaning the panel has one **C** face, one **D** face, and is laminated with exterior glue. For exposed cornices, **C-C** plugged is a good choice. It offers one **C** face in which the defects have been removed and plugged with solid veneer, offering a good surface for painting. The most common thickness is 1/2 inch, but 5/8 inch or even 3/4 inch is used in certain high-load applications.

A relatively new alternative to plywood is oriented strand board (OSB). OSB panels are manufactured from long, thin strands of wood, oriented so that their grains are all running the same direction. The strands then are mixed with resin and cured under heat and pressure into a stable, uniform board. The panels then are treated with a wood preservative for good weather resistance. It is available in 4-×-8-foot panels, and in most of the same thicknesses as plywood. When you are using OSB for sheathing, be sure that you still use plywood for exposed cornices.

First apply the panels to the overhang, using the **C-C** plugged grade if necessary. Start the first course with a full panel, continuing with full panels for the entire length of the roof. Start the second course with a half panel, so that the joints are staggered over different rafters, then continue with full panels to the end. (See Fig. 13-4.) Continue staggering the joints of each course by alternating full and half panels in each course, making certain that the joints always fall over a rafter.

Nail the panels to the rafters with 6d or 8d nails. Space the nails 6 inches apart along the edges and 12 inches apart everywhere else.

For open-beam ceilings, 2-inch No. 1 grade tongue-and-groove lumber is the best choice. It provides a structurally solid roof, a good base for the roofing materials, and an attractive appearance to the room below. Be certain the size of the lumber being used for sheathing is correct for the spacing of the beams in the roof.

Begin the application at the bottom of the roof, with the tongue of the board facing toward the top of the roof. Secure each board with two 16d nails driven into each rafter, and be certain any splices fall over the center of a beam.

INSTALLING COMPOSITION SHINGLES

Composition shingles are installed with flat-headed, galvanized roofing nails. Use 1 1/4- or 1 1/2-inch-long nails for new work, 1 3/4-inch or longer nails for reroofing. Each square of roofing will require approximately 2 1/2 pounds of nails.

Underlayment

After the sheathing is completed, cover it with an underlayment of 15-pound, alphalt-impregnated felt (Fig. 13-5). Felt is sold in 36-inch-wide rolls that cover three or four squares. The "15-pound" designation refers to the felt's weight per square. The waterproof felt provides an additional layer of protection against leaks, and should never be omitted when you are shingling over new sheathing. When you are shingling over existing composition shingles that are in relatively good condition, you usually can omit the felt.

To help the roof shed water away from the cornices and overhangs, a drip edge is often installed along with the felt (Fig. 13-6). Galvanized sheet-metal drip edges are available in a preformed **L** shape, in various sizes to accommodate new roofing or reroofing. Install one at the eaves, directly on the roof sheathing, then cover it with the felt. Install the side drip edges on top of the felt.

Starting at the one edge at the bottom of the

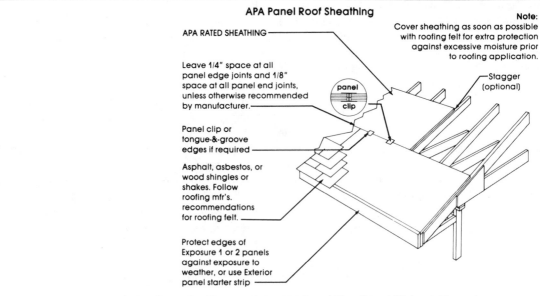

APA Panel Roof Sheathing

APA RATED SHEATHING ——

Leave 1/4" space at all panel edge joints and 1/8" space at all panel end joints, unless otherwise recommended by manufacturer. ——

Panel clip or tongue-&-groove edges if required ——

Asphalt, asbestos, or wood shingles or shakes. Follow roofing mfr's. recommendations for roofing felt. ——

Protect edges of Exposure 1 or 2 panels against exposure to weather, or use Exterior panel starter strip ——

panel clip

Note: Cover sheathing as soon as possible with roofing felt for extra protection against excessive moisture prior to roofing application.

—— Stagger (optional)

Recommended Uniform Roof Live Loads for APA Panel Sheathing with Long Dimension Perpendicular to Supports[c]
(APA RATED SHEATHING and APA Structural I RATED SHEATHING)

Panel Span Rating	Panel Thickness (in.)	Maximum Span (in.)		Allowable Live Loads (psf)[d]							
		With Edge Support[a]	Without Edge Support	Spacing of Supports Center-to-Center (in.)							
				12	16	20	24	32	40	48	60
12/0	5/16	12	12	30							
16/0	5/16, 3/8	16	16	55	30						
20/0	5/16, 3/8	20	20	70	50	30					
24/0	3/8, 7/16, 1/2	24	20[b]	90	65	55	30				
24/16	7/16, 1/2	24	24	135	100	75	40				
32/16	15/32, 1/2, 5/8	32	28	135	100	75	55	30			
40/20	9/16, 19/32, 5/8, 3/4, 7/8	40	32	165	120	100	75	55	30		
48/24	23/32, 3/4, 7/8	48	36	210	155	130	100	65	50	35	
48 oc[e]	1-1/8	60	48				375	205	100	65	40

(a) Tongue-and-groove edges, panel edge clips (one between each support, except two between supports 48 inches on center), lumber blocking, or other.

(b) 24 inches for 1/2-inch panels.

(c) When roofing is to be guaranteed by a performance bond, check with roofing manufacturer for minimum thickness, span and edge support requirements.

(d) 10 psf dead load assumed.

(e) Span Rating applies to APA RATED STURD-I-FLOOR "2-4-1".

Recommended Minimum Fastening Schedule for APA Panel Roof Sheathing

Panel Thickness (in.)	Nailing[c]			Stapling[a] [b]		
		Spacing (in.)		Leg Length (in.)	Spacing (in.)	
	Size	Panel Edges	Intermediate		Panel Edges	Intermediate
5/16	6d	6	12	1-1/4	4	8
3/8	6d	6	12	1-3/8	4	8
7/16, 15/32, 1/2	6d	6	12	1-1/2	4	8
19/32, 5/8, 23/32, 3/4, 7/8	8d	6	12[d]	—	—	—
1-1/8, 1-1/4	8d or 10d	6	12[d]	—	—	—

(a) Values are for 16-ga. galvanized wire staples with a minimum crown width of 3/8 inch.

(b) For stapling asphalt shingles to 5/16-inch and thicker panels, use staples with a 3/4-inch minimum crown width and a 3/4-inch leg length. Space according to shingle manufacturer's recommendations.

(c) Use common smooth or deformed shank nails with panels to 1 inch thick. For 1-1/8-inch and 1-1/4-inch panels, use 8d ring- or screw-shank or 10d common smooth-shank nails.

(d) For spans 48 inches or greater, space nails 6 inches at all supports.

37

Fig. 13-3. Recommendations for plywood roof sheathing (Courtesy of American Plywood Association).

Fig. 13-4. Installing plywood roof sheathing. Note the staggered joints (Courtesy of Senco Products, Inc.).

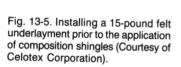

Fig. 13-5. Installing a 15-pound felt underlayment prior to the application of composition shingles (Courtesy of Celotex Corporation).

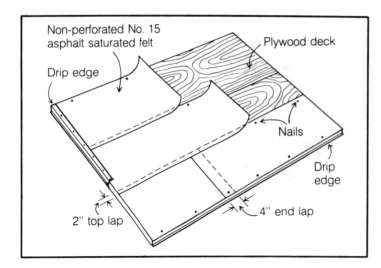

Non-perforated No. 15 asphalt saturated felt

Plywood deck

Drip edge

Nails

Drip edge

2" top lap

4" end lap

Fig. 13-6. Typical sheathing and drip-edge requirements for a composition roof (Courtesy of Asphalt Roofing Manufacturers Association).

roof, roll out about 3 feet of felt. Carefully align it with the edge and bottom of the roof, and secure it with roofing nails or staples. Continue unrolling it to the other roof edge, and cut if off with a utility knife.

The bottom edge of the second row of felt should overlap the top of the first row by 2 inches, as should each succeeding row. Remember that when you are installing any materials on a roof, always start from the bottom and work up, and always be certain that each row or course overlaps the one below it. If the felt becomes too short to reach from edge to edge, overlap the end to end seam by at least 4 inches.

In areas where winter icing is a problem, the installation of protection against ice-dam formation is necessary. (See Fig. 13-7.) Simply install an extra layer of 15- or 30-pound felt, extending at least 36 inches up from the line of the outside wall (not the end of the overhang). In areas with severe icing problems, 90-pound roll roofing is recommended, or you can use a special membrane.

Shingles

After you have completed the underlayment, install a starter course of shingles at the eave line. (See Fig. 13-8.) Cut the tabs off of a regular shingle, then trim 6 inches off one end. This procedure ensures that the tabs and the end joints of the first

course of full shingles will be staggered from the joints in the starter course. Install this shingle flush with the side and bottom drip caps, so that the self-sealing strip of adhesive on the shingle is nearest the bottom of the roof. Continue along the bottom of the roof to the other edge, using full shingles with the tabs removed. The nails should be placed about 6 inches apart, just above the self-seal line.

Begin the first course and all succeeding courses on the same side you began the starter course. Use a full shingle, and align it with the side and bottom drip cap edges. If you did not use a bottom drip cap, allow the first course of shingles to overhang the bottom edge of the roof by about 1/2 inch to help shed water. Continue placing full shingles, abutting them end to end, until you reach the other end of the roof. Cut the last shingle off flush with the drip cap.

Place four nails in each shingle (Fig. 13-9), 1/2 inch up from the top of the tab cutouts. Two nails should be placed approximately 1 inch in from each end, and the other two should be placed directly above each tab cutout. Maintain this nailing pattern for the entire roof to ensure that each succeeding course covers the nails in the course before it.

For the second course, trim 6 inches off the end of one shingle, again ensuring that the joints and tab cutouts are staggered. (See Fig. 13-10.) Align the shingle so that the bottom edges are in line with the tops of the tab cutouts on the shingle below it,

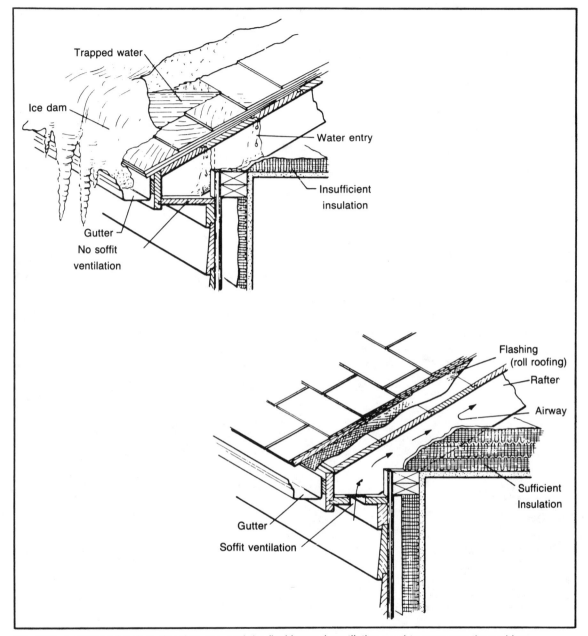

Fig. 13-7. A common ice-dam situation, top, and the flashing and ventilation used to overcome the problem.

then nail it in place. Finish the row with full shingles. Each course is installed in the same manner, with the exception of the length of the starting shingle, as follows.

Although these types of shingles are virtually self aligning, it is good practice to strike a chalk line between the edges of the roof about every fifth course, to help ensure that the courses are remaining straight. Measure from the bottom of the roof at one edge to the top of the tabs on the last com-

165

Fig. 13-8. Installing a composition shingle starter course (Courtesy of Celotex Corporation).

166

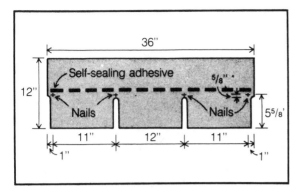

Fig. 13-9. Recommended nailing pattern for composition shingles (Courtesy of Asphalt Roofing Manufacturers Association).

pleted row. Repeat on the other side. The two measurements should be the same. If they aren't, "cheat" one side down slightly until they are, then snap the chalk line between these two points and follow it with the bottoms of the shingles on the next course.

The third course starts by removing 12 inches from a full shingle; the fourth course starts with 18 inches removed; the fifth course with 24 inches removed; and the sixth course with 30 inches removed. The seventh course then starts again with a full shingle. This pattern staggers the cutouts over the center of a tab on each course, and causes six courses to be installed before the butt joints at the ends of the shingles are in line with each other again. Save the pieces cut off for use at the other end of the course, or for making hip and ridge shingles.

Valleys

Install a 36-inch-wide strip of 50- or 90-pound roll roofing in the valleys, on top of the underlayment felt (Fig. 13-11). Nail the strip at the outer edges only, taking care not to place nails in the central portion of the valley.

Continue installing shingles on one side of the valley, allowing them to extend at least 12 inches past the valley centerline and onto the other side of the valley. (See Fig. 13-12.) Do not nail these shingles any closer than 6 inches to the centerline

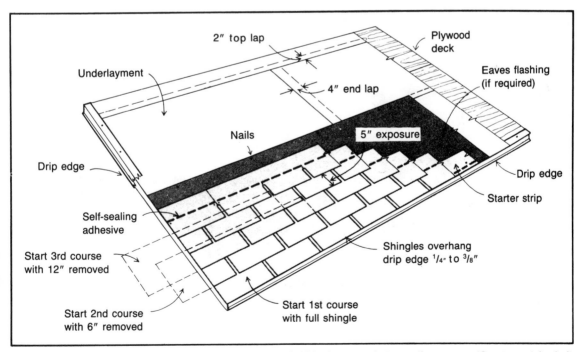

Fig. 13-10. A typical composition roof installation, showing the 6-inch stagger between the courses (Courtesy of Asphalt Roofing Manufacturers Association).

167

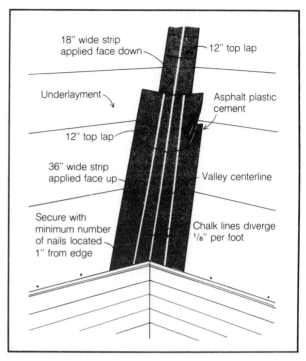

Fig. 13-11. Using a 90-pound roll roofing for valley flashing (Courtesy of Asphalt Roofing Manufacturers Association).

18" wide strip applied face down

12" top lap

Underlayment

Asphalt plastic cement

12" top lap

36" wide strip applied face up

Valley centerline

Secure with minimum number of nails located 1" from edge

Chalk lines diverge 1/8" per foot

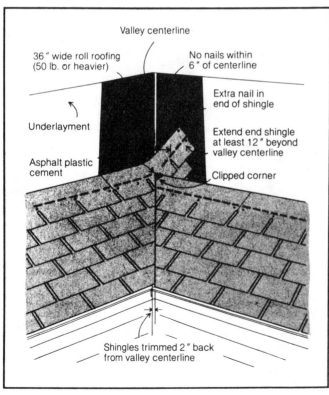

Valley centerline

36" wide roll roofing (50 lb. or heavier)

No nails within 6" of centerline

Extra nail in end of shingle

Underlayment

Extend end shingle at least 12" beyond valley centerline

Asphalt plastic cement

Clipped corner

Shingles trimmed 2" back from valley centerline

Fig. 13-12. Closed valley construction. The shingle courses on the left overlap the valley, then the courses on the right abut to within 2 inches of the valley centerline (Courtesy of Asphalt Roofing Manufacturers Association).

of the valley. Measure over 2 inches from the centerline at the top and bottom of the valley, on the side not yet shingled. Snap a chalk line between these two points.

Begin shingling second side of the roof toward the valley. Cut the end shingle of each course on an angle so that it is in line with the chalk mark. Be careful not to cut or nail into the valley.

Vent Flashings

Any protrusion through the roof requires the installation of flashing to prevent the roof from leaking at that point. Prefabricated aluminum, plastic, rubber, or sheet-metal flashings are available for most of the plumbing and ventilation pipes that extend through a roof (Fig. 13-13). Plumbing vents are left open on top, while mechanical vents and flues use a two- or three-piece flashing with a cap. You should purchase the proper type of flashing at

the time that you buy the pipe, vent, or flue. All penetrations of the roof must be complete before roofing begins.

Install the shingle courses until they reach the vent pipe, then cut the next shingles to go around or over the pipe. (See Fig. 13-14.) Now slip the flashing over the pipe, so the bottom of the flashing flange overlaps the shingles. Continue roofing, cutting each course to fit neatly around the pipe. Install all succeeding courses over the flashing flange. As an extra precaution, you can set the flange and the shingles around the pipe in asphalt roofer's cement.

Step Flashings

Flashings also are required where the shingles meet a vertical surface, such as a wall, chimney, or skylight curb (Fig. 13-15). These flashings, called *step flashings*, are approximately 7 inches long and 10 inches wide, folded along the 7-inch dimension

Fig. 13-13. A prefabricated metal roof jack with a tight-fitting rubber collar.

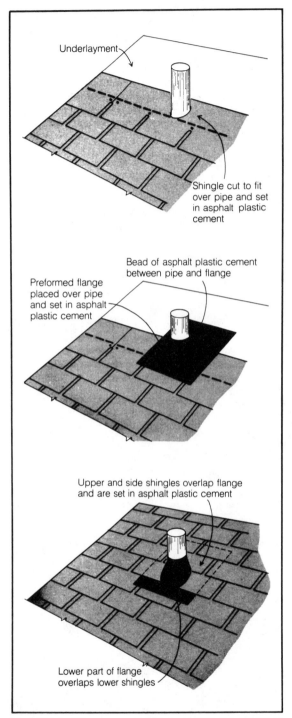

Underlayment

Shingle cut to fit over pipe and set in asphalt plastic cement

Preformed flange placed over pipe and set in asphalt plastic cement

Bead of asphalt plastic cement between pipe and flange

Upper and side shingles overlap flange and are set in asphalt plastic cement

Lower part of flange overlaps lower shingles

Fig. 13-14. The recommended procedure for shingling around a roof jack (Courtesy of Asphalt Roofing Manufacturers Association).

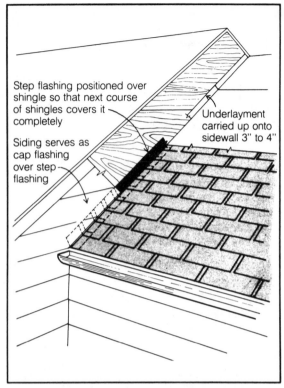

Step flashing positioned over shingle so that next course of shingles covers it completely

Siding serves as cap flashing over step flashing

Underlayment carried up onto sidewall 3" to 4"

Fig. 13-15. The use of step flashings at the intersection of a roof and a wall (Courtesy of Asphalt Roofing Manufacturers Association).

into an L shape. These flashings can be purchased from some roofing suppliers and sheet-metal shops, or you can cut your own from lengths of prebent flashing material.

Starting from the bottom, set one piece of flashing so that it sits on the roof deck and also extends up the wall. Secure it by driving one or two nails into the sheathing at the top, then extend the roofing course over the flashing up to the wall. A dab of roofing cement placed between the bottom of the shingle and the top of the flashing will improve the shingle's wind resistance.

Install the next piece of flashing so that it overlaps the top of the previous one by 2 inches, then cover it with the next shingle course. Continue alternating flashings and shingles until you reach the top of the wall. Then install the finish siding on the wall so it overlaps the tops of the step flashings. The siding should be held above the angle of the

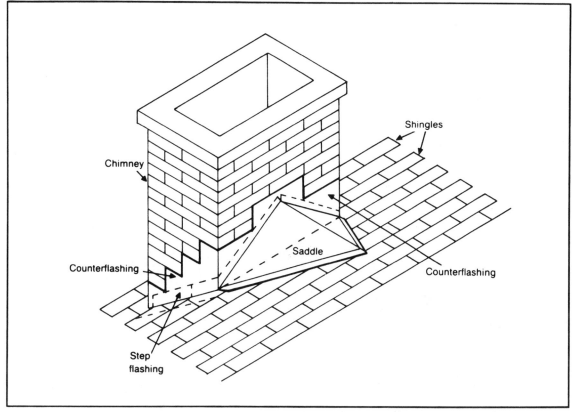

Fig. 13-16. Step flashing and counterflashing used at a masonry chimney. The saddle behind the chimney prevents the buildup of snow and debris, and facilitates better rain runoff.

step flashings by about 1 inch, to allow for good drainage.

For skylights and masonry chimneys (Fig. 13-16), cap and base flashings must be used also. Install the base flashing first, and set it so that it is on top of the lower courses of shingles. Install the step flashings, as just outlined, along both sides, then install the cap flashing so that it overlaps the top step flashings. Then install the upper row of shingles to cover the roof deck flange of the cap flashing.

When you are installing flashings or shingles, always remember that the drainage is from the top of the roof to the bottom, and that upper courses and flashings must always overlap lower courses and flashings. These rules will help you to avoid confusion at some of the tricker stages of installing roofing.

Hip and Ridge

Hips and ridges are finished off with hip and ridge shingles. You can purchase these separately, or you can cut them from regular three-tab shingles (Fig. 13-17). Cut through the shingle at the tabs, angling each cut back slightly.

Start by covering the hips, working from the bottom up, so that the ridge shingles will overlap the top of the hips. Bend the first shingle and center it over the hip, setting it low enough on the roof to overlap the eaves. Secure it with two nails, one on each side about 5 1/2 inches up from the bottom and 1 inch in from the sides. Set the next one so that about 5 inches of the first one is exposed to the weather. Continue in this manner to the top of the hip, and repeat for the other hips. (See Fig. 13-18.)

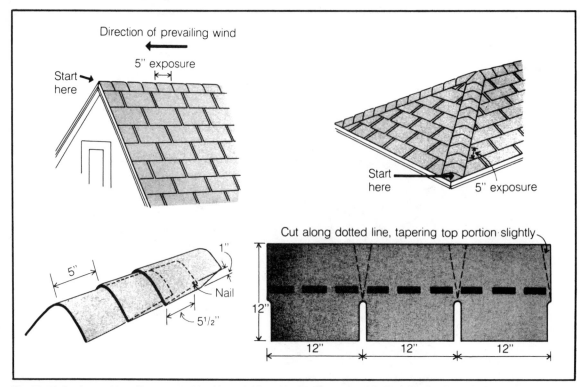

Fig. 13-17. Cutting and installing composition hip and ridge shingles (Courtesy of Asphalt Roofing Manufacturers Association).

To speed installation and ensure a straight line, measure the distance from the center of the hip to the bottom of the hip shingle. Transfer this measurement to the top of the hip, and snap a chalk line between the two points. Follow this line with the edges of the shingles.

If the ridge is parallel with the direction of the prevailing winds, you should start the ridge shingles from the end of the roof away from the prevailing wind for maximum wind resistance. Continue applying shingles to the other end of the ridge, and set the last one with roofer's cement. If the ridge is perpendicular to the prevailing wind, start from each end and work toward the middle. Overlap the meeting point with a full shingle and set it in roofer's cement.

INSTALLING WOOD SHINGLES AND SHAKES

While there are similarities between the installa-

tion of composition shingles and wood, there are also a number of differences. Wood is not as uniform, especially in the case of shakes, and it is not self-aligning, as are composition shingles. The smaller size of wood shingles and shakes means a much greater number of pieces per square, and their random widths require more installation time.

Wood shingles are installed using 3d box nails for the 16- and 18-inch shingles, and 4d for the 24-inch shingles. 6d nails are used with wood shakes. Each square will require 2 to 2 1/2 pounds of nails.

Installing Wood Shingles

Wood shingles are installed without underlayment felt or drip caps. (See Fig. 13-19.) Begin the installation at the bottom edge of the roof with a starter course of No. 4 shingles, overlapping the eaves by about 1 inch to ensure good drainage over the cornice. Space the shingles approximately 1/4

Fig. 13-18. Securing composition shingles on the ridge (Courtesy of Celotex Corporation).

inch apart to allow for expansion, and secure them with two nails driven about 3/4 inch in from each side. Use only two nails per shingle, regardless of the shingle's width.

Cover the starter course completely with the first course of regular shingles. Close attention must be paid to the joints between the shingles to ensure that each one falls over a solid shingle below. Place each shingle so that the joints are offset by at least 1 1/2 inches from the joints in the course below it. At least two rows of shingles should separate the courses before you allow the joints to fall in line again. Pick and choose among the different widths of shingles in the bundle to find the proper combinations of overlaps.

The weather exposure of the shingles varies with the length of the shingle being used. When you are nailing, place the nails so that the succeeding course will cover the nail head by no more than 1 inch. Also, because the rows are not self-aligning, some sort of guide must be used to keep the shingles straight. A length of board temporarily tacked to the roof works best, enabling you to rapidly install the shingles by simply abutting them against the board. Snapping a chalk line for each course also works well.

Installing Wood Shakes

Shakes are installed essentially the same as wood shingles, except than an 18-inch-wide strip of 30-pound felt, called a *shake liner*, is used be-

Begin by laying a strip of 36-inch-wide, 15- or 30-pound felt at the eaves and nailing or stapling it down. Next, install a strip of 18-inch shake liner, positioning it up from the eaves a distance equal

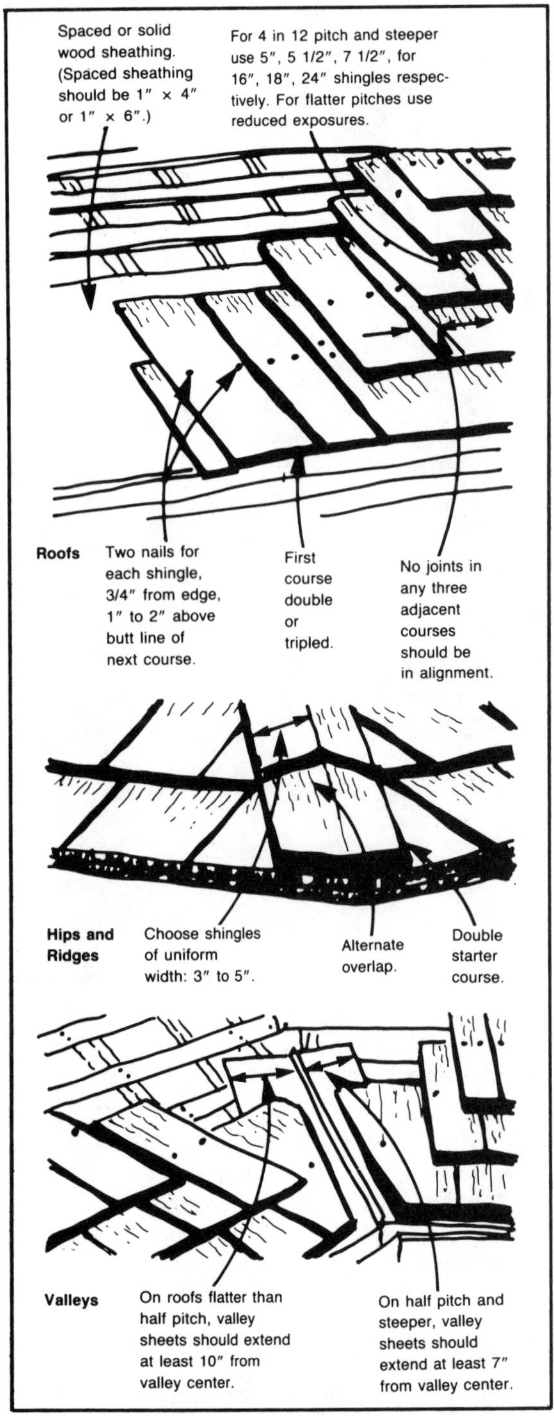

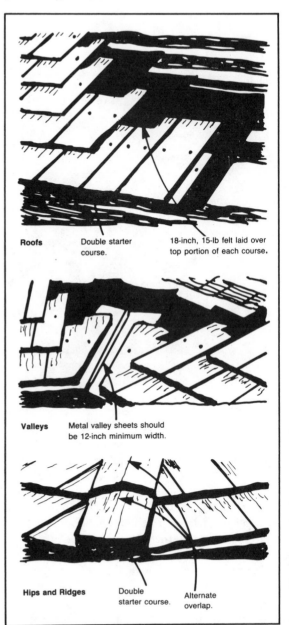

Spaced or solid wood sheathing. (Spaced sheathing should be 1″ × 4″ or 1″ × 6″.)

For 4 in 12 pitch and steeper use 5″, 5 1/2″, 7 1/2″, for 16″, 18″, 24″ shingles respectively. For flatter pitches use reduced exposures.

Roofs Two nails for each shingle, 3/4″ from edge, 1″ to 2″ above butt line of next course.

First course double or tripled.

No joints in any three adjacent courses should be in alignment.

Hips and Ridges Choose shingles of uniform width: 3″ to 5″.

Alternate overlap.

Double starter course.

Valleys On roofs flatter than half pitch, valley sheets should extend at least 10″ from valley center.

On half pitch and steeper, valley sheets should extend at least 7″ from valley center.

Fig. 13-19. Recommended procedure for installing wood shingles (Courtesy of Red Cedar Shingle & Handsplit Shake Bureau).

Roofs Double starter course.

18-inch, 15-lb felt laid over top portion of each course.

Valleys Metal valley sheets should be 12-inch minimum width.

Hips and Ridges Double starter course.

Alternate overlap.

Fig. 13-20. Recommended procedure for installing wood shakes (Courtesy of Red Cedar Shingle & Handsplit Shake Bureau).

to twice the weather exposure of the shakes. For example, if you are installing 24-inch shakes with a 10-inch weather exposure, which is fairly common, you should position the felt 20 inches up from the eaves. The bottom edge of the next strip will be 10 inches up from the first, as will each succeeding row. You can save considerable time by rolling out several courses of paper at once. Tack the felt down on the top edge only because the tops of the shakes will slide under it.

Install the shakes in the same manner as the wood shingles, paying close attention to the positioning of the joints between the shakes and securing them with two nails each. Position the shakes about 1/4 to 3/8 inch apart. As you apply each course, position the shakes over one layer of felt and under the layer above that (Fig. 13-21). Approximately the top 4 inches of the shake should be covered by the felt.

Valleys

Prefabricated, galvanized sheet-metal valleys are used with both wood shingles and shakes. The

Fig. 13-21. Installing wood shakes using an air stapler (Courtesy of Senco Products, Inc.).

valley sheets are 10 feet long, and are nailed to the sheathing starting from the bottom up. Overlap each sheet by at least 2 inches, and do not nail within 6 inches of the centerline of the valley. If desired, you may paint the valley sheets before you install the roofing to blend them in better.

Cut the shingles at an angle as they reach the valley, matching the angle so that it parallels the centerline of the valley metal. Approximately 1 to 2 inches of metal should remain exposed on either side of the centerline. Remember not to nail too close to the center of the valley. A small circular saw with a fine-toothed blade works well, or you can use a handsaw or utility knife. You will find it easiest to use wide shingles at the valley, and to cut and install them first, then work out onto the rest of the roof.

Flashings

The procedure for installing flashings is the same for wood as for composition. Cut the shingles neatly around the vent pipes, and be sure the flashings are set so that the bottom part of the flange is on top of the shingles, and the upper part is beneath the shingles. Step, cap, and base flashings are all used in the same manner. In areas with severe winter weather, precautions must be taken to prevent the formation of ice dams at the eaves.

Hip and Ridge

The easiest and best looking way to cover hips and ridges is with preassembled hip and ridge shingles. They consist of two uniform-width, tapered shakes, overlapped along one edge and nailed together to form a V. The overlapped area is then beveled for a finished appearance. A rather time-consuming alternative is to select uniform-width shakes or shingles and make your own.

The hip and ridge shingles should be installed so that the overlaps alternate. This is the way that the bundles are packaged at the factory, making selection of alternating laps quick and easy.

Install the wood hip and ridge shingles in the same manner as the composition ones, doing the hips first and working from the bottom up. The ex-

posure to the weather should be the same as that for the rest of the shingles. Because you are nailing through both the hip and ridge shingles and the regular shingles, longer nails will be necessary in order to penetrate the sheathing.

REROOFING

In many cases, it is possible to apply new roofing directly over the existing roofing material. New composition shingles can be laid over either old composition shingles (Fig. 13-22) or wood shingles; wood shingles can be laid over composition; and shakes can be laid over either (Fig. 13-23). Because of the size and random texture of shakes, new roofing material cannot be installed over them.

Most building departments limit the number of roof layers on a house to three, and sometimes to two. Applying more layers can place too much weight on the roof structure.

Prepare the old roof to receive the new one by first nailing down or cutting away all loose, curled, or lifting shingles. Replace any missing shingles, and remove any loose or protruding nails. Finally, sweep down the entire roof with a stiff push broom.

Reroofing with Composition Shingles

Prepare the first course of shingles by cutting away the tabs, then cutting off enough of the top edge so that the height of the shingle is equal to the weather exposure of the first existing course (Fig. 13-24). Remove 3 inches from the edge of the first shingle, and apply it with self-sealing adhesive toward the bottom. Finish out the rest of the starter course with full-length shingles similarly cut down in height.

For the first regular course, begin with a full-length shingle. Cut the bottom edge off so that the shingle will be the correct height to extend from the bottom edge of the starter course to the bottom edge of the third course of existing shingles. Finish out this course with full-length shingles cut down in height. The nailing pattern is the same as for new work.

The second regular course uses shingles of full height, and begins with a shingle that has had 6

Fig. 13-22. Reroofing over a composition roof with new composition shingles (Courtesy of Coletex Corporation).

Fig. 13-23. Reroofing over a composition roof with wood shakes (Courtesy of Red Cedar Shingle & Handsplit Shake Bureau).

inches cut off the length. This method will shorten the weather exposure of the first course, but with the tops of the new shingles abutting the bottoms of the old ones, exposure will be automatic, and the new roof will be smooth and even. (See Fig. 13-25.) This method will work over old composition shingles or old wood shingles having a 5-inch exposure. Reroofing over other exposures is done as for new roofing, but the finished appearance will not be as smooth.

Begin the third course by removing 12 inches from a full-height shingle, and continue the courses in this manner, shortening each starter by 6 inches until the seventh course, when you'll start over with a full-length shingle.

Reroofing with Wood Shakes or Shingles

Prepare the old roof by following the steps given at the beginning of this section, then remove a 6-inch-wide strip of the old roofing at the eaves and along the gable edges. Fill in this area with lumber that is equal in thickness to the surrounding roofing. Tear off the old ridge covering and replace

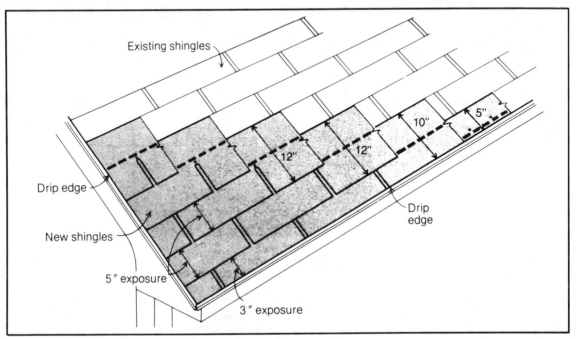

Fig. 13-24. Recommended procedure for reroofing over composition shingles (Courtesy of Asphalt Roofing Manufacturers Association).

Fig. 13-25. Installing new composition shingles so that each new course abuts to the bottom of each old course for a smoother roof (Courtesy of Senco Products, Inc.).

it with lengths of beveled cedar siding having its thin edge pointing down the roof.

Place a strip of lumber over the existing valley metal, then install a new valley over the wood. The wood keeps the two valleys separate and prevents the possibility of corrosion.

For wood shingles, no underlayment felt is necessary. Begin with a starter course as before, then continue up the roof in the same manner as for new work. Shakes also are applied as for a new roof, with a 36-inch-wide felt underlayment at the eaves, and 18-inch shake liner between each course.

New flashings are used at each roof penetration, and new hip and ridge is installed after the shingling is complete.

CONNECTING TO AN EXISTING ROOF

In cases where the existing roofing is still in good condition, it is only necessary to tie into the old shingles with the new ones.

If the old roof is only one layer thick, the top of the sheathing on the addition should be positioned to be flush with the top of the existing

179

sheathing. If the old roof has two or three layers of roofing, it will be necessary to raise the sheathing to a point where the new shingles and the top layer of the old shingles will coincide. You can raise the sheathing when you frame the roof by raising the new ridge and rafters, or by shimming between the rafter and the roof sheathing. A third alternative is to raise the level of the new roofing by first laying down one or two layers of 90-pound roll roofing with butted (not overlapping) seams, then applying the new shingles over it. Remember that offsetting the sheathing in this manner might present alignment problems when it again is time to reroof.

Starting from the top and working out from the intersection of the addition and the existing house, tear back each course of existing roofing to expose a shorter section of the course below it. When you reach the bottom of the roof, the old roofing should have the appearance of a set of stairs, with each course of roofing torn back a little farther than the one before it (Fig. 13-26).

From this point, roofing proceeds as if it were a new roof. Underlay the new deck as required, then place the necessary starter course. Begin roofing by abutting to the end of the first existing course and working out to the edge of the addition. Each succeeding course will in this manner cover the transition seam in the course below it. The whole key to reroofing properly is the proper alignment of the roof decks to make the level of the new roofing even with the level of the old one.

SKYLIGHTS

Skylights have grown in popularity in recent years,

Fig. 13-26. Stepping the old shingles back, left, to allow new roofing to be patched in. A metal bracket in the center holds a 2 × 6 for working more safely on the steeply pitched roof.

180

enabling homes to become lighter and more airy and open. Adding one to the addition, or to the existing house, can be done easily at the time of roofing.There are two basis styles of skylights—domed and flat—and both are constructed from glass or molded-acrylic sheets set in a metal frame. The domed models offer more area, resulting in a greater amount of light entering into the room. They also tend to be somewhat "self-cleaning," in that their curved shape allows rainwater to wash away accumulated dirt. Circular and pyramid shapes are variations of the domed style. Flat skylights offer the advantage of being a little less obtrusive on the roof, as a result of their lower profile. (See Fig. 13-27.) Single, dual, and triple glazing are available in both styles from most manufacturers.

Average sizes range from a 12-inch square to a 48- × -96-inch rectangle, with a variety of sizes in between. The height of the domes range from about 4 inches to 8 inches. If the house has a trussed roof, the skylight cannot be wider than the spacing between the trusses, which is usually 24 inches. Since each truss is engineered as a self-supporting unit, you should not cut or alter it to accommodate a larger skylight without first consulting an engineer.

In choosing a skylight, use the smallest size that will do the job. This practice saves on the initial purchase price, and most importantly, it saves energy. A dual-glazed skylight is rated at less than R-2, so it becomes a rather large cold spot in a ceiling rated at R-19 or more.

Skylights are also available as fixed or operable. Fixed units are the least expensive, but operable units can be opened in the summer to allow hot air trapped at the ceiling to escape. Choices among operable skylights include manual operation, usually via a crank, or electric operation from a remote switch, with a manual override in case of emergency.

Most skylights are available in the following shades:

☐ Clear glazing, which offers the most light but also has the greatest amount of heat loss and gain

☐ Translucent white, which offers a more subdued light and a slightly better resistance to heat loss

☐ Tinted, usually a gray or bronze shade, which reduces glare but colors the light to some degree

Light Shafts

If the room that you intend to illuminate with the skylight has an *open ceiling* (one that is simply the underside of the actual roof), you can install the skylight without needing to construct a light shaft. This is by far the simplest installation, and it offers the maximum amount of light and a view of the sky. Operable units are usually recommended, especially for a second-floor room, since these direct skylights often add a considerable amount of heat to the room on a summer day.

For conventional ceilings, a light shaft must be provided that connects the skylight to the room. (See Fig. 13-28.) The light shaft is usually constructed of 2- × -4 lumber, and is covered on the inside with wood or drywall. Painting the drywall with gloss white paint will reflect even more light into the room. These shafts take one of three forms:

☐ *Straight*, in which the shaft drops vertically from the roof to the ceiling and is the same dimension as the skylight itself. This type is the easiest to construct, but, because of its offset angle to the skylight, offers the least amount of light.

☐ *Angled*, where the shaft is parallel to the pitch of the skylight. It, too, is the same dimension as the skylight, but its straight-in angle offers more light than a straight shaft. Angled shafts also are used to connect two locations that cannot otherwise be aligned, such as when the skylight must be installed in a particular spot, i.e., between two trusses, and the shaft opening is likewise limited to a particular location on the ceiling.

☐ *Splayed*, or pyramid, in which the ceiling opening is larger than the skylight opening in width, length, or both. This type, although a little harder to construct, is the most popular, simply because it allows a smaller skylight to illuminate a larger area.

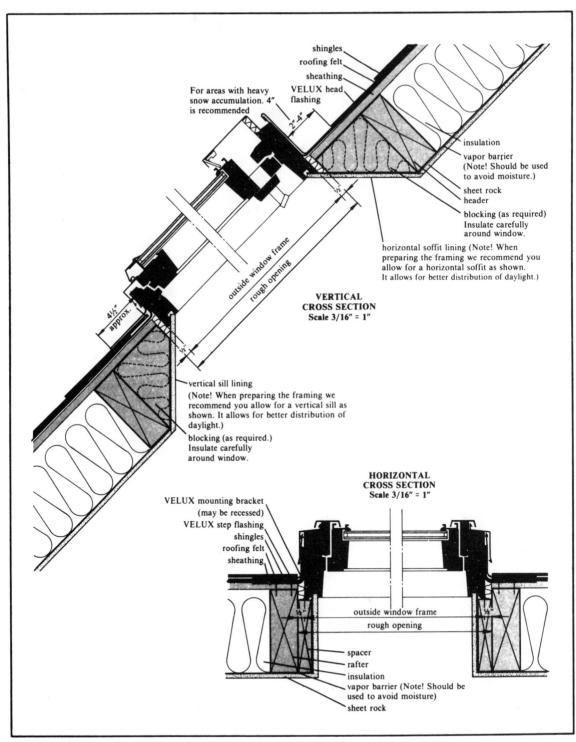

shingles
roofing felt
sheathing
VELUX head flashing

For areas with heavy snow accumulation. 4" is recommended

2"-4"

insulation
vapor barrier
(Note! Should be used to avoid moisture.)
sheet rock
header
blocking (as required)
Insulate carefully around window.

horizontal soffit lining (Note! When preparing the framing we recommend you allow for a horizontal soffit as shown. It allows for better distribution of daylight.)

outside window frame
rough opening

1/2

VERTICAL CROSS SECTION
Scale 3/16" = 1"

4½" approx.

1/2

vertical sill lining
(Note! When preparing the framing we recommend you allow for a vertical sill as shown. It allows for better distribution of daylight.)

blocking (as required.)
Insulate carefully around window.

HORIZONTAL CROSS SECTION
Scale 3/16" = 1"

VELUX mounting bracket (may be recessed)
VELUX step flashing
shingles
roofing felt
sheathing

outside window frame
rough opening

1/2

1/2

spacer
rafter
insulation
vapor barrier (Note! Should be used to avoid moisture)
sheet rock

Fig. 13-27. Cross sections of a typical double-pane flat skylight (Courtesy of Velux-America, Inc.).

182

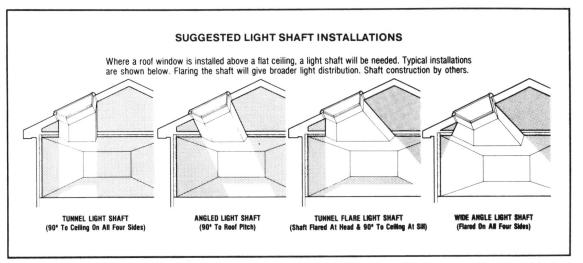

SUGGESTED LIGHT SHAFT INSTALLATIONS

Where a roof window is installed above a flat ceiling, a light shaft will be needed. Typical installations are shown below. Flaring the shaft will give broader light distribution. Shaft construction by others.

TUNNEL LIGHT SHAFT
(90° To Ceiling On All Four Sides)

ANGLED LIGHT SHAFT
(90° To Roof Pitch)

TUNNEL FLARE LIGHT SHAFT
(Shaft Flared At Head & 90° To Ceiling At Sill)

WIDE ANGLE LIGHT SHAFT
(Flared On All Four Sides)

Fig. 13-28. Typical skylight shaft configurations for bringing natural light through an attic into a room (Courtesy of Andersen Corporation).

Constructing a Light Shaft

First, decide on the desired ceiling opening. Take into consideration the overall room size and how much light you need, then select an opening of appropriate size. Remember, an opening that will lay in between the ceiling joists will require the least amount of framing.

Mark the opening on the ceiling, using a framing square and straightedge to ensure a square, accurate layout. Drive a small nail through the drywall at each corner, then go up into the attic and check for obstructions such as electrical wires, pipes, etc. While you're up there, move the insulation back away from the area of the opening.

The next step is to mark the underside of the roof for the skylight opening. Use a plumb bob to transfer each corner of the ceiling opening up to the roof sheathing. Refer to the manufacturer's specifications for the proper roof opening for your skylight, and mark this opening size on the sheathing also. Use the ceiling opening marks as a guide for laying out the roof opening, aligning the second opening to the first in accordance with the type of shaft you intend to use. Drive a 16d nail up through each corner of the roof layout.

From below, use a drywall saw to cut out the ceiling opening. If the opening falls directly between the two joists, use lumber of the same dimen-sion as the joists and install a cross piece between the joists at each end of the ceiling cutout. Be sure the crosspieces are installed square to the joists.

If the opening necessitates cutting a joist, first construct temporary supports between the floor and the ceiling to carry the cut joists during framing. Cut and box the joists with headers and trimmers as with any other ceiling opening. (See Fig. 13-29.)

Locate the four protruding nails on the roof, then carefully remove the shingles in an area 12 inches beyond these marks. Cut out the roof sheathing between the four corner marks. Using lumber of the same size as the rafters, frame in the opening using the same procedures as for the ceiling opening.

Using 2- × -6 lumber, build a box, called a *curb*, with inside dimensions equal to the size of the hole you cut in the roof. Apply a thick coating of waterproof roof mastic to the sheathing around the opening and secure the curb to the roof, toenailing it down to the rafters. Seal the corner joints in the curb with roof mastic also.

Many manufacturers offer a one-piece flashing to fit the curb dimensions of their skylights, or you can have one made at a sheet-metal shop. To install the flashing, first replace the roof shingles on the downslope side of the opening until they reach the curb. Apply a bead of roof mastic around the

183

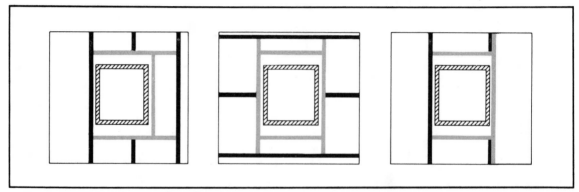

Fig. 13-29. Three different methods of boxing between ceiling joists for a skylight (Courtesy of Velux-America, Inc.).

underside of the flashing, then fit the flashing over the curb so that the bottom lip is over the bottom course of shingles. Work from the downslope side up and replace the remaining shingles, covering the side and top lips of the flashing.

Frame between the two openings with 2- × -4 lumber, angled as necessary to make the connection. Then finish off the inside of the shaft as desired.

The final step is the installation of the skylight itself. Apply a bead of clear silicone sealant or foam weatherstripping tape to the top edge of the curb, then press the skylight unit down into place. The flashing on the skylight will overlap the one-piece flashing that you installed earlier. Using corrosion-resistant screws or aluminum-screw nails with rubber washers, fasten through the predrilled holes in the skylight frame into the wood curb.

Windows and Doors

Windows and doors make a major contribution to the architectural style of a home, and their selection is not something that should be taken lightly. There are a number of door and window types and styles from which to choose, and the selection needs to take into consideration energy efficiency, cost, appearance, and style. The style should be consistent with the rest of the house.

The wrong window style can ruin the look of a carefully planned and constructed addition, and doors that don't match the rest of the house tend to point out which areas have been added. Of course, you won't necessarily have to shop the used building material stores to match a leaky double-hung window. A little shopping around and some common sense will allow you to mix new styles with old ones and still achieve an addition that blends in naturally with the rest of the house.

DOORS

Selecting doors for the addition is a little easier than selecting windows, since whatever style was used

originally on the house is probably still around today. (See Fig. 14-1.) Door styles have not changed to any great degree in many years. The big changes are in the materials, which stems from the growing interest in energy efficiency.

Door Styles

To begin, there are two basic door styles: flush and panel (Fig. 14-2). A *flush door* consists of a four-piece framework, onto which sheets of various materials, called *door skins*, are glued. The skins might be of real wood veneer in a variety of hardwood and softwood grades, or of hardboard that has been embossed with a grain pattern or covered with a photographic paper that simulates the look of wood grain. Moldings often are added to the flush faces of the door for decorative effect.

In addition, flush doors can be *solid core*, meaning that the space between the door skins is solid lumber or particleboard, or *hollow core*, meaning that the space is empty except for strips of corregated material which give some rigidity to the

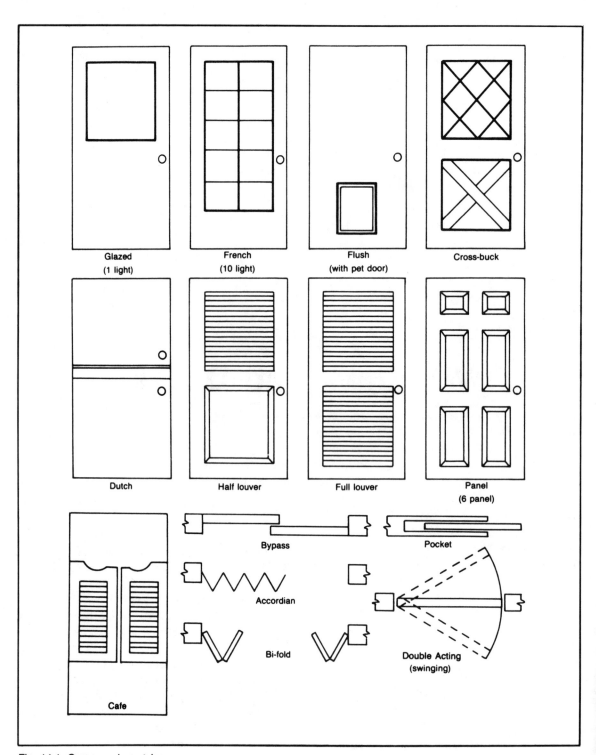

Fig. 14-1. Common door styles.

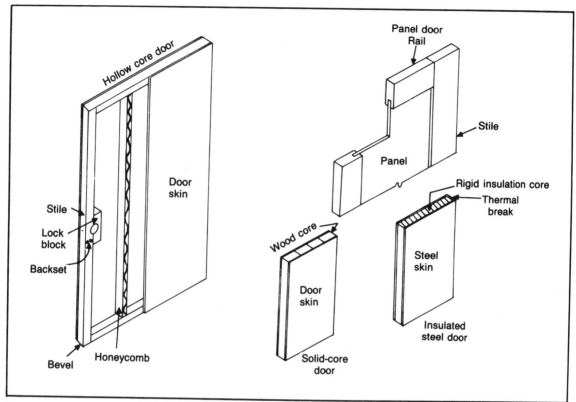

Fig. 14-2. Panel and flush door parts.

skins. Hollow-core doors should be used only for interior applications.

A *panel door* contains four or more slotted, interlocking frame pieces assembled around a central panel or panels of wood. The door is designated by the number of panels it contains, as a one-panel door, a four-panel door, etc. The panels can be either flat, or beveled to give a raised appearance. A number of styles are available, including ones with carved panels and other decorative effects. Panel doors are available in a variety of hardwoods and softwoods, and are usually more expensive than flush doors.

French doors, a variation of the panel door, contain one or more panes of glass in place of the wood panels. *Louvered doors* are also a form of panel door, having a series of angled slats between the vertical stiles of the door.

A new variation is the *insulated door*, which has

been developed in recent years to provide an exterior door with a higher R-value than standard wood doors. Something of a cross between traditional flush and panel doors, most insulated doors are constructed from a two-piece stamped steel frame. The two sections of steel are separated by a strip of material that does not readily conduct heat, usually rubber or plastic. This material, called a *thermal break*, reduces the natural tendency of metal to conduct heat, thereby improving the performance of the door. Sandwiched between the steel panels is a solid core of rigid-foam insulation, which is the reason for the door's high R-value.

Insulated steel doors are usually sold prehung, with an attached magnetic weatherstripping similar to that used on a refrigerator door. When closed, the weatherstripping attaches itself securely to the door, providing a very effective seal. The steel panels are either flat, like a flush door, or stamped

187

with a raised panel effect to simulate a panel door.

In addition to high energy efficiency, insulated steel doors offer excellent security. They are somewhat more expensive than most comparable wood doors. Perhaps their biggest drawback is the fact that they can only be painted, sacrificing the warm, natural beauty of a wood door.

A new door on the market offers a compromise between the wood and the steel doors. Made of fiberglass, these doors contain a solid foam core like the steel doors, but with face panels that have been carefully detailed to look like real wood. The fiberglass will accept stain almost like wood, allowing it to be customized to match the home's existing doors. Although still rather expensive, it does offer one more choice for some applications.

Standard Door Sizes

Doors are manufactured in two standard thicknesses: 1 3/4 inches for exterior use and 1 3/8 inches for interior use. The standard manufactured height is 6 feet 8 inches, although 7-foot doors are available for special applications. In addition to these standard heights and thicknesses, certain standard widths are also commonly available. These are 2-foot, 2-2, 2-4, 2-6, 2-8, 2-10, 3-0, and 3-6. Not all dealers carry all sizes, although 2-6 through 3-0 are almost universally stocked. Other sizes are available by special order, but as with any nonstandard item, the cost jumps considerably. For economy, and to ensure easy availability, always plan around standard sizes.

Doors can be purchased separately, in which case you'll receive the door only, with no cutouts for the lockset or hinges and no jambs; or prehung, meaning that the door is bored and hinged using a special machine, and then mounted on a fully assembled set of jambs. Boring and mortising a door is a very exacting task requiring special tools, so for almost all applications purchasing a door prehung will save a tremendous amount of time and labor, and also will ensure that the door is perfectly hung.

When you are ordering doors prehung, you will have three other considerations in addition to door size. One is the boring you wish for the lockset. The standard is a 2 1/8-inch-diameter hole, centered 40 inches down from the top of the door and 2 3/8 inches in from the face (called the backset). Any deviation from these standards will need to be specified.

Secondly, you will need to specify the jamb width. Jamb width varies with the type of wall construction, and should be equal to the thickness of the wall studs plus the combined thicknesses of the finished wall-covering materials. For example, a very common jamb size is 4 9/16 inches, which allows for a 2- x -4 stud (actual width is 3 1/2 inches) and a layer of 1/2-inch drywall on each face.

The final consideration is which way you want the door to swing. (See Fig. 14-3.) Doors are specified by visualizing yourself standing in front of the door and having it swing out away from you. In this manner, if the hinges are on the right, it's a right-hand door. If they're on the left, it's a left-hand door.

Interior and Exterior Doors

For exterior use, a door needs to be of a sturdier construction than one intended for interior use, both for security and for weather resistance. For this reason, you should only use 1 3/4-inch-thick doors for exterior applications. In addition, use waterproof glue in the assembly process to ensure resistance to weather damage.

In addition to insulated steel and fiberglass doors, which are designed specifically for exterior use, solid-core wood doors and most panel doors are also fine for exterior applications. Hollow-core

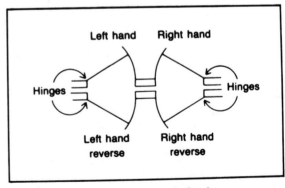

Fig. 14-3. How to specify the hand of a door.

doors offer no security protection, and are typically not constructed with exterior glue. Some types of panel doors utilize very thin wood panels, and again are not suitable for exterior use from a security standpoint.

INSTALLING A PREHUNG DOOR

Prehung doors are supplied as a unit, with the side and head jambs (the door frame) preassembled and the door already hinged in place. Precut casing (four legs and two heads) usually is supplied with the door also. Install the entire frame unit in the rough opening without disassembly. Use tapered wooden shims or wood shingles to plumb and level the frame as necessary during installation. (See Fig. 14-4.)

Remove the temporary nails that held the door fastened to the jamb during shipping, and slide the frame into the opening. Use a level to check that the floor in the opening is level. If it isn't, insert a shim under one of the jamb legs to raise it. Place the level against the underside of the head jamb, and tap the shim in until the frame is level.

Now place the level against the hinge jamb leg, and check to see if the frame is plumb. Use shims as necessary between the jamb leg and the trimmer stud to bring the entire leg into plumb. Plumb the entire hinge leg first. When that side is plumb, work on the strike leg, using both the level and a visual sighting of the gap between the door and the jamb legs as a guide. A uniform space of approximately 1/8 inch should exist all the way around between the door and the frame.

If a large amount of shimming is necessary between the jamb and the stud, you should install the shims from both sides so that they overlap and slide over each other. This method shims both sides of the frame equally, preventing the framing from being twisted. When the door and frame are positioned correctly, nail through the jamb and shim into the trimmer stud using 8d or 10d finishing nails. Open and close the door to check its operation. Use a sharp handsaw to cut the protruding ends of the shims off flush with the face of the wall.

Install exterior prehung doors in essentially the same manner as interior units. The only difference

Pre-hung door units are readily available in standard size door openings. They are made to accommodate various wall thicknesses and door swing directions.

The unit is set into the rough door opening.

Use level to check if floor is plumb.

If floor is not plumb, shim below one side of unit, or trim one jamb leg to make unit level

Slide unit into door opening and visually check the clearance between the jamb and the door.

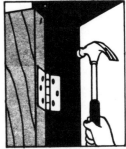

If an approximate ⅛" space is not uniform around total door, the unit is not square. Shim between jamb in order to square unit. Place shims between jamb and stud to secure unit and nail jamb thru shim into stud with 2½" finishing nails.

Check clearance by opening door to see that it fits properly. Apply casing ¼" from edge of jamb as described in "Casing Application" section.

Fig. 14-4. Installing a prehung door unit (Courtesy of Wood Moulding and Milling Producers Association).

45° ANGLE BAY UNIT SIZES

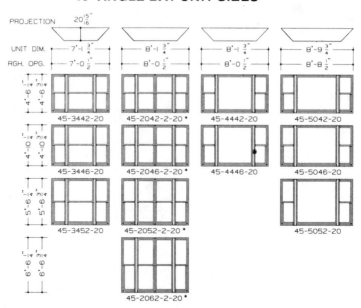

PROJECTION 20 15/16"

| UNIT DIM. | 7'-1 3/4" | 8'-1 3/4" | 8'-1 3/4" | 8'-9 3/4" |
| RGH. OPG. | 7'-0 1/2" | 8'-0 1/2" | 8'-0 1/2" | 8'-8 1/2" |

45-3442-20   45-2042-2-20 *   45-4442-20   45-5042-20

45-3446-20   45-2046-2-20 *   45-4446-20   45-5046-20

45-3452-20   45-2052-2-20 *   45-5052-20

45-2062-2-20 *

Perma-Shield® Patio Doors

White or Terratone

Arrow indicates direction panel opens, as viewed from exterior.

*Unobstructed glass sizes shown in inches.

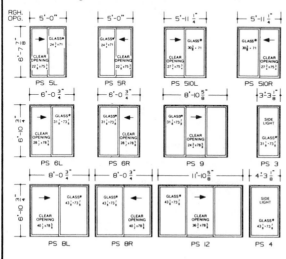

| RGH. OPG. | 5'-0" | 5'-0" | 5'-11 1/4" | 5'-11 1/4" |

PS 5L   PS 5R   PS 510L   PS 510R

| 6'-0 3/4" | 6'-0 3/4" | 8'-10 5/8" | 3'-3 3/8" |

PS 6L   PS 6R   PS 9   PS 3

| 8'-0 3/4" | 8'-0 3/4" | 11'-10 5/8" | 4'-3 1/8" |

PS 8L   PS 8R   PS 12   PS 4

Perma-Shield® Narroline® Double-hung Windows

White or Terratone

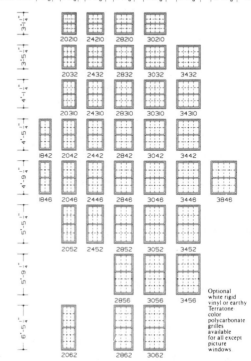

| RGH. OPG. | 1'-10 7/8" | 2'-2 1/8" | 2'-6 1/8" | 2'-10 1/8" | 3'-2 1/8" | 3'-6 1/8" | 3'-10 1/8" | RGH |

20210	24210	28210	30210
2032	2432	2832	3032	3432
20310	24310	28310	30310	34310
1842	2042	2442	2842	3042	3442
1846	2046	2446	2846	3046	3446	3846
2052	2452	2852	3052	3452
2856	3056	3456
2062	2862	3062

Optional white rigid vinyl or earthy Terratone color polycarbonate grilles available for all except picture windows

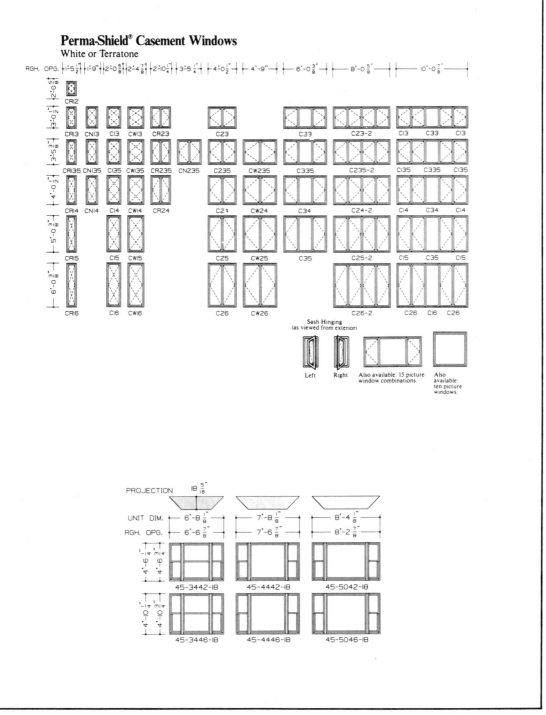

Fig. 14-5. A sampling of the window sizes and styles available from one manufacturer (Courtesy of Andersen Corporation). (Continued from page 190.)

arises when the unit comes with the exterior casing or molding already in place, which is fairly common. In this case insert the door frame into the opening from the outside. You will need to have a second person hold the exterior trim flat against the outside wall while you shim the frame. Insert the shims from the inside, and secure the frame as described previously.

WINDOWS

At first glance, the number of window choices might seem a bit bewildering. However, like doors, there are certain standard materials and configurations (Fig. 14-5), and making the basic choices one at a time will make the whole selection process easier.

Probably the biggest difference between the windows you'll be looking at and the ones that are already in your home is energy efficiency. Windows have always been a cold spot, and today, when compared to the higher R-values being achieved in the walls, that cold spot is even more noticeable. Window manufacturers have made great strides to improve the performance of their windows. Like doors, the window styles themselves have not really changed, so the chances are quite good of finding a new, energy-efficient window that offers a visually pleasing match with the existing house.

Window Materials

Wood has always been the traditional material for window frames. Because of rising labor costs, it was overshadowed in the 1960s and 1970s by aluminum, which was mass-produced in standard sizes and which offered lower cost and easier installation. Steel also was used to some extent in window manufacturing, but not to the same degree as aluminum. Today, wood is making a comeback, and both wood and aluminum windows are available in a wide variety of sizes and styles. In addition to the considerations of matching the existing windows, the choice between wood and aluminum is primarily one of cost, appearance, and energy performance. Each material has its strengths and weaknesses, and the advantages of one are the disadvantages of the other.

An aluminum window is made by extruding molten aluminum in certain cross-sectional shapes, then cutting it into standard lengths. The pieces are assembled into a frame, then an aluminum and glass sash is added in one of various configurations. The sliding sash is the most common. The window can be left its original silver color, called a *mill finish*, or colored by painting or a chemical process called *anodizing*. Bronze is probably the most widely used standard color for aluminum, but virtually any color is available by special order.

It is this fast, standardized manufacturing process that keeps the cost of aluminum windows relatively low. In addition, the windows are very easy to install, never need painting, and can weather the elements virtually forever with no deterioration of the frames or sashes.

The two drawbacks to aluminum windows are energy efficiency and appearance. Aluminum, like any metal, is an extremely good conductor of heat. During cold weather, the temperature of the aluminum frame drops rapidly, and any moisture in the house will readily condense on the cold frames, often forming frost or even ice. To counter this problem, manufacturers of aluminum windows recently have introduced thermally broken frames. The frame is actually two pieces of aluminum separated by a strip of rubber, plastic, or other material that resists heat movement. These types of frames perform well, but the added cost sometimes can be substantial.

The other drawback of aluminum windows is a matter of individual taste. As with doors, many people will not settle for any material other than wood for appearance. If all of the windows in your house are wood, colored aluminum might blend in quite well, depending on how much separation there is between the new windows and the old ones.

Wood windows are still constructed in virtually the same manner as they've always been, except that modern manufacturing techniques have replaced much of the hand labor in an effort to keep costs down. Clear grades of softwoods, especially pine, fir, and hemlock, are used almost exclusively in today's windows. Several styles are available; casement and single hung are the most common.

The advantages of wood windows are the same as the drawbacks of aluminum: energy efficiency and appearance. Wood is a material that is naturally low in heat conductance, so the frame stays much warmer than an aluminum one. Although condensation may still appear on the glass itself, it is eliminated on the frame. As far as appearance is concerned, few materials, if any, can match natural wood for warmth, style, and beauty. However, although aluminum windows often can be installed in a house with existing wood windows and still look good, wood windows are often not a very good blend with the basic, lower cost sliding aluminum windows used on many houses in the last two decades or so.

Aluminum's strengths are, again, wood's weaknesses. Wood is not naturally resistant to weather, and must be protected in some way to ensure long life and good performance. Painting the exteriors is one way of providing protection, but this method is time consuming and must be redone every few years. A fairly new technique is to clad the outside of the wood with colored aluminum or vinyl. This method offers excellent weather protection, and the factory-baked colors are permanent. This method adds to the cost of the window, however, and wood windows are already more expensive than aluminum.

Window Styles

Windows, both aluminum and wood, are available in a variety of styles, which makes matching to your existing windows a lot easier. Remember that when you are using aluminum windows, you need to trim out the inside window openings afterward with individual pieces of wood or drywall. With wood windows, it's often necessary to order attached jambs of the proper width, as with pre-hung doors. Be sure to ask your supplier about the jamb details when you are purchasing wood windows.

The most common window styles on the market follow.

☐ *Single and Double Hung.* Double-hung windows were the standard in wood windows for many years. (See Fig. 14-6.) In the traditional double-hung style, two vertically sliding sashes were fixed in tracks in a wood frame (Fig. 14-7). The lower sash slides up and to the inside of the upper sash, while the upper sash slides down on the outside.

Each sash is connected by a cord to iron weights suspended in a cavity in the wall. The weights counterbalance the weight of the sash to prevent it from dropping. In later years, different sash-holding methods were used in place of the weights to make the construction and installation of the windows easier. Today, most windows of this type, in both aluminum and wood, are single hung. The lower sash opens vertically over and to the inside of the upper sash, which remains fixed. In most cases, single-hung windows will match well with older style double hungs.

☐ *Sliding.* This is the standard style for aluminum

Fig. 14-6. Double-hung window styles (Courtesy of Andersen Corporation).

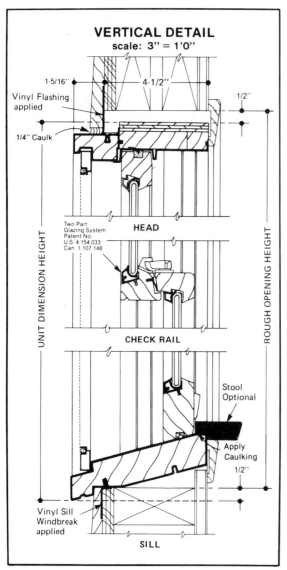

VERTICAL DETAIL
scale: 3" = 1'0"

1-5/16"   4-1/2"   1/2"

Vinyl Flashing
applied

1/4" Caulk

Two Part
Glazing System
Patent No.
U.S. 4,154,033
Can. 1,107,148

HEAD

UNIT DIMENSION HEIGHT

ROUGH OPENING HEIGHT

CHECK RAIL

Stool
Optional

Apply
Caulking
1/2"

Vinyl Sill
Windbreak
applied

SILL

Fig. 14-7. Cross section of a modern dual-pane double-hung window (Courtesy of Andersen Corporation).

windows. It consists of two equally sized sash units, one of which slides horizontally over and to the inside of the other one, which is fixed. In larger units, a fixed center panel is used, with two sliding sashes opening over it from each side. Although less common, sliding wood windows are also available.

☐ *Casement.* A casement window contains a sash that is hinged on pins at the top and bottom corners of one side of the frame (Fig. 14-8). A crank is used to open them outward, pivoting them on these pins (Fig. 14-9). Steel was a fairly common material for earlier casement windows. Wood is the most common material for casements today, but aluminum styles are also available. As with a door, casement windows close tightly against a frame and can be very effectively weatherstripped. For this reason, today's casements are the most energy efficient of all the window styles.

☐ *Awning.* Awning windows have a sash that is hinged on pins at the two top or two bottom corners, and opens outward (Fig. 14-10). Most awning windows utilize a fairly small sash in combination with a larger, fixed sash above it.

☐ *Bay and Bow Windows.* These types of windows are actually composed of several window units that project out from the face of the wall. A bay window contains three units, one of which is parallel to the wall. The other two are set at an angle to the back one, usually 30 or 45 degrees. (See Fig. 14-11.) A variation of this window is the box bay, in which the three units are at right angles to each other, forming a three-sided box. Bay windows can be factory constructed as a three-window unit ready for installation, or can be simply three individual windows set in separately framed openings. In most cases, the back window is fixed while the two side units are casement, but a number of different combinations are available.

A bow window is similar to a bay window, except it is made up at the factory out of several narrow sashes set at slight angles to each other to form a curve. Bow windows usually contain all fixed sashes, although sometimes the first sash on each side is a casement.

ENERGY-EFFICIENT WINDOWS

Glass is used in windows because it does not obstruct or discolor visible light. It also does little to obstruct heat flow, being a naturally poor insulator. As energy conservation has become a major factor in today's housing design and construction,

Fig. 14-8. Common casement window configurations (Courtesy of Andersen Corporation).

much attention has been given to how to make windows more energy efficient. Frames, as just described, are only one aspect of how well a window performs. The other consideration is the glass itself.

The first major improvement was *double glazing*, which today is virtually standard and is required by most building codes. Double glazing is achieved by setting two panes of glass in a common seal with a space between them that contains a vacuum. This dead air space acts as an insulator between the glass panes, keeping the inner pane warmer and slowing the loss of heat through the glazing.

A logical next step was to add a third pane, called *triple glazing*, creating a second air space. The resulting window, while offering improved performance over double glazing, has the problem of blocking some of the visible light that was the whole reason for having the window in the first place. *Quad pane glazing*, which utilizes two thin panels of transparent plastic or other material between two panes of glass, further improves the performance while affecting the visible light about as much as triple glazing.

Another energy alternative is the use of glass coatings or additional inner films. These windows, known as *low emissivity* (low-e) windows, affect the amount of heat that the window emits, or loses. One concept, Heat Mirror, is to suspend a thin layer of polyester that has been treated with metal oxide between two panes of glass. This third layer allows light in the visible range and the near infrared range, which is the range of solar heat, to pass through the glass. It selectively blocks most of the

ultraviolet range, which is responsible for fading carpets and drapes. More importantly, it also blocks the far infrared wavelengths, which is the heat radiated by people and objects. In warm climates, the coating can be altered to block rather than admit the near infrared wavelengths, reducing unwanted solar heat gain.

Another recent step perfecting low-e windows is the application of the metal oxide coating on the glass itself. It is hoped that this method will lower the cost of the window by eliminating the third inner film, while increasing the amount of emitted visible light and further reducing the emission of desirable heat within the structure.

Whether high-performance windows or coatings are worth the higher initial cost depends on how much glazing the addition will have and where it's located. An addition with a large amount of south glass and some solar storage mass, for example, might be able to trap and hold enough winter solar heat with high-performance windows to offset the need for additions to the home's existing heating system. Another plus to these types of windows, one not measured in dollars and cents, is the increase in comfort that results from the warmer glass. In most cases, it will be necessary to consult with your designer to make the necessary calculations as to how much various types high-performance windows will save in both heat and operating dollars.

INSTALLING WINDOWS

Most windows are designed to be installed on the

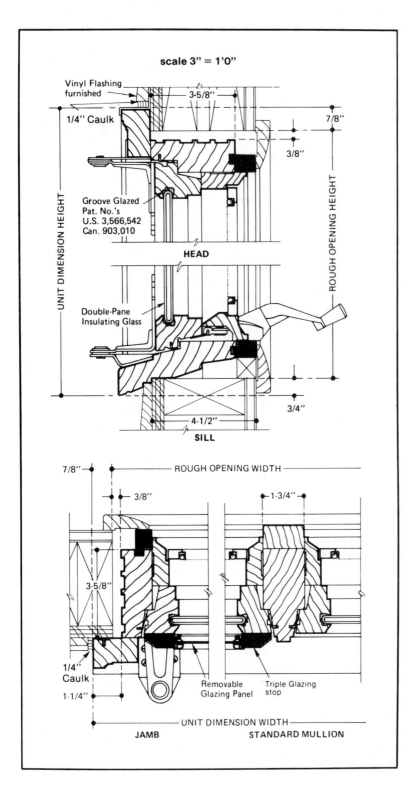

scale 3" = 1'0"

Vinyl Flashing
furnished

1/4" Caulk

3-5/8"

7/8"

3/8"

UNIT DIMENSION HEIGHT

ROUGH OPENING HEIGHT

Groove Glazed
Pat. No.'s
U.S. 3,566,542
Can. 903,010

HEAD

Double-Pane
Insulating Glass

3/4"

4-1/2"

SILL

7/8"

3/8"

ROUGH OPENING WIDTH

1-3/4"

3-5/8"

1/4"
Caulk

1-1/4"

Removable
Glazing Panel

Triple Glazing
stop

UNIT DIMENSION WIDTH

JAMB

STANDARD MULLION

Fig. 14-9. Cross section of a dual-pane casement window (Courtesy of Andersen Corporation).

Fig. 14-10. Awning windows (Courtesy of Andersen Corporation).

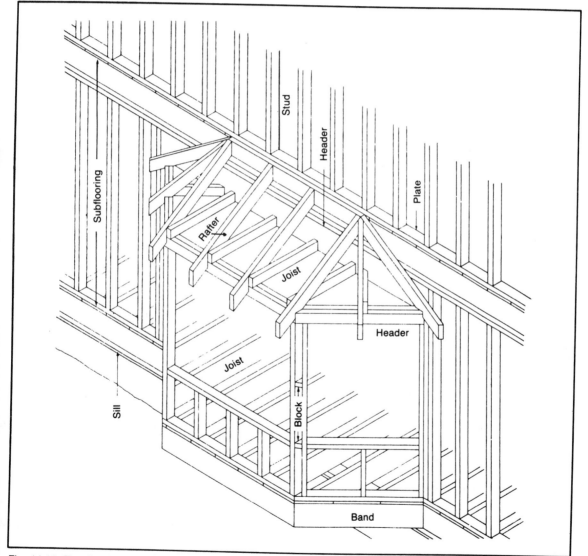

Fig. 14-11. Framing for a bay window parallel with the floor joists (Courtesy of National Forest Products Association).

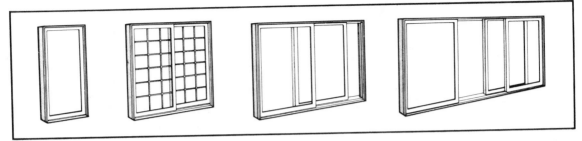

Fig. 14-12. Sliding glass door styles (Courtesy of Andersen Corporation).

rough framing or wall sheathing, before the installation of the finished siding. Make certain the rough opening is square and of the correct size before you begin the installation of the window.

Aluminum windows come equipped with a flange around the outside, called a *nailing fin*. Apply a bead of caulk to the inside face of this flange, then have a helper lift the window and set it in the opening from the outside. Check the window from the inside to see that it's centered both vertically and horizontally in the opening, and that it's plumb, level, and square. You can use shims as necessary to support the window in the desired location.

Secure the window by simply nailing through the fin into the wall framing. Use a nail that is long enough to penetrate through the fin and the sheathing and into the framing by at least 1 inch. Nail the two sides and the bottom, placing the nails about 2 to 4 inches from the corners and 12 inches apart after that. Most manufacturers recommend that the top fin not be nailed, since distortions of the header under load could be transferred to the window and possibly break the glass.

Wood windows are installed in much the same way. Most wood windows come with a finish molding attached to the outside of the window frame. This molding acts in the same manner as the nailing fin on the aluminum window, providing a stop against the wall and a surface for nailing. Caulk around the inside surface of the molding, then install the window in the opening and position it. Nail through the molding with 8d or 10d galvanized finishing nails. Remember that the molding will remain visible as a finished trim piece, so take care that it isn't damaged.

If you are using plywood siding as the finish

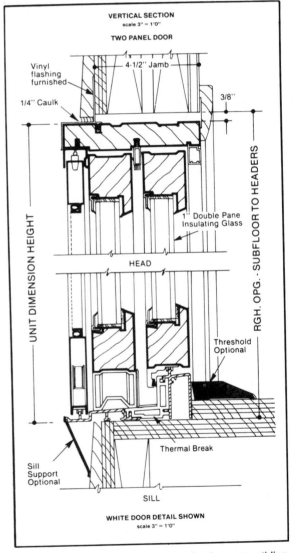

Fig. 14-13. A vertical cross section of a dual pane sliding glass door (Courtesy of Andersen Corporation).

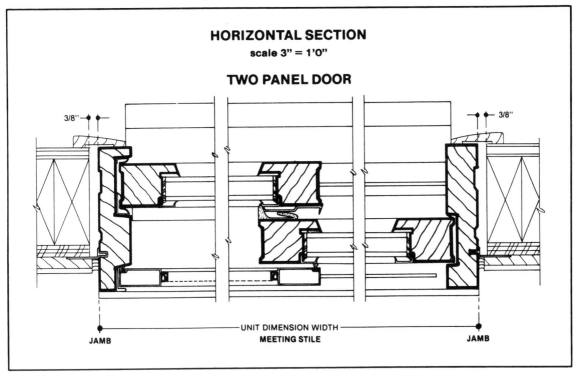

HORIZONTAL SECTION

scale 3" = 1'0"

TWO PANEL DOOR

3/8"

3/8"

UNIT DIMENSION WIDTH

JAMB   MEETING STILE   JAMB

Fig. 14-14. A horizontal cross section of a dual-pane sliding glass door (Courtesy of Andersen Corporation).

siding material and are installing wood windows with attached moldings, you might need to install the windows after the siding is in place to achieve a good finished appearance. Consult with the manufacturer or supplier for the correct installation sequence.

SLIDING GLASS DOORS

Sliding glass doors (Fig. 14-12) are actually more of a window than a door, consisting almost entirely of glass in a horizontally sliding wood or aluminum frame (Figs. 14-13 and 14-14). Wood units come completely preassembled, requiring at least two people for the installation. Caulk and set the unit in the opening as with a regular window, then position it and nail it in place through the outside moldings.

Aluminum sliding glass doors are shipped as two glass sections and a disassembled frame. Begin by laying out the four pieces of the frame, applying a thin bead of caulk to the joints. Assemble the frame pieces with the screws provided. Apply a bead of caulk to the floor where the unit will sit, as well as to the nailing fin. Position the assembled frame in the opening. Check it carefully for plumb and level, then nail it to the framing.

Set the fixed panel in place by lifting it up into the frame channel, then swinging it in and allowing it to drop into the lower channel. Secure it with the screws and clamps provided. Set the sliding panel in the channels in the same manner; install the restraining hardware that prevents the door from being lifted out from the outside; then install the latch assembly. Check the sliding unit for proper operation, and be certain the door is contacting the weatherstripping at all points along its edges.

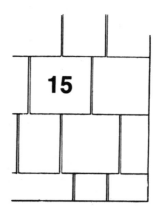

Siding

With the framing and roofing complete and the windows and exterior doors in place, the last stage of enclosing and weatherproofing the addition is the installation of the exterior siding. Here again, proper selection and installation of the siding material is crucial to achieving an addition that blends in with the rest of the house. No single step in the process of constructing a room addition has more visual impact than the installation of the siding.

Although the choices of siding materials are many and varied, matching the existing siding, or at least approximating it, shouldn't present any problems. Most siding materials and patterns that you're likely to encounter on an old house are still available today, although some might take a little hunting down.

The first step in selecting the siding for your addition is to determine exactly what type is existing, and to decide if you will match to that or, like roofing, reside the entire house. Residing is a big job, and is usually necessary only if the existing siding has deteriorated to a point beyond repair. In most cases, repair, washing, and repainting will be sufficient.

CORNICE CONSTRUCTION

Before you install the siding, you should complete the cornice construction. Because the siding abuts the underside of the cornice, completing this step first will make the installation of the siding easier and neater. There are a number of different types and styles of cornices, depending on the overall architectural style of the house. Your choice of a cornice design needs to be influenced by what's existing on your house.

Cornices are classified as *open* (Fig. 15-1), in which the rafter tails and the underside of the roof sheathing is visible; *closed* (Fig. 15-2), in which additional framing and sheathing are used to conceal the rafter tails; and *close* (Fig. 15-3), in which the rafter tails are cut off flush with the wall and the siding conceals the cut ends.

A close cornice is the easiest to construct, con-

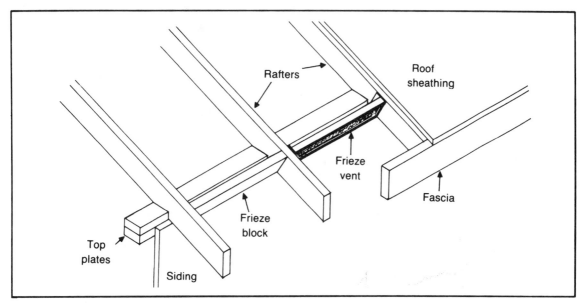

Fig. 15-1. Framing for an open cornice.

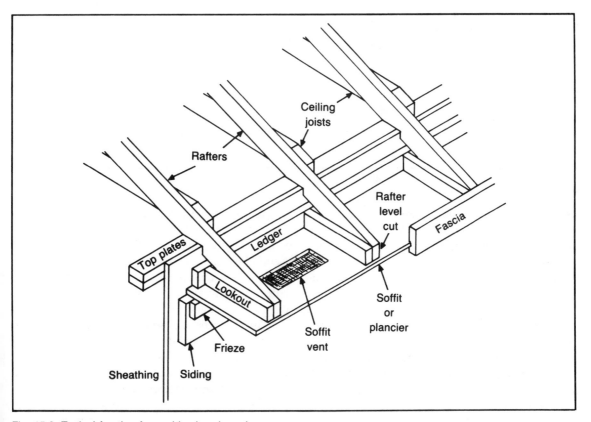

Fig. 15-2. Typical framing for a wide closed cornice.

201

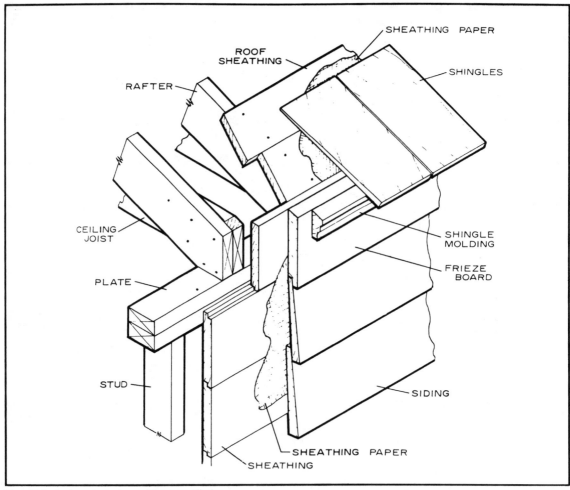

Fig. 15-3. A closed cornice, without ventilation.

sisting of little more than a frieze board and shingle molding at the top of the wall. It offers no weather protection for the wall itself, however, and so is not often used.

Open cornices are common on more contemporary houses, especially ones using roof trusses. The rafter tails overhang the outside wall, and a fascia board covers the ends of the tails. Frieze blocking and frieze vents enclose the spaces between the rafters or trusses, and the siding abuts the underside of this blocking. (See Fig. 15-4.) A molding is sometimes used over the joint between the siding and the blocking.

The most difficult and perhaps the most attrac-

tive of the cornice designs is the closed, or *box*, cornice. One type of closed cornice is constructed by simply covering the underside of the rafters with a soffit board. A fascia board covers the ends of the soffit and the tails, and the siding extends up to the soffit, usually with a molding to conceal and decorate the joint.

Another type of closed cornice utilizes lookouts that extend horizontally from the rafter tails to the wall. (See Fig. 15-5.) Nail the soffit directly to the underside of the lookouts, and use a frieze board or molding where the siding meets the soffit. A simpler variation is to allow the rafter tails to overhang slightly, then cut the undersides off horizontally.

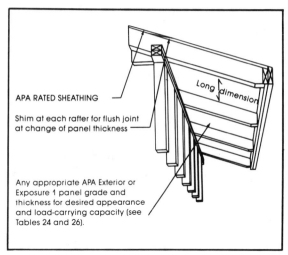

APA RATED SHEATHING

Shim at each rafter for flush joint
at change of panel thickness

Any appropriate APA Exterior or
Exposure 1 panel grade and
thickness for desired appearance
and load-carrying capacity (see
Tables 24 and 26).

Long dimension

Fig. 15-4. Plywood sheathing on an open soffit (Courtesy of American Plywood Association).

APA Panels for Closed Soffits
(Long dimension across supports)

Maximum Span (in.) All Edges Supported	Nominal Panel Thickness	Species Group	Nail Size and Type[a]
24	11/32″ APA[b]	All Species Groups	6d nonstaining box or casing
32	15/32″ APA[b]		6d nonstaining box or casing
48	19/32″ APA[b]		8d nonstaining box or casing

(a) Space nails 6 inches at panel edges and 12 inches at intermediate supports for spans less than 48 inches; 6 inches at all supports for 48-inch spans.
(b) Any suitable grade of Exterior panel which meets appearance requirements.

APA RATED
SHEATHING

Protect edges of
Exposure 1 or 2 sheathing
against exposure to
weather

Any appropriate grade of
APA-EXT plywood for soffit

Continuous screened
vent or louvered vent

Leave 1/8″ space at all panel
end and edge joints. Support
all panel edges.

Long dimension

Fig. 15-5. Recommended plywood grades and nailing schedule for closed-cornice construction (Courtesy of American Plywood Association).

A soffit board conceals the underside of the rafter, while a fascia covers the ends. (See Fig. 15-6.)

WOOD SIDING BOARDS

Wood has always been a popular material for siding. It is durable, attractive, and available in many patterns and styles. If it is properly maintained, it will last for years. A huge variety of styles, sizes, and patterns of siding boards have been manufactured over the years. If the type used on your house is not readily recognizable, the best procedure is to take a small sample to some of the lumberyards in the area and see if they can match it up.

In some instances, you might need to have a quantity of the siding specially milled in order to get an exact match. Milling can add substantially to the cost of the siding, and usually entails a wait of 2 weeks or more, so scour the lumberyards first and try to find a match. If the pattern is really hard to find, you might want to check with used building material suppliers, or perhaps with an older carpenter who has built in the area for a long time. They often can lead you to more obscure sources for matching your siding.

Siding Styles

The Western Wood Products Association

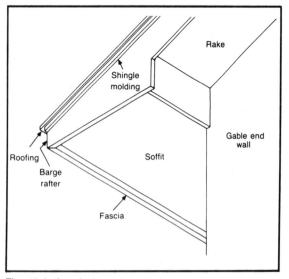

Fig. 15-6. A typical cornice return used on a gable end.

203

(WWPA) oversees the milling of several standard siding patterns (Fig. 15-7), and its mills are also usually a source of special patterns and custom milling. Following are some of the patterns offered by the WWPA.

☐ *Boards.* These are square-edged boards available in a variety of widths and thicknesses, with either a smooth or rough-sawn face. They are applied vertically using one of three methods: *board and batten*, in which wide boards are placed on the wall, then the joints are covered with narrow boards; *batten and board*, which is the reverse of this pattern, with the narrow boards put up first; and *board on board*, which utilizes fairly wide, equal-sized boards. No matter which pattern you use, make sure the boards overlap by a minimum of 1 inch.

☐ *Channel.* These boards are milled in a variety of widths with a wide rabbet along one face edge and a narrower rabbet along the opposite back edge. They can be installed vertically or horizontally and produce a 1 1/4-inch-wide channel, similar to a batten-and-board style, when

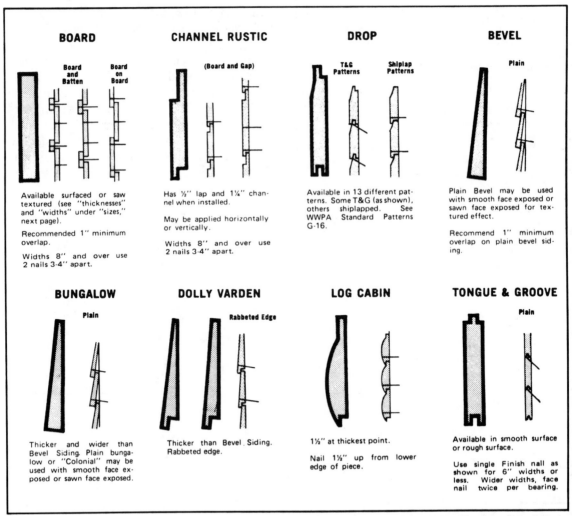

Fig. 15-7. Standard Western Wood Products Association siding patterns (Courtesy of Western Wood Products Association).

the edge rabbets are overlapped.

☐ *Drop.* WWPA offers 13 different standard patterns of drop siding designed for horizontal applications. Some types have tongue-and-groove edges; other types are shiplap. When installed, the edges overlap and form a slightly curved or beveled surface along one face edge.

☐ *Bevel, Bungalow.* Bevel siding boards vary from 4 to 6 inches in width, tapering down in thickness from bottom to top. They typically have one smooth face and one rough face, and can be used with either face exposed for the desired decorative effect. This type of siding is designed for horizontal use, with the thick bottom edge of one board overlapping the thinner top edge of the preceding board by about 1 inch. Bungalow siding is the same as bevel, but in wider boards ranging from 8 to 12 inches.

☐ *Dolly Varden.* A siding similar to bevel siding, only thicker and with a rabbeted bottom edge that overlaps the top edge of the preceding board.

☐ *Log Cabin.* This siding is designed to approximate the look of uniform individual logs. They have a curved face, with a flat lip on one face edge and a rabbet on the opposite back edge. They are installed horizontally with the rabbet overlapping the flat lip.

☐ *Tongue and Groove.* These are boards of various widths and thicknesses, having tongue-and-groove edges. Most are installed horizontally, although some types also can be installed vertically.

In addition to these types of individual boards milled from solid wood is siding made from plywood, hardboard, and other materials that closely approximate solid lumber. A variety of patterns and styles are available, many in strips that are milled to resemble two or more individual boards. They offer the advantage of faster installation time and less tendency to warp.

Installing Siding Boards

Siding boards are almost always installed over wood sheathing, in order to provide solid backing for the individual boards. Solid wood siding should have a moisture content as close to that of the region where it's being installed as possible, in order to minimize the problems of shrinkage. If the siding is being brought in from another region, it's best to have it on the job site several weeks before installation to allow it to adjust somewhat to the condition in which it's being applied.

Priming and painting of the siding should be done before it's installed, for several reasons. Laying the boards out on sawhorses makes the application of the primer and paint much easier. Also, since the boards are lying flat, there's much less tendency for the paint to run. Painting the boards one at a time also allows the ends and edges to be completely covered, which seals the board to minimize swelling and warpage. It also ensures that if the boards should shrink or warp, an unpainted area won't be exposed.

Cover the sheathing with an air and moisture barrier, such as kraft or felt paper. Check with the building department for the exact requirements for your area. The sheathing paper should be applied from the bottom up, with each succeeding layer overlapping the one below it by about 2 inches. Side laps should overlap by 4 inches. Staple the paper to the sheathing as needed to hold it in place until the siding material is applied.

Additional blocking is usually required when you are installing vertical siding in order to provide sufficient nailing supports. Blocking should be installed approximately 36 inches OC. Horizontal siding is adequately supported by the wall framing, and can be nailed to the studs on 16-inch centers, or with sheathing over studs on 24-inch centers.

Begin the installation of vertical siding at one inside or outside corner, and cover one entire wall at a time. Joints should fit smoothly and tightly. Horizontal siding is always applied from the bottom up, just like roofing, to ensure complete weather-tightness. Bevel siding requires the installation of a starter strip under the bottom of the first course (Fig. 15-8), so that the course will be beveled away from the wall to match the subsequent courses. Follow the manufacturer's recommendations for the size of the starter strip, and for the

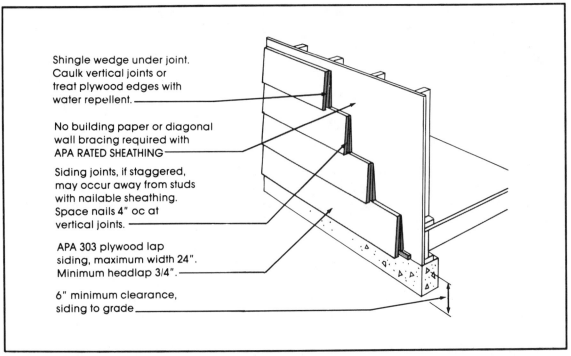

Shingle wedge under joint.
Caulk vertical joints or
treat plywood edges with
water repellent.

No building paper or diagonal
wall bracing required with
APA RATED SHEATHING

Siding joints, if staggered,
may occur away from studs
with nailable sheathing.
Space nails 4" oc at
vertical joints.

APA 303 plywood lap
siding, maximum width 24".
Minimum headlap 3/4".

6" minimum clearance,
siding to grade

Fig. 15-8. Horizontal bevel siding over plywood sheathing. Note the starter strip, which establishes the bevel under the first course (Courtesy of American Plywood Association).

amount of the overlaps between courses.

For the installation of horizontal siding, the use of a story pole is a good idea. It speeds the layout, and helps to ensure that all of the courses are the same on each wall. To make a story pole, measure the distance from where the bottom of the first siding board will be to the underside of the soffit, then cut a straight length of lumber to this length. Divide this length into spaces equal to the exposed face of the siding. Adjust the overlaps of the siding until the spacing on the pole comes out even, but do not plan on lapping the siding less than the minimum requirements. Mark these divisions on the piece of lumber.

To use the story pole, hold it at each inside and outside corner of the building, so that the top of the pole is against the bottom of the soffit. Transfer the marks from the pole to the wall. Repeat the procedure at both sides of each window and door opening. Snap a chalk line between the marks to establish the level lines necessary to guide the siding. To ensure accuracy over long spans, stretch out the chalk line and hold it near the center, then snap it to each side.

For inside corners, horizontal siding usually is abutted to a piece of 2- x -2 lumber, installed vertically in the corners (Fig. 15-9). This method provides a clean transition in the corner and eliminates a tremendous amount of cutting and fitting of the individual boards. For outside corners, two vertical corner boards are the most common choice. This method will work for either horizontal or vertical siding. With either type of siding, you also can miter the boards individually to form a corner. Another alternative for horizontal bevel siding is the use of preformed metal corners (Fig. 15-10), which lock under the bottom lap and then are nailed to the top of the boards, where the next board will cover the nails.

At windows, doors, and other openings, you can abut the siding directly to a trim board placed next to the opening, or you can abut it loosely to the opening and then cover it with a trim board mounted on top of it. The best procedure is always

Fig. 15-9. Using a 2- x -2 strip as a transition molding where shingle siding abuts a stone wall.

move it, allowing the transition to begin from a full-width board.

You should remove existing horizontal siding in individual courses back to an original joint, and then start the new siding run from there. Do one course at a time, tearing back the old siding, abutting the new, and completing that course for the length of the wall. If there are no joints in the old siding, or if too much siding would be wasted, cut random joints in the old siding as starting points for the new runs. Do not simply cut one vertical line of joints, because such joints are both hard to conceal and difficult to seal against the weather. Instead, stagger the joints as they would have been during the original installation. Cut the joints to fall over the existing studs so that good support can be

to follow the size and style of the trim used on the rest of the house. Caulk the siding carefully where it abuts the inside corners, and at all window and door openings. Use a good grade of caulk for the easiest application and longest life.

Transitions

Where the new siding abuts to the old, care must be taken to prevent the joint from being obvious. With vertical siding, carefully abutting the siding together is usually sufficient for a clean transition. If the last siding board on the old wall has been ripped down to fit the corner, you should re-

Fig. 15-10. Metal corners used over horizontal bevel siding.

provided for both ends of the siding. Caulk the transition joints as an added precaution.

SHEET SIDING

Probably the most common material for sheet siding is plywood. (See Fig. 15-11.) Plywood siding is assembled with exterior glue for good weather resistance, is dimensionally stable (making it resistant to warping and buckling), adds greatly to the structural stability of the building, and is fast and easy to install. Douglas fir, cedar, southern pine, and redwood are the most common species of wood for the face veneer, and the American Plywood Association (APA) lists several different patterns. (See Fig. 15-12.)

☐ *Texture 1-11*. Commonly called *T 1-11*, this is one of the most popular of the plywood siding types. It has parallel grooves running with the panel's long dimension, 1/4 inch deep, 3/8 inch wide, and 4 or 8 inches OC. It is available in 19/32- and 5/8-inch thicknesses, with shiplapped edges.

☐ *Channel Groove*. Similar to T 1-11, with 1/16-inch-deep grooves, 3/8 inch wide, 4 or 8 inches OC. Thicknesses are 11/32, 3/8, and 1/2 inch, with shiplapped edges.

☐ *Rough-Sawn*. This type of plywood has a lightly rough-sawn texture running across the grain, and is available with or without grooves. Lap siding styles are available, as are full sheets. Common thicknesses include 11/32, 3/8, 1/2, 19/32, and 5/8 inch.

☐ *Kerfed Rough-Sawn*. A type of rough-sawn panel with a pattern of vertical, narrow, saw kerfs. These grooves are usually 4 inches OC, although grooves on multiples of 2-inch centers are also available. Common thicknesses are 11/32, 3/8, 1/2, 19/32, and 5/8 inch, with shiplapped edges.

☐ *Brushed*. These panels have a brushed or relief-grain texture, which accents the natural grain pattern of the face veneer. They are usually available without grooves in 11/32-, 3/8-, 1/2-, 19/32-, and 5/8-inch thicknesses.

☐ *Reverse Board and Batten*. This type of panel has a rough-sawn or coarse-sanded face, with deep, wide grooves. The grooves are 1/4 inch deep, 1 to 1 1/2 inches wide, and spaced 8, 12, or 16 inches OC, with shiplapped edges.

☐ *Medium Density Overlay (MDO)*. MDO plywood has a special smooth or texture-embossed resin face coating that creates an excellent surface for painting. It is available in panels without grooves, in T 1-11 or reverse board-and-batten style, or in a V-grooved pattern, with grooves 6 or 8 inches OC. It is also available in factory-precut lengths for use as a lap siding. Common thicknesses are 11/32, 3/8, 1/2, 19/32, and 5/8 inch.

In addition to plywood, siding panels are commonly available in OSB and hardboard, both of which have been textured for a realistic wood grain appearance. These panels are usually available in many of the same styles as the APA panels. Whether plywood or one of the other materials, the common sheet sizes are 4 × 8, 4 × 9, and 4 × 10 feet.

Installing Sheet Siding

Siding sheets are installed vertically, either over sheathing or directly on the studs. Some patterns also may be installed horizontally. Apply a covering of paper first, as with the siding boards.

Begin the installation from the same corner that you started your stud layout (Fig. 15-13) to ensure that the panel edges fall directly over the studs. With shiplap panels, start so that the edge of the panel that is rabbeted on the back face is at the corner. The other edge of the panel will cover almost the entire stud, which is fine. When the next panel is put in place, the shiplap rabbets will overlap. When you nail along the edge of the second panel, the nails will be in the center of the stud. A 1/8-inch space usually is recommended at all panel edges to prevent distortion from swelling. Nails should be placed 6 inches OC along the edges and 12 inches OC at the intermediate supports.

Wherever possible, select siding panels in an adequate length to eliminate horizontal joints. In areas such as gable ends where horizontal joints are

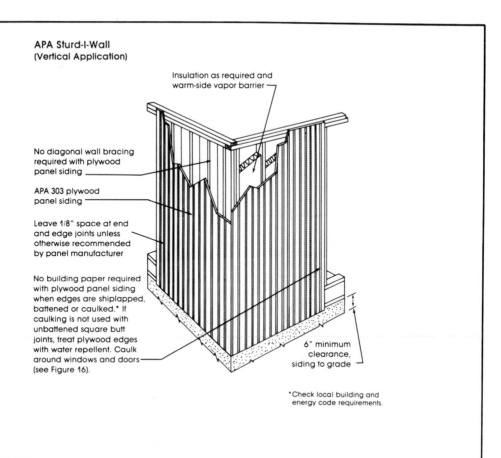

APA Sturd-I-Wall
(Vertical Application)

Insulation as required and warm-side vapor barrier

No diagonal wall bracing required with plywood panel siding

APA 303 plywood panel siding

Leave 1/8" space at end and edge joints unless otherwise recommended by panel manufacturer

No building paper required with plywood panel siding when edges are shiplapped, battened or caulked.* If caulking is not used with unbattened square butt joints, treat plywood edges with water repellent. Caulk around windows and doors (see Figure 16).

6" minimum clearance, siding to grade

*Check local building and energy code requirements.

APA STURD-I-WALL Construction
(Recommendations Apply to APA 303 Plywood Siding Direct to Studs and Over Nonstructural Sheathing)

Plywood Panel Siding Description (All species groups)	Nominal Thickness (in.)	Max. Stud Spacing (in.)		Nail Size (Use nonstaining box, siding or casing nails) (a) (b)	Nail Spacing (in.)	
		Face Grain Vertical	Face Grain Horizontal		Panel Edges	Intermediate
APA MDO EXT	11/32 & 3/8	16	24	6d for panels 1/2" thick or less; 8d for thicker panels.	6(d)	12
	1/2 & thicker	24	24			
APA 303 SIDING – 16 oc EXT (including T1-11)	11/32 & thicker	16	24			
APA 303 SIDING – 24 oc EXT	15/32 & thicker (c)	24	24			

(a) If siding is applied over sheathing thicker than 1/2 inch, use next regular nail size. Use nonstaining box nails for siding installed over foam insulation sheathing.

(b) Hot-dipped or hot-tumbled galvanized steel nails are recommended for most siding applications. For best performance, stainless steel nails or aluminum nails should be considered. APA tests also show that electrically or mechanically galvanized steel nails appear satisfactory when plating meets or exceeds thickness requirements of ASTM A641 Class 2 coatings, and is further protected by yellow chromate coating.
Note: Galvanized fasteners may react under wet conditions with the natural extractives of

some wood species and may cause staining if left unfinished. Such staining can be minimized if the siding is finished in accordance with APA recommendations, or if the roof overhang protects the siding from direct exposure to moisture and weathering.

(c) Only panels 15/32" and thicker which have certain groove depths and spacings qualify for 24 oc Span Rating.

(d) For braced wall section with 11/32" or 3/8" siding applied horizontally over studs 24" oc, space nails 3" oc along panel edges.

Fig. 15-11. Recommendations for the use of plywood siding (Courtesy of American Plywood Association).

unavoidable, a special galvanized sheet-metal flashing, called a *Z-bar or Z-metal*, is used to seal the joint. The flashings are available in 10-foot lengths, and in various leg dimensions to fit the different thicknesses of siding. Side-lap the flashings by 2 to 4 inches when you are making up longer lengths.

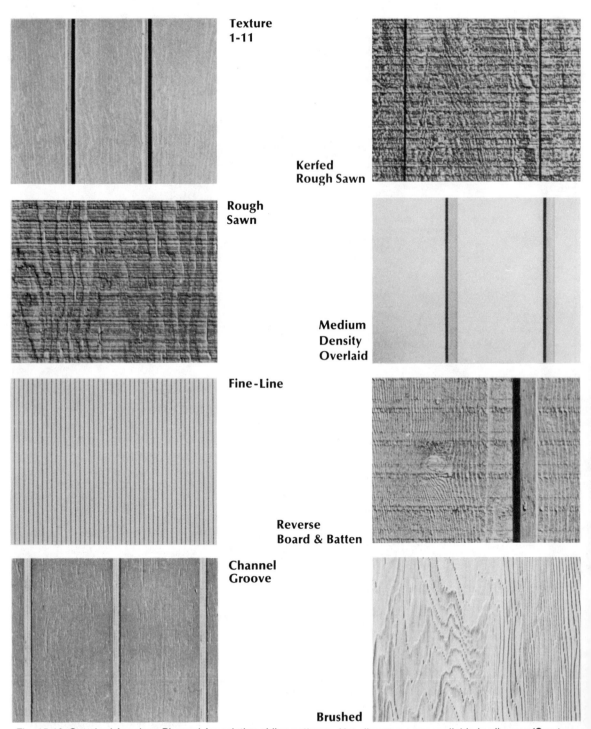

Texture 1-11

Kerfed Rough Sawn

Rough Sawn

Medium Density Overlaid

Fine-Line

Reverse Board & Batten

Channel Groove

Brushed

Fig. 15-12. Standard American Plywood Association siding patterns. Not all patterns are available in all areas (Courtesy of American Plywood Association).

Fig. 15-13. Installing plywood siding (Courtesy of American Plywood Association).

After all of the lower panels are in place, install the Z-bar so that the bottom leg extends out and over the lower panels, and the upper leg is flat against the studs. Then install the upper panel on the lower one, covering the upper leg of the flashing. The lower leg remains exposed, and can be painted or covered with wood trim as desired.

Because of the size of the sheets, cutting accurate mitered corners or butting cut edges around openings is extremely difficult (Fig. 15-14), so wood trim is commonly used at the outside corners and around openings (Figs. 15-15 through 15-18). Inside corners are simply abutted to each other and then caulked. Caulk all window and door openings also.

Transitions

Sheet-siding transitions are done like the transitions for vertical siding boards. One edge of the new panel is simply abutted against the edge of the last original panel. If you're using siding with shiplap edges, the last original panel will need to be torn out to get back to its rabbeted edge.

An alternative is to simply abut the panels together and then cover the joint with a piece of wood trim. This is the simplest way of making the transition, but the least visually appealing. The vertical wood trim that covers the seam is a dead giveaway as to where the addition starts, no matter how well everything else has been matched.

SHINGLES AND OTHER SIDING MATERIALS

Shingles, either of wood, asbestos-cement, or other materials, can be used as an exterior siding. They offer fairly easy installation, and can be applied over furring strips as a means of residing an entire house.

Installing Wood Shingles

Wood shingles are essentially the same for siding applications as they are for roofing. There are also side-wall shingles made specifically for siding applications. They are cut from clear cedar or redwood, and have a combed surface texture. They are boxed in 1 square units, and some types come preprimed for easy painting.

Wall shingles are installed in much the same manner as any horizontal siding. They need to be applied over a solid subsurface, usually sheathing, which has been papered first. You can use a story pole (Fig. 15-19) to align the courses from wall to wall, and to speed the layout of the horizontal chalk lines. You can use a single-course application, in which the exposure is limited to about half the length of the shingle (Table 15-1), or a double-course application, which allows greater exposure (Table 15-2).

Single-Course Application

Begin the application from the bottom of the wall with a layer of #3 wood shingles (Fig. 15-20). Install the first course of shingles over this starter course, extending the bottom of the shingles about 1/2 inch below the bottom of the starter course. Hold each shingle in place with two galvanized nails, driven above the line of the next course so that the nail heads will be covered. After laying up the first course, snap a chalk line at the level of the bottom of the next course. In order to maintain a straight row, tack a straightedge along this line and set the shingles on it as you install them.

Take care to install each course so that the butt lines do not align with the butt lines in the course below it. There should be a space of about 1/8 inch between each shingle, and you should maintain an offset of approximately 1 1/2 inches between the joints of one course and the joints of the one below it.

You can abut outside corners to each other and then cut them on a slight taper to match the bevel of the course. An alternative is to use premade sheet-metal corners, which slip over the shingle corner and are attached above the line of the next course. Metal corners speed the installation and offer good impact resistance, thus preventing the corner from being damaged. Abut inside corners to a 2- x -2 corner board, applied vertically in the corner. Also abut the shingles to finish moldings applied around window and door openings.

Double-Course Application

Double-course application involves the use of

Fig. 15-14. Cutting plywood siding around an opening (Courtesy of American Plywood Association).

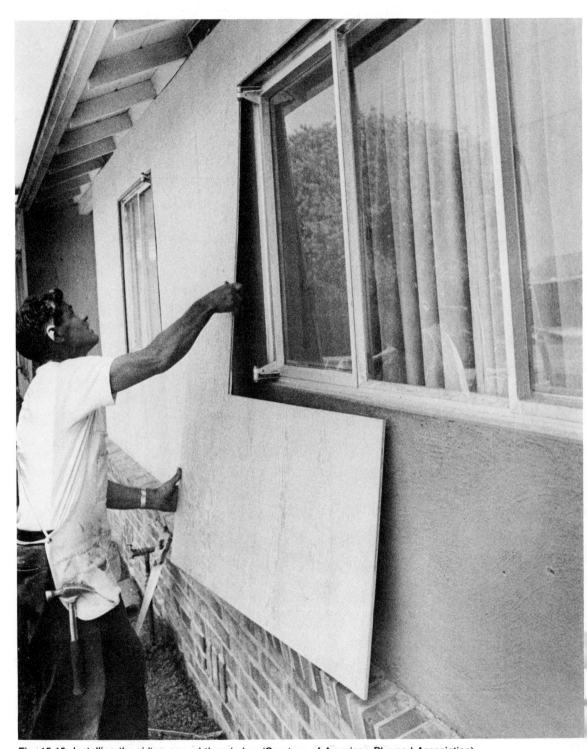

Fig. 15-15. Installing the siding around the window (Courtesy of American Plywood Association).

Fig. 15-16. Trimming the window (Courtesy of American Plywood Association).

Fig. 15-17. Trimming an opening (Courtesy of American Plywood Association).

a layer of #4 shingles under each course of siding shingles (Fig. 15-21). This method allows more exposure between the courses, while still maintaining the necessary doubled thickness of wood at all points. Exposure for 16-inch shingles is 12 inches, and exposure for 18-inch shingles is 14 inches, or as recommended by the manufacturer.

Begin with a starter course of #3 shingles, then add a second start course directly over the first, overlapping the joints. Then lay the first shingle course over the doubled starter course, again overlapping the joints and allowing the shingles to protrude 1/2 inch over the bottom of the starter courses.

Unlike single-course shingles, double-course

shingles are installed with exposed nails. Place two nails in each shingle, 3/4 inch in from each edge and approximately 1 1/2 inches up from the butt line. For shingles over 8 inches in width, place a third nail in the center of the shingle.

Snap a chalk line for the placement of the second course, and install a straightedge along it (Fig. 15-22). Using the straightedge as a guide, install a course of #3 shingles 1/2 inch above the line. Hold the undercourse shingles in place with a staple or one 3d nail. Install the second course of finished shingles in line with the straightedge, covering the undercourse. Proceed up the wall in this manner, first installing an undercourse and then following it with the finished shingles. Corners and openings

Fig. 15-18. Installing trim at an outside corner (Courtesy of American Plywood Association).

Fig. 15-19. Using a story pole to transfer measurements for the layout of shingle siding (Courtesy of Red Cedar Shingle & Handsplit Shake Bureau).

are installed in the same manner as for single-course applications.

STUCCO

Stucco is a mixture of cement, sand, lime, and water that is applied wet over a prepared surface in a series of coats. Stucco is very durable and weather resistant, although it is prone to cracking with time. It can be painted with most types of paint, or the final coat can be colored with powdered cement colors for a permanent color coating.

Stucco requires the use of a cement mixer, so you can mix quantities of material on the job site as needed. Do not mix more than you can apply in a short time. Stucco is a very labor-intensive siding to apply, and might or might not be within the range of the do-it-yourselfer. Consult with a stucco supplier or watch a contractor installation before deciding if it's something you feel comfortable undertaking.

Table 15-1. Recommended Exposure for Single-Course Siding Shingles.

LENGTH & TYPE	MAXIMUM EXPOSURE	ONE-BUNDLE COVERAGE
16″ Shingle	7 1/2″	37 sq. ft.
18″ Shingle	8 1/2″	38 sq. ft.
24″ Shingle	11 1/2″	38 sq. ft.
18″ Shake	8 1/2″	17 sq. ft.
24″ Shake	11 1/2″	23 sq. ft.

(Courtesy of the Red Cedar Shingle & Handsplit Shake Bureau)

Table 15-2. Recommended Exposure for Double-Course Siding Shingles.

LENGTH & TYPE	MAXIMUM EXPOSURE	ONE-BUNDLE COVERAGE
16″ Shingle	12″	60 sq. ft.
18″ Shingle	14″	63 sq. ft.
24″ Shingle	16″	53 sq. ft.
18″ Shake	14″	28 sq. ft.
24″ Shake	20″	40 sq. ft.

(Courtesy of the Red Cedar Shingle & Handsplit Shake Bureau)

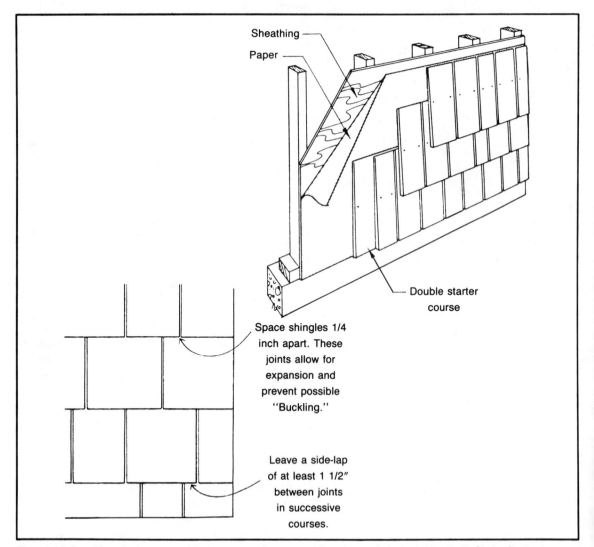

Sheathing

Paper

Double starter course

Space shingles 1/4 inch apart. These joints allow for expansion and prevent possible "Buckling."

Leave a side-lap of at least 1 1/2″ between joints in successive courses.

Fig. 15-20. Installing single-course siding shingles (Courtesy of Red Cedar Shingle & Handsplit Shake Bureau).

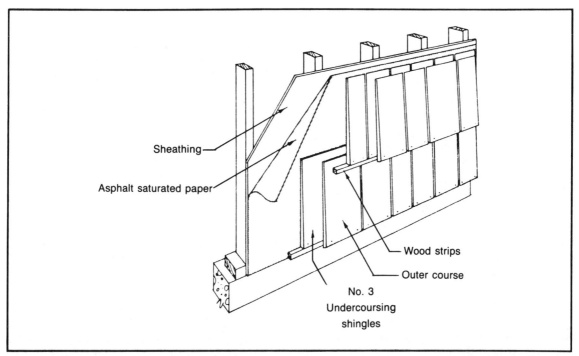

Fig. 15-21. Installing double-course siding shingles (Courtesy of Red Cedar Shingle & Handsplit Shake Bureau).

Fig. 15-22. The use of a straightedge makes alignment of the siding shingles much faster and more accurate.

Installing Stucco

Proper backing is required to support the stucco. This backing can be wood sheathing or *line wire*, a series of galvanized or stainless steel wires stretched horizontally on 6- or 8-inch centers.

After the line wire or sheathing is in place, cover the walls with 15-pound felt, lapped the same as for roofing felt. Next, install a layer of stucco netting, which resembles chicken wire, using special furring nails. *Furring nails* are large-headed aluminum or galvanized nails with a thick fiber washer under the head. Install the nails so that the stucco netting is trapped between the washer and the nail head, securing the netting and holding it away from the wall. In this way, the wet stucco can pass through the netting and into the space between the netting and the wall, ensuring a good bond.

Use special corners, manufactured from wire mesh, to form and strengthen the outside corners. On horizontal surfaces, such as the underside of a soffit, use expanded metal lath in place of the netting to provide a stronger backing. Place wooden stucco molding around windows, doors, and other openings. This molding has a deep rounded groove along one edge. When you install the stucco, push it into the groove in the molding, forming a good bond with the wood to prevent cracking along these joints. Leave the wood exposed as trim and paint it later.

Apply the first layer of stucco with a trowel and press it solidly against and through the netting. It should be a thick enough coat to completely embed the netting. As the stucco dries, even it out and "scratch" it with a special long, grooved trowel. Roughening the surface in this manner ensures a good bond between the first coat and the second coat.

After the first coat has dried, apply the second coat in the same manner, troweling it on in an even, uniform thickness. Depending on the installation, you can apply stucco in two or three coats. The third coat is usually a texture coat. If two coats are used, texture the surface of the second coat slightly at it dries by rubbing it with a wood block. This procedure rubs away some of the surface cement and creates a fine, sandy texture.

If you are applying three coats, smooth the second coat out and let it dry. Apply the third coat by thinning the stucco somewhat and troweling it on in patches or swirls to create a pleasing surface texture.

Another common texture is *dashing*, which is done with a thick brush, called a *dashing brush*, that resembles a stiff broom. Dip the brush into wet, thinned stucco, and then "spray" it on the wall by flicking the brush bristles with a stick. This procedure covers the surface with a thin layer of small globs of stucco, which creates a nice texture when painted.

Transitions

For a good transition with stucco, break the existing stucco back from the intersection with a hammer in a random line that obscures the exact line along which the old and new meet. Remove all of the loose stucco from the netting, and leave the netting intact. If possible, undercut the old stucco so that the new material can be worked under it, minimizing the chances of a crack forming along the seam. Interweave the new netting with the old as much as possible, using galvanized wire to tie the two together.

Trowel the stucco over the intersection in the netting, feathering the second coat out slightly onto the old material. When texturing, pay particular attention to the seam between the two surfaces and apply the texture to hide it as much as possible.

MASONRY SIDING

Masonry is another common siding material, and the type and style of masonry varies in different parts of the country. This type of siding can be bricks (Fig. 15-23) or stone, either in the form of solid masonry walls or, more commonly, a masonry veneer (Fig. 15-24). Masonry veneers are one unit thick over a base of plywood or sheathing boards.

Installing Masonry

Usually you will pour a concrete footing at the

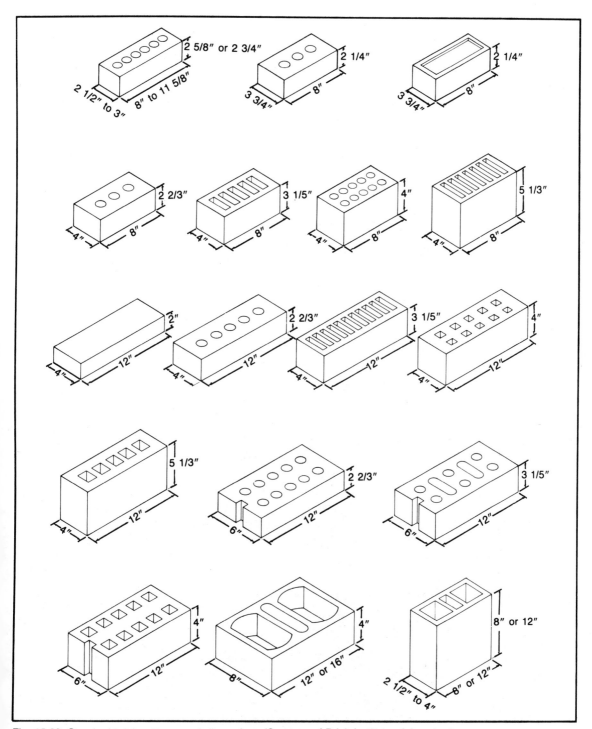

Fig. 15-23. Standard brick patterns and dimensions (Courtesy of Brick Institute of America.)

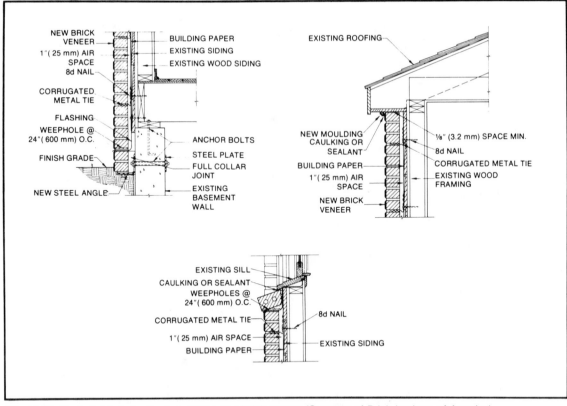

Fig. 15-24. Typical details for the installation of a brick veneer (Courtesy of Brick Institute of America).

Fig. 15-25. Tying a new stone veneer into an existing one takes careful fitting.

Fig. 15-26. After marking the stone, it is cut using an electric masonry saw.

base of the wall to serve as a level, weight-bearing platform from which the veneer is started. Then lay up individual courses, with L-shaped ties inserted at regular intervals to secure the masonry to the sheathing.

Transitions

Brick veneer must be broken back into alternating courses, then the new bricks are started from the end of each old course. Extreme care must be taken to align the course and keep the size of the new mortar joints consistent with the size of the old ones. The transition for stone is done in much the same way, with enough old stone being removed to provide a random seam for starting the new material.

Stone and brick transitions require a solid knowledge of masonry installations to be done properly. (See Figs. 15-25 and 15-26.) Mortar composition, brick and stone type and color, joint size, and many other factors go into making a transition that blends in well. Determining the best transition is usually beyond the scope of the do-it-yourselfer, and is best left to an experienced mason.

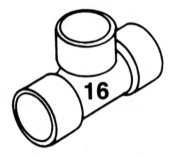

Plumbing Systems
and Connections

As plumbing systems have become more standardized and today's plumbing materials have become easier to work with, much of the basic plumbing work on a room addition falls within the realm of the do-it-yourselfer. Before attempting any work on the system, however, you need to understand how the system works and how to tie into it safely.

Every building has two complete and separate systems: the hot and cold water system, which supplies potable (clean) water to the building for normal cooking and cleaning; and the drain, waste, and vent *(DWV)* system, which removes nonpotable water and solid waste from the building and conveys it to a disposal site.

HOT AND COLD WATER SYSTEM

Water is supplied to the home via a main supply line from the source, be it a municipal water system or a private well. A main shutoff valve, located on the main line just before or after it enters the house, is used to close off the supply when work

on the home's plumbing system becomes necessary. It's important to know the exact location of this valve, and to ensure that it's in proper working order.

After the cold water enters the home, it branches off into smaller diameter lines to feed various fixtures. Typically, the main water supply line is of a fairly large diameter, usually 1 or 1 1/4 inches. It drops down to 3/4 inch for the main branch feeder pipes that go to various parts of the house, reducing again to 1/2-inch pipe for the lines that actually supply the fixtures. These diameters will vary with the water pressure, the number of fixtures being fed off the line, and the distance the line has to run.

At a point near where the main supply enters the house, a 3/4-inch branch line is taken off to bring cold water into the water heater. The water heater, typically a 30- to 50-gallon tank with a gas burner or electric elements, warms the water and stores it until a demand for it exists. A 3/4-inch hot-water line leaves the tank, and hot water is supplied to the fixtures through branch lines, which run parallel with the cold-water lines. When hot water is drawn off by opening a faucet at one of the fixtures, cold water enters the water heater to replace it, thereby maintaining pressure in the hot-water system and keeping the tank full.

In planning any additions to the plumbing system, it helps to take the time to study the existing plumbing layout and determine what the lines are and what they feed. You will need to know what line you're planning to tap into, and whether that line will be large enough to feed the intended addition. For example, tapping into a 1/2-inch line might be adequate for a short run to supply a garden faucet, but a bathroom addition will require that a new branch line be taken off a 3/4-inch or even a 1-inch cold-water line in order to supply enough volume of water. A 3/4-inch line, near the water heater if possible, will need to be tapped for the bathroom's hot-water supply.

If the proposed bathroom addition is quite a distance from the existing water heater, or if a fairly substantial increase in hot-water capacity is needed, the addition of a second water heater is worth considering. All that is required is a 3/4-inch supply line of cold water and a fuel source. In remodeling, it is often easiest to use electricity for the new water heater, since it eliminates the need for gas lines and flue vents. Place the new water heater in or near the new bathroom to minimize piping runs and heat loss. You also can place it next to the existing tank if you're merely looking to increase capacity. You also can increase capacity by simply replacing a small, outdated water heater with a new, energy-efficient model of larger size.

DRAIN, WASTE, AND VENT SYSTEMS

The other plumbing system in a house is the DWV system (Fig. 16-1). It is a carefully designed system of interacting pipes that allow for the removal of liquid and solid waste, and for venting of the system. Once again, knowing what the lines are and where they go is essential before you tap into one.

Drain Lines

Trace the lines starting at the fixtures and work

back out of the house. The drain lines are the ones that connect directly to a sink, bathtub, shower drain, washing machine, or other fixture containing only liquid waste. Drain lines are usually 1 1/4, 1 1/2, or 2 inches in diameter, and are intended to carry liquid waste only, never solids.

For example, a bathroom sink is connected to a short piece of pipe called a *tailpiece,* which in turn enters a curved section of pipe called a *trap.* A small amount of water is always held in the curved section of the trap, which is below the level of the drain line. This standing water, called the *trap seal,* prevents gas and odors from the sewer from entering the house through the fixture. The other end of the trap is connected to the drain line, which feeds directly into a waste line.

Waste Lines

Waste lines, typically 2- and 3-inch-diameter pipes, are designed to carry both liquid and solid waste. They receive the liquid discharge from the drain lines, and are also connected directly to toilets and kitchen sinks, from which they receive both liquid and solid waste. The waste lines then discharge into a 4-inch line, called the *main building sewer* or *house sewer,* which conveys the waste out of the house and discharges it into a septic tank or municipal sewer system.

The drain and waste portions of the DWV system operate on gravity flow to remove waste from the building. Each line, starting from the fixtures, is angled down slightly from perfectly level. This angle, called the *pipe's fall,* is usually equal to 1/8 to 1/4 inch of fall per 1 foot of run. This angle must be fairly consistent. If there is not enough fall, the waste will not flow smoothly. If there is too much fall, the liquid waste will drain much faster than the solids, creating the risk of the solids becoming lodged in the line.

Fall is a critical consideration in the placement of new fixtures and lines. (See Fig. 16-2.) Each new line must be placed so that it can drain down into an existing line, which can present problems in some installations. Sewage pumps can force the waste uphill, but they should be considered only as a last resort. Check with your local plumbing

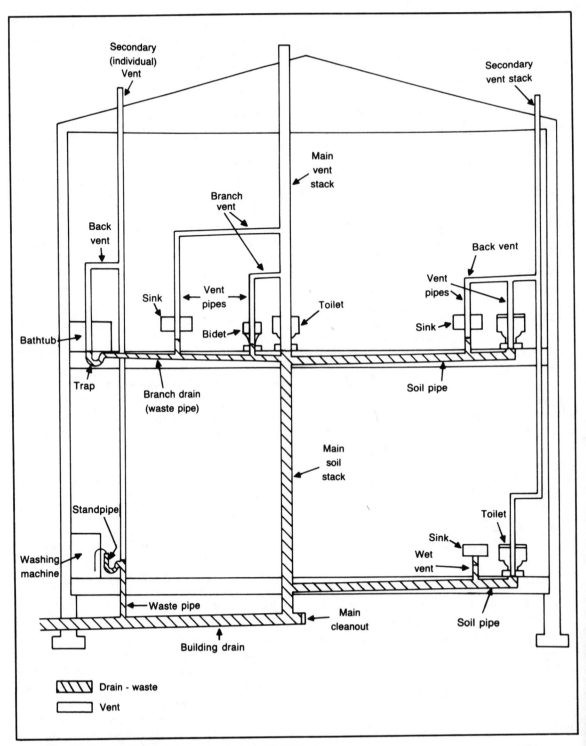

Fig. 16-1. A typical residential drain, waste, and vent system.

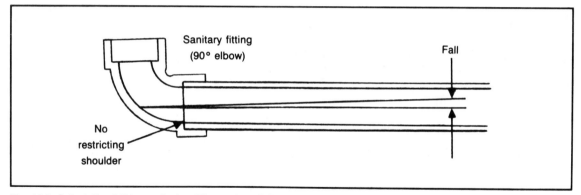

Fig. 16-2. Calculating fall in a soil pipe. The sanitary fittings used with soil lines have no restricting shoulder to obstruct the flow of waste.

department for sizing, restrictions, and other information.

When you are adding a new plumbing run, it is necessary to tap into a waste line or main sewer line, not a drain line. Drain lines are intended to serve one fixture only, and cannot be doubled up. Also, the line you tap needs to be large enough to handle the intended load. A toilet, for example, needs to drain into a 3- or 4-inch line. Code will not allow it to empty into anything smaller. A sink, on the other hand, can empty into any line 2 inches or larger. Adding to a building's DWV system takes careful study and planning in order to ensure that both the new system and the existing one function properly.

Vent Pipes

The third portion of the DWV system are the vent pipes. Vent pipes begin at the level above the drain and waste lines, and are not intended to carry waste of any sort. Extending up through the roof, vents provide the atmospheric pressure necessary for the drain and waste system to operate.

In many installations, the *main vent stack,* one large pipe usually 3 inches in diameter, extends up through the roof from a central waste line, called the *main soil stack.* Other vents from other fixtures connect to the vent stack and vent through it, eliminating the need for several penetrations of the roof.

For one new fixture, such as the addition of a washing machine, the vent can extend individually through the roof, or it can tie into an existing vent stack. For several new fixtures, as in the case of a new bathroom, it is best to run a secondary vent sack. This secondary vent, like the main vent stack, is one large line out through the roof, into which the other vents in the room connect.

SEPTIC SYSTEMS

Many homes in areas not served by municipal sewer systems have a private sewage disposal system, which is almost always in the form of a septic tank. Cesspools, which receive the solid and liquid waste from a building, allowing the liquid to seep out while retaining the solids for later removal, are now illegal in most areas for health and safety reasons.

A septic system consists of a watertight concrete, metal, or fiberglass box, called a *septic tank,* (Fig. 16-3) and a series of liquid disposal pipes. The septic tank receives all the waste from the building via the main sewer line. Solids settle to the bottom of the tank, where they are broken down by bacterial action. Liquids pass through a solid line at the other end of the tank, into a distribution box, and from there into a series of perforated drain lines. The drain lines are laid out in gravel-lined trenches, called a *leach* or *disposal field* (Fig. 16-4). The liquid waste is slowly drained out of these lines to be filtered by the gravel as it disperses down into the soil.

Septic systems are rated by their capacity in gallons, which is an indicator of the volume of waste

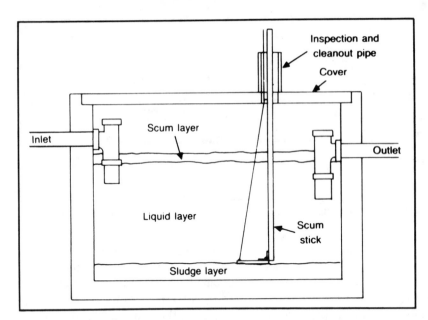

Fig. 16-3. A typical septic tank.

they can handle. The Uniform Plumbing Code rates the size of a house by the number of bedrooms it has, and relates that to the capacity of the septic tank. For example, a one- or two-bedroom house requires a septic tank with a minimum capacity of 750 gallons, a three-bedroom house requires 1,000 gallons, and a four-bedroom house requires 1,200 gallons. An additional 150 gallons of capacity is required for each additional bedroom.

When you are adding on to a house with a sep-

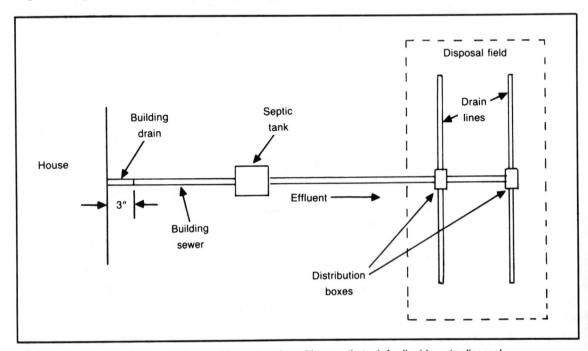

Fig. 16-4. A drain field and drain lines used in conjunction with a septic tank for liquid-waste disposal.

tic tank, the plumbing or building department might wish to verify that the size of the septic tank and the length of the drain lines are adequate to handle the increased load imposed by the addition. Verify this information with the proper authorities before the addition begins, since expensive additions to the septic system might be required.

PLUMBING MATERIALS

Unlike other parts of the addition, the materials you use for any new plumbing do not have to be the same as the existing materials. As a result of the ready availability of transition fittings, the materials available for use on the addition are virtually unlimited. The materials you decide on are a matter of choice, and some are easier for the nonprofessional to use than others.

Water Lines

For new water lines, the most common choice today is copper pipe. Copper does not rust or corrode like galvanized pipe. It is also lightweight, relatively inexpensive, and easy to work with. It is joined with slip fittings, (Fig. 16-5), which are attached by soldering, a technique that's easy to learn. No threading is required, and alterations can

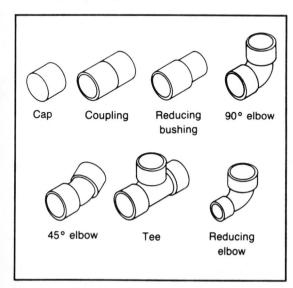

Cap   Coupling   Reducing   90° elbow
                   bushing

45° elbow   Tee   Reducing
                    elbow

Fig. 16-5. Some of the variety of common slip fittings for use with copper pipe.

be performed quickly and easily.

Copper pipe is found in four basic types, each carrying a letter designation and a color-coded stripe on the pipe's side for easy identification.

☐ *Type K.* Thick-walled pipe, color-coded green; used primarily for underground installations.
☐ *Type L.* Medium-walled pipe, color-coded blue; used in some underground installations and in above-ground locations where higher water pressures might be encountered.
☐ *Type M.* Thin-walled pipe, color-coded red; the most common residential pipe. It is for above-ground installations only, and is commonly limited to water pressures of 100 PSI or less.
☐ *Type DWV.* Larger diameter medium-walled pipe, color-coded yellow; sometimes used in drain, waste and vent installations.

In addition to these four rigid pipes, called *hard-supply pipes,* types K and L are also available as *soft-supply pipes,* meaning they are soft tempered and can be bent, allowing the use of fewer fittings. Type K is used for above-ground and some below-ground installations, while Type L is for above-ground use only. Color coding is the same as for hard-supply pipe.

The old standard for water lines was galvanized iron pipe, and it's still widely in use today, especially for remodeling. This type of pipe requires the use of threaded fittings (Fig. 16-6), and each piece of pipe must be individually threaded after it is cut to length. You can purchase a pipe threader if you have an ongoing need for one, or you can rent one fairly inexpensively as the need arises.

Plastic pipe for water lines is relatively new, and is not yet accepted by most building officials. Widely used in mobile home construction, plastic pipe is inexpensive, very easy to cut and join, and extremely lightweight. It requires more support than rigid metal pipes, and some of the compatible plastic valves and fittings have not reached the high level of quality and reliability that metal fittings have. If you intend to use plastic pipe, check with the plumbing department for any restrictions, and be certain to use a plastic that is rated for both hot- and cold-water use, such as polybutylene.

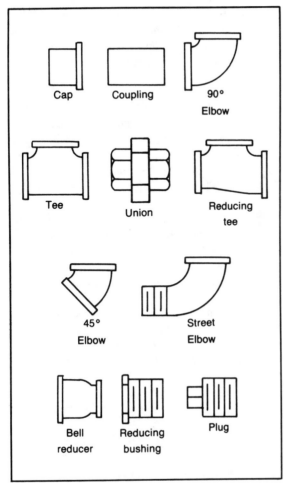

Fig. 16-6. Common threaded fittings for use with threaded metal pipe.

DWV Lines

Plastic pipe for DWV use, specifically pipe formulated from acrylonitrile-butadiene-styrene (ABS), has become widely accepted in recent years, and is probably your best choice for new work. ABS is a rigid black plastic, sold in 20-foot lengths in 1 1/2-, 2-, 3-, and 4-inch diameters. It is joined with special ABS slip fittings, which require no threading and are attached using liquid solvent cement. ABS pipe is quite light when compared with other DWV pipe, is extremely easy to cut and join, and requires no special tools. Alterations to it are easy, involving only cutting the pipe and gluing in a new fitting.

Cast-iron pipe was used for many years in residential work, and, like galvanized iron pipe, is still widely used today. The older style of cast-iron pipe was joined using special cast-iron fittings that were flared out on each end to receive the pipe. The end of the pipe was inserted into the flared hub on the fitting, and the joint was packed with oakum or other packing material, then sealed with molten lead. Today, most cast-iron pipe and fittings are joined using no-hub connectors, which consist of a neoprene sleeve and a screw-activated clamp.

Cast-iron pipe requires a special cutter, which is actually a type of chain with steel cutting wheels in it. To use the cutter, wrap the chain around the pipe, then tighten it with the tool's racheting handle until the pipe snaps. You can rent soil pipe cutters, also called *chain cutters,* as needed.

For smaller diameter drain pipes, copper or galvanized iron pipe was sometimes used. Galvanized pipe for DWV use is cut and threaded exactly like water pipe, and is joined with threaded fittings. Copper DWV pipe is cut and soldered like copper water lines. It is a very durable, corrosion-resistant pipe for this use, but is quite expensive in the larger diameter sizes.

TRANSITIONS AND CONNECTIONS

Commonly available at plumbing and hardware stores is a variety of transition fittings which make it possible to easily go from one material to another, or from one size to another, or both. These transition fittings are specifically designed for this use, and they are the only type of fittings you should use to ensure safe, problem-free connections.

Water-Line Transitions

Probably the most common water-line transition between dissimilar materials is joining copper pipe to galvanized pipe. If the joining is done incorrectly, a chemical reaction takes place between the copper and the zinc used in the galvanizing, causing the joint to be slowly eaten away until it finally fails.

There are two basic ways to correctly join copper pipe to galvanized pipe. The first is to make the transition through a third material—brass— which will not react adversely to either the copper or the zinc. There are a variety of ways to use brass, depending on the particular installation. For example, you can solder a copper slip-to-female fitting onto the copper pipe, screw a connector onto the galvanized pipe, then connect the two with a brass nipple. You also can use one of the many types of elbows or T's designed for the purpose, which have a slip fitting on one end and a threaded fitting on the other.

The second transition method, and probably the most effective, is through the use of a device called a *dielectric union*. Slip one half of the union over the end of the copper pipe and solder it in place. The other half has a female thread to attach to the end of the galvanized pipe. A thick rubber washer fits between the two halves, keeping the dissimilar materials separated while still forming a seal between them. A nylon washer inside the lock nut separates the copper side of the union from the lock nut itself for further protection. Installation is quick and easy, and you have the added benefit of a union fitting in case disassembly of the pipes ever becomes necessary.

If a dielectric union is installed on a cold-water line that is used as a ground for electrical or telephone equipment, the rubber washer inside the union breaks the pipe's continuity, making it ineffective as a ground. To prevent this situation, it's necessary to attach a standard electrical ground clamp to the pipes on either side of the union, and run a piece of #6 bare or green-jacketed copper wire, called a *jumper* or *bond wire*, between the clamps (Fig. 16-7). You also should use this precaution anytime a water pipe is broken up by a nonmetallic object, such as when you are installing a water filter with a plastic casing.

A variation on the use of brass to make a safe connection between copper and galvanized pipe is the flexible water line. Constructed of copper, it has a brass locknut with an insulating nylon bushing inside. It is useful for installing such devices as water heaters or water softeners, since the pipe's flexibility greatly simplifies alignment of the connections. Flexible water line is available in different lengths, and either with locknuts at both ends, or with a locknut on one end and a slip fitting for direct soldering to copper pipe on the other.

To adapt plastic to copper or galvanized pipe, use a slip-to-thread adaptor. Simply glue this fitting onto one end of the plastic pipe, then screw

Fig. 16-7. A bond wire being used around a plastic water filter to ensure ground continuity.

it into an appropriate male or female fitting on the other pipe. Be certain the fitting is compatible with the type of plastic pipe being used.

For copper pipe, a wide variety of transition and adaptor fittings are commonly available. Slip-to-thread fittings, either male or female, adapt the copper pipe for use with threaded fittings, allowing the transition from copper to plastic or the connection of brass plumbing fixtures. Reducing couplings are used to join two pipes of different diameters, and reducing bushings will slip into a fitting such as a T to adapt it to a smaller pipe size. T fittings for use with two different diameter pipes are available in several sizes and outlet combinations.

Galvanized pipe adapters are also available in several different sizes and styles. Female-threaded bell reducers will connect two different sizes of pipe, while male/female threaded bushings are used to adapt a larger size fitting to a smaller diameter pipe. Reducing T's and elbows are also available in a variety of size combinations.

For pipe runs where future disassembly is anticipated, unions are used to connect the pipes to each other, or to a fixture or appliance. Every union works basically the same way, employing one or more removable locknuts to join the two ends of pipe. Slip unions are available for soldering to copper pipe, and threaded ones are used to connect galvanized pipes. Slip unions are also available for plastic or unthreaded galvanized pipe. This type consists of two locknuts, two washers, and a connecting body. The pipe ends slip into the body, and the nuts are tightened down to compress the washers and form a seal.

Always be certain to use the correct glue or thread sealer for the type of connection you're making. Read the label for the manufacturer's instructions and recommended applications.

Soil-Line Transitions

A very common situation created by remodeling is the need to connect ABS soil pipes to cast-iron, clay, transite, or whatever other type of pipe was used in the house originally. For this purpose, a band clamp similar to that used with no-hub cast-iron pipe is used (Fig. 16-8). It consists simply of a metal sleeve with two worm-drive or screw clamps, and an inner sleeve made of rubber. Rubber transition gaskets of various thicknesses can be inserted into the inner sleeve to make up the difference in the outer diameters of the pipes being joined.

To adapt ABS to galvanized pipe, slip-to-thread adapters are used. One end of the fitting is designed to slip over the end of the ABS pipe, or into an ABS fitting, and be glued into place. The other end has a female or male thread to make the connection to the threaded pipe. Use Teflon tape or a Teflon-based compound on the plastic threads, since most other compounds are petroleum-based and can cause deterioration of the plastic over time.

A variety of adapters are available for changing from one diameter to another in pipe of the same material. You can use elbows and Ts with inlets in two different sizes when you are changing the direction of the run or tapping a branch line off the main. For straight runs, use an adapter bushing, which is inserted into a coupling or other fitting to step down the pipe diameter.

To make the transition between two pipes that are both of different sizes and different materials, use a band clamp with the appropriate adapter gaskets to connect the dissimilar materials first, then step down the size. You're less likely to encounter leaks or assembly problems using this method.

The use of a split-case adapter can simplify tap-

Fig. 16-8. Band clamps being used to tie new ABS plastic pipe into a cast-iron cleanout fitting.

ping a threaded pipe off an existing ABS line without needing to cut the pipe. Place the two halves of the heavy plastic case around the existing pipe and secure them in place with two worm-drive clamps. Next, drill a hole through the threaded side opening in the case and into the pipe. Tighten down the clamps to compress various rubber O-rings in the case, thus ensuring a watertight seal. Then screw a pipe into the side opening to take off for the new line.

Drain lines, such as those used under a sink, are usually connected by means of a slip fitting, which employs a locknut and a rubber or nylon washer. Insert the pipe into the end of the fitting, and tighten down the locknut to compress the washer. These fittings are available in plastic or chrome-plated metal, and in several different forms, including straight connectors, 45- and 90-degree elbows, tailpiece extensions, and various types of traps. Adaptor washers are also available that allow a 1 1/4-inch pipe to be inserted into a 1 1/2-inch fitting.

PLUMBING PROCEDURES

Every remodeling project can create a number of different plumbing situations, each of which needs to be analyzed and solved as it arises. The tools, procedures, and techniques are basic to every application, requiring only the selection of the proper materials and fittings for the specific situation.

It's often easiest to complete the work on the addition first, treating it as any new plumbing installation. Work down and in the direction of the transition and tie in with the existing house. The transition method you select depends on the materials being joined, using the proper fittings as outlined in the previous sections. Remember that the connections will need to be made with the proper pipes in the proper location to ensure adequate water pressure and the proper fall for the drain and waste lines.

If the addition has a crawl space, you should complete some of the underfloor rough plumbing before you install the subfloor, thus simplifying the installation. Tack a 2 × 4 to the floor joists to indicate the exact location of any interior walls that con-

tain plumbing, and work from these locations to align the pipes. Rough in the rest of the plumbing after the walls are up. In the case of a slab floor, all of the underslab plumbing needs to be in place and tested before the slab is poured.

The plumbing department usually will require that all new DWV lines be pressure-tested before they are enclosed or covered in any way. To make this test, insert a test ball in the lowest end of the new line, and cap off all other outlets or plug them with test plugs. You must have one of the vent lines in place. Then insert a garden hose in the end of the vent (Fig. 16-9). Fill the system with water from this point, and check all of the joints for leaks. This procedure might vary with different inspectors, and yours might or might not want to be on hand dur-

Fig. 16-9. Pressurizing a DWV system by filling the lines through the new vent.

ing the test, so check with him first.

Working with ABS Pipe and Fittings

As mentioned earlier, ABS pipe is quite simple to work with. The pipe can be cut with any fine-toothed handsaw, or with a hacksaw. Be careful to cut the end of the pipe square, not at an angle. You can use a miter box to guide the saw if desired. After you make the cut, brush or file away any burrs that might interfere with the pipe's insertion into the fitting.

When you are measuring the pipe for cutting, remember to allow for the fittings. First, measure the total length from the centerline of one fitting to the centerline of the next fitting. Next, measure the distance from the centerline of the fitting to the inside of the shoulder. Subtract this distance from the total length needed. Repeat the subtraction for the fitting on the other end. Dry-fit the pipe and fittings to check for proper alignment before you glue.

ABS pipe and fittings (Fig. 16-10) are joined with ABS cement, a thick, black liquid available in cans that have a small brush attached to the inside of the lid. Using the brush, coat both the inside of the fitting and the outside of the pipe with cement, then press the pipe fully into the fitting. Work quickly to install and position the fitting because the cement sets within a few seconds.

Installing DWV Lines

Drain, waste, and vent lines are usually installed first, since it is easier to work the smaller diameter water lines around the DWV pipes than it is to work the DWV pipes around the water lines. For a large plumbing installation such as a bathroom, it's common to run a 3-inch line directly from the location of the toilet, then tie the other drain lines into it.

A fitting called a *closet bend* is used at the floor to start the turn from the toilet into the waste line.

First screw a closet flange to the subfloor, if it's in place, then attach the closet bend to it. If the subfloor is not in place, extend the closet bend above the line of the joists a distance equal to the thickness of the subfloor, and add the flange later.

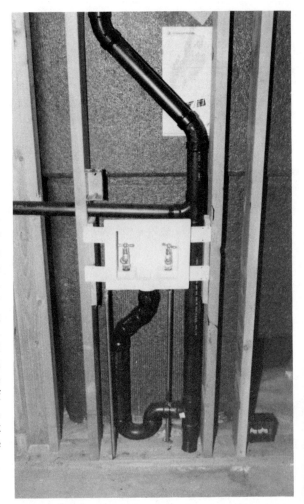

Fig. 16-10. ABS pipe and fittings simplify drain and vent systems such as this one for a new washing machine.

The closet flange contains two or more slotted holes for the insertion of the toilet bolts, and it is to this flange that you will attach the toilet later. Check with the toilet supplier for the correct rough-in dimensions for the flange, which is usually 12 inches out from the finished surface of the back wall (Fig. 16-11).

From the flange, the closet bend turns back toward the wall behind the toilet, and enters a special fitting which resembles an elbow. It has a 3-inch inlet and outlet, and a second, 2-inch outlet at the curve of the elbow, from which the vent stack is

234

Fig. 16-11. A closet bend and sanitary Y fitting used to plumb for a new toilet. A plastic test plug is glued in the top of the closet bend.

can take these vents through the roof individually or tie them into the vent stack that comes off the toilet. (See Fig. 16-12.) Use sanitary T's to connect the vents to the vent stack, remembering that the direction of flow for the side outlet of the elbow is always in the direction that the waste will flow.

Working with Copper Pipe and Fittings

Copper pipe can be cut with either a hacksaw or a tubing cutter (Fig. 16-13). Tubing cutters are the preferred method of cutting because they leave a square end. If you're using a hacksaw, take care

taken off. From the bottom of the elbow, add another 90-degree elbow, facing in the direction of the tie-in with the existing house.

Add bathtub, shower, and sink lines next. You'll need to refer to the manufacturer's specifications for the exact locations and sizes of all the rough-ins. Sinks usually are installed with a fitting called a *sanitary* T, which resembles a standard T except that the side inlet flows into the fitting in one direction only. Since the third side of the T becomes the start of the vent, this fitting allows water from the drain to only flow into the waste line, not into the vent. The bottom side of the T points toward the underfloor, and piping is taken off of it to tie into the main waste line installed earlier. Make all connections to the main waste line with sanitary T's also, to keep the flow going in one direction only.

Tubs and showers extend directly down through the floor, then enter a trap. For slab floors, use a fixed trap with solid joints. For crawl-space applications, use a removable trap so that it can be taken off as necessary to clear obstructions.

Extend vents off the top of each T fitting. You

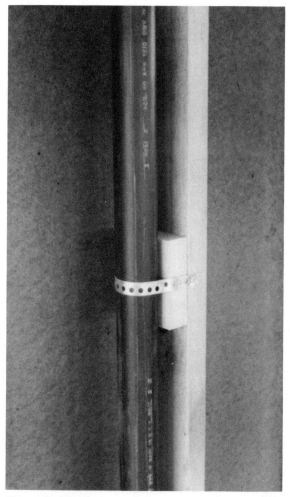

Fig. 16-12. Plumber's tape being used to strap a vent pipe in place.

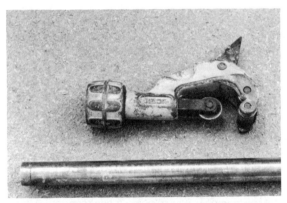

Fig. 16-13. A piece of copper pipe and a commercial tubing cutter. The retractable reamer at the top is used for cleaning burrs from the inside of the cut pipe.

that your cut is square and that the pressure of the saw does not distort the pipe. After cutting, remove the burrs from inside the cut end. Most tubing cutters have a small, fold-out reamer for this purpose. A half-round file also will work well.

It is extremely important that the pipe and fittings be completely clean where they are to be joined, since solder will not stick to oxidized or dirty pipe. Using emery cloth, steel wool, or one of the special wire brushes made for copper pipe, polish the end of the pipe until it is bright and shiny, making sure you clean the entire area that will be inserted into the fitting. Clean the inside of the fittings in the same manner, and be certain that both the fittings and the pipe are round and free of dents.

Using a small brush, apply a generous coating of paste flux to the polished end of the pipe. The flux prevents the pipe from oxidizing during heating, and allows the solder to flow more easily. Insert the pipe into the fitting, and support the joint so that it remains together and correctly aligned while soldering.

With a propane torch, begin to heat the joint.

Apply the tip of the flame to the joint and allow it to heat thoroughly. The trick is to heat the joint just enough to melt the solder; don't overheat it. Pull the flame away, and touch the tip of the solder to the joint. Use 50/50 solder (50 percent tin, 50 percent lead). If the joint is properly heated, you will notice the solder being rapidly drawn into the joint; if not, remove the solder and apply more heat. Do not use the flame itself to melt the solder. Before the solder hardens, wipe the joint with a wet cloth to cool it and remove excess flux. Use a scrap of sheet metal, or even an old cookie sheet, to protect any wood or other combustibles near the area where you're soldering. You are holding an exposed flame, so work cautiously.

When you are repairing or adding to an existing run of pipe, shut off the water supply, open the lowest faucet in the house, usually an outside hose bibb, and allow the lines to drain. Draining the lines is very important in repair work, because water left in the lines will prevent the pipe from reaching the temperature necessary for soldering.

Try to prepare and solder all the joints in a fitting at one time (i.e., both ends of an elbow); otherwise the heat you are applying to one joint might loosen the other one. If it's not possible to do all the joints at once, wrap the existing ones with a wet cloth while you are soldering the new one. To disassemble an existing joint, heat it until the solder becomes liquid, then gently tap it apart with a hammer. Clean any previously soldered pipe or fittings thoroughly before reusing them.

If a joint refuses to take the solder, stop. Allow the pipe and fittings to cool, disassemble them, then thoroughly reclean and reflux them before you try again. The most common causes of failed joints are out-of-round or dented pipes or fittings, incomplete cleaning, lack of flux, or improper heating of the joint.

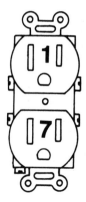

Electrical
Systems and Connections

As with plumbing, the advent of standardized fittings and nonmetallic sheathed cables such as Romex has greatly simplified electrical wiring for the average do-it-yourselfer. Extending or adding new circuits and installing new appliances and other electrical devices is now a fairly straightforward undertaking.

Remember that improper electrical wiring can be extremely dangerous, and is a leading cause of household fires. If you are at all unsure of a procedure, or in doubt about the correct materials to use, consult with a qualified electrician or your electrical inspector. Also, don't overlook the need to have an electrical permit on the job, and to have the electrical wiring inspected at the rough and final stages. These precautions are for your own safety.

HOW THE ELECTRICAL SYSTEM WORKS

Before beginning any actual wiring, you should know a little bit about how the electrical system in your house works. Knowing what the various parts of the system do and how they interrelate can save

you time and help you avoid mistakes.

Volts, Amperes, and Watts

There are three terms commonly heard when referring to the current flowing through your home's electrical system: volts, amperes, and watts. To understand the terms, visualize the flow of electricity through the wires as being the flow of water through a pipe.

The *volt* is a measure of electrical potential, which is probably better understood as electrical pressure. It is this pressure that causes the current to flow. Just as the water pressure in a pipe would be measured in pounds per square inch, electrical pressure is measured in volts. You most commonly will hear volts, or voltage, associated with total potential pressure in a circuit or device, for example, a 120-volt circuit or a 240-volt appliance.

An *ampere* (amp) is a measure of how much current is flowing through a wire or electrical device, just as gallons are used to express how much water is flowing through a pipe or a faucet. Individual circuits and devices are rated in amps to indicate the largest amount of current that the circuit or device is intended to handle. The current flow should never exceed the amperage rating.

A *watt* is a unit of measurement of electrical power, which can be determined by the simple formula:

$$\text{Volts} \times \text{Amps} = \text{Watts}$$

Many devices, such as light bulbs, are rated in watts. By knowing the wattage of a particular device, you will know how much electricity that device is consuming when it's in use. It is this unit of measurement that is the basis for how you are charged for the electricity you use.

If you were purchasing water based on how much you used at any given time, it might be measured and sold in gallons per hour. Likewise, you purchase electricity based on how much you use. On your electric bill, you will see the term *kilowatt hour,* or kWh, which is how the electric company measures and sells electricity. A kilowatt is 1,000 watts, and 1,000 watts used for 1 hour is equal to 1 kilowatt hour.

For example, suppose you are using a small heater that is rated at 2,000 watts. If you use the heater for 1 hour, you would consume 2,000 watts per hour, or 2 kilowatt hours of electricity. If you are paying 8 cents per kilowatt hour, using the heater for 1 hour would cost you 16 cents.

An Electrical Circuit

In order for electrical current to flow, it must have a complete, continuous path from its beginning, which is the source of the power, through the device using the power, such as a light bulb, and then back to where it began. This complete path is called a *circuit.* No matter how confusing a set of wires might look, this principle remains the same; the current goes out and comes back.

In today's residential wiring, a two-wire cable is commonly used. Within the common outer jacket are contained two individually wrapped wires, called *conductors.* As prescribed by the National Electrical Code (NEC), the two conductors are color-coded. One conductor is white, and the other is black, or any color other than white, gray, or green. The black wire is always *hot,* meaning it carries the current. The white wire is neutral, and provides the return path for the current, completing the circuit.

Grounding

The NEC requires that all new circuits be grounded, and a third conductor, color-coded green, is provided within the cable along with the white and black for this purpose. The ground wire is a safety device, independent of the neutral wire, and during normal operation of the circuit it does nothing. It comes into use only when a problem occurs.

If the hot wire in the circuit were to become dislodged, or if its insulation were to wear or break away, the bare wire could come into contact with metal components within the circuit, such as a metal box or the trim on a light fixture. In that event, the entire metal part would become charged, and anyone touching the metal would receive a shock.

The ground wire connects all the metal parts of the circuit through to the neutral bus bar in the service panel, and from there to the earth, usually through a ground conductor connected to a cold-water pipe. In the event of a problem with the hot conductor, the potentially dangerous current is carried harmlessly to the earth.

Including the ground wire in the cable with the hot and neutral wires makes grounding the entire system quite simple. Within each box, the ground wires are tied together to make the ground continuous, and they also are connected to whatever device is installed in the box, such as a receptacle. Grounded receptacles (Fig. 17-1) have a ground screw, colored green, which is provided for the attachment of this wire. The screw is in turn connected to a third opening on the face of the receptacle. When a tool, appliance, or other electrical device having a grounded plug is plugged into the receptacle, the grounding protection is continued on to the tool. Should a wire come loose within the tool and touch the metal case, the user is protected against shock.

238

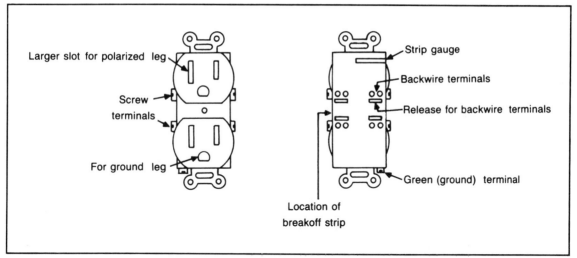

Fig. 17-1. A grounded receptacle. The D-shaped hole accepts the ground prong on a grounded plug, and is tied to the grounding screw.

Alternating Current

Alternating current (ac) is electrical current that regularly reverses its direction of flow, flowing first in one direction, then reversing to flow in the other direction, then reversing back. There is a short period between each reversal when no current is flowing at all. This alternating of current flow originates at the power source, and is done to allow the electricity to be transmitted over long distances.

Each two reversals of direction is called a *cycle*, and the number of cycles per second is referred to as the *frequency* of the current. The unit of measure for electrical cycles is *hertz* (Hz), and 1 hertz is equal to 1 cycle per second. Household current in the United States is 60 cycle, meaning the current makes two complete reversals of direction 60 times each second. It is the speed of these reversals that makes the current appear to be continuous.

RESIDENTIAL WIRING SYSTEM

Electricity originates at power-generating stations, and is transmitted to electric utility companies for sale and distribution to the utility's consumers. The utility erects and maintains power transmission lines, and extends wires from its lines to service each individual building. That service might be from overhead, which is probably the most common type, or from underground. (See Fig. 17-2.)

Overhead service conductors drop down from the transmission lines to connect with the home's service entrance conductors, which extend up within a piece of conduit that passes through the roof. Underground service is becoming more popular, since it eliminates the unsightly overhead wires. With this type of service, the conductors extend in conduit down one of the utility poles from the transmission lines, or are brought to the site completely underground, buried in a trench. They are then brought up through conduit to enter the service panel from underneath. In both cases, the utility company provides the lines up to the service panel, after which all of the wiring and equipment is provided and maintained by the homeowner.

The service is also described as being two-wire or three-wire. *Two-wire service,* which is no longer being installed, has one 120-volt hot conductor and one neutral conductor. This type of service only provides 120 volts of power to the house. In all new and remodeled installations, a *three-wire service* is used, providing two 120-volt hot conductors and one neutral. This type of service gives the house the potential for 240-volt power, which is needed for many of today's appliances.

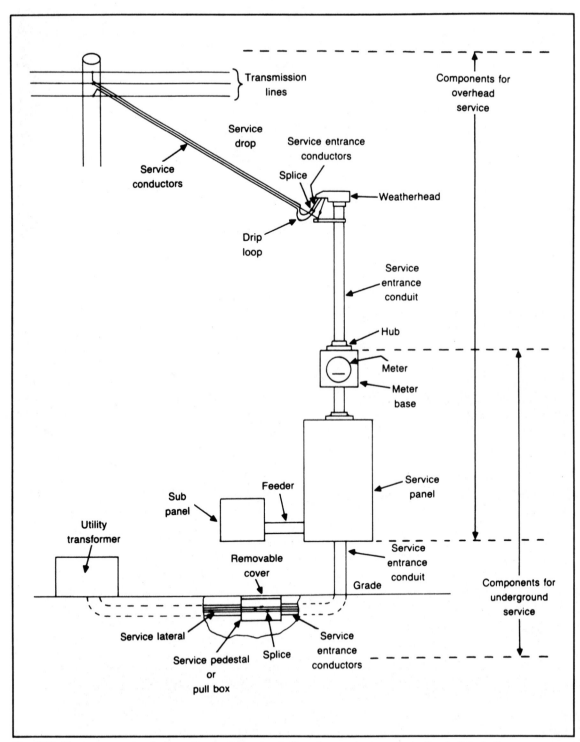

Fig. 17-2. The components of an overhead service, top half, and an underground service, bottom half.

The Service Panel

After the electrical current arrives at the house, it passes first through an electric meter, which is provided, installed, and sealed by the utility company. (See Fig. 17-3.) The meter measures and records the number of kilowatt hours of electricity being consumed by the home. This reading is the basis from which you are billed each month.

From the meter, the electricity enters the service panel itself (Fig. 17-4), which might be one unit with the meter or separate from it. (See Fig. 17-5.) The service panel takes the incoming current and distributes it to each of the branch circuits in the house. A main disconnect switch (Fig. 17-6), which today is usually a circuit breaker but in older homes might be a large handle or a pull-out fuse block, controls all of the current entering the panel. Shutting this switch shuts all power to the house at one time.

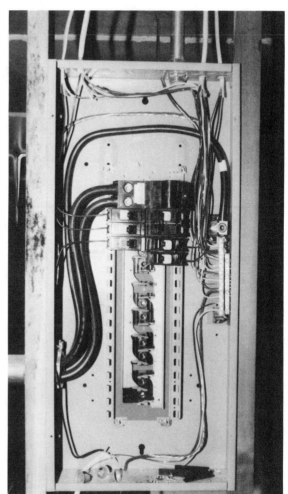

Fig. 17-4. A typical 200-amp service panel. Heavy wires at the left come in from the meter base.

The main disconnect switch is rated in amperes, which is the total capacity of the entire service panel. Service panels are usually available in 100-, 125-, and 200-amp sizes. Today, most people install a 200-amp service panel, even if that is more capacity than they need at the time, since it will accommodate additional load in the future if the need arises.

From the main disconnect switch, the current travels down two metal bars, called the *hot bus bars*. (See Fig. 17-7.) Individual circuit breakers are snapped onto these bars to route the electricity into the various branch circuits. Each hot bus bar car-

Fig. 17-3. A meter base, into which the electric meter is placed. Heavy wires at the top extend down from the service entrance, enter the four clips that hold the meter, then exit through the back to the service panel.

Fig. 17-5. A separate meter panel. The conduit at the top extends up to the roof, and contains the service entrance cables.

ries 120 volts. For a 120-volt circuit, use a single-pole circuit breaker, which contacts only one of the bus bars. For a 240-volt circuit, use double-pole circuit breakers, which contact both bus bars. Then connect the hot wires for the branch circuits to the screw terminals on the circuit breakers.

The service panel also contains a neutral bus bar, which is connected to a service ground. The ground source might be a metal cold-water pipe in the home's plumbing system, a steel rod driven into the ground, or a piece of reinforcing steel set in the building's foundation. Some states require a double service ground, utilizing two ground wires to both the ground rod and the cold-water pipe.

The neutral bus bar contains a series of holes and screws. Insert each of the neutral and ground wires in each of the branch circuits into one of the holes, and then secure them by tightening a screw down onto each wire.

Capacity of the Service Panel

If your new addition requires a number of new circuits, especially appliance circuits that draw a lot of current, the existing service panel might not have the capacity to handle the increased load. The components within a service panel are all sized to the panel's maximum capacity, which is usually reflected in the amperage rating of the main service disconnect switch. The amperage of the main disconnect switch is stamped on the breaker itself, and the panel capacity is printed on a label contained somewhere within the panel enclosure.

In some cases, the panel might be rated for a higher capacity than the size of the main circuit breaker. In this event, you can increase the capacity of the panel to handle additional circuits by changing out the main breaker. Before you can do so, the utility company will need to remove the electric meter to disconnect the current into the panel.

If the panel and the main disconnect are rated the same, which is usually the case, then you will need to change the entire service panel. For this procedure, the utility company must disconnect the service conductors that feed the old panel and reconnect them to the new panel. (See Fig. 17-8.) All of the existing circuits then must be transferred over to the new panel, and new circuits added as needed.

In either of these cases, the quantity and intricacy of the wiring involved is usually out of the realm of even the most advanced do-it-yourselfer. If you have any doubts or questions about the capacity of the panel, have it checked by an electrician before you attempt to add new circuits. If the main breaker or the entire panel needs to be changed, have the electrician do it. You then can

Fig. 17-6. The main service disconnect breaker, top right, connected to the conductors coming in from the meter base. Note the grounded bushing on the conduit, bottom center.

safely add the new circuits yourself, if you desire.

CALCULATING LOAD

To accurately determine the total electrical load on the system, most electricians perform a simple mathematical load calculation. Doing this calculation yourself will enable you to combine the existing circuits with the additional proposed circuits to determine if the existing panel will handle the combined load.

All of the calculations are based on the wattage requirements of each circuit. The total wattage requirement is divided by the voltage of the service to determine the service panel's required amperage. Some circuits are simply assigned an average wattage for calculation purposes, while others are determined by the wattage rating listed on an ap-

pliance's nameplate. The following example is based on a typical electrically heated home having a combined area for the house and addition of 1,500 square feet.

First, the general lighting and receptacle load is figured at 3 watts per square foot:

1,500 square feet × 3 watts   4,500 watts

Next, a minimum of two kitchen appliance circuits and one laundry circuit are figured in at 1,500 watts each:

1,500 watts × 2 kitchen circuits = 3,000 watts
1,500 watts × 1 laundry circuit = 1,500 watts

Dedicated (individual) circuits for major appliances

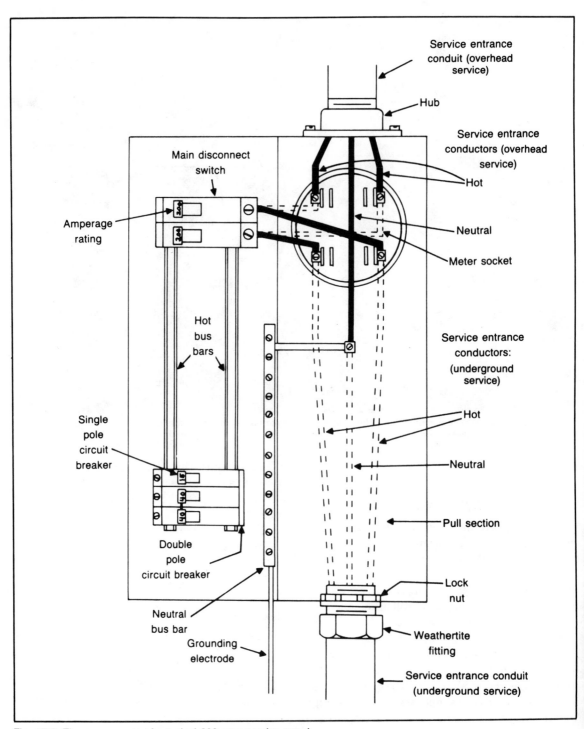

Fig. 17-7. The components of a typical 200 amp service panel.

Fig. 17-8. A utility company lineman changing a service drop from the old service conduit, left, to the new service conduit.

are added in next, based on their nameplate rating:

Range	12,000 watts
Dryer	5,000 watts
Water heater	2,500 watts
Central furnace	20,000 watts
Air conditioner, wall mount, 2 @	
1,500 watts each	3,000 watts
TOTAL	51,500 watts

Since it reasonably can be assumed that not all of the circuits will be at full capacity at any one time, only the first 10,000 watts are calculated at full load. The remaining watts are calculated at 40 percent of capacity:

First 10,000 watts @ 100%	10,000 watts
Remaining 41,500 watts @ 40%	16,600 watts
TOTAL LOAD	26,600 watts
26,600 watts ÷ 230 volts	115.65 amps

In order for the service panel to handle the combined anticipated load of the existing house and the addition, a panel capacity of approximately 116 volts is required. A 125-amp panel will work, but a 200-amp panel would be a wiser choice, allowing for future expansion.

This is a simple but reasonably accurate forecast of the home's electrical needs. Your calculations are still subject to the approval of the building department, whose calculation methods might be different from these, but these calculations give you a good place to start. Include a copy of these calculations when you apply for your electrical permit to show the building department the basis for your choice of panel size.

TRANSITIONS AND CONNECTIONS

As with plumbing, there are a number of components and materials on the market that simplify the wire-to-wire connections and transitions involved in remodeling. Use only approved components, and never attempt a connection you're not completely sure of.

Wire-to-Wire Connections

Of obvious importance is how to properly join two wires. If you are connecting wires of the same material, such as copper to copper or aluminum to aluminum, the wire nut is probably the easiest and most secure connection method. Wire nuts are available in a variety of sizes, depending on the gauge of the wire and the number of wires being joined. After you have stripped the insulation from the ends of each of the conductors, twist the bare ends together with a pair of pliers. Place the proper-sized wire nut over the ends, and twist it firmly into place. No bare wire should be visible after the wire nut is attached.

Should you need to join copper and aluminum wires together, you must take care to use a connector that keeps the two wires from touching. The two most common methods are the split-bolt connector and the junction block.

The *split-bolt connector* is a special bolt with a long slot cut in the shaft. Insert the wires to be joined into the slot. The wires are kept separated by a small, sliding metal plate. Tighten a nut onto the shaft, sandwiching the wires and the plate to make the connection. Then securely wrap the bolt with electrical tape.

The *junction block* is simply a metal bar with setscrews. Insert the wires into holes in the block, and tighten down the setscrews to hold them in place. The blocks are designed so that the holes are separated by metal, keeping the wires from touching. Both the split-bolt connector and the junction block are suitable for joining copper to copper or aluminum to aluminum.

When you are connecting aluminum wire to anything, whether to a junction block, a terminal, or an appliance, it's important to coat the exposed wire with a special compound to prevent oxidation. Most compounds are a thick, greaselike substance, and all you need to do is spread some on the wire

before you make the connection.

Grounding Connections

For making ground connections within an outlet box, the easiest method is to use a crimp sleeve, also known as a *bullet connector* because of its resemblance to a small shell casing. Slip two or more ground wires into the sleeve. Then, crimp down the sleeve with a standard crimping tool to make the connection.

To ground a metal box, two methods are common. One is to use a *ground clip*, a simple spring steel clip that snaps over the side of the box, trapping the ground wire against the box for a positive connection. The second is to use a *pigtail*, a short, green-coated wire attached to a green screw. Drive the screw into a threaded hole on the back of the box, marked *gr* on most boxes. Tie the other end of the wire in with the rest of the grounds in the box.

For attaching a ground wire to a galvanized or copper water pipe, a special ground clamp is available. Place the two serrated jaws of the clamp on either side of the pipe, then secure the clamp with the two attached screws. Insert the ground wire into a hole on the top of the clamp, and use a setscrew to hold it in place.

Two sizes of ground clamps are commonly available: small, for 1/2-, 3/4-, and 1-inch pipe; and large, for 1 1/4-, 1 1/2-, and 2-inch pipe. A different ground clamp is used for securing a ground wire to a rod that has been driven into the earth. This type of clamp is merely a metal ring with an attached bolt, which is slipped over the rod. The wire goes between the rod and the ring, and both are held in place by tightening the bolt.

To provide grounding protection for threaded, rigid-metal conduit, bonding bushings are available. These bushings have an attached grounding screw. (See Fig. 17-6.) The bushing is screwed onto the end of the conduit above the locknut, then a ground wire can be run from any convenient ground source to the screw terminal on the bushing. Bond bushings are commonly used on the underground feeder conduit that is connected to a service panel.

Conduit and Cable Connectors

The number of connectors and fittings designed for use with the various types of conduit and electrical cables is extensive, and can vary considerably with the requirements of each individual installation.

Cable connectors, also known as *Romex connectors* or *looms,* provide a means of entering the box without contacting the rough sides of the knockout hole, and also provide a clamp for securing the cable to the box. After you have removed an appropriate knockout from the box or panel, insert the threaded end of the connector into the hole, and secure it from the inside with the locknut. Then feed the cable through the connector into the box, and secure it in place by tightening down the two screws on the attached clamp. A variety of sizes are available to accommodate different knockout and cable sizes. Plastic and metal snap-in connectors are also available, as are double connectors, which allow two cables to enter the box through the same knockout.

The three most common types of conduit used in residential wiring are electromechanical tubing (commonly known as EMT or thinwall), flexible conduit, and Sealtite. Each has its own specific connector, but all work basically the same way. After you have removed the desired knockout, secure the connector to the box with a locknut, then secure the conduit to the connector. Standard thinwall connectors and flex connectors use one or more setscrews to lock the conduit in place, while weathertight thinwall and Sealtite connectors use a compression ring and washer with a locknut to ensure a watertight seal.

As sometimes happens, a knockout might be removed from a box or panel in error, or perhaps the only unused knockouts available in the box are too large for the fitting you wish to use. Knockout plugs, available in all the standard knockout sizes, can be used to seal off an unneeded hole. For a hole that's too large, knockout reducing rings are available in a variety of standard size combinations. The rings are used in pairs—one inside the box and one outside—and are held in place by the connector and locknut.

Electrical Boxes

Most basic metal electrical boxes can be converted for a variety of applications through the use of specially designed adapters. For example, you can use a standard four square box as a junction box by adding a blank cover, or as a receptacle box by fitting it with a single or double plaster ring.

Use metal hanger bars to adapt a box for use with a light fixture, or to allow it to be placed between studs. Spread apart the adjustable bar and secure it to the joists or studs, then attach the box to the bar with a locknut through the box's rear center knockout. Then slide the box along the bar to the desired location, and lock it in place by tightening the nut. Open-back extension rings are made in sizes to mate with most standard metal boxes. They are used when remodeling increases the thickness of a wall, or when extra capacity is required to accommodate additional wiring.

ADDING A NEW CIRCUIT

If your addition requires new circuits and you've either updated the panel or determined that its capacity is adequate to handle the increased load, you might wish to undertake the installation of the new circuits yourself. In most cases, installing new circuits is a fairly straightforward procedure. As mentioned earlier, however, never undertake an installation you're not completely comfortable with, and always have the electrical inspector check it for safety.

Wire

Wire size and type are important considerations when you are installing a new circuit, so a working knowledge of how wire is described will be helpful. An individual wire, called a *conductor,* is rated by its diameter, or *gauge,* according to American Wire Gauge (AWG) standards. The larger the gauge number, the smaller the wire. When two or more conductors are grouped together in a common outer jacket, they form a *cable.* Cables are designated by wire gauge, number of wires in the cable, insulation type, and inclusion or exclusion of a ground wire.

Generally speaking, most 120-volt circuits will require three wires: one hot (black), one neutral (white), and one ground (green or bare). A 240-volt circuit usually will need one more hot wire (commonly red). In recent years, these combinations of individual conductors have been grouped together into cables and bound by another layer of thermoplastic insulation for ease in handling and more resistance to damage. Technically named *nonmetallic sheathed cable,* or type NM, you will often hear it referred to by the trade name Romex. When you are ordering this type of cable, refer to it by gauge first, then number of conductors, then whether or not you wish a ground wire; for example, "12/2 with ground."

Circuit Size

You will need to determine the specific requirements for the circuit you wish to install. The first thing to decide is how big the circuit must be, in terms of amperes. General lighting and plug circuits are usually 15 amps, and kitchen circuits are usually 20 amps. If you are installing a special-use circuit, such as one for a specific tool or appliance, you can determine the circuit size from the manufacturer's specifications. The required amperage is given on a plate attached to the unit itself, or in the instructions accompanying the unit. If the amperage is not given but wattage is, use the formula:

$$\text{Watts} \div \text{Volts} = \text{Amps}$$

The proper circuit breaker and gauge of wire are the next considerations. Circuit breakers are rated and labeled according to the maximum amount of amperage they can be used with, and are commonly found in 15-, 20-, 30-, 40-, 50-, and 60-amp sizes for most branch circuits. Using the amperage determined earlier, select a breaker that is rated as close to that amperage as possible, but no smaller. Therefore, a circuit requiring 12 amps would use a 15-amp breaker, but a circuit of 16 amps would need a 20-amp breaker.

Because the types and styles of breakers available on the market vary widely among brands, it is best to note the manufacturer and the general size and shape of the existing breakers (a simple sketch might help). Take this information to any electrical or hardware store, where the staff will be able to select the right one for your service panel.

The amperage of the circuit breaker determines the size of the wire:

15 amps	14 gauge
20 amps	12 gauge
30 amps	10 gauge
40 amps	8 gauge
50 amps	6 gauge

(Note: These gauges are for standard thermoplastic insulated copper wires.)

Conduit and Cable

Your decision on the type of wire to use is dependent on how you intend to get from the panel to the location of the new unit. In general terms, there are three different ways in which you can get a wire from one place to another. The easiest and least expensive method is to use Type NM cable, running it where the cable will be concealed from weather and abrasion.

If the wire must be installed outside or in a place where normal activities might subject it to damage, you must encase it in conduit. Conduit is available in several different forms, again dependent on where it will be used, and in diameters of 1/2 inch up to 6 inches. For areas where a high degree of support or impact resistance is needed, use rigid metal conduit, which is used just like metal plumbing pipe. Burial and some outdoor uses require rigid plastic conduit, which is joined by either threaded fittings or glued, slip-fit connectors. Flexible metal conduit can be used in areas where a number of bends or angles will be encountered, and is commonly referred to as *flex* for indoor use, and *Sealtite* for outside or wet locations.

Probably the most commonly used type of conduit is EMT, usually called *thinwall*. Thinwall conduit is a light, inexpensive metal tube that easily can be cut and bent to shape as needed. Cut it with a hacksaw, then use a round file to remove any burrs inside the cut end that might damage the wire being pulled through it. Use a conduit bender when you are bending the tube to avoid crimping it.

For short runs of conduit or for transitions, such as running cable exposed in the attic and then entering conduit to come down a wall, Type NM cable will work fine. For longer runs, it is much easier to pull the wires through the conduit if you use individual conductors, which eliminates the bulk of the cable's outer jacket. The most common type of wire for this use is Type TW (thermoplastic weather-resistant), and is available in the same gauges and colors as the conductors used in Type NM.

The third method is burial. Depending on local frost and soil conditions, and any building code restrictions, you can bury rigid plastic conduit or directly bury the cable. A special sunlight- and weather-resistant cable is made for this application. In this cable, called Type UF (underground feeder), the conductors are encased in solid plastic. This is the only type of cable you should use for direct burial.

Wire or cable of almost any type can be bought by the foot, or by the box, usually in 100-, 250-, and 500-foot lengths. Buying it by the box is cheaper and more convenient, unless you have no use for what is left over.

Often, especially in remodeling work, a combination of two or three of these methods is necessary. Your considerations include the easiest and most direct route to the panel, and the way you will enter the panel itself once you get there.

Installation Procedures

Type NM cable can be run in the walls, attic, underfloor, or any other protected area. (See Fig. 17-9.) When you are running the cable through walls, you should drill holes in the center of the stud, to eliminate the chance of the wire being damaged by a nail when you install the siding or drywall.

In the attic or under the floor, use cable staples to secure the cable neatly along the joists, out of the way of potential contact. Most building codes require that cables installed in attics be run in areas

Fig. 17-9. Type NM cable, here being used overhead for a fluorescent light fixture.

with 3 feet or less of headroom, to prevent possible damage from being stepped on.

Leave at least 6 inches of excess where the cable enters a box to allow for hookups. Secure the cable within 8 inches of the box with a cable staple, and do not use the same staple to secure more than one wire. (See Fig. 17-10.)

Before you start any work on the panel itself, shut the power off by switching off the main service disconnect breaker. Next, remove the protective metal cover to expose the wiring inside. (See Fig. 17-11.) Then, decide through which knockout you wish to enter the panel, and remove it.

If you're using cable to enter a flush-mount panel, snap a metal or plastic cable connector into the hole. For a conduit installation, attach the conduit to the panel which an appropriate conduit connector, and secure the conduit to the wall using straps. Then simply pass the cable through the conduit into the panel. Remember that you will need at least 2 to 3 feet of cable at the panel for hookups.

Snap the new circuit breaker onto the bus bars.

Fig. 17-10. Securing type NM cable to the studs next to an outlet box.

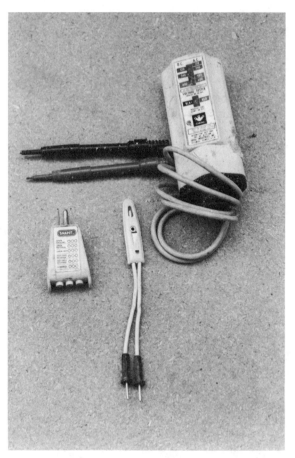

Fig. 17-11. Electrical test equipment for checking whether a circuit is live. The plug-in tester, left, also will tell if a circuit is correctly polarized and grounded. The simple tester in the center will light up if a circuit is live. The professional tester, right, also can determine the amount of voltage in the circuit.

Next, strip the outside jacket from the cable, then route the hot wire(s) to the breaker. A single-pole, 120-volt breaker will have one screw for the single hot wire, while a double-pole, 240-volt breaker will have two screws. It doesn't matter which screw gets which hot wire. Use wire strippers to strip off about 3/8 inch of insulation, and secure the wire(s) under the screw(s). Route the neutral and ground wires to the neutral bar, and secure them under any unused screws on the bar. If you're using one of the larger types of cable, such as Type SE (service entrance), the conductors might be aluminum instead of copper. If so, use great care not to nick the wires when you are stripping off the insulation, and remember to dip the exposed wires in a corrosion inhibitor before securing them under their respective screws.

Remove the appropriate knockout from the panel cover to accommodate the new breaker, then replace the cover. Be sure to label indelibly on the cover what circuit the new breaker controls.

PREPARING FOR INSPECTIONS

Electrical malfunctions are a major cause of residential fires, so electrical codes and inspections can be pretty strict. Remember that the electrical inspectors are there to ensure your safety. Pay close attention to any suggestions they might make or corrections they might require, and don't hesitate to ask questions if you are not completely sure of something. The following checklist will help you prepare for the rough wiring inspection and minimize any mistakes. Show it to the building department when you take out your electrical permit and have them check it against local code requirements for your area.

- ☐ Exterior walls are enclosed on the outside, and the roof and roofing are completed.
- ☐ On the common wall between the house and the garage, all boxes are metal and not over 16 square inches in size. All penetrations are properly sealed.
- ☐ Receptacle outlets are provided: within 6 feet of the start and finish of any wall, with at least one every 12 feet thereafter; on any usable wall space 2 feet wide or greater; on counter spaces 12 inches wide or greater in kitchens and dining rooms; in bathrooms adjacent to the sink; outside (at least one); in the basement and attached garage; in the laundry area.
- ☐ Separate branch circuits are provided: 20 amp for laundry; 15 amp lighting circuit for each 500 square feet of floor or fraction thereof; 20 amp for dishwasher and/or garbage disposal; minimum 15 amp for furnace motor; 30 amp for clothes dryer; minimum of two 20-amp small appliance circuits for receptacles in the kitchen, pantry, breakfast room, dining room, and family room. Divide the receptacles evenly between the two circuits.
- ☐ Nonmetallic sheathed cable is supported within 8 inches of the boxes and at intervals not exceeding 4 1/2 feet.
- ☐ Outlet boxes are of sufficient size to provide free space for all of the conductors. Use a box with at least 2 cubic inches of capacity for #14 AWG wire, 2.25 cubic inches for #12 AWG.
- ☐ Six inches of free conductor are provided at each box for connections.
- ☐ Ground fault circuit interrupter (GFCI) receptacles are installed on all outdoor and bathroom outlets.

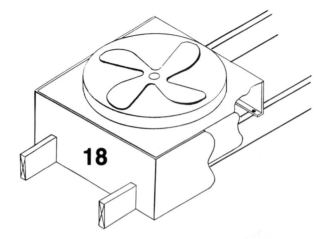

18

Heating, Ventilating, and Air Conditioning

The heating, ventilating, and air conditioning systems within a home, known collectively as the *HVAC system* or simply as the mechanical equipment, comprise the entire system of air-handling and air-conditioning equipment. This equipment varies widely from house to house, and includes the furnace, permanent room heaters, ducts, fans, vents, filters, humidifiers, and other related equipment. Portable appliances such as movable room heaters and window air conditioners usually do not fall within the HVAC system, although permanently mounted room air conditioners will be included in this chapter.

Heating and cooling systems fall into two broad catagories: central and zone. *Central systems* have one, or in larger homes more than one, centrally located furnace or air conditioning units, which supply conditioned air to the entire home through a series of air ducts. Zone systems have several individual, independently controlled units, which treat the air in one room or area of the house.

The type of heating and air conditioning system you intend to use in the addition depends primarily on the size and type of the existing heating system, and the size of the addition. Unlike many of the other considerations in the construction of the addition, what you use in the new rooms does not necessarily need to be an extension of the existing system.

CENTRAL SYSTEMS

The furnace currently being used in your home might be fueled by electricity, gas, oil, coal, or wood. The fuel is supplied to a central furnace unit and consumed to heat the air within the furnace, which is then fan-forced or gravity-fed into the rooms through ducts. Cool air is taken from within the house and returned to the furnace for reheating, ensuring a continuous supply and cycle of heated air.

In some systems, water takes the place of air as the heat-delivery medium. The furnace heats the water and delivers it, as a hot liquid or in the form of steam, though a series of closed pipes to individual radiators in the rooms. This system depends largely on the proper balance between the room units for efficient operation. Adding to these systems should be done only under the inspection and guidance of a professional.

Central air conditioning is electrically powered, and most commonly uses a *split system,* with an indoor evaporator unit located in the furnace plenum and an exterior condensing unit. The two separate units are connected by two large, flexible copper tubes. A refrigerant, usually Freon, is circulated through the system via the tubes. The refrigerant enters the evaporator as a liquid, where it is allowed to expand and change state into a gas. The expansion process draws heat from the surrounding air, and the resulting cooled air is blown into the house through the ducts. The refrigerant leaves the house as a gas to enter the outdoor unit, where a compressor compresses it back into a liquid. The compression process causes the refrigerant to give off its heat, and a condensor distributes that heat to the surrounding outside air. As a liquid again, the refrigerant passes back into the house to repeat the process.

Heat pumps, a relatively new and energy-efficient innovation, use this same process in reverse to heat the house. Air, even in frigid temperatures, contains a certain amount of heat energy. The expansion process of the refrigerant draws this heat from the outside air and circulates it into the house. Backup electric heaters, which are contained within the unit and come on in stages, provide auxiliary heat as needed in periods of extreme cold. The process can be reversed in the summer, allowing the heat pump to act as an air conditioner also. (See Fig. 18-1.)

If your home is equipped with a central heating system of adequate capacity, the simplest method of heating the addition is to extend new ducts off the existing system as needed. This method requires no expensive new equipment, and the new duct runs are a fairly simple matter for the do-it-yourselfer. In the event of a very large addi-

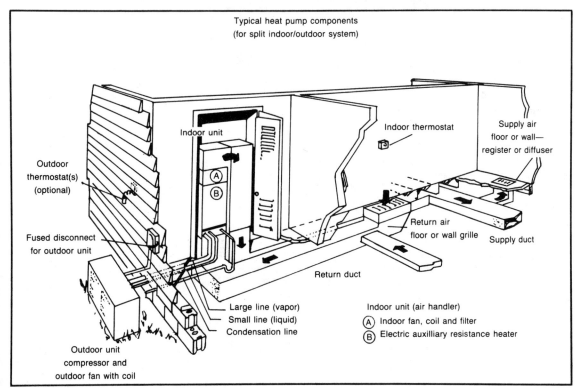

Fig. 18-1. The basic operation of a heat pump (Courtesy of Pacific Power and Light).

tion, say one of over 1,000 square feet, a whole new central system dedicated to the addition would be the best choice.

Furnace Capacity

As with the electrical system, the key factor is system capacity. You will need to determine if the furnace is large enough to handle the addition, and at what point to tie into the duct work.

The furnaces originally installed in many homes were somewhat oversized to compensate for heat losses through uninsulated areas and through leaks around windows, doors, and other areas. This additional capacity, on the average, is enough to heat two additional bedrooms. Whether or not this extra capacity actually exists, however, is not always easy to determine.

One indicator is how well your furnace has performed in the past. Has it always been capable of easily maintaining a comfortable temperature in the house, or does the furnace seem to always be running while the house remains chilly?

Another factor is how much energy-related work has been performed on the house in the past. Have the attic and underfloor areas been insulated? Has weatherstripping been applied to all the doors and windows? Has caulking been carefully applied wherever potential air leaks were spotted? In an older home, the furnace had to be oversized to compensate for all this loss. Stopping the loss enables the furnace to work more efficiently, and often can give it the extra capacity for handling new areas.

Different sizing rules apply for different furnace types. For example, a rule of thumb for electric furnaces is to allow 10 to 12 watts of furnace capacity for each square foot of floor area, which in an energy-efficient house can be as much as twice the capacity needed. If you have an electric furnace, check the wattage on the furnace nameplate, then compare it to the square footage of the house, both with and without the addition. Other sizing formulas are available from the utility company that supplies your furnace fuel.

When in doubt, your best bet is to consult with a heating contractor. For a modest service call fee, he can examine the furnace, evaluate both its ca-

pacity and its condition, and advise you on the feasibility of adding a new duct run.

Duct Systems

There are two types of duct systems commonly employed in residential installations: the *radial,* or *perimeter system,* and the *extended plenum system.* Take a moment to familiarize yourself with the layout of your duct system, and determine where each of the ducts go and what they do.

A radial system (Fig. 18-2) consists of registers placed around the building's outside walls, usually under a window so that the warm air can counteract the natural convection currents around the cold

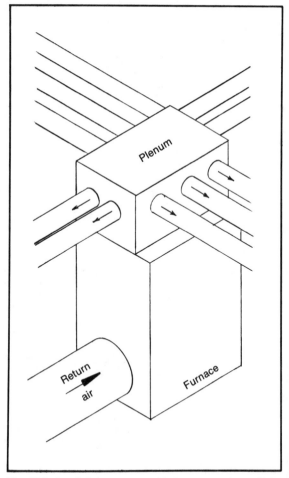

Fig. 18-2. A radial duct system. All ducts extend out off the plenum.

glass. Each register is served by a duct that extends directly off the *plenum chamber* (the warm air distribution box attached to the outlet side of the furnace) in as straight a line as possible. In some cases, one large duct might extend out from the plenum and branch into two smaller ducts for individual registers. This system, because of its economy of fittings and labor, is the most common.

In the extended plenum system (Fig. 18-3), a large rectangular duct extends off the plenum, usually in a straight line that runs the length of the building. Individual ducts extend off this main plenum duct to serve each register. This type of system offers less resistance to air flow and easier arrangement of the registers, and is more common in larger buildings with greater heat requirements.

Each of these systems have two types of ducts:

supply ducts and *return ducts*. Supply ducts carry the warm air from the furnace to the rooms. They can be identified as extending off the supply, or *outlet,* side of the furnace. They also will feel warm when the furnace is operating. Supply ducts, or the plenum on the supply side of the furnace, are the starting points for a new duct run.

Return ducts carry cool air from the house to the furnace for reheating. These ducts attach to the return, or *inlet,* side of the furnace, and feel cool. In many houses there is only one, large-diameter, centrally located return duct, which serves the entire house. Larger homes might have two or more returns. If you are adding duct runs to an existing furnace and the addition is fairly large, you also should consider adding a new return duct from the addition to ensure best circulation.

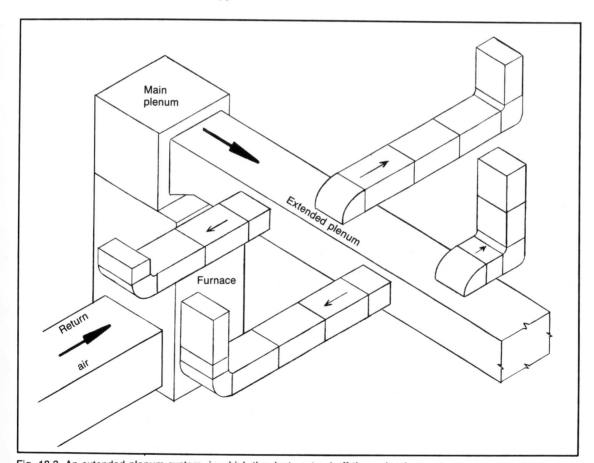

Fig. 18-3. An extended plenum system, in which the ducts extend off the main plenum duct.

ADDING A NEW DUCT RUN

If you've determined that the furnace has the capacity to handle the new ducts, you'll next need to map out the duct runs and determine their sizes. Duct sizing is critical to proper performance, and must take into consideration the size of the area being heated, the length of the run, and the number and type of fittings.

First, carefully study the layout of the existing furnace, and determine at what points you can tap into the system. For a radial system, new ducts must originate directly from the plenum. Each of the existing ducts is carefully sized to handle only the room it's supplying, and would not have the capacity for another duct. Extended plenum systems, on the other hand, can be tapped anywhere along the main plenum duct.

Next, determine where you will place the registers. Consider the room's size and layout, doors and traffic patterns, and, in the case of floor registers, furniture placement. Try to establish a location where the incoming heat will best circulate into the room. With the starting point on the plenum and the location of the registers in mind, lay out the duct run. The run should be as straight as possible because each elbow and fitting causes a friction loss in the air movement through it. If the losses are high enough, you must use larger ducts to compensate for them. Make a sketch of the intended run, including all necessary turns, all joist locations, the direction of the run, and all appropriate dimensions.

You'll need to take this sketch, along with information on the sizes of the rooms and the size of the furnace, to a heating supply outlet or sheet-metal shop. Consult with a specialist to verify if your existing furnace has the capacity to service the additional area, and have him determine the number and size of the ducts and registers necessary for the addition. He has the necessary charts and formulas for figuring out the friction loss for each fitting, and can perform the calculations you need quickly and accurately. You might be charged a small fee for all these calculations, but it's worth it. In many cases, the fee will be credited to you if you buy your supplies from that shop.

Your new duct run will consist of four basic components: the *starter* or *take-off collar*, a sheet-metal fitting which connects the duct pipe to the plenum; a *register boot*, which makes the transition from the duct pipe to the register; the *register*, which is the visible grill that directs and controls the air flow; and the *duct pipe*, with any necessary elbows or other fittings. The shop where you are purchasing your supplies can provide you with all the necessary components.

Starting and Ending the Run

Begin the installation by marking the size of the boot on the floor or ceiling, then check the attic or underfloor area for obstructions. Drill a hole in each corner of the marked area, and use a jigsaw to cut out the opening. Fit the boot into the hole with the duct inlet opening facing back toward the furnace. Secure the boot to the joists, providing wooden backing between the joists if necessary. Secure the register over the boot with screws. For floor registers, it's a good idea to caulk the area between the boot and the floor to prevent the entry of cold air from under the house.

If you have a radial system, select a convenient area on the plenum chamber and mark the size of the starter collar. Place the edge of a screwdriver blade against the sheet metal in the center of the marked area, and tap it with a hammer. This procedure will start a hole in the plenum, allowing you access to cut out the rest of the opening with sheet-metal snips. The plenum might be lined with rigid insulation, which you must cut out with a utility knife, taking care that the cutout doesn't fall back into the furnace. Insert the starter collar into the hole until its raised shoulder is flat against the plenum, then reach into the collar and secure it by bending the tabs back against inside of the plenum.

If you have an extended plenum system, mark the location of the take-off collar on the main plenum duct, and cut it out as just outlined. Place the flange on the bottom of the collar into the hole until the upper flange rests on the duct. Reach into the collar and bend the flanges over, then secure the collar to the duct by placing sheet-metal screws through the outer flanges.

The final step in installing the new run is to connect the duct pipe between the collar and the boot. There are two types of pipe to choose from—rigid and flexible—each with its own advantages and disadvantages. Choose whichever type is better suited to the particular installation.

Rigid Pipe

Rigid pipe is sturdy and inexpensive, but requires the use of elbows for each change in direction. The pipe comes in various lengths and diameters, and is shipped opened out with a locking snap seam along the edges (Fig. 18-4). Cut the pipe with sheet-metal snips while it still opened out, then form it into a round pipe and secure it by snapping the lock edges together. Once snapped, the connection is permanent, and any further cutting must be done carefully with a hacksaw. Each length of pipe has one straight end and one crimped end. Crimping the end of the pipe allows it to slip into the straight end of the next pipe or fitting for making connections. If the crimped end is cut off, use a pair of crimping pliers to make a new end that can be inserted into the next pipe. Always assemble the pipe so that the crimped end is facing away from the furnace.

Adjustable elbows, movable to any angle from 0 to 90 degrees, are the fitting most commonly used for direction changes. All pipe-to-pipe and pipe-to-fitting connections are joined with sheet-metal screws. Use three screws per connection, equally spaced around the diameter of the pipe. After assembly, seal all of the joints, including the snap-lock seams, with a good-quality duct tape to prevent heat loss through the connections.

Horizontal runs of rigid pipe should be supported at least every 10 feet. Perforated metal plumber's tape works well for this application. Wrap the tape around the pipe once, leaving one long end. Secure the tape to itself by placing a screw and nut through two overlapping holes, or by weaving an 8d nail through the holes. Then support the duct pipe by nailing the long end of the tape to the joists.

Flexible Pipe

Flexible pipe is essentially a long, spiraling coil of wire lined with plastic sheeting on the inside and

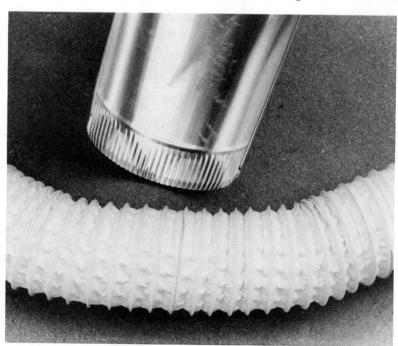

Fig. 18-4. Rigid and flexible pipe.

insulation on the outside (Fig. 18-5). It is more expensive than rigid pipe, and has a somewhat higher degree of friction loss, but its flexibility eliminates the need for elbows. No special tools are required, and it's the easiest pipe for the do-it-yourselfer to work with.

The pipe is joined to itself and to fittings with a special collar, which comes attached to one end of each pipe. The other end is a crimped sheet-metal collar similar to the end of a rigid pipe. Slip the crimped end of one pipe or fitting into the collar, and tighten it down with a screwdriver. Seal all joints with duct tape.

Because of its flexibility, care must be taken to keep the duct extended out straight. Do not allow it to become crimped. You must support

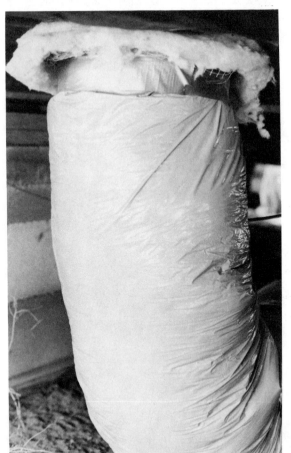

Fig. 18-5. A flexible heating and cooling duct.

horizontal runs every 4 feet with 2-inch-wide sheet-metal or plastic strapping. Plumber's tape is too narrow, and will cause the pipe to crease around it, partially obstructing the air flow.

TRANSITION AND CONNECTION FITTINGS

Many fittings for use with round, square, and rectangular sheet-metal pipe are available prefabricated in standard sizes and configurations. Special fittings can be made up inexpensively at a sheet-metal shop.

Among the standard fittings to be found in many plumbing supply and heating and air conditioning supply outlets are starter collars and take-off collars, which are available for all standard round and rectangular duct sizes.

Connections between ducts can be made in a number of ways. Straight connectors will attach two lengths of equal-diameter flexible or rigid pipe, or use a reducer to connect two unequal sizes. Square-to-round transitions are used when going from square or rectangular pipe to round pipes of various diameters. Several different size combinations of both the reducer and the square-to-round are available.

T and Y fittings allow the installation of runs that branch off from a main line. They can be purchased with all the outlets of equal diameter, or with different diameters to allow a size transition to be made for the branch run. For direction changes, you can use adjustable elbows, which give you an infinite variety of angles from 0 (straight) to 90 degrees (Fig. 18-6).

For heating or air conditioning ducts, standard size boots simplify the transition from a round duct pipe to a rectangular register. They are made in several different combinations of round and rectangular sizes to fit standard duct and register dimensions. Various styles are available depending upon the intended application, including straight, end, and 90-degree configurations.

BASIC HEATING SYSTEM MAINTENANCE

Adding a new duct increases the load on the furnace, and this is a good time to perform some main-

Fig. 18-6. An adjustable sheet-metal elbow.

tenance on the heating system. Routine maintenance, no matter how simple, will keep the system working at peak efficiency and minimize energy use.

Heat Anticipators

The basic function of the thermostat is to sense when the temperature of the air in the room falls below a certain, preset level. When it does, a low-voltage electrical signal is sent to the furnace, turning it on. The furnace warms the air to the desired level, which is again read by the thermostat. Then another signal is sent which turns the furnace off.

In actual practice, the operation of the thermostat is a little more involved. If the thermostat simply told the furnace to come on when it got too

cold, the fan would begin blowing while the burners were still warming up, forcing cold air into the house. Likewise, if the furnace got the command to stop at the moment the thermostat read the right temperature, warm air still rising from the burners after they shut down would cause the room temperature to rise higher than the desired setting.

Both these situations affect the home's comfort level, and also waste energy. This is where the heat anticipator (Fig. 18-7) comes into play. When the air temperature drops below the preset level, the burners alone are activated. When temperatures inside the furnace reach a certain point, the fan is triggered to begin circulating the warmed air into the house. The anticipator reads the rising temperature, and signals the burners to shut down in advance of reaching the desired room temperature, allowing the fan to continue pushing the warm air still in the furnace into the room, achieving the preset temperature. As the furnace air temperature drops, the fan shuts off automatically.

In order to work properly, the heat anticipator needs to be set correctly. Remove the cover from the thermostat. Inside you will see a small dial or

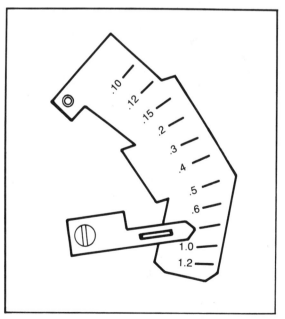

Fig. 18-7. A typical thermostat heat anticipator. The numbers indicate amperage settings.

scale with a pointer next to it. The scale is marked in amps, usually ranging from .10 to around 1.2. Move the pointer until it indicates the proper setting, which is equal to the amperage of your furnace's primary control circuit. This amperage is listed on the furnace's specification plate, or in the owner's manual. If you can't find it, call the dealer and request the correct setting.

Cleaning

Shut off the power, and remove the front cover or inspection plates from the furnace. Using a shop vacuum or a small broom, clean out the accumulation of dust and dirt from around the fan and the heat elements. Check carefully for frayed wires or loose connections, and call a serviceman for repairs if you encounter any. Check the filter to see if it needs to be replaced, then reinstall the covers.

Next, go to each room and remove the registers. Clean each one thoroughly with a brush or vacuum, and then vacuum any accumulated dust out of the boot. If your registers have movable louvers, check them for proper operation, adjusting or lightly oiling them if necessary. Check the return air grill also, vacuuming out any dust. Some types have a filter here, too, so replace it if necessary.

Energy experts have proven that a substantial amount of heat loss occurs in and around the duct system of a forced air furnace, particularly if the ducts are located under the floor. If you have floor registers, remove them and check the area where the floor has been cut out to accommodate the sheet-metal boot. Chances are you'll find gaps between the metal and the wood, substantial ones in some cases. These gaps let cold air enter from the crawl space, so close them up with sealant, preferably from underneath (Fig. 18-8). Because of the expansion and contraction of the sheet-metal boots, it's best to use a flexible silicone sealant.

Check the boots and the duct pipes. All the joints should be securely covered with duct tape, and the entire system should be wrapped with insulation.

ZONE HEATING SYSTEMS

A good alternative to installing new ducts in a room addition is to use zone heaters. Individually installed and controlled, these heaters allow one room or zone to be heated independently of the others. They are easy and convenient to install, and provide only the heat that's necessary for that zone, which is good from both a comfort and cost standpoint. In addition, they are quite inexpensive when compared to an entire new central system.

Zone heaters are available in a wide range of

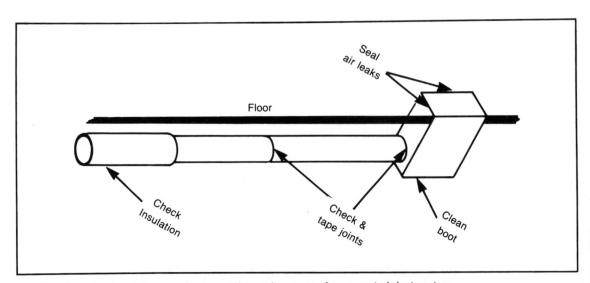

Fig. 18-8. Some of the routine maintenance points to be aware of on a central duct system.

types, and styles, and most can be installed easily by the do-it-yourselfer. Depending on the type, they can be installed just about anywhere, including the walls, floor, ceiling, or even in cabinets.

Electric Systems

The most commonly used zone heaters for remodeling situations are electric. They are easy to install, requiring the running of only a single cable. They are also quiet, and clean, and require no ducting. There are several forms of electric heaters, each suited to a particular application.

Baseboard Heaters. A baseboard heater is a long, strip heater, ranging in length from 2 to 8 feet. Several units can be joined end to end for longer runs. They are attached to the wall at floor level, like a baseboard. Some types have a thermostat built into the heater; other types are wired through a wall thermostat which operates on either low or line voltage. Split systems for heating and cooling are also available (Fig. 18-9).

Wall Heaters. A wall heater is a square or rectangular unit, with a wide range of sizes and wattages. It consists of a small fan, which blows over a resistance coil, and has either an attached or a separate thermostat. Most wall heaters have three main components: the can (Fig. 18-10), which is installed in the wall during the rough wiring stage; the heat and fan element unit (Fig. 18-11), which is installed in the can; and the finish trim panel (Fig. 18-12). Wall heaters can be installed in virtually any wall, and one model is made to fit in the toe kick underneath a cabinet.

Ceiling Heaters. A variation of the wall heater, a ceiling heater is a small, fan-forced unit that is recessed into the ceiling, especially in bathrooms. Some types are made up in combination with a light or an exhaust fan.

Radiant Heaters. Radiant heaters take the form of either cables placed in the ceiling, or decorative wall- or ceiling-mounted panels. They rely on the natural radiation of heat from a warm surface to a cold one, and provide a very gentle, silent source of heat. Their only disadvantages is that anything blocked from a direct line of sight to the heater will not be warmed.

Cove Heaters. A relatively new type of radiant heater, the cove heater is a long strip with a concave face, designed to be placed on the wall where it meets the ceiling. Cove heaters are usually white to blend in unobtrusively with the surrounding wall and ceiling. Once again, they heat only objects in a direct line of sight.

Hydronic Systems

Hot-water, or *hydronic,* heaters offer yet another alternative. Available primarily in baseboard or wall-mounted units, they tap the home's hot-water plumbing system as a source of heat. Hot water passes through coils within the unit, warming a series of heat exchanger fins. A fan blowing across the fins extracts the heat and forces it into the room. Although still relatively easy to install, they do involve some plumbing work, and should be located as close to a hot-water line as possible for maximum efficiency.

The unit can be tapped into the house plumbing in one of three ways. If the home is heated with hot water already, it can be tapped into the supply and return lines coming from the boiler. For an existing steam heat system, the piping is installed below the normal water level. It draws off hot water from the boiler, but is low enough that steam will not be drawn in.

The third method, for homes with heat sources other than hot water or steam, is to tie into the domestic hot-water lines. A T is placed in any convenient hot-water pipe to supply the heater. The return line from the heater ties into the cold-water line where it enters the water heater. A check valve is installed on the return line to prevent cold water from being drawn into the heater when it's not in operation.

FIREPLACES AND WOODSTOVES

Wood has been a source of home heat since man's earliest days, and it is still popular today. Depending on the type of addition you're building, wood heat might be worth considering. Wood heat can take the form of a primary heat source, back-up heat on especially cold days to take some of the load

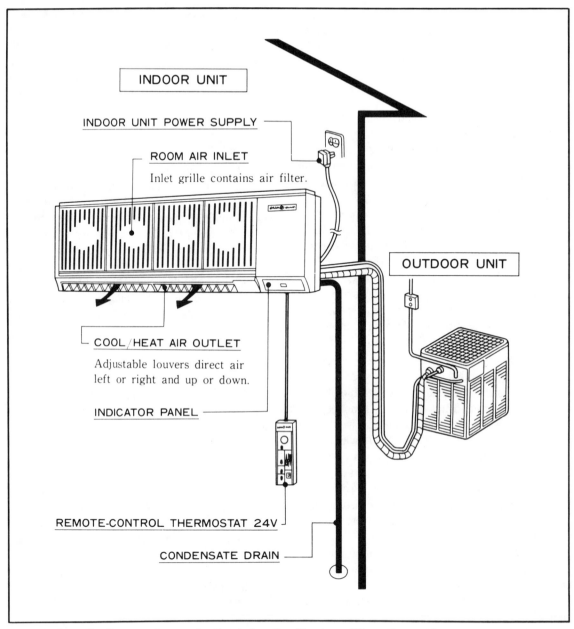

INDOOR UNIT

INDOOR UNIT POWER SUPPLY

ROOM AIR INLET

Inlet grille contains air filter.

OUTDOOR UNIT

COOL/HEAT AIR OUTLET

Adjustable louvers direct air
left or right and up or down.

INDICATOR PANEL

REMOTE-CONTROL THERMOSTAT 24V

CONDENSATE DRAIN

Fig. 18-9. A small split system for zone heating and cooling (Courtesy of Trane Company).

off the other heaters, or simply as a nice addition to a room's ambiance when entertaining, or for special evenings. No matter what the source or its intended use, few things can replace the warmth and atmosphere of a wood fire.

Because of rising energy costs, wood heat has

enjoyed a fresh growth of popularity in recent years. The result is a tremendous selection of wood-burning appliances, many of which have become extremely energy efficient. When you are considering wood heat as the home's primary heat source, however, don't overlook the problems of supplying

Fig. 18-10. The enclosure for an electric wall heater.

the wood. All too often, wood heat is considered "free" after the initial purchase of the unit, but whether you purchase wood or cut it yourself, it's far from free, and you must consider these costs when you are making the final decision.

Fireplaces

The traditional wood-burning unit has always been the fireplace. For appearance and atmosphere, it can't be beat. For efficiency as a heat source, it leaves a lot to be desired.

Fireplaces draw in room air to support the combustion of the wood, and the smoke is exhausted up the chimney. As much as two-thirds of heat energy produced by burning the wood is lost directly up the chimney. In addition, the constant need for combustion air causes a slight and often uncomfortable draft across the floor of the room.

Fig. 18-11. The heat element and fan unit placed inside the enclosure.

Fig. 18-12. The trim plate and thermostat assembly.

It also takes the air you've been heating with the regular furnace and expels it up the chimney.

Traditionally, fireplaces have been built of solid masonry (Fig. 18-13), an exacting and labor-intensive task. If you are having a fireplace installed, be certain that the mason doing the work is skilled and experienced specifically in building fireplaces, since poor design and construction will

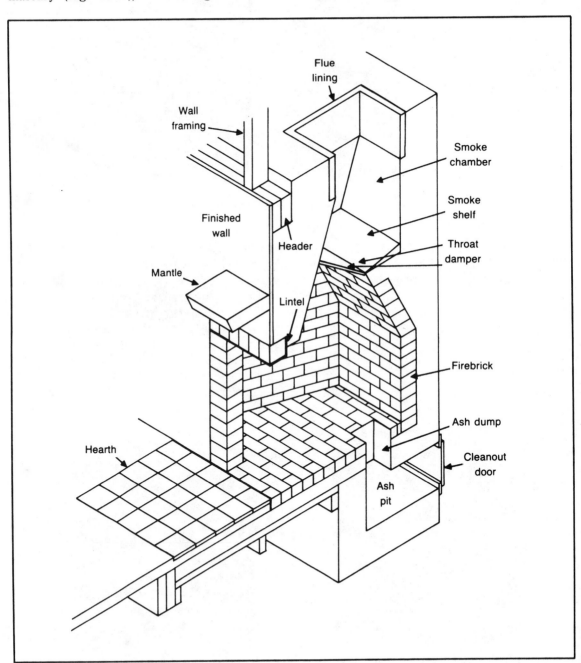

Fig. 18-13. A cross section of the complex masonry involved in constructing a fireplace.

multiply the fireplace's inherent faults.

An alternative to the solid masonry fireplace is the freestanding, or *zero-clearance*, fireplace. It is offered in many styles, and installing one is primarily a matter of setting the unit in the desired location and ducting it out through the roof. It's imperative that you follow the manufacturer's instructions for clearances, and use only approved, multiwall pipe. Installing the fireplace or the pipe too close to combustible surfaces is a major cause of household fires.

Wood Stoves

An extremely popular alternative to the fireplace is the wood stove (Fig. 18-14). Airtight and with a large metal surface area, these units make much better use of the heat energy in the wood. Fires burn longer, and much more usable heat is obtained. A tremendous variety of styles are available to suit any decor, and a popular option is the glass door, which provides energy efficiency while not sacrificing the traditional enjoyment of watching the burning wood.

Wood stoves are installed essentially like freestanding fireplaces. They must be placed on a noncombustible surface, such as a brick or synthetic hearth pad, and specific clearances must be maintained from other combustibles. Once again, special pipe is used for venting, and great care must be taken to provide the necessary clearances from wood framing. (See Fig. 18-15.)

When you are selecting the size of the woodstove, don't try to heat too large an area with it. Most units are rated by the manufacturer according to the area they theoretically will heat, and these numbers can be misleading. They rely on unobstructed access for the heat to flow from room to room. They are also sometimes based on rooms with 7-foot ceilings, which are quite uncommon in most homes but make the woodstove appear to be more efficient than it really is.

Another problem with purchasing a large woodstove is that it often will overheat the room it's in before producing enough heat to warm the rooms farthest away from it. A better sizing strategy is to place the unit in a room where a relatively con-

Fig. 18-14. An airtight wood stove with a glass door. Note the fireproof hearth pad on which the stove is sitting.

stant level of heat is desired, such as a living room or family room, and size it for the two or three rooms immediately surrounding it. Use baseboard heaters or other zone heating to warm rooms such as bedrooms, where a lower level of heat is usually desirable.

ZONE COOLING

For homes with zone heating, adding a central cooling system is usually impractical. Duct runs would be required as for a central furnace, and the mechanical equipment is quite expensive. An alter-

Fig. 18-15. A special transition fitting that maintains the proper clearance between the wood stove's flue pipe and wood framing members.

Using the case as a guide, frame the rough opening into the wall as you would a window opening. Provide an electrical outlet directly under the opening to prevent the need to run the cord for long distances. Most air conditioners require a dedicated circuit, so check with the manufacturer's instructions.

Slip the case into the opening, and position it so that the case protrudes out from the inside wall a distance equal to the thickness of the finished wall material. Secure it by screwing it into the surrounding framing. Some units come predrilled for wall mounting; others require that you drill holes through the case. Be certain you place the screws where the heads will not interfere with the operating portion of the unit as you slide it back in.

After you have completed the siding and interior wall finish, carefully caulk around the outside of the unit to seal off any air leaks. On the inside, the drywall can be taped tight to the case, or you can trim around the case with moulding that matches the rest of the interior trim.

During the winter, seal the unit to prevent cold air from working its way in through the exhaust louvers on the outside of the case. This operation can be done neatly and easily with a reusable winter cover, sized to fit the case. They can be purchased wherever you bought the air conditioner, or through several different retail and mail-order outlets. If you can't find a cover, seal the unit with heavy black plastic sheeting and duct tape.

WHOLE-HOUSE FANS

If your house seems warm and stuffy in the summer but air conditioning seems too drastic a solution, consider installing a whole-house fan (Fig. 18-16). A relative newcomer on the home improvement market, a whole-house fan can provide an alternative to expensive air conditioning, or can act side by side with your existing cooling system to cut electricity costs. It has the added advantage of providing you with a year-round ventilating system that can rapidly clear your house of smoke, odors, and that wintertime "staleness."

The operating principle is quite simple. The fan is recessed into the ceiling and covered by an un-

native, which uses the same principles of zone heating to cool by zones, is the room air conditioner. Units can be purchased in sizes that will cool small individual rooms or large, multiroom areas.

Most room air conditioners actually are designed for installation in a window, but this option has a number of drawbacks. Use of the window as a source of ventilation is lost, as is much of the natural light that the window admits. The unit is difficult to fit and seal into a window. If it is not taken out during the winter, it allows a lot of cold air to move around it. Also, in most cases, it has an unfinished, added-on look.

The alternative is to mount the unit in the wall.

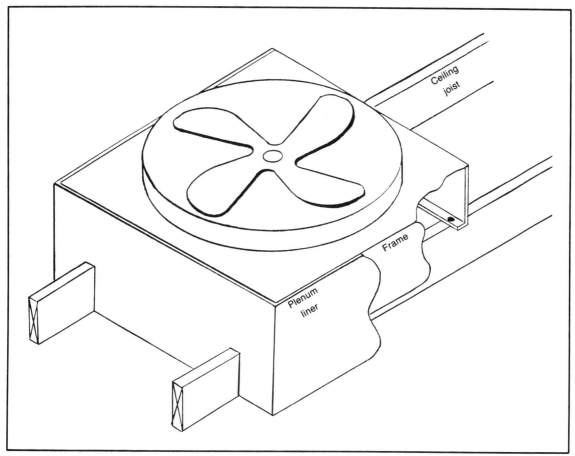

Fig. 18-16. A whole-house fan with plenum liner.

obtrusive white shutter panel. Even as the outside air temperature drops toward evening, your house retains the heat it accumulated during the day. By opening the windows and activating the fan, cool outside air is swept into the house, forced up into the attic, and out through the attic vents. The inside air temperature is lowered, both by the infusion of outside air and by the removal of hot attic air.

Several manufacturers offer these fans in kits, designed for simple installation by the average do-it-yourselfer. The most common sizes are 30 and 36 inches, and all are 120 volts for easy wiring. The 30-inch fans have a rating in the range of 5,100 to 5,500 cubic feet per minute (CFM) range, and are adequate for homes up to about 1,800 square feet. The 36-inch fans, at 6,800 to 7,000 CFM, will han-

dle homes of about 2,300 square feet. Multiple units in different areas might be required for larger homes. The fans can provide a complete change of air in the house in as little as 10 minutes, but the air movement, especially on low speed, resembles no more than a gentle breeze. The cost is comparable to a small, one-room air conditioner, and the operating costs are much lower.

A typical kit contains the fan, which is already mounted with motor and belt; the shutter panel, which contains a series of spring-loaded shutters that open and close automatically when the fan is started or stopped; a two-speed or variable-speed switch; complete installation instructions, with ceiling hole-cutting template; and an ingenious plastic plenum liner, which is the key to the unit's simple installation.

Select a location on the ceiling that is centrally located in the house for best air flow. If you're installing it in an existing ceiling, use the template supplied with the kit to mark and cut a hole in the drywall, leaving the ceiling joists exposed. Lift the fan up into the attic through the hole, center it over the opening, and fasten it to the top of the joists. Most kits provide rubber cushions, which mount between the fan's frame and the joists to provide isolation from vibration and noise. Run a wire to the unit, following the manufacturer's power requirements, and wire it into the unit's junction box.

The plenum liner simplifies the installation. Following the instructions on the liner, cut out the slots to fit your joist size and spacing. Wrap the liner around the fan, then attach it to the frame with the clips provided. The liner's design eliminates the need to cut the joists and frame a hole for the fan. Mount the shutter to the ceiling.

For most efficient operation, be certain that your home has sufficient attic vents to allow the fan-forced air to escape the attic. Extra roof or side-wall louvers are simple to install, if needed. During the winter, remove the ceiling louver and slip in a precut piece of rigid-foam insulation to prevent a cold spot in the ceiling. Run the fan occasionally on sunny winter days also to quickly remove stale inside air. Remove the insulation before operation.

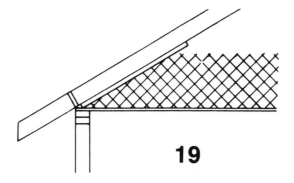

19

Insulation and Energy Conservation

Even though your room addition might represent only a small portion of the total square footage of your house, you should not overlook good insulation and other energy conservation measures. A properly insulated house can stop as much as 75 percent of the home's heat loss. With insulation, like weatherstripping, even a little will help. Partial insulation added to an existing home can still cut your heat loss by up to 30 percent.

The addition is no longer really an addition at this point. It's part of the house, and as such, its performance affects the performance of the rest of the home. Low insulation levels here will make the whole heating system work harder, and drafts around new windows and doors will be felt throughout the house.

To understand how to keep the entire house warmer and more comfortable, and to save heating and cooling costs at the same time, you should understand how heat moves and how it is lost from a seemingly solid structure. You will also hear a number of different terms associated with energy efficiency, some of which you might not be familiar with, so understanding them also will be helpful.

BASICS OF HEAT TRANSMISSION

Heat is a form of energy, created by the movement of molecules. Heat will always travel in one direction—from a warm surface to a colder surface—and it does so in one of three ways: by convection, radiation, or conduction. Knowing how heat moves is essential in knowing how to stop, or at least slow, its movement. (See Fig. 19-1.)

Convection. As a liquid or a gas, such as air, takes on heat, it expands and becomes lighter, causing it to rise. As it rises and cools, it becomes more dense and heavy, and falls. This natural rising and falling is called convection. If the heated air is confined to a relatively small area, these natural air movements take on a circular pattern, called a *convection current.*

Radiation. Every heated object gives off energy in the form of infrared waves, which will travel naturally from the heat source to an object having a lower surface temperature. This is radiated heat, an example of which would be the

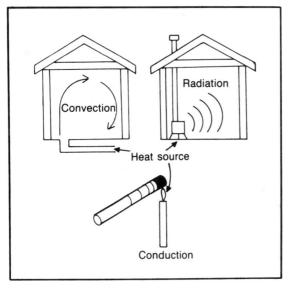

Fig. 19-1. The three primary forms of heat transfer.

warmth you feel on your body when you are standing in front of a hot stove, or in direct sunlight.

Radiated heat is line of sight. For example, imagine you are standing in front of a camp fire on a cold night. The front of you, which is at a lower temperature than the fire and which is directly exposed to the fire's heat, feels warm. The heat is moving from the warmer surface, the fire, to the colder surface, your body. The back of you, sheltered from the fire but still at a higher temperature than the surrounding air, feels cold. Again the heat is moving from the warm surface, your body, to the cold surface, the night air.

Conduction. While convection and radiation involves the transference heat through the movement or disruption of the surrounding air or liquid, conduction is the movement of heat between molecules within a solid object, or within air or liquid, without such disruption. As the molecules are heated, their speed of movement increases, and they give off energy. This energy causes adjacent molecules to heat and move faster. This process is repeated until, given enough time, the entire object will achieve the same temperature. An example of conduction would be a metal rod held in a flame. The end in the flame will heat first, then the

heat will pass down the rod to the other end.

This concept is of primary importance in construction, since it is by conduction that heat inside a building will pass through the walls, floor, and ceiling to the cooler areas on the other side. Thermal insulation is incorporated into a building in order to eliminate as much of this heat transfer, called *conduction loss,* as possible.

The Four Values of Heat Resistance

Every material has some resistance to heat flow, most commonly known simply as its *resistance value,* or *R-value.* How resistant a material is depends primarily on the number of air cells it contains. These minute cells resist heat transfer by convection because the air space is too small to allow movement. Transfer by radiation is resisted because very little of the heat striking the dead air space is transmitted to the opposite surface. Transfer by conduction is lessened because continuity of the molecules within the material is broken up by the dead air.

How well a material permits or resists heat flow is the main criterion used to evaluate that material as a thermal insulation. For this reason, four values have been developed which make the evaluation and comparison of different materials much easier. Although R-value may be the only term you're familiar with, the other three, particularly U-value, are all important.

K-value. This is the basic measurement of heat transfer, dealing with a uniform size and thickness of material. It is the number of BTUs of heat that will pass through 1 square foot of a material 1 inch thick in 1 hour, at a temperature difference of 1 degree Fahrenheit between the surfaces. The lower the K-value, the less heat will pass through that material, and the better it is as an insulator.

C-value. Since not all materials can be tested at a uniform thickness of 1 inch, C-value is used as a measurement of heat movement through standard thicknesses, such as 1/2-inch drywall or 3/4-inch plywood. It is defined as the number of BTUs that will pass through 1 square foot of a material of actual standard thickness in 1 hour, at a 1-degree temperature difference between the two surfaces. The lower the C-value, the better the material is as an insulator.

U-value. Since some objects are made up of several different materials having different heat-transfer characteristics, such as a window, a door, or an entire wall, U-value measures the heat movement through the combined materials in a building component or section. (See Fig. 19-2.) U-value is defined as the number of BTUs that will pass through 1 square foot of a combined building component or section at a temperature difference of 1 degree between the surfaces. The lower the U-value, the more effective the component is in resisting heat flow. U-value is used almost as much as R-value in construction, and you will often see windows and doors rated by the manufacturer in U-values instead of R-values.

R-value. The most common of the terms, R-value measures a material's resistance to heat flow. (See Appendix E.) The higher the R-value, the better the material is as a thermal insulator. Since R-value measures how well a material stops heat flow, it is the opposite, or reciprocal, of the C-, K-, and U-values, which measure how well a material permits heat flow. Therefore, the following conversion formulas can be used:

$$1/K = \text{R-value per inch of a uniform material}$$
$$1/C = \text{R-value of the standard form and thickness of a material}$$
$$1/U = \text{R-value of a combined building component or section}$$
$$1/R = \text{U-value}$$

Vapor Barriers

The other element in effective insulation is the vapor barrier. Warm, moist air trying to escape the inside of a building will collide with cool, dry air trying to enter. This collision takes place within the insulated area and results in condensation. This condensation wets the insulation, substantially reducing its insulating value, and also becomes a potential source of damage to the wood framing.

This situation is why a vapor barrier is needed.

Placed on or over the side of the insulation that faces the heated area of the building, the vapor barrier prevents moist air from passing through it. This moist air, turned back into the building, helps the building to retain its heat, and also needed humidity.

In residential construction, vapor barriers are commonly achieved through the use of insulation that is faced on one side with asphalt-impregnated paper or with reflective foil. Newer techniques are being developed in which unfaced insulation is used to fill the wall, floor, or ceiling cavity, and a continuous covering of polyethylene (plastic sheeting) is used to cover the entire surface. Done correctly, this latter method is very effective in stopping a large number of small air leaks, which makes for a tighter, warmer building.

Vapor barriers also are used on the outside of the building, underneath the siding. Should moisture pass through the siding material, either as airborne water vapor or as an actual liquid, the outside moisture barrier helps stop the underlying sheathing and framing from being damaged.

INSULATION MATERIALS

Insulation is commonly available in several different materials, and in three basic forms, depending on its intended application.

Batts and Blankets. Batts and blankets are flexible strips of insulation, designed to fit between structural members. (See Fig. 19-3.) Batts are sold in precut lengths, usually 4 or 8 feet, while blankets are sold in long rolls. Both types come faced with kraft paper or foil to be held in place with staples, or unfaced to be held in place by friction against the framing members on each side. Batt and blanket insulations are sold in two widths: 15 inches for use with studs on 16-inch centers, and 23 inches, for 24-inch OC framing. Insulation in this form is used in unfinished wall cavities, in ceilings, and in underfloor areas. It is also commonly used for wrapping pipes and ducts. Remember that the paper facing on batt and blanket insulation is combustible,

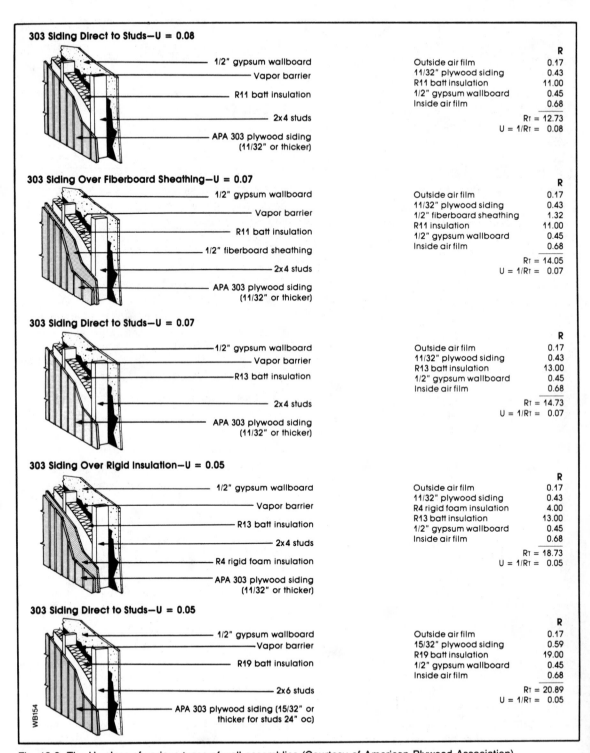

303 Siding Direct to Studs—U = 0.08

- 1/2" gypsum wallboard
- Vapor barrier
- R11 batt insulation
- 2x4 studs
- APA 303 plywood siding (11/32" or thicker)

	R
Outside air film	0.17
11/32" plywood siding	0.43
R11 batt insulation	11.00
1/2" gypsum wallboard	0.45
Inside air film	0.68
	R_T = 12.73
	$U = 1/R_T$ = 0.08

303 Siding Over Fiberboard Sheathing—U = 0.07

- 1/2" gypsum wallboard
- Vapor barrier
- R11 batt insulation
- 1/2" fiberboard sheathing
- 2x4 studs
- APA 303 plywood siding (11/32" or thicker)

	R
Outside air film	0.17
11/32" plywood siding	0.43
1/2" fiberboard sheathing	1.32
R11 insulation	11.00
1/2" gypsum wallboard	0.45
Inside air film	0.68
	R_T = 14.05
	$U = 1/R_T$ = 0.07

303 Siding Direct to Studs—U = 0.07

- 1/2" gypsum wallboard
- Vapor barrier
- R13 batt insulation
- 2x4 studs
- APA 303 plywood siding (11/32" or thicker)

	R
Outside air film	0.17
11/32" plywood siding	0.43
R13 batt insulation	13.00
1/2" gypsum wallboard	0.45
Inside air film	0.68
	R_T = 14.73
	$U = 1/R_T$ = 0.07

303 Siding Over Rigid Insulation—U = 0.05

- 1/2" gypsum wallboard
- Vapor barrier
- R13 batt insulation
- 2x4 studs
- R4 rigid foam insulation
- APA 303 plywood siding (11/32" or thicker)

	R
Outside air film	0.17
11/32" plywood siding	0.43
R4 rigid foam insulation	4.00
R13 batt insulation	13.00
1/2" gypsum wallboard	0.45
Inside air film	0.68
	R_T = 18.73
	$U = 1/R_T$ = 0.05

303 Siding Direct to Studs—U = 0.05

- 1/2" gypsum wallboard
- Vapor barrier
- R19 batt insulation
- 2x6 studs
- APA 303 plywood siding (15/32" or thicker for studs 24" oc)

	R
Outside air film	0.17
15/32" plywood siding	0.59
R19 batt insulation	19.00
1/2" gypsum wallboard	0.45
Inside air film	0.68
	R_T = 20.89
	$U = 1/R_T$ = 0.05

WB154

Fig. 19-2. The U-values of various types of wall assemblies (Courtesy of American Plywood Association).

Fig. 19-3. Fiberglass blanket insulation (Courtesy of Georgia-Pacific Corporation).

and should not be left exposed. Common batt and blanket materials are:

☐ Fiberglass. Long filaments of spun glass, loosely woven and cut into various widths and thicknesses. The R-value in batts is approximately 3.1 per inch.
☐ Rock Wool and Slag Wool. This is granite rock or furnace slag that has been melted at temperatures between 2,500 and 3,000 degrees Fahrenheit and processed into a thick, woollike material. It has an R-value of approximately 2.9 per inch.

Loose Fill. Loose fill is any of a variety of insulation materials that are provided in loose, bulk form, usually in bags, to be poured, blown, or placed by hand into walls or attics. Common loose-fill materials include:

☐ *Fiberglass.* This is the same material as that used in batts, but it's left loose in small clumps. It is placed by blowing using a special, high-power blower and a large-diameter hose. The R-value of fiberglass as a blown material drops to about 2.2 per inch.
☐ *Cellulose.* Paper products, primarily recycled newsprint or wood fibers, which are shredded and milled into a fluffy, low-density material, then treated with fire-retardant chemicals, usually boric acid. Cellulose can be blown in using commercial blowers like those used for fiberglass, or it can be blown using do-it-yourself machines which are rented or loaned through retail distributors. Cellulose is also commonly used for blowing into closed, uninsulated wall cavities. Its R-value is around 3.7 per inch.
☐ *Rock Wool.* The same material as that used in batts, but left loose for blowing. The R-value is approximately 2.9 per inch.
☐ *Perlite.* A volcanic material, expanded 4 to 20 times by heating to produce a light, cellular material in pellet form. It is placed by pouring and then raking level to the desired thickness. Its R-value is about 2.7 per inch.
☐ *Vermiculite.* A material having numerous thin layers that expand under heat in accordion-like

folds, producing lightweight pellets. It can be used alone as a poured, loose-fill insulation, or can be mixed in plaster or concrete. It has an R-value of approximately 2.2 per inch.

Rigid Boards. Rigid boards is thermal insulation in the form of rigid sheets, either with square or tongue-and-groove edges, for use on roofs, wall surfaces, and stem walls, and under slabs. (See Fig. 19-4.) The sheets are usually 2 × 8 feet or 4 × 8 feet, and come in several different thicknesses. Several different materials are used in producing rigid boards, and all of the following ones are combustible. Whether you are using them inside or outside, they should not be left uncovered.

☐ *Extruded Polystyrene.* Polystyrene beads are fed

Fig. 19-4. Rigid boards being used to insulate the outside of a wall (Courtesy of Celotex Corporation).

274

into an extruder and melted into a thick fluid, which is then injected with a mixture of gases to foam the fluid into a mass of bubbles. Heat and pressure are applied and the mixture is shaped by the extruder into a solid board. It has an R-value of about 5.2 per inch, and is suitable for below-grade and under-slab use. Above grade, it should be protected from constant exposure to sunlight, which might cause degradation over time. (See Fig. 19-5.)

☐ *Molded or Expanded Polystyrene.* In this process, polystyrene beads are poured into a mold, then heated. The beads swell to fill the mold and fuse together into a solid form. Because it is lower in density and its cells do not contain gases, it has a lower R-value, about 3.6 per inch, and is more brittle then extruded polystyrene. This material often is referred to as *beadboard,* and is also commonly used in such items as ice chests and coffee cups. This type of insulation should not be used in below-grade applications.

☐ *Polyurethane and Polyisocyanurate.* These are plastic polymers that are formed into boards using a process similar to that for extruded polystyrene, but using somewhat different chemicals. The resulting foam sheet contains a number of gas-filled cells, and offers a high R-value. Polyurethane insulation is rated around R-6 per inch, and polyisocyanurate is approximately R-7.5 per inch.

INSTALLING INSULATION

There are several areas of the addition, and the existing house if possible, that should be well insulated for maximum comfort and greatest energy saving. They include the ceiling, floor, walls, water pipes, and ducts. If portions of the existing house are not insulated or have skimpy insulation, consider upgrading them at the same time.

For most people, installing insulation is not the most pleasant task they encounter during the course of construction. Some types of insulation, such as loose fiberglass, can be installed only with special blowing equipment, and usually must be left up to a contractor. Blanket insulation is easy for most do-it-yourselfers, but if the money you're saving is not substantial, you might want to leave this job to the contractors also.

You will need only basic hand tools to install blanket insulation: a tape measure, a utility knife,

Fig. 19-5. Sheet-metal flashing used to cover rigid-foam insulation used above grade.

a staple gun, and portable lighting. Temporary floor boards installed across the ceiling joists will give you a more comfortable and stable working platform, and lessen the risk of damaging the ceiling.

You should always wear protective clothing, particularly when you are working with fiberglass. Wear long pants, a long-sleeved shirt, gloves, and some sort of respirator to avoid breathing in the tiny floating fibers. If you are particularly sensitive to fiberglass, take the added precaution of wearing a shirt or sweatshirt with a hood to prevent fibers from finding their way in around your neck, and use duct tape to tape the area between your shirt sleeves and your gloves.

Ceiling Insulation

Of all the areas you'll be insulating, the ceiling is where most heat is lost, so the levels of insulation there will be the greatest. Many codes now require R-38 in the ceiling, which is a good level. If your local codes do not specify the exact level, plan on installing at least a minimum of R-30, with R-38 being preferable. It's a very good idea to bring the insulation level in the existing attic up to R-38 also.

Before you actually install the insulation, you'll need to perform some preliminary work. First of all, you need to protect the soffit or frieze vents with

insulation baffles so that they are not covered with insulation (Fig. 19-6). Simply place a piece of plywood, drywall, heavy cardboard, or other material across the rafters wherever there is a vent (Fig. 19-7). The baffle should extend down to the plate, and up to approximately 2 inches above the finished level of the insulation. If desired, you can use two or more thicknesses of insulation batts around the entire perimeter of the attic, where they will act as both an insulation baffle for the vents and a dam to contain loose-fill insulation. Place a similar dam around the attic access hatch to contain the loose-fill insulation.

Any fixtures or flues that produce heat, including ceiling fans, ceiling heaters, recessed lights, doorbell transformers, chimney flues, flues for combustion appliances, and other similar objects, need to be protected from being covered by insulation. If they are covered, a tremendous amount of heat can build up under the insulation, creating a high risk of fire. Even insulation that is noncombustible, such as fiberglass, must be kept away from these fixtures, since the heat buildup could cause wooden structural members to catch fire.

Using thin-gauge sheet-metal, which can be purchased in rolls at most lumberyards, construct a dam around each of these fixtures and flues. (See

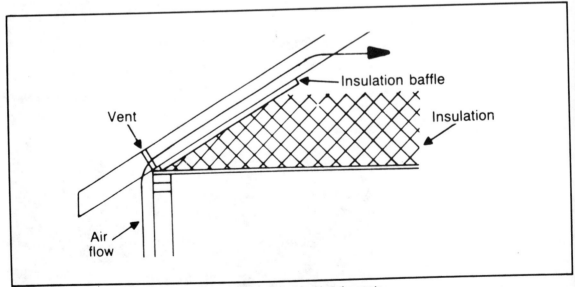

Fig. 19-6. An insulation baffle used to keep insulation from blocking the vents.

Fig. 19-7. Plywood insulation baffles used between the joists.

Fig. 19-8.) The dam should be of a sufficient size to provide at least 3 inches of clearance around the fixture, and it should extend at least 4 inches above the insulation level. Secure the dam to the ceiling or to the rafters to prevent it from being knocked loose during the insulation process.

Check to see that all exhaust fans are vented completely out of the attic. Exhaust fans draw moisture from inside the house, and this moisture can cause a number of problems if it is allowed to enter and remain in the attic. In addition to wetting the insulation, which drastically reduces its effectiveness, attic moisture can stain ceilings and cause serious damage to wooden structural members.

Vent all fans through the roof to the outside, using flexible dryer hose or other types of rigid or flexible pipe. Terminate the vent in an approved, weatherproof flashing and cap. Follow this procedure for bath fans, laundry room fans, kitchen range hoods and fans, clothes dryer vents, and any other fans that vent into the attic.

Another precaution against moisture damage is the installation of a vapor barrier. If you have not yet covered the ceiling with drywall or other finish material, you can install batt insulation from underneath. In this case, the facing on the batts acts as the vapor barrier, and should be installed facing

Fig. 19-8. Dams being used to protect a flue pipe, right, and the attic access opening, bottom.

down, toward the heated portion of the room.

Another alternative is to cover the bottom side of the ceiling joists with 6-mil plastic sheeting, which is stapled directly to the joists. Extend the sheeting down the walls 12 inches, and try to maintain at least 12 inches of overlap at all seams. Press the sheeting tightly into the corners, and take care to install it smoothly so that it will not interfere with the later installation of ceiling finish materials. This type of vapor barrier will work with either unfaced batt insulation, or with blown insulation after the ceiling materials are installed.

If the ceiling material is already in place, you have two choices for a vapor barrier. You can place batt insulation with an attached vapor barrier between the joists. Make sure the vapor barrier faces down toward the heated space. A more effective method is to install long strips of plastic sheeting between the joists, running parallel with them and lapped at least 2 inches up the sides. Staple the plastic to the sides of the joist, and overlap the seams by 12 inches.

Most people prefer to have insulation blown into the ceiling (Fig. 19-9), although this is typically not a do-it-yourself project. If you are having a contractor do the work, you can prepare the attic as outlined previously and save some of the installation costs, or you can have the contractor do the whole job. Blown insulation offers the advantage to fast installation, and you are assured that the entire attic area is completely and uniformly covered.

For the do-it-yourselfer, the best alternative is blanket insulation. After you have prepared the attic, begin at one corner and place the end of a roll of R-19 insulation between the ceiling joists, overlapping the top plate if possible. Unroll the insulation and tuck it neatly down between the joists. Install full rolls in long strips first, then go back and fill in with short pieces as needed, abutting the pieces tightly end to end. Using a utility knife, cut the insulation as needed to fit neatly around dams, bridging, and other obstacles. Remember to keep the vapor barrier facing down.

When you have filled all of the joist spaces, start at the same corner and install a second layer of R-19, on top of and perpendicular to the first. This second layer will give you a total of R-38 in the entire attic, and by running perpendicular to the joists, it covers the gaps and seams in the first layer. Use unfaced insulation for the second layer, to avoid doubling the vapor barrier and possibly trapping moisture between the layers.

Loose-fill insulation is another possibility, although its cost might be prohibitive. Prepare the attic first, then install the loose-fill material by simply pouring it in place. Pour it to the thickness recommended by the manufacturer for the R-value you're trying to achieve, then use a board or a garden rake to level it.

Wall Insulation

For unfinished wall cavities, batt or blanket insulation is the common choice, both for the contractor and the do-it-yourselfer. Use whatever thickness of insulation is compatible with the width of the studs, usually R-11 for 2-×-4 studs and R-19 for 2 × 6s. Use precut batts if their length suits the height of the wall cavities, or cut blanket insulation to the proper length. You will find it easiest to cut the insulation by placing it, with the vapor

Fig. 19-9. Blown fiberglass insulation.

Fig. 19-10. Blanket insulation used between wall studs. Flanges are stapled to the insides, not to the face of the studs.

barrier side down, on a scrap piece of plywood or drywall, then compressing it along the line of the cut with a board. Using the board as a guide, cut through the compressed insulation and the vapor barrier with a sharp utility knife.

Press the insulation between the studs, with the vapor barrier facing the heated side of the room.

Unfold the stapling flanges, and secure the insulation by stapling through the flanges into the sides of the studs (Fig. 19-10). This is a little more work than stapling the flanges to the face of the studs, but it ensures that the facing and the staples will not interfere with the finished wall-covering material.

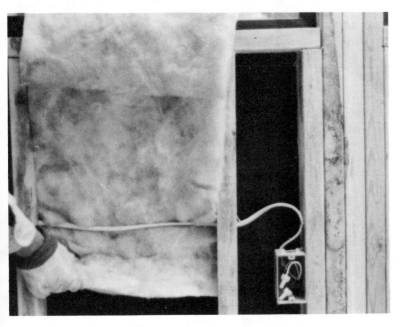

Fig. 19-11. Fitting the separated piece of insulation over both sides of an electrical wire.

When all of the full width stud spaces have been filled, cut narrow strips as necessary to fill in the other spaces. You won't have stapling flanges to work with here, so cut the insulation a little wider than the space so that friction will hold it in place.

Where you encounter electrical wiring running through the walls, separate the insulation near the center, and work part of it behind the wire while leaving the rest to cover the front (Fig. 19-11). This procedure prevents the insulation from bunching over the wire, which could cause a bulge in the finished wall, and ensures a uniform thickness of insulation on both sides of the wire. Trim the insulation neatly around electrical boxes (Fig. 19-12); don't just compress it around the boxes, which causes uninsulated gaps. Work carefully around any plumbing, filling in around the pipes as thoroughly as possible.

An alternate method is to use unfaced insulation, which is held in place by friction, then cover the wall with plastic sheeting. Although considerably more work, this method creates a very effective vapor barrier, which gives the added advantage of stopping a considerable amount of air infiltration.

Attic kneewalls are insulated in the same manner, as are the spaces between rafters in a sloping ceiling. Some codes require a 1-inch ventilation space over the top of insulation being installed in sloping ceilings, so check with the building department first.

Floor Insulation

Underfloor insulation is most effective when it is placed directly up against the underside of the subfloor. An easier option is to simply insulate the stem walls, but this still allows a tremendous amount of heat to be lost through the floor into the crawl space. You should insulate the floors over garages and unheated basements also. R-19 is the accepted standard thickness for these applications.

To begin, cover the ground in the crawl space with a vapor barrier. (See Fig. 19-13.) The vapor barrier prevents ground moisture from dampening the insulation, and also prevents heat absorption by the soil. By installing the ground cover first, you also provide yourself with a cleaner place to work.

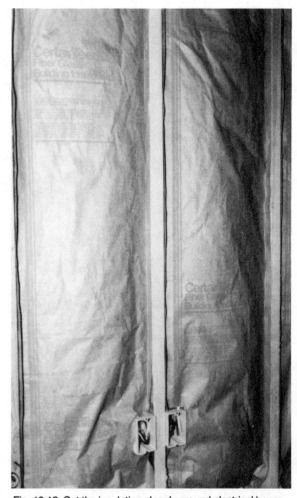

Fig. 19-12. Cut the insulation cleanly around electrical boxes.

Place 6-mil black plastic sheeting directly on the ground, allowing it to lap up the stem walls approximately 6 inches. Glue the plastic to the stem wall with a compatible adhesive, or hold it against the wall with bricks. Lap it up the sides of the piers, but do not allow the plastic to touch any wood members. Side and end seams should overlap by 6 inches.

There are several options for holding the insulation in place, and you should select whichever one seems the most comfortable for you to do. Sheets of wire mesh or chicken wire are one possibility, or you can lace string or wire across the joists on 12-inch centers. Use rustproof wire or rotproof

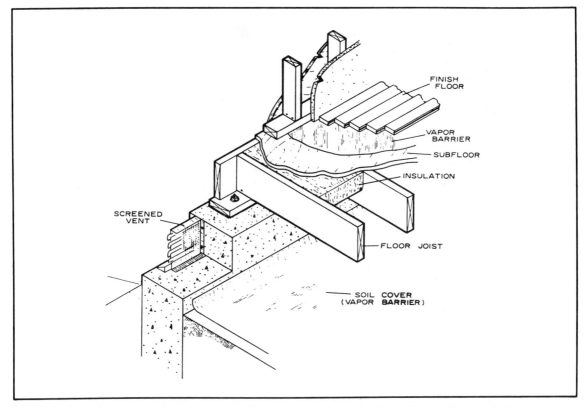

Fig. 19-13. A plastic vapor barrier being used in the crawl space in conjunction with underfloor insulation.

string to be sure that the installation will last. Some manufacturers offer specific materials for installing underfloor insulation, including nylon mesh and spring steel bars which span between the joists.

A simple and less expensive method, favored by many contractors, is to nail thin wood strips, such as lath sticks, to the underside of the joists (Fig. 19-14). Use galvanized nails, and place the strips on 18-inch centers.

Start at one corner of the crawl space and place the insulation between the joists, unrolling and installing a strip about 5 feet in length. Remember that the vapor barrier on the insulation always faces the heated area, so in this case it would be up, toward the house. Secure the insulation with whatever material you've chosen, then roll out another 5 or 6 feet. Continue in this manner until the entire floor has been insulated, and insulate the underfloor areas in the existing house, also.

Roof and Slab Insulation

Two areas of the home that are difficult to insulate using conventional methods are concrete slabs and roofs having no rafter spaces, as in the case of an open-beam ceiling. Rigid insulation is the proper choice for both of these applications. However, since only extruded polystyrene is moisture resistant, it should be used under the slab. Extruded polystyrene also has the necessary bearing strength to handle the load imposed on it by the weight of the concrete. Roof or slab insulation details should be clearly shown on the plans so that you can be certain they meet local codes.

For a slab with a separate stem wall, you can insulate the inside of the stem wall before you put the fill material in place (Fig. 19-15), or you can insulate the outside of the stem wall (Fig. 19-16). A more effective alternative is to insulate under the entire slab, and also the area between the stem wall

Fig. 19-14. Underfloor insulation, placed between the floor joists and held in place with wood lath strips.

and the edge of the slab. For monolithic slabs, place the insulation under the entire slab area, and insulate the outside of the footing, too.

To insulate under a slab (Fig. 19-17), first put all the under-slab plumbing and wiring in place, and backfill and compact the slab area. Place the insulation boards directly on the compacted fill, then cover it with a vapor barrier of 6-mil plastic sheeting. Then pour the concrete directly on the vapor barrier.

Roof insulation is placed after the decking has been completely installed. (See Fig. 19-18.) Nail furring strips, equal in thickness to the thickness of the insulation boards, to the decking on 24-inch centers. Cut strips of rigid insulation to fit between the furring, then cover the entire area with plywood sheathing before you apply the roofing. Some codes limit the total thickness of the furring, and therefore the amount of insulation, so check with local building officials first.

Pipe and Duct Insulation

Ducts, water pipes, and hydronic pipes should not be overlooked, either under the floor or in the attic. Both of these areas remain considerably colder than the temperature of the pipe or duct, so

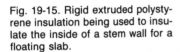

Fig. 19-15. Rigid extruded polystyrene insulation being used to insulate the inside of a stem wall for a floating slab.

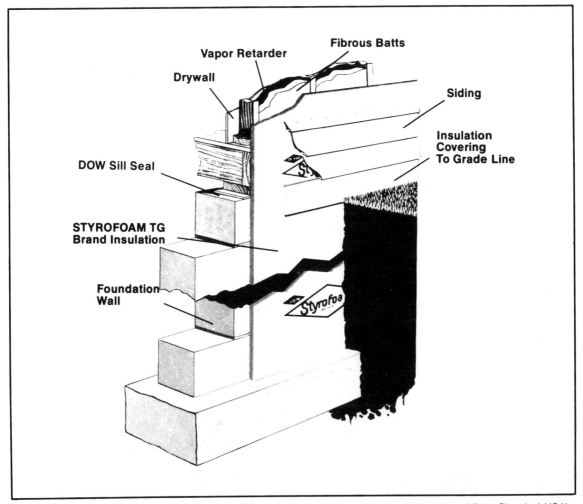

Fig. 19-16. Rigid insulation being used to insulate the outside of a foundation wall (Courtesy of Dow Chemical USA).

the heat movement between the warm pipes and the cold air is substantial. This situation is especially true for heating ducts, and you can be throwing away a lot of heating dollars on uninsulated ducts.

Heat ducts should be wrapped with a layer of unfaced R-11 blanket insulation. Before insulating, check to see that all of the joints are securely taped with duct tape. Starting at the plenum, tie the end of the roll around the duct, using wire or string. Continue to wrap the insulation spirally around the entire length of the duct, abutting or slightly overlapping the edges. Secure the insulation with

spirally wrapped string or wire as necessary. Insulate all the plenums, ducts, and boots in the entire system, and don't forget any exposed ducts or plenums in the garage, basement, or other unheated area.

Wrap water pipes in the same manner, using an R-11 blanket that has been separated into two half thicknesses. (See Fig. 19-19.) An alternative is the preformed hollow foam tubes manufactured specifically for water pipes. Purchase these tubes according to the outside diameter of the pipe being wrapped, and install them by opening the lengthwise slit in the tube and placing it over the

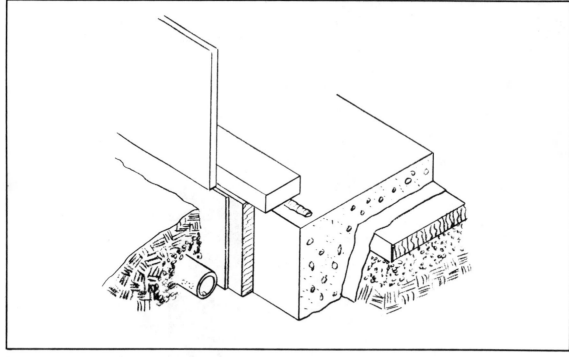

Fig. 19-17. Rigid insulation (shaded area) and vapor barrier being used under and beside a monolithic slab.

pipe. Abut each piece tightly to the one before it, and tape all the joints. Finally, install a water-heater jacket on the water heater.

STOPPING AIR LEAKS

Air infiltration, the movement of air into and out of the house through a myriad of tiny cracks and

Fig. 19-18. Rigid-foam insulation used between furring strips to insulate a roof.

284

Fig. 19-19. Fiberglass insulation being used to wrap water pipes.

gaps, can be a substantial source of heat loss. In leaky older buildings, it can account for as much as 40 percent of the home's heat loss.

There are a number of areas where leakage can be stopped, both during construction and on the finished house and addition. Caulking is the primary weapon against air infiltration; in fact, it has been estimated that a truly tight house can use as much as five times as much caulk as a conventional house. When compared to the return in comfort and energy saving, caulking is probably the wisest, least expensive investment you will make in your home.

Caulking Materials

Rapid advances in the construction chemical market have resulted in a huge variety of special-purpose caulking and sealing compounds. Although the advances have greatly improved the working ease and useful life of these products, the choices can be confusing. For the most part, you get what you pay for with caulks and sealants. As the price

goes up, usually so does the warranty, the ease of use, and the flexibility, which is the key to long life.

Caulking compounds are used in sealing joints in wood, metal, masonry, and various other materials. They are generally less expensive than sealants, have a shorter life span, and are somewhat less flexible. The basic types of caulking follow.

Oil-Based Caulk. This is the least expensive and most difficult type of caulk to use. It is paintable and will work with most building materials, but tends to dry out quickly. If the package does not specifically list the caulk's ingredients, it is most likely an oil-base composition. Coverage is about 20 lineal feet of 1/4-inch bead per tube.

Acrylic Latex Caulk. This compound is commonly known as a "painter's caulk," since its primary application is the sealing of cracks and gaps before painting. It is usually white, although colors are becoming popular. It will work with most common building materials and is moderately flexible, but should not be used for filling large gaps, or in areas of substantial expansion and contraction between materials. Life expectancy averages 10 years.

Silicone Acrylic Caulk. Also labeled as acrylic latex with silicone, this type of caulk is similar to acrylic latex, but has silicone added for increased flexibility. It is compatible with most materials, and can be painted after 30 to 60 minutes. This compound is a good-quality, reasonably priced caulk for a variety of general-purpose sealing jobs. It is commonly available only in white or clear. The life expectancy is 20 to 25 years.

Butyl Rubber Caulk. This is a flexible, rubber-based compound that is used as a painter's caulk, or as a sealant for movement areas. It is available in white or colors and can be painted after 7 days. Life expectancy is about 15 years.

Adhesive Caulk. In addition to being an effective caulk, this compound also has the adhesive ability to handle such jobs as setting loose ceramic tile or repairing cracked porcelain. It goes on white but dries clear, and will adhere to most common building materials. It is waterproof and flexible, and has an average life expectancy of about 15 to 20 years.

Sealants

Sealants differ from caulks primarily in their flexibility and longevity. They are especially good in situations of high expansion and contraction: in areas that get a lot of wear, movement, or weather exposure: and between dissimilar materials. Some of the common sealant types follow.

Silicone Sealant. This versatile sealant is available in several forms for different applications. The general-purpose compound is waterproof, bonds to almost anything, can handle temperatures down to -40 degrees Fahrenheit, and is extremely flexible, with life expectancies of up to 50 years. Most types are safe for use in areas where it will contact food or drinking water. Check the label for specific details. Most types are clear, and cannot be painted unless specifically noted on the label. A white bathroom sealant, designed for sealing around tubs, showers, and sinks, is also available. It's extremely waterproof, flexible, and long lasting. For repairing cracks or sealing expansion joints in concrete, mortar, stucco, and other masonry, use the light gray concrete and masonry sealant. Coverage for each type is about 50 feet of 3/16-inch bead per tube.

Gutter and Lap Sealant. Designed specifically for metal, this compound will seal gutters, flashings, truck bodies, etc. It is durable and flexible, with a good temperature range. Most types are white, but can be painted after about a week.

The applications, warranties and other details will vary among brands, so always check the label. Pay close attention to the manufacturer's instructions to ensure an effective, long-lasting application.

Areas to Seal

During construction, it is easy to caulk a number of areas that would be difficult or impossible to reach after the addition is complete. Keep a caulking gun and several tubes of good-quality caulk or sealant available during construction, and don't be afraid to use it.

During the framing stages, be sure to seal the area between the sill plate and the stem wall, using either caulking or a foam sheet sill sealer. Seal the subfloor to the joists with construction adhesive, which not only will stop air from coming up from the crawl space, but will ensure a squeak-free floor. Also, apply a bead of caulk underneath the rim joist where it sits on the sill plate.

Caulk underneath the bottom exterior wall plates by applying a bead to either the plate or the subfloor just prior to standing the wall. Repeat the caulking process for the rim joist, subfloor, and exterior wall plates at each subsequent floor.

In addition to caulking under the nailing flange on the windows, you will need to seal the space between the finished window trim and the rough framing, as well as the area between exterior door frames and the wall framing. Depending on the size of the gap, you can seal this area using fiberglass insulation, or, better yet, expandable foam caulking in cans. Apply the foam according to the manufacturer's instructions, then trim off any excess with a sharp knife after it dries to avoid interfering with the finished wall covering.

When the rough plumbing and electrical wiring is complete, it's important to seal all of the penetrations through the upper and lower wall plates. Be sure to seal the interior walls as well as the exterior walls, since any wall cavity will act as a chase for cold air leaking in from the crawl space. Caulking can be used for small gaps, but foam will work best for larger areas. The need for sealing around penetrations can be minimized by taking care to drill holes to the exact size when you are doing the rough wiring and plumbing. In some cities, there are companies that will come out at the rough-framing stage and foam all the penetrations, including around windows and doors. The fee is usually reasonable, and might be worth the investment if you have a number of areas to seal.

On the outside, caulk the area between the bottom of the siding and the lowest framing member, to prevent air from working its way up behind siding. Caulk the top siding board against the framing in the same manner. Caulk carefully around window and door trim, and any openings in the siding, such as around faucets, conduit, etc.

Carefully weatherstrip all exterior doors, and be certain the weatherstripping on the windows is in place and effective. If possible, purchase your exterior prehung doors with the weatherstripping already in place as an integral part of the door. Otherwise, any of the better quality do-it-yourself weatherstripping kits on the market will do the job.

Inexpensive foam gaskets behind the receptacle and switch plates, again on both the interior and exterior walls, will finish the sealing on the inside after the drywall is installed. Also caulk as many areas on the existing portion of the house as possible. In addition to the comfort and energy-saving factors, the house will be easier to paint; the paint will last longer; and you will provide important weather protection for all the wood members.

House Wraps

In addition to careful caulking and sealing, the use of a house wrap on the exterior of the addition might be worth considering. Fairly new on the market, house wrap products such as DuPont's Tyvek are installed over the exterior of the wall framing or sheathing, and are specifically designed for stopping air leakage behind the siding. The material is vapor permeable, and is not intended to act as a vapor barrier. House wraps come in a 10-foot-wide roll, and contain enough material to wrap an average size house. If your addition is large enough, a house wrap might be worth the investment.

Begin at one corner of the addition, or where the addition meets the house. Align the bottom of the roll so that it overlaps the top of the stem wall, and staple it in place. Have a helper slowly roll out the material while you follow behind and staple it in place. Wrap the entire addition in one piece, if possible.

If the material needs to be seamed, as on a gable end or a two-story area, lap the upper sheet over the lower one, and staple the seam. For a truly airtight barrier, seal both the seams and the joint between the house wrap and the stem wall with mastic. At window and door openings, cut the material diagonally from corner to corner, fold it into the opening, and staple it to the framing.

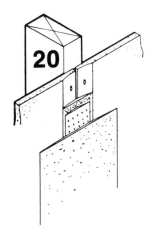

Interior Walls and Ceilings

With the addition completely framed and enclosed, and with all the wiring, plumbing, and insulation in the walls, it's time to look toward enclosing the interior. This procedure requires a solid base over which other interior finish materials, such as paint or wallpaper, can be applied.

PLASTER

For many years, plaster was the common interior finish material. Plaster is a hard, smooth, and highly fire-resistant mixture of Portland cement, lime, sand, and water, often with gypsum and other materials added. It is site-mixed and applied wet. It is also rather time consuming and, for the amateur, difficult to apply correctly.

Plaster requires a base material, called *lath,* which is applied over the framing. Prior to about 1950, wood lath strips were applied horizontally with small spaces between them. When the wet plaster was applied, it would ooze between the cracks and dry, locking the lath and plaster to-

gether. In more recent construction, gypsum lath panels, usually 16 or 24 inches wide and 48 or 96 inches long, took the place of the wood. Regular perforations in the lath panels acted in the same manner as the spaces between the wood lath to bond the wet plaster. A base coat was applied over the lath by spray or by hand with a trowel and allowed to dry, then one or two finish coats were applied. It was essential that a uniform thickness be maintained, and that the final coat be completely smooth.

From perforated gypsum lath panels, it became a logical time- and money-saving step to simply make the panels solid, and then just worry about finishing off the joints between the sheets. This process became known as *drywalling,* since the interior finish was achieved with dry sheets instead of wet plaster. Drywall has today almost completely replaced plaster as an interior finish material, and the uniform sheets and improved taping materials now on the market make it something the do-it-yourselfer can quickly learn to handle.

DRYWALL

The drywall serves as a base for almost any finish material you choose to apply, including paint, prefinished paneling, wallpaper, ceramic tile, or wood or masonry veneers. About the only exception would be solid wood or wood panels in thicknesses over 1/2 inch, which can be applied directly over the studs if desired.

Drywall sheets, known variously as wallboard, gypsum board, gypsum wallboard, plasterboard, and by the common brand name Sheetrock, are constructed from a continuous layer of gypsum wrapped with heavy paper on the two faces and the two long edges. Depending on the intended application, additional materials can be added to the gypsum to make it more resistant to water or fire damage. There are three commonly available thicknesses—3/8, 1/2, and 5/8 inch—and two common sheet sizes—4 × 8 feet and 4 × 12 feet. The 3/8-inch thickness is used in remodeling over other materials, such as plaster, and might not be commonly available in all areas.

The sheets might have square, beveled, rounded, or tongue-and-groove edges, but beveled edges are by far the most common. The bevel is placed on the face side of the sheet during the manufacturing process, and runs along the two long edges. When the sheets are installed, the beveled edges form a recess, which makes it easier to conceal the taped seams.

Another common drywall designation is Type X, which you might see called out specifically on your plans in certain areas. Type X drywall has asbestos fiber added to make the sheets fire resistant, and 5/8-inch Type X will give a 1-hour fire wall. The building code requires the use of 5/8-inch Type X drywall on garage walls that are common with living spaces, on the underside of interior stairways, between separate but connected living spaces, such as apartments, and in various other locations.

Checking the Framing

Before you begin to install the drywall, you need to carefully check the framing for any warps. With plaster, irregularities in the framing could be compensated for when applying the wet material, but the drywall panels follow the contours of the framing with no room for correction.

One method of checking the framing is to stand at the corner of a wall, right against the framing, and sight down it at the middle, looking for studs that bow in or out vertically. Another method is to hold a long, straight 2 × 4 against the face of the studs, or to stretch a string across them. Repeat the procedure for all the walls, and also sight the ceiling. Use a lumber crayon or soft pencil to mark any obvious deviations.

To correct a bowed stud (Fig. 20-1), use a handsaw and cut well into the edge of the stud, on the side opposite the bow (the concave side). While a helper pushes against the bowed side, opening up the cut, drive a wedge into the cut to hold the stud straight. Nail a 1 × 3 or a strip of plywood to each side of the stud to reinforce the cut. For badly

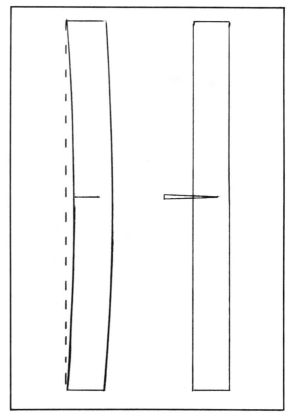

Fig. 20-1. Cutting a bowed wall stud, left, then shimming it to keep it straight.

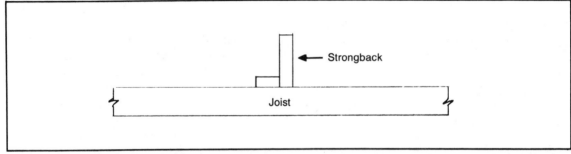

Fig. 20-2. The use of a strongback to support ceiling joists.

warped studs, two or more cuts might be necessary, reinforced by a continuous board along both sides.

On the ceiling, a joist that is bowed down often can be corrected with the installation of a strongback, provided the area above the joists is an attic or other unused space. (See Fig. 20-2.) Select a straight 2 × 6 or 2 × 8, long enough to span across the joists between two plates if possible. Nail a 2 × 4 to one face along one edge, forming an L-shape. Then place the two boards on top of and perpendicular to the joists, with the 2 × 4 flat on the joists and the 2 × 6 on edge. Wedge a 2 × 4 between the floor and the underside of the joist to raise it level with the others, then screw down through the 2 × 4 into the joist to hold it up. Special nails with two points bent at opposite angles, called *strongback ties,* can be used in place of the 2 × 4. Simply wedge up the joist temporarily, then use the strongback tie between the 2 × 6 and the joist.

If the addition of a strongback is not possible because another floor is above the joists, you usually can cut and shim the bowed joist straight following the same procedure as for the wall studs, subject to the approval of the building inspector. Use 2 × material on both sides of the cut for reinforcement.

For a joist that is bowed up, stretch a string across the faces of all the joists. Using the string as a guide, place shims on the bottom side of the joist as necessary to provide a straight plane for the drywall.

Working with Drywall

Drywall sheets are installed with the long dimension perpendicular to the studs and joists, and must be cut so the ends fall over the center of a framing member. Depending on the dimensions of the area to be covered, the use of 12-foot sheets might eliminate some of the end-to-end seams, and therefore save on taping and finishing. For example, you could cover a 12-foot room in one length and with no seams using a 12-foot sheet. If, however, you used 8-foot sheets, you would need 1 1/2 sheets and have one seam. A 24-foot span would use two 12-foot sheets and one seam, or three 8-foot sheets and two seams. The disadvantage with 12-foot sheets is their weight and awkwardness, which makes them a little trickier to install.

Use a utility knife to cut the drywall. Keep a sharp blade in the knife at all times, changing it as it becomes dull or dirty. Using a straightedge as a guide, score the face side of the sheet with the blade, cutting through the paper and slightly into the core. Snap the sheet away from the cut to break the core, then cut through the back paper to separate the piece. For small cuts of 1 inch or less, cut through both faces before you try to snap off the piece.

After you have snapped off the piece, the gypsum core usually will be somewhat ragged. You should smooth this edge to allow for a clean fit between sheets. A Surform plane (Fig. 20-3) works quite well for this operation, requiring only a few quick passes to smooth the rough edge. A homemade alternative is to wrap a piece of metal lath around a block of wood. Coarse sandpaper on a block of wood also will work, but it tends to clog quite quickly.

The use of a straightedge is important when

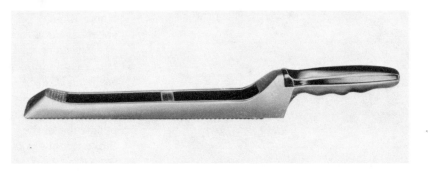

Fig. 20-3. A surform plane used for smoothing the rough edges of cut drywall (Courtesy of Stanley Tools, Division of The Stanley Works, New Britain, CT 06050).

you are cutting drywall in order to create a straight, square edge. A drywall square, which is actually a 4-foot-long aluminum T square specially made for this purpose, works the best. Simply measure and mark the sheet at the length you need, place the head of the square on the edge of the sheet at the mark, and use the T square blade as a guide for cutting. For lengths over 4 feet, mark the sheet twice and use the T square from each end, or use a chalk line and a straight board to guide the cut.

For cutting outlet holes and other small openings in the sheet, use a drywall saw (Fig. 20-4). Similar to a keyhole saw, a drywall saw has a series of coarse teeth and a pointed end with a wooden or plastic handle. Place the point against the face of the sheet within the area of the cut and tap the handle to drive the saw into and through the sheet, then cut out the opening. An electric drill with a hole-saw or wood-boring bit also will work for cutting openings, as will a reciprocating saw. (See Fig. 20-5.) Always cut from the front side to avoid tearing the face paper.

You can install drywall sheets using either screws or nails. Special flathead drywall screws are made for this purpose, and are the only type you should use. Install the screws with a drywall screw gun, which can be purchased or rented. The gun has an adjustable clutch that regulates how deep the screw is driven, and should be set so that the screw head is just below the surface of the sheet but does not tear through the paper face. Screws are more expensive, but they offer the advantage of better holding power, virtual elimination of "nail pops," and somewhat increased installation speed over nails. They are especially recommended for ceilings that have a floor above them. Incidentally, drywall screws are slender and very strong, making them ideal for a variety of general woodworking jobs also.

If you are using nails, use only drywall nails, which are designed for this purpose. They are galvanized to resist the moisture present in the joint compound, and have a cupped head, which holds the compound and makes them easier to conceal.

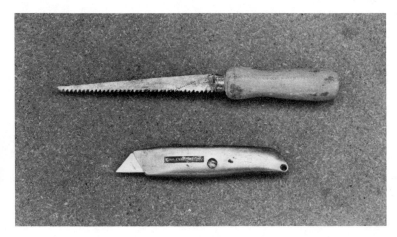

Fig. 20-4. A drywall saw (top) and a retractable utility knife.

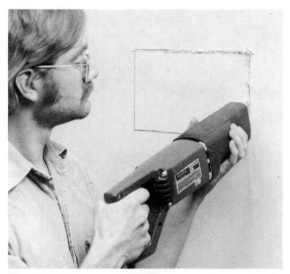

Fig. 20-5. Using a reciprocating saw to cut an opening in drywall (Courtesy of Skil Corporation).

It is very important to drive the nails straight into the sheet to the proper depth, without tearing the face paper. Using a hammer with a crowned (slightly convex) face, the last blow should set the nail head slightly below the surface of the sheet. The hammer creates a slight concave depression, called a *dimple* (Fig. 20-6). This dimple receives the joint compound, allowing the nail head to be concealed and finished off flush with the surrounding sheet. If you drive the nail too deep, you will tear the paper, making the holding power of the nail practically nil. If you do not drive the nail enough, you will leave the head exposed, preventing it from being concealed during the taping process. If this is your first attempt at installing drywall, you might want to practice with some scrap lumber and drywall to get a feel for how deep to drive the nail or screw.

For 1/2-inch drywall, use 1 1/4-inch nails or screws. This size will work for 5/8-inch sheets also, but 1 1/2- or 1 5/8-inch fasteners are much preferred for 5/8-inch sheets because they offer greater holding power. Install the fasteners 8 inches apart on the walls and 7 inches apart on ceilings.

Installing Drywall Sheets

Install drywall sheets on the ceilings first, where their edges can be supported by the wall sheets. Take a moment to first mark the location of each ceiling joist on the wall plates, using a lumber crayon or a dark pencil. In this way, you can easily find the joists for nailing after they have been concealed by the drywall sheet.

Begin at one corner, working out in a line perpendicular to the joists. Measure from the wall to the center of the joist closest to but less than 8 feet from the corner (or 12 feet for 12-foot sheets). Cut your sheet 1/4 inch shorter than this measurement to allow for framing irregularities. Make this 1/4-inch allowance a habit. Gaps will be covered during finishing, and you will eliminate the need for a lot of trimming.

Drywall is heavy—about 1.8 pounds per square foot, or almost 58 pounds for a 4- × -8-foot, 1/2-inch-thick sheet. In addition to its weight, the size of the sheet and its flexibility make it awkward to handle alone. (See Fig. 20-7.) For ceiling installations, you'll need a strong helper. The sheets go up faster, and alignment is easier. Provide short benches, scaffolds, or ladders for each of you to work from. Most professionals use an adjustable bench that is set so it's just tall enough to allow them to brace the sheet against the joists with their head, leaving both hands free for nailing. You might be able

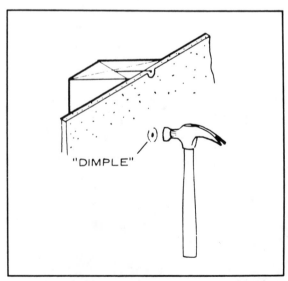

Fig. 20-6. Creating a dimple when hammering in drywall nails.

Fig. 20-7. Using a commercial boom truck to deliver drywall to a second-story addition. Arranging for delivery and placement of drywall can save a lot of extra labor.

to rent one of these benches, or you can easily make a simple one at a fixed height from scraps of lumber and plywood.

Grip a sheet at each end, placing your hands on the outside edges. Make sure the sheet is face down. Working in unison with your helper, climb onto the benches or ladders and place the sheet against the joists, then slide the end of the sheet into the corner. Check to see that the other end is squarely over the center of a joist. Brace the sheet against the joists with your head, and drive enough nails to secure it in place, then finish off the nailing pattern for each joist. Always nail off the entire sheet before you move on to the next one.

If no help is available, you can use a wooden prop for one end while you lift and nail the other end, but this method makes alignment of the sheet somewhat awkward. The best answer for a one-person installation is a drywall jack (Fig. 20-8), which is available at most rental yards. Place the drywall sheet face down on the arms of the jack. Turn a large wheel to raise the sheets to within about 1/2 inch of the ceiling. Wheels on the bottom of the jack make positioning the sheet quite simple. When the sheet is properly aligned, turn the wheel again to press it firmly against the joists, where it is securely held while you fasten it in place. Drywall jacks are quite inexpensive to rent, and the safety and convenience inherent in their use might

Fig. 20-8. Using a drywall jack to place a sheet of drywall against the ceiling. Note the adjustable bench, right.

make renting one worthwhile even if you have a helper.

If your framing was laid out correctly, the remaining sheets in the first row should go up with no cutting until you reach the opposite wall. For the second row, start at the same wall and measure to the center of the joist closest to but less than 4 feet from the wall. Begin the third row with a sheet cut to the same length as the first one. Staggering the joints in this manner makes them easier to conceal and provides a smoother finished ceiling.

When the ceiling is completely done, begin on the walls. Install the sheets horizontally on the upper half of the wall first, perpendicular to the studs. Use the same techniques of measuring, cutting, and securing as just described. Staggering the seams is not necessary here, since the joints are much less obvious on the walls than they are on the ceiling. Install the full sheets and large pieces first, setting aside all of the smaller scraps. Use the scraps as you go along to fill in the smaller areas. This method will save you time and material over cutting out small fills from full sheets.

Avoid ending a sheet directly against the edge of a door or window. This method places the seam directly above the jambs, where the repeated opening and closing of the door or window probably will crack it. Try, instead, to span the opening with a sheet and then cut out the opening later, or if a joint is necessary, abut the sheets above the center of the opening.

When you are installing the bottom sheets, first cut the sheet to size and set the bottom edge on the floor, leaning the sheet against the wall in the proper position. Set a pry bar or a tapered piece of wood over a short piece of pipe on the floor, under the panel. Operate it with your foot as a lever, lifting the sheet up to abut the upper piece and leaving your hands free for nailing. Manufactured drywall levers, designed for this purpose, are available from most drywall suppliers.

There are a variety of methods of marking the location of electrical outlets and other openings for cutting. One is to coat the face of the electrical box with chalk, then press the drywall sheet against it.

This method transfers the box location to the sheet, but necessitates cutting from the back side.

The most straightforward method, and probably the safest, is to measure off the wall or the preceding sheet to all sides of the box, then transfer these measurements to the face of the sheet. These measurements should be exact, without a 1/4-inch allowance. After you set the sheet in place, if the opening is too small you can trim it out easily with a utility knife. If you make a mistake and cut the opening a little too big, you can take up the gap later. If the opening is considerably oversized or poorly located, cut a new sheet.

Outside corners should be finished off with metal corner beads, which are available wherever you purchased your drywall. Trim and smooth the drywall at the corners for a good fit with no protrusions or gaps, then seat the bead over the corner joint. Nail the bead in place carefully, alternating nails from one side to the other so as not to distort it; you want to maintain a nice, straight line on the corner.

For curved corners, such as over an archway, use tin snips to cut from the edge to the center bead, spacing the cuts about 1 inch apart. Cut one edge only, and install the bead with the cut edge on the top side of the curve. The numerous cuts will enable you to easily bend the metal to the desired configuration.

Remember that drywall installation is heavy, tiring work. It doesn't all need to be done at once, so be careful not to exceed your physical limits.

TAPING AND TOPPING

Finishing drywall is not particularly difficult; it just requires a little patience and practice to learn the techniques. You will need a 6-inch taping knife, a 12- or 14-inch taping knife, a mud pan, sanding pad, and sandpaper. All of these tools are available through your drywall supplier. The sizes of the taping knives just noted are pretty universal, but what you decide to use is a matter of personal preference. Some professionals use knives with larger blades for faster finishing, but they require more skill to use. Select a size with which you feel comfortable.

In addition to the tools, you will need joint compound and joint tape. Joint compound is available premixed, usually in 12- or 50-pound quantities, or as a dry powder to which you add water. The dry powder has a longer shelf life, since you only mix what you need. However, the premixed compound, which is ready to use right from the bucket, eliminates the problem of mixing the powder to the right consistency, and is the choice of most professionals.

Joint compound is available in all-purpose, taping, and topping formulas. The all-purpose mixture is suitable both for taping and applying the subsequent finish coats, and is fine for most uses. If you have a lot of finishing to do, use the special-purpose compounds. The taping compound is used to embed the tape and cover the nail heads. The topping compound is somewhat thinner and softer, allowing it to go on smoother and sand with less effort. Do not use topping compound for taping or over nail heads because it does not have the necessary strength and adhesion qualities.

Joint tape is a heavy, nonadhesive paper tape 2 inches wide and available in 60-, 250-, and 500-foot rolls. It has a slight ridge down the cen-

Fig. 20-10. Embedding the joint tape in the compound (Courtesy of the Foundation of the Wall and Ceiling Industry).

ter, enabling it to be creased easily for taping corners. As a rough estimate, each 150 square feet of drywall will require 12 pounds of compound and 120 feet of tape, but the amount can vary widely depending on the installation.

Tape the flat seams first, beginning with the ceiling, and then do the corners. Until you gain some speed, apply compound to only one seam at a time. Begin by filling your pan about half full with joint compound. Working from the pan, apply a layer of compound to the seam with the 6-inch blade. Hold the blade at a fairly flat angle to the ceiling, leaving a nice layer of joint compound that is not too thick (Fig. 20-9). This is the bedding coat, into which the tape will be placed.

Be certain that the entire seam is coated with compound, and that there are no dry spots. Keep the knife and pan clean and free of debris at all times; don't scoop up any dropped compound and put it back in the pan. If the compound becomes dirty, discard it, since small bits of dirt and other debris will prevent you from getting a smooth coat.

Start at one end of the seam and press the end of the tape into the compound (Fig. 20-10). Unroll

Fig. 20-9. Placing a layer of joint compound for bedding the tape (Courtesy of the Foundation of the Wall and Ceiling Industry).

the tape along the seam, pressing it lightly into the compound every 2 to 3 feet to hold it in place. Be certain the tape stays centered over the seam. When you reach the end of the seam, use your knife as a straightedge and tear the tape off cleanly.

Return to the starting point and use the 6-inch blade to embed the tape into the compound. Hold the blade at about a 45-degree angle to the face of the drywall, and apply enough pressure to smooth the tape and work out all of the bubbles. Continue to scrape your blade along the edge of the pan to remove excess compound. In this way, you will save a lot of sanding later and conserve material.

Finally, apply a skim coat of compound over the tape. Don't worry about trying to completely conceal it; that step will come later. Keep the compound smooth, scraping off the excess and returning it to the pan. The more perpendicular you hold your knife, the more compound you'll remove and the smoother the joint will be. Experiment with different angles until you're comfortable with one that smoothes the compound without removing too much.

When all of the flat seams are taped, do the corners. For inside corners, apply about a 4-inch-

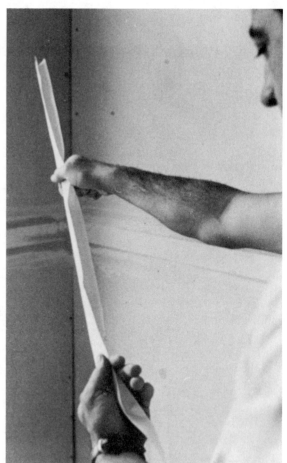

Fig. 20-12. Folding the joint tape along its performed crease, prior to using it in the corner (Courtesy of the Foundation of the Wall and Ceiling Industry).

Fig. 20-11. Applying joint compound in an inside corner (Courtesy of the Foundation of the Wall and Ceiling Industry).

wide layer of compound to each side of the corner (Fig. 20-11), then crease the tape between your fingers and place it in the corner (Fig. 20-12). Use the 6-inch blade to smooth it into place as you did for the flat seams, keeping the tape centered in the corner. Special corner trowels are available that smooth both sides of the corner at the same time. They take a little getting used to, and you might want to experiment with one to see if you like it.

For outside corners, no tape is necessary. Simply cover the metal corner bead by resting one corner of your knife edge on the bead and the other on the wall. Let the knife ride along the bead and the wall, filling in the area beneath the blade with compound (Fig. 20-13). Covering corner metal consumes a lot of compound in relation to the other seams, so keep your knife and mud pan full.

After you do the corners, you'll want to cover the heads of the fasteners. Scoop up some joint compound on one corner of the knife and run a bead over a line of about four to six nails at one time. Then, again holding the blade at a 45-degree angle, simply scrape off the excess, filling in each of the dimples.

Allow the compound to dry for at least 24 hours, or as recommended by the manufacturer. You will need to maintain a temperature of at least 50 degrees Fahrenheit in the room in which you're

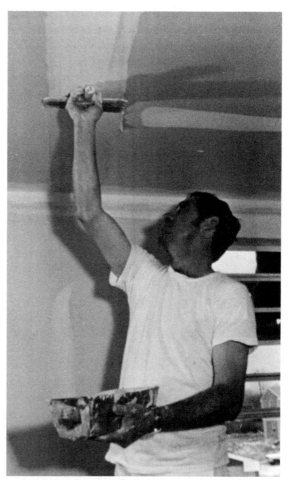

Fig. 20-14. Using a 12-inch blade to apply a topping coat of joint compound (Courtesy of the Foundation of the Wall and Ceiling Industry).

working, using heaters if necessary. The compound is water based, so be certain it is not allowed to freeze or the joints will fail. Make sure the compound is completely dry before you apply the next coat.

Apply the second coat, which can be either all-purpose or topping compound, with a wider taping knife. (See Fig. 20-14.) You can use the 12-inch blade, or you might find a 10-inch one easier to use.

Use the blade at a low angle to spread on a layer of compound over the entire seam. Then, with the blade more vertical, go back over the seam and smooth it out. Remember that each time you lift or twist the blade, you move the compound beneath

Fig. 20-13. Applying joint compound over metal corner bead (Courtesy of the Foundation of the Wall and Ceiling Industry).

it, causing slight irregularities. For the smoothest results, try to cover as much of the seam as possible in one continuous movement. Keep scraping your blade clean on the edge of the pan, and keep scraping excess compound off the walls to minimize sanding. Top the inside and outside corners, and go over the nail heads again. By the time you are finished with the second coat, none of the tape should be visible.

After the second coat has dried, sand it as necessary. Rubber-backed drywall sanding pads work quite well for this step, and offer the advantage of precut, easily changed sandpaper. A pole-mounted version with a swiveling head is also available for sanding ceilings and the upper parts of walls, and also for sanding the lower wall areas without stooping. (See Fig. 20-15.) A regular sanding block also will work.

Sanding drywall compound produces a very fine dust, so you should wear an approved face mask while you are sanding. Electric sanders seem to aggravate this dust problem and also can tear into the face paper on the drywall, so avoid the temptation to use one for this job. Remember to cover the doorways leading to other rooms with plastic sheets and masking tape, provided you have enough other ventilation in the room where you're working, to keep the dust problem elsewhere to a minimum.

Apply the third coat as you did the second, using a 12- or 14-inch blade. Some people find it easier to use a 12-inch cement trowel and a hawk, as are used in plastering. This choice again is a matter of personal preference, and requires a little experimentation. You should feather out the third coat as much as possible to blend the seam into the surrounding area and, again, to minimize sanding. If the seam you are finishing is one where two tapered edges meet, it is sufficient to merely fill in this recess with compound; extending it farther onto the surrounding sheet will just necessitate further sanding later.

For untapered butt joints, it is necessary to build the compound up to a somewhat greater thickness, allowing the seam to be sanded in such a way that the compound is feathered out onto the sheet

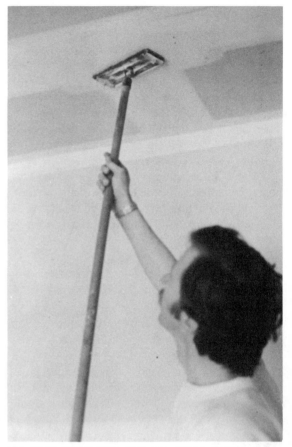

Fig. 20-15. Sanding the final coat of joint compound with a pole-mounted pad sander (Courtesy of the Foundation of the Wall and Ceiling Industry).

without cutting into the underlying tape. (See Fig. 20-16.) Don't overdo it, however; remember that the ultimate goal is a flat seam that blends in totally with the surrounding sheet.

Finish off the outside corners a third time also, applying the compound as you did for the first two coats. The inside corners and nail heads are usually all right with two coats, unless you notice obvious deficiencies while you are sanding. When the final coat is dry, sand it as necessary, concentrating on blending the edges into the surrounding wall area.

TRANSITIONS

Once again, you must deal with the transition be-

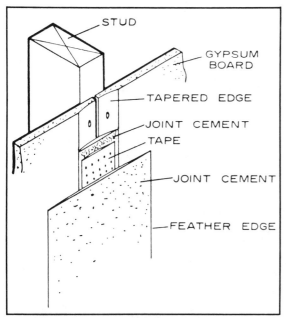

Fig. 20-16. The stages of taping and topping involved in finishing out a drywall joint.

tween the old and new wall and ceiling surfaces. In newer homes, where 1/2 drywall was used, the transitions shouldn't present any problem. Simply abut the new material carefully to the old, then tape the resulting seam. Slight irregularities might be present at the transition line and require several coats of joint compound to smooth out.

If you are abutting new drywall to existing plaster, the difference in the thicknesses can cause

problems. Plaster usually was applied in a 3/4-inch thickness, but in areas where the plaster was being used to even out irregularities, it could be considerably thicker or thinner than that.

Take the time to carefully measure the thickness of the lath and plaster at several points along the transition line, and write the measurements on the wall or ceiling at the point they were taken. This will give you a guide for matching the new material smoothly to the old.

Probably the easiest way to make the transition is to use 5/8-inch drywall. If the plaster measurements are fairly consistent at 3/4 inch, tack a layer of 1/8-inch shim material to the stud or joist at the transition point to bring the two surfaces level. Wood veneer, paneling, linoleum strips, or any other material of the proper thickness will work fine. If you don't wish to go to the added expense of installing 5/8-inch drywall, you can use the same methods with 1/2-inch drywall. Place a 1/4-inch shim on all the joists or studs of the wall or ceiling area being matched, or simply place a 1/4-inch shim on the first stud or joist, then a 1/8-inch shim on the next one, allowing the new surface to gently slope up to the old one.

If the thickness of the plaster varies widely, the lath might have pulled away from the underlying framing. Try reattaching it by nailing or screwing through the plaster, recessing the heads of the fasteners as much as possible. (See Fig. 20-17.) Recheck your measurements afterward to see if the

Fig. 20-17. Renailing a cut plaster edge to secure it to the joists before fitting the drywall.

Fig. 20-18. After installing the drywall and abutting it to the plaster as well as possible, fill in any broken areas in the plaster prior to taping.

problem has been corrected. As a last resort, you might need to place individual shims of varying thicknesses at different points along the transition in order to align the surfaces.

If the line of the plaster has broken away in various places along the transition line, as a result of damage sustained during the tear-out (Fig. 20-18), you might need to fill in the missing areas before you tape the joint. Install the new drywall first, abutting it to the plaster in as straight a line as possible. Using patching plaster or a filler material such as Fixall, fill in the missing areas and level them off with the surrounding plaster.

After the patches are dry, you can tape the joint with regular joint compound and joint tape. Apply as many coats of joint compound as necessary to get a smooth blend, feathering each coat farther out onto both surfaces (Fig. 20-19). Texturing, wallpaper, or other surface coverings will further hide the transition.

TEXTURING

If the drywall is to be painted later, you might want to consider texturing the walls. (See Fig. 20-20.) Texturing covers minor imperfections in the taping and topping, and because of its hiding power, speeds the finishing process. Applying a texturing

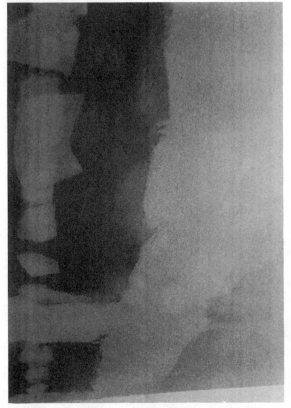

Fig. 20-19. The smoothly finished transition joint, ready for texturing and painting.

Fig. 20-20. A textured wall and ceiling, ready for painting. The wall at the right will be wallpapered, so the texturing was omitted.

ish simply by blending a texture additive into paint, or you can create heavy swirls with thickened joint compound. In new homes where a large amount of wall and ceiling surface is to be textured at once, the texturing material is usually applied by spraying with a special machine. This machine creates an attractive, uniform surface texture of small splotches, which if done correctly, can be applied after only one coat of joint compound on the drywall.

For hand-texturing, you can create a surface somewhat similar to that applied by the spray gun through a method known as *skip troweling*. Mix clean water with all-purpose or topping compound to thin it to a consistency similar to molasses, then add a small quantity of very fine sand, no more than about 1 teaspoon.

To apply the texture, pour the thinned joint compound mixture into the mud pan. Dip a 12-inch taping knife into the pan vertically. As you remove it, you will notice thick drips of the material hanging on the end of the blade. With a quick flip of the wrist, bring the knife into a vertical position with the blade up. This action will cause the drips to flip back onto the compound clinging to the blade. It is these random drips of compound that are actually applied to the wall as the sand in the mixture causes the blade to "skip," or bounce, across the surface of the drywall.

To apply the texture, hold the blade lightly against the wall so that the side of the blade with the splotches of compound is against the drywall. Lightly move the knife across the wall with very little pressure on it, allowing it to bounce and leave a random pattern of joint compound on the drywall. (See Fig. 20-21). Continue to dip the blade into the pan and apply the texture with random, curving movements of the knife. After you have covered about 50 or 75 square feet of wall, go back and lightly stroke a clean blade over the texturing, knocking down any high spots and evening out the surface. As you work, continue to add water to the mixture to prevent it from becoming too thick.

Skip-troweling is quite simple, but usually requires a little practice to get the feel for it. Pick a spot that is fairly concealed, such as the inside of

over the transition between old and new walls and ceilings can blend the two surfaces together, obscure the transition lines, and cover cracks and deficiencies in the old wall surfaces.

In addition, texturing imparts a pleasing appearance to the finished wall, providing an interesting blend of light and shadow that is a visual relief from a stark, flat wall surface. It can create different visual moods in the rooms, or can add contrast between different areas, or between the walls and the ceiling.

There are many types and styles of texture, limited only by the imagination of the person applying the texturing. You can apply a light sand finish

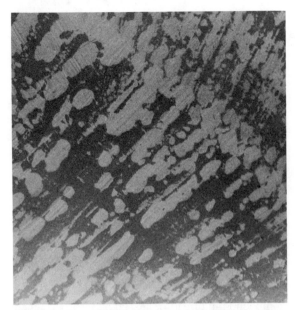

Fig. 20-21. The proper texture pattern left by skip troweling.

a closet, and practice there for awhile. Apply the texture to a small area, then simply scrape it off and return it to the pan, if you're not happy with the results. Keep trying until you're comfortable with the technique before you apply it to the more visible areas in the room.

If you don't like the appearance of skip-troweling, you can use one of several other textur-ing techniques. They include:

☐ Dipping a stiff brush in thinned joint compound, then running a stick or a piece of pipe across the end of the bristles to spray the compound on the wall.

☐ Troweling a thick layer of joint compound on the wall, then "swirling" it with the end of a paintbrush.

☐ Applying random splotches of joint compound with a heavy sponge, crumpled wax paper, a brush, or other objects.

☐ Applying stiff, heavy peaks of texture in a Med-iterranean style, using commercially available texturing compounds.

☐ Adding coarse sand to joint compound that has been thinned to the consistency of paint, then applying it with a heavy paint roller for a sand texture.

☐ Using a carpet roller to apply thickened paint or thinned joint compound, creating a light tex-ture commonly known as *stippling*.

The choices are many, and you should try a few to find the right look for your house. If you are hav-ing a contractor do your drywalling, ask to see some samples of his texturing, or take a look at a house he has done. Texturing can add a lot of visual in-terest to a room, as long as it's a texture you're happy with.

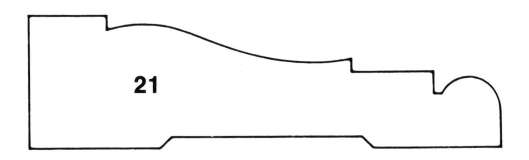

21

Interior Trim, Stairs, and Cabinets

One of the most enjoyable and satisfying aspects of a room addition is the interior finish work. All of the framing, roofing, and other rough work is behind you, and the walls are enclosed. Now the addition really begins to come together.

No matter what different finishing materials you're using for the addition, wood is almost sure to be one of them. Window and door trim, baseboards, ceiling moldings, wall trim, paneling—in these and many other areas, wood adds a touch of warmth and class. Wood is also a nice material to work with. It cuts nicely, finishes well, and fastens easily, and even the beginning do-it-yourselfer can get a nice finished product with a minimum of tools.

The old adage for finish work is "measure twice, cut once," and it's well worth remembering. Trim material is expensive when compared with framing lumber, and almost all of the joints you make will be visible. Take your time, measure carefully, then take a moment to verify your measurements before you cut.

MATERIALS

There is a tremendous variety of materials available for use as interior trim, or you can combine materials or cut your own if you need a special piece. Closely study the style and material used in the rest of the house, and let that be a guide in selecting materials for the addition. As with most of the other visible aspects of the addition, the interior trim should match up for the best overall finished appearance. (See Fig. 21-1.)

Most molding patterns (Fig. 21-2) are available in both hardwood and softwood, and the prices and availability will depend on the area in which you live. You should select clear grades if you intend to stain or varnish the trim. In some cases, depending on the quality, No. 1 material might work fine and save you some money, if you don't mind working around some small imperfections.

If you will paint the trim, No. 1 grades will be fine. Some moldings are also available with *finger-joints,* small scraps of clear lumber that are con-

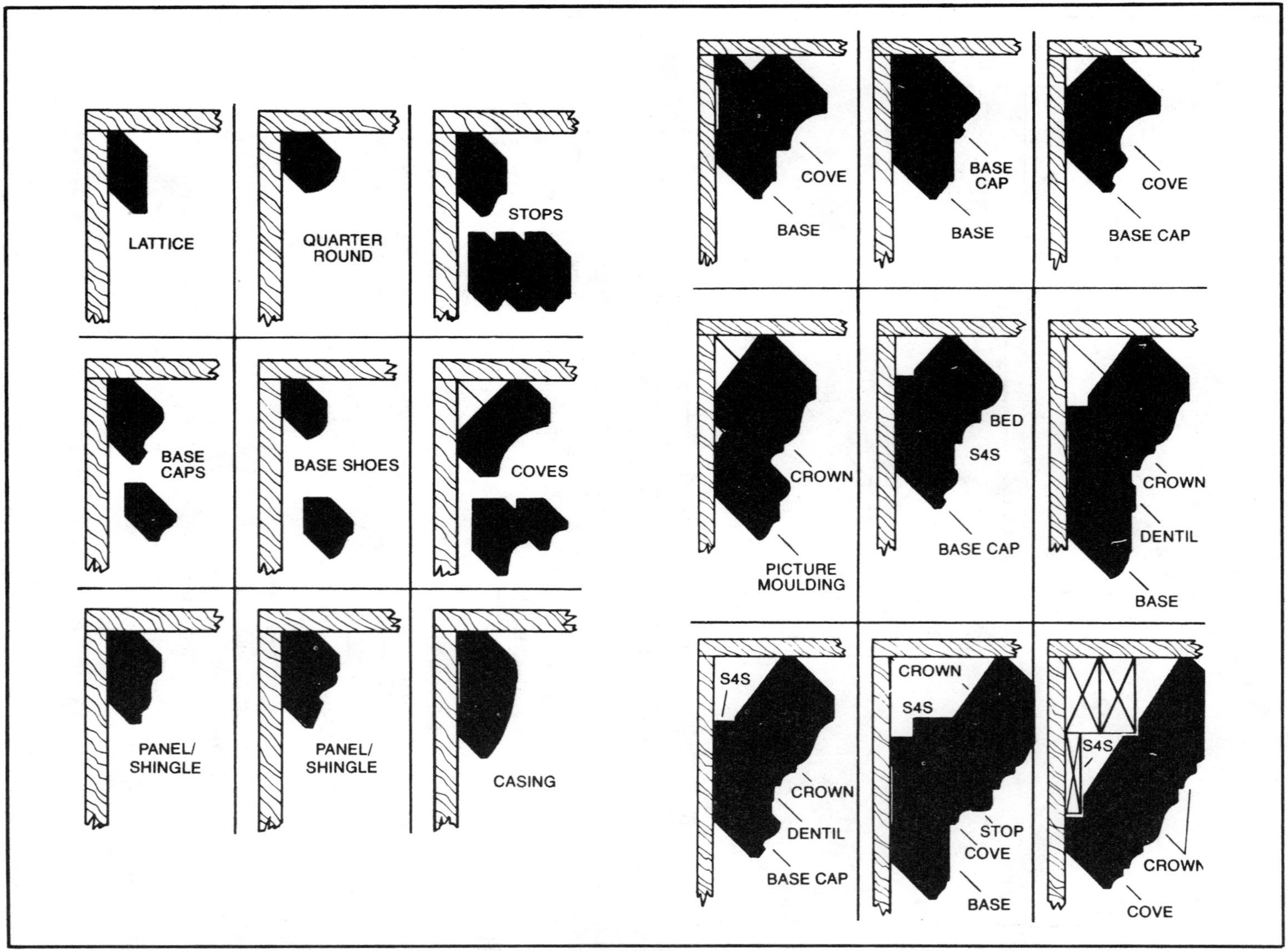

Fig. 21-1. Combining moldings to create a new look or to match up to what's existing (Courtesy of Wood Moulding and Millwork Producers Association).

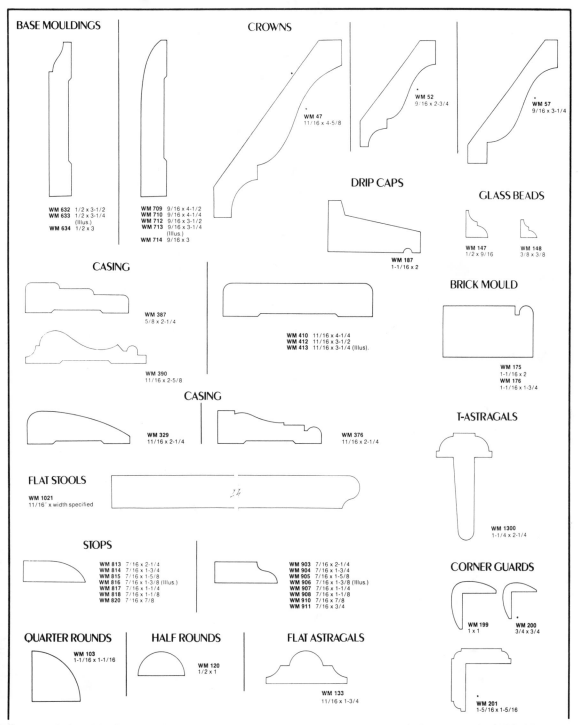

BASE MOULDINGS

WM 632 1/2 x 3-1/2
WM 633 1/2 x 3-1/4
(Illus.)
WM 634 1/2 x 3

WM 709 9/16 x 4-1/2
WM 710 9/16 x 4-1/4
WM 712 9/16 x 3-1/2
WM 713 9/16 x 3-1/4
(Illus.)
WM 714 9/16 x 3

CROWNS

WM 47
11/16 x 4-5/8

WM 52
9/16 x 2-3/4

WM 57
9/16 x 3-1/4

DRIP CAPS

WM 187
1-1/16 x 2

GLASS BEADS

WM 147
1/2 x 9/16

WM 148
3/8 x 3/8

CASING

WM 387
5/8 x 2-1/4

WM 390
11/16 x 2-5/8

WM 410 11/16 x 4-1/4
WM 412 11/16 x 3-1/2
WM 413 11/16 x 3-1/4 (Illus.)

BRICK MOULD

WM 175
1-1/16 x 2
WM 176
1-1/16 x 1-3/4

CASING

WM 329
11/16 x 2-1/4

WM 376
11/16 x 2-1/4

T-ASTRAGALS

WM 1300
1-1/4 x 2-1/4

FLAT STOOLS

WM 1021
11/16" x width specified

STOPS

WM 813 7/16 x 2-1/4
WM 814 7/16 x 1-3/4
WM 815 7/16 x 1-5/8
WM 816 7/16 x 1-3/8 (Illus.)
WM 817 7/16 x 1-1/4
WM 818 7/16 x 1-1/8
WM 820 7/16 x 7/8

WM 903 7/16 x 2-1/4
WM 904 7/16 x 1-3/4
WM 905 7/16 x 1-5/8
WM 906 7/16 x 1-3/8 (Illus.)
WM 907 7/16 x 1-1/4
WM 908 7/16 x 1-1/8
WM 910 7/16 x 7/8
WM 911 7/16 x 3/4

CORNER GUARDS

WM 199
1 x 1

WM 200
3/4 x 3/4

QUARTER ROUNDS

WM 103
1-1/16 x 1-1/16

HALF ROUNDS

WM 120
1/2 x 1

FLAT ASTRAGALS

WM 133
11/16 x 1-3/4

WM 201
1-5/16 x 1-5/16

Fig. 21-2. Some of the many molding patterns available for interior trim and finish work (Courtesy of Wood Moulding and Millwork Producers Association).

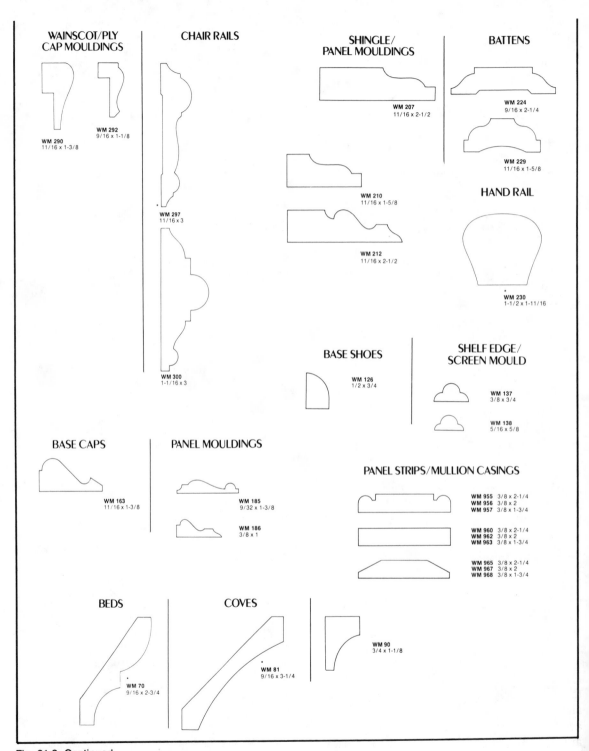

WAINSCOT/PLY CAP MOULDINGS

WM 290
11/16 x 1-3/8

WM 292
9/16 x 1-1/8

CHAIR RAILS

WM 297
11/16 x 3

WM 300
1-1/16 x 3

SHINGLE/ PANEL MOULDINGS

WM 207
11/16 x 2-1/2

WM 210
11/16 x 1-5/8

WM 212
11/16 x 2-1/2

BATTENS

WM 224
9/16 x 2-1/4

WM 229
11/16 x 1-5/8

HAND RAIL

WM 230
1-1/2 x 1-11/16

BASE SHOES

WM 126
1/2 x 3/4

SHELF EDGE/ SCREEN MOULD

WM 137
3/8 x 3/4

WM 138
5/16 x 5/8

BASE CAPS

WM 163
11/16 x 1-3/8

PANEL MOULDINGS

WM 185
9/32 x 1-3/8

WM 186
3/8 x 1

PANEL STRIPS/MULLION CASINGS

WM 955   3/8 x 2-1/4
WM 956   3/8 x 2
WM 957   3/8 x 1-3/4

WM 960   3/8 x 2-1/4
WM 962   3/8 x 2
WM 963   3/8 x 1-3/4

WM 965   3/8 x 2-1/4
WM 967   3/8 x 2
WM 968   3/8 x 1-3/4

BEDS

WM 70
9/16 x 2-3/4

COVES

WM 81
9/16 x 3-1/4

WM 90
3/4 x 1-1/8

Fig. 21-2. Continued.

nected with a series of interlocking joints, like fingers. The joints are strong and the moldings are well milled, offering you good savings while still providing you with an excellent trim for painting.

There is usually a fair amount of waste with trim, because of the miter cuts and the number of odd-length pieces that need to be cut and fit around the windows, doors, baseboards, and other areas. Depending on the size of the material and the number and type of cuts you'll be making, you should allow anywhere from 10 percent to 20 percent waste when ordering. Trim lumber is expensive, so you might wish to order only the minimum that you think you'll need, then purchase a few more pieces to finish up if the need arises. If you intend to purchase trim in this way, make certain that additional matching material is available when you place your initial order.

WORK SPACE

When you get to the trim stage on your addition, take a moment and set yourself up a work area. A sheet of 3/4-inch plywood set on two sturdy sawhorses of convenient height will work well as a temporary table for your miter box, portable table saw, and other tools. Set it up in the middle of a room where it will be handy, but out of the way. Then run a multioutlet extension cord to it, and install a small clamp light. Set out all of your screws and nails, tools, and other finish materials, using small boxes or cans to organize everything in a way that's convenient for you. You'll find that a little effort expended here will save you many hours of searching for supplies and fumbling with moldings, and it also eliminates the need to work on your knees on the floor.

FINISH WOODWORKING
AND WOODWORKING TOOLS

For most of the finish trim work you'll be doing on the addition, the hand and power tools you've used all along will be sufficient, with a few specialized additions. Most of the additional tools you'll need are quite inexpensive, and will always come in handy.

Miters and Miter Boxes

One tool you will need is a miter box. There are a number of areas where wood needs to be joined in a miter, and a miter box is about the only way to make the necessary cuts accurately. Miter boxes range from very simple to very elaborate, in both hand and electric models. You can rent a miter box if this is your only woodworking project. If, however, you plan other projects in the future, you might wish to invest in a good one and add it to your workshop collection. You'll always find a use for it.

For a few simple cuts, you can get by with the basic model. This is simply a U-shaped box with saw cuts in the sides at 45 and 90 degrees. It might be made of wood or plastic. You simply set the piece of wood you wish to cut inside the box, then set a fine-toothed handsaw or backsaw in the cuts and use them as a guide. The two drawbacks to this type of miter box are that it is not always very accurate, and it limits you to only 45- and 90-degree cuts. If you wish to make a miter at an angle other than these, the box won't help you.

A considerable improvement is the type of miter box that has an attached backsaw (Fig. 21-3).

Fig. 21-3. Professional-quality miter box with an attached back saw (Courtesy of Stanley Tools, Division of the Stanley Works, New Britain, CT 06050).

The saw is suspended on spring-loaded arms over the saw table, and can be adjusted to any angle. Most of these types of miter boxes are highly accurate, and the stiff, fine-toothed backsaw makes smooth, clean cuts. The electric version of this, the power miter box, has an interchangeable circular saw blade, usually 8, 9, or 10 inches in diameter, and the angles can be adjusted as desired.

No matter which type of miter box you use, test the miters with some scrap wood before you cut your finish moldings. Simply cut a 45-degree miter on two boards, hold the cuts together, and place a framing square next to them. If the square indicates that the resulting joint is at 90 degrees, then the box is accurate. If not, it needs to be adjusted. On miter boxes that are adjustable, simply set the angle of cut in or out (to 44 or 46 degrees, for example). On miter boxes with fixed saw cuts, use the tip of a shingle or other thin shim between the molding and the box to "tip" the cut to the proper angle. You will need to do some experimentation on pieces of scrap to get it just right.

Remember when you are mitering moldings and other trim that the miter cut creates a certain amount of waste on each cut. You will need to take this waste into consideration when you are ordering the wood. The amount wasted on each cut is equal to the width of the piece being cut, plus an allowance for the width of the saw blade. If you have a number of cuts to make, you can easily waste several feet of wood.

Nail Sets and Nail Spinners

Nail sets are another necessary item. They are quite inexpensive, and are sold individually or in a set of three, which give you the complete size range for any job you'll encounter. To avoid damaging wood moldings and to make the nails as unobtrusive as possible, use finish nails of the smallest size possible that still gives you the necessary length for good penetration.

Drive the nail to within 1/4 inch of the surface, then use the nail set. Select a tip size that is close to but slightly smaller then the size of the nail head. Place the tip of the nail set squarely against the head of the nail, and use light hammer blows to drive the nail just below the surface of the board.

If you are working with hardwoods or very small moldings, you should always predrill the wood to prevent it from splitting. Use a drill bit that is the same size or slightly smaller than the nails you're using. If you're lacking a drill bit, just use a nail of the same size as you're using on the moldings. Snip off the head, sharpen the point, and use it in your drill in place of the drill bit. Simply discard it when it becomes dull or bent.

Another handy tool for this purpose is the nail spinner. (See Fig. 21-4.) Place the tool in the chuck of the drill, and insert a finish nail in the end, point out. Place the point of the nail against the molding, and activate the drill. The drill will "spin" the nail into the wood, leaving just the head exposed for finishing off with a nail set. Nail spinners cost just a few dollars at most hardware stores, and can save you quite a bit of time if you have a lot of moldings to install.

Coping Saw

A coping saw is a type of handsaw with a deep throat and a thin, narrow, replaceable, fine-toothed blade. Coping saws are useful for cutting fine scrolls, intricate patterns, and other curved work in fairly thin materials. In finish work, you can use a coping saw to make coped joints in baseboards and moldings where they meet at 90-degree inside corners. This type of joint, a little more time consuming then a standard miter joint, usually fits tighter and will adapt better to irregular corners.

For coped joints, install one entire wall of baseboard first, using square-cut ends. You should cut

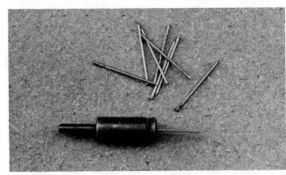

Fig. 21-4. A nail spinner for installing finish nails.

the baseboard just slightly longer than is needed. Bow out the center, place the ends of the board in the corners, and allow the center to spring back naturally against the wall, tightly pressing the ends of the board into the corners.

Cut the intersecting piece at a 45-degree angle, as you would for any mitered joint. (See Fig. 21-5.) Set the molding on a bench or worktable and hold or clamp it steady. Starting at the top of the board, use the coping saw to carefully cut along the face contour. Darken the corner where you'll be cutting with a pencil to make the contour easier to follow. Start the saw out at 90 degrees to the back of the board, then angle it slightly to about 85 degrees as you cut. The finished cut should fit tightly against the other baseboard at the front and top, which are the exposed cuts, and be angled slightly back at the rear of the piece, which is hidden. This sounds like a difficult cut, but it's actually quite simple, and a few trial cuts on some scrap will quickly give you the hang of it.

Measuring

Measuring moldings and trim is much more crucial than measuring framing pieces. The joints are quite visible, and since most trim is rather expensive, a lot of miscuts can become quite costly.

Inside measurements are the trickiest. You can use a folding rule with an extension rod. Fold out the sections of the rule one at a time until they almost reach the opposite wall, then slide out the extension rod to touch the wall. Add the measurements shown on the folding sections to the measurement shown on the extension rod to get the total inside wall-to-wall measurement.

The only drawback to folding rules is that they are relatively short. An alternate method for longer areas is to use a regular retractable tape measure. Start at one corner and measure out to a convenient whole number on the tape, say 12 feet. Mark the wall at this point. Now measure from the opposite corner to this point. If the second measurement is 3 feet 2 1/4 inches, adding the two measurements will give you the total inside measurement of 15 feet 2 1/4 inches.

When you are measuring any finish material,

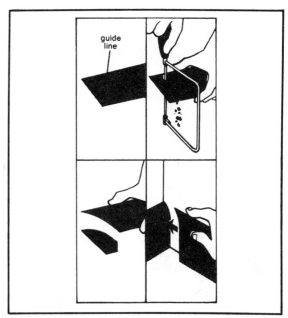

Fig. 21-5. Cutting a coped joint in a baseboard (Courtesy of Wood Moulding and Millwork Producers Association).

don't forget to allow for the waste generated by the cuts. For example, suppose you want to cut a 12-foot board into three exact 4-foot lengths. Marking the board into 4-foot pieces and then cutting it will make each piece short by the width of the cut.

Cutting

You should always cut trim using a fine-toothed saw blade. The finer the teeth, the slower the blade will move and the finer the cut surface will be. If the cut needs to be extremely accurate, mark it with a sharp knife instead of a pencil, since the width of the pencil lead can be enough to throw off a really precise cut. If the piece is being crosscut (cut across the grain), score it slightly with the knife to prevent it from splintering along the grain when you are cutting.

Plywood and other thin veneers should be cut with a very fine toothed crosscut saw if you're doing it by hand, or with a plywood blade if you are cutting it with a circular or table saw. Because of the direction of movement of the blade's cutting teeth, be sure to cut the piece face up if you're using a handsaw (Fig. 21-6) or table saw, and face down if you're using a circular saw. For panels with thin or fragile veneers, apply masking tape along the line of cut. Remove the tape immediately and carefully after you have completed the cut.

When you are using a handsaw or circular saw for ripping, use a saw guide for an accurate line. A saw guide is simply a sturdy, straight board clamped to the piece being cut with C-clamps at each end. Clamp the board on the side of the piece that you'll be using, not on the scrap side. That way, if your saw should waver off the edge of the board, the miscut will be into the scrap and not the finished piece.

Always completely support the piece you are cutting (Fig. 21-6). Support is especially important for long pieces, since the weight of the piece being cut off will crack the board across the saw kerf before the cut is finished, often ruining the piece you intended to use. You must support plywood and large panels at several points to prevent the cut from tipping in or out and closing the kerf, which causes the saw to bind and can throw off the line of cut. Worse yet, it can cause a dangerous kickback when you are using a circular saw.

Scribing

Quite often you will encounter the need to fit a straight surface against an irregular one. This situation could be a piece of paneling abutting the edge of a brick fireplace, or a piece of molding being used against a wavy plaster corner. In these instances, you must scribe the board so that its contours match up to those of the irregular surface.

The easiest way to do scribing is with an inexpensive compass, the type with the small tube that holds a replaceable pencil. Abut the straight piece, for example a sheet of paneling, against the irregular edge. Be sure the sheet is plumb, and tack it to the wall if necessary to hold it in this position. Sight along the gap between the sheet and the corner, locate the widest point, and set the compass to this width.

Starting at the top, hold the steel point of the compass against the corner and place the pencil point on the paneling. Slowly move down the wall, keeping the compass point against the corner and the pencil point in contact with the paneling. Let the steel point follow each jog and irregularity in the wall corner, which will automatically transfer them in pencil onto the sheet. The pencil line then serves as a cutting guide to create an edge on the paneling that will exactly match the wall corner.

WALL PANELING

A popular choice for an interior finish, either for an entire room or just as an accent on one wall, is wood paneling. Wood paneling can take the form of wood strips or veneers, solid boards, or prefinished plywood panels. Whatever your choice, install wood paneling first, before baseboards, door and window casing, or any other trim. This method will allow you to trim out the paneling at the same time as the rest of the room, and make the installation simpler and neater.

You should purchase wood paneling, in board or sheet form, about 2 weeks before you need it, if possible. Stack the paneling in the room where you will install it, using small spacers to keep the pieces separated and allow an even air flow around them. This procedure allows the wood to dry and become acclimated to the temperature and humidity conditions in which it will be installed, which minimizes shrinkage and warpage after the material is up. Protect the faces of prefinished paneling with cardboard or other material to prevent them from becoming scratched during stacking and handling.

Installing Individual Boards

If you are installing boards horizontally, you can attach them directly to the studs. Apply thin wood over a backing of drywall or other solid material to provide adequate support. Vertical boards will require horizontal blocking between the studs on 24-inch centers to provide a nailing surface, or you can attach 1-×-2 or 1-×-3 furring strips horizontally across the studs. Stain or paint the paneling boards first. Laying them out on sawhorses or other supports greatly simplifies the application of the finish.

Vertical Boards. Begin the installation of

Fig. 21-6. Proper cutting of a veneered panel with a handsaw. The panel needs to be supported well to prevent damage as the cut is completed (Courtesy of Georgia-Pacific Corporation).

vertical boards at one corner. Hold the first board in place against the corner, and check it carefully with a level to see if it's plumb. If it isn't, tip it away from the corner until it is, then check to see how big the gap is. If the gap will be covered by a molding, or by the boards being installed on the cross wall, then this first board can be installed as it is. Otherwise, you'll need to plane the board so that it fits against the corner. In either case, it's essential that the first board be installed perfectly plumb, or the entire finished wall will appear to be leaning.

Work out from the first board, carefully fitting each subsequent board against the one before it for a clean line. Face-nail the boards using finish nails driven into the studs, furring, or blocking. Install two nails for boards up to 6 inches wide, and three nails for wider boards.

For a symmetrical appearance, measure the finished width of one board and divide that into the total width of the wall. If this calculation shows that you will be left with a small fill at one end, split the difference between the two corners to even out the finished appearance. For example, suppose you intend to cover a 13-foot-wide wall with 7-inch boards. Thirteen feet is 156 inches, which when divided by 7 means you will need 22 boards, and you'll be left with a fill of 2 inches. Rather than have a 7-inch board in one corner and a 2-inch board in the other, use a 1-inch board in each of the corners.

Horizontal Boards. Install horizontal boards either from the floor up or from the ceiling down. Follow the same procedures as for vertical boards, checking the first board against the floor or ceiling and trimming it as necessary to be sure it's perfectly level. If desired, split the difference between fills at the floor and ceiling as just described. Fasten the boards with finish nails driven into the studs.

Installing Prefinished Paneling

Prefinished paneling is commonly sold in 4- × -8-foot sheets. You can install sheets of 3/8-inch thickness or greater directly over studs on 16-inch centers (Fig. 21-7), but you must apply thinner materials over a drywall backing.

Colors and face grains on prefinished paneling can vary considerably. It's a good idea to lean the panels up against the walls in the location they'll be installed, then stand back and take a look at how they match up. Move the sheets around as necessary to create a pleasing flow of grain and color. When you're satisfied with the look, start at one corner and number each panel sequentially on the back as a guide for when you install them.

Prefinished paneling can be installed with nails, panel adhesive, or a combination of both. For a nailed installation, install the nails into each stud, keeping them about 16 inches apart. Many types of paneling have vertical grooves or dark decorative areas on the face. Drive the nails into these areas if possible for best concealment.

If you're using panel adhesive, follow the manufacturer's instructions carefully. Apply the adhesive in vertical lines to the studs or the drywall backing, keeping the lines 12 to 16 inches apart and covering a section of the wall only one panel wide. Hold the panel in place and tack it with a couple of nails at the ceiling, holding it 4 to 6 inches away from the wall at the bottom with a block of wood. Let the panel remain in this position until the adhesive becomes tacky. For some types of adhesive, it is recommended that you first push the panel against the wall and then pull it away.

After the recommended time has elapsed, remove the block and carefully press the panel into contact with the wall. Using a rubber mallet or a hammer and a thickly padded block of wood, tap over the entire surface of the panel to get a good bond. Drive the ceiling nails the rest of the way in, and add additional nails as you feel are necessary.

DOOR CASING

Casings are used to cover the gap between the door frame and the rough framing that surrounds the opening. Select a casing material that is compatible with the other moldings in the room, and that is consistent with the look you are trying to achieve. A standard 6-8 door will require two 7-foot pieces and one 3-foot to 3 1/2-foot piece (depending on the door width) per side.

Begin by marking the reveal on the edge of the door frame. (See Fig. 21-8.) The standard reveal is 1/4 inch, but it can be adjusted to suit your own

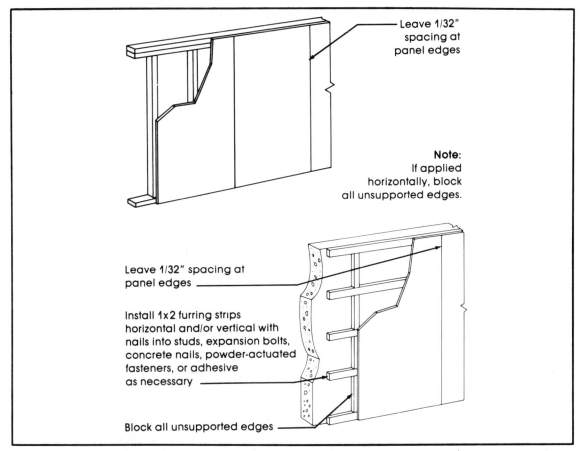

Leave 1/32" spacing at panel edges

Note:
If applied horizontally, block all unsupported edges.

Leave 1/32" spacing at panel edges

Install 1x2 furring strips horizontal and/or vertical with nails into studs, expansion bolts, concrete nails, powder-actuated fasteners, or adhesive as necessary

Block all unsupported edges

Fig. 21-7. Recommendations for installing plywood paneling directly to the wall studs (Courtesy of American Plywood Association).

preference. Using a combination square, a marking gauge, or a rabbeted piece of wood, mark both jamb legs and the head jamb with a sharp pencil.

Set the end of one piece of side casing on the floor, in line with the marked reveal. If the finish flooring has not been laid and you are using linoleum, tile, or hardwood, place a scrap of the flooring down first, then set the casing on it. This procedure will leave a gap under the casing that the flooring can slide into, simplifying its installation.

Mark the casing at the point where it crosses the reveal line on the head jamb. Cut the casing on a miter at this point, then tack it into place with just a couple of nails, driven only partially in. Repeat the procedure for the other side.

Check the door frame to see that it's square.

If it is, measure the distance between the insides of the casings and cut the top casing to this measurement. Test-fit it, and finish nailing all three casings into place.

If the door frame is not square, you'll need to cheat a little on the top casing miters. Cut one end at the approximate angle needed (44 or 46 degrees for example) and test-fit it by holding the miter against the side casing and lining up the bottom of the casing with the reveal mark on the head jamb. When you have a good fit on one end, repeat the procedure on the other end, but leave the casing long. Test-fit this second cut, and when you have both angles right, cut the piece to length. You usually can get away with cheating on the angle up to about 2 degrees; beyond that the miters on the

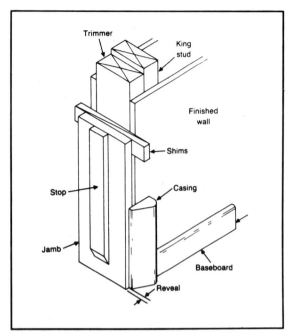

Fig. 21-8. Typical trim work around a door frame. Note the reveal, usually 1/4 inch, between the face of the jamb and the edge of the casing.

side casings also will need to be adjusted to prevent the finished joint from being noticeable.

An optional installation method is to square-cut the joints on the casings. This method was common with older, wide materials. Measure each side casing to the reveal mark on the head jamb as just described, then cut them off square. Tack both pieces in place, and measure the distance across the casings from outside to outside. Cut the top casing to this length, then fit and secure all three pieces. Decorative blocks also can be used in the corners, to which all three casing pieces abut.

If the door jambs are slightly too wide for the width of the opening, the mitered or square cut corners might tip back, thus opening up the joint. Watch for this condition while you are installing the casings, and slip a small shim behind the joints as necessary to correct it. If the shim makes the gap between the casing and the wall substantially too wide, you will need to place a wooden strip between the wall and the back of the casing. Remember that the edge of this strip will be exposed, so select a suitable material.

If you are using wide casing material, hollowing out the back will greatly simplify its installation over slightly uneven walls. Some material comes this way, or you can simply run it through a table saw, face up, and dado out the back. Dado to a depth approximately one-fourth the thickness of the board, and to within about 3/4 inch of each side. Remember that if you are square-cutting the corners, you cannot dado the top casing all the way to the ends, or the dados will show. Start and stop the cuts short of the ends.

WINDOW CASINGS AND TRIM

Window casings serve the same purpose and are installed in the same manner as door casings. If the jambs did not come preassembled with the window, as is the case with most wood windows, then you will need to enclose the opening with jamb material before you apply the casings.

The easiest way to enclose the opening is to simply build a box and slip it into the window opening, similar to installing a prehung door frame. Building the jambs in this manner speeds the installation, and ensures that all of the joints in the jambs are secure and well joined, and that the assembly is square in the opening. You will find this method an improvement over installing the jamb pieces one at a time.

First, measure the exact width and height of the window opening. Check these measurements in several areas to be certain the opening does not vary to any great degree. Next, measure the distance from the face of the window frame to the face of the finished wall surface. Check this measurement in several areas, also. Rip your jamb material to this dimension, and sand it smooth with a belt sander or a pad sander.

Cut the two jamb legs to the height of the window opening minus 1/4 inch. Cut the top and bottom jambs to the width of the window opening minus twice the thickness of the jamb material, and minus 1/4 inch. Assemble the four pieces into a box, nailing the side jambs onto the top and bottom jambs. The resulting box should be 1/4 inch less than the opening in both directions.

Slip the box into the opening and shim it so that

it is square, plumb, and level. (See Fig. 21-9.) The face of the box should be flush with the finished wall surface. Secure the box in place by nailing through the shims with finish nails, as you would a prehung door frame. Finally, install the casing with a 1/4-inch reveal, using either mitered or square-cut corners, as you did with the door casing.

Some windows have drywall applied directly to the framing around the two sides and the top of the opening, and therefore use no jambs and casings. In this case, a wooden window sill, called a *stool,* is commonly used over the bottom member of the framing. Select a stool material that is approximately 1 inch wider than the distance from the face of the window to the face of the finished wall. Cut it 2 inches longer than the distance between the drywalled sides of the opening.

Mark the distance from the window to the finished wall on the face of the stool at each end, and measure in a distance of 1 inch from each end. Cut out the resulting notch, and fit the stool to the opening. Finish by installing a trim piece, called an *apron,* under the stool. The apron covers the rough edge of the drywall and gives a nice finished look to the entire installation. Leave the apron shorter than the length of the stool and cut the ends either square, rounded, or at any pleasing angle.

A combination of these two methods also looks nice. (See Fig. 21-10.) First, install the stool over the bottom member of the rough opening. It should overhang each side of the opening by the width of the casing plus about 3/4 inch. Construct a three-sided box, and install it in the opening, shimming it so that it is square and the two side legs are parallel to each other. Use two side casings, resting them on the stool and showing a 1/4-inch reveal. Next, install a top casing, just like around a door. An apron beneath the stool finishes off the installation.

BASEBOARDS

Baseboards are used to finish off the area at the bottom of the walls, where they meet the floor. They are not essential, but they add a professional finished touch to the room while protecting the wall from damage, and should be included in your plans for finishing off the room.

You should coordinate the selection of the baseboard material (Fig. 21-2) with your choices for all the rest of the moldings. Massive baseboards do not look quite right with slender door casings, and vice versa. If you are using wide baseboard material, it should have a hollow back for easy installation and a flush fit against the wall. There are several styles

Fig. 21-9. Shimming the window frame box to make it plumb and level.

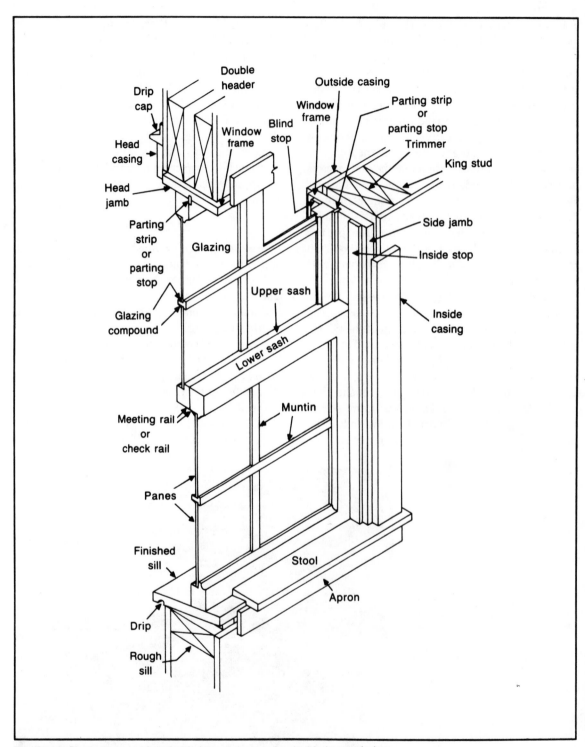

Fig. 21-10. Stool, apron, and casing being used around a double-hung window.

of hollow-backed baseboards available, or you can dado your own material as described previously.

You can miter or cope the inside corners, but you will need to miter the outside corners. If the baseboard is rectangular in section, you might wish to use square-cut corners, although miters will still look better. Another interesting alternative is to use blocks at all the corners, then abut the baseboards to the blocks with square cuts.

If you are installing wall-to-wall carpet, you will usually install the baseboards first, then abut the carpet to them. With other types of flooring, you might wish to install the baseboards after you have laid the flooring. This method simplifies the installation of the flooring by allowing the baseboard to cover the area between the edge of the flooring and the wall. Another alternative, popular in older houses but not done as much today, is to first install the baseboard, then the flooring. Then install another molding, called a *base shoe*, to cover the edge of the flooring.

If you are using wide, square-topped material for baseboard, you might wish to consider an additional molding, called a *base molding* or *base cap*. (See Fig. 21-11.) This piece of trim sits on top of the baseboard, adding a nice decorative effect while covering any small gaps that might exist between the baseboard and the wall.

STAIRS

Stair construction represents a combination of both rough and finish carpentry. There are several types of stairways, depending on the size of the area and the desired finished appearance (Fig. 21-12).

In some instances, you will construct the rough carriages for the stairs during the wall framing stage, then finish them out with the rest of the trim. You can purchase most of the finish parts prefabricated. If you desire, you can purchase the entire stairway in prefabricated, knocked-down form, custom cut to your specifications. Other manufacturers offer stock size units that fit given rough openings and ceiling heights. You also can purchase stairways for special situations, such as a spiral staircase for a confined area, in stock and custom sizes. A prefabricated unit is often your best bet, espe-

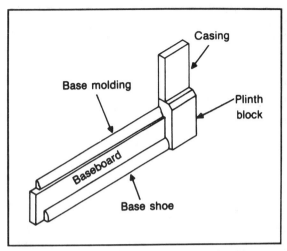

Fig. 21-11. Base molding being used on top of a wide baseboard. The plinth block adds an elegant finishing touch.

cially if the sizes or configurations are at all out of the ordinary. Check with your local lumberyard for sources of manufacturers.

Ratio of Riser to Tread

If the size of the risers and treads are not already specified on your plans, you will need to make these calculations based on the existing conditions. It's important to maintain the correct ratio between the two, so that the stairway looks and feels right. (See Fig. 21-13.)

The ideal riser height is between 7 1/2 and 7 3/4 inches, with a tread width of around 9 1/2 to 10 inches. As a rule of thumb, the tread width multiplied by the riser height should equal between 72 and 75. For example, a 9 1/2-inch tread with a 7 3/4-inch riser would equal 74, and a 10-inch tread with a 7 1/2-inch riser would equal 75. Both fall within the range of an ideal ratio.

Another rule is that the tread width plus twice the riser height should equal approximately 25. In the two examples just given, both of the combinations would equal exactly 25 (9 1/2 + 7 3/4 + 7 3/4 and 10 + 7 1/2 + 7 1/2).

Working from these ideal riser heights, you can calculate the number of steps between floors. If you have a ceiling height of 8 feet, you will need to figure the height of the second-story joists, along with

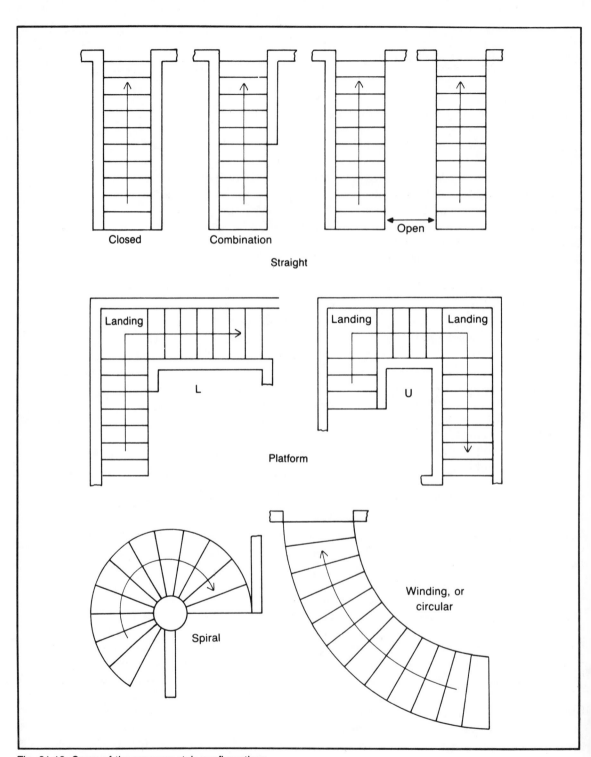

Fig. 21-12. Some of the common stair configurations.

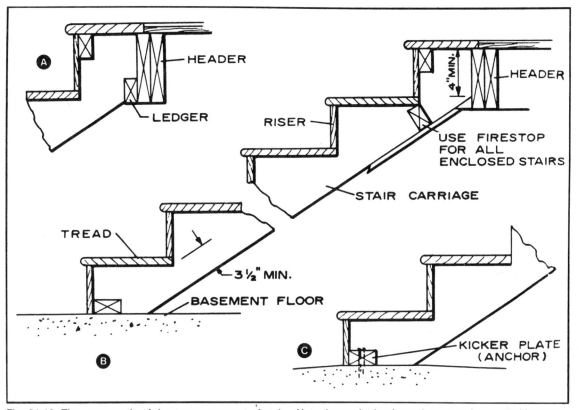

Fig. 21-13. The proper ratio of rise to run on a set of stairs. Note the methods of attachment at the top and bottom.

the subfloor and finished floor. If this measurement added another 12 inches, you would have a total from one floor to the next floor of 9 feet, or 108 inches. A common number of stairs for a main stairway is 14, so you can check your riser height by dividing 108 by 14. The answer is 7.7 inches, which falls with the range of an ideal riser height.

The stairway will have one less tread than risers, so if the stairway has 14 risers, it will have 13 treads. If the tread width is 9 1/2 inches, the entire horizontal run of the stairs will be approximately 124 inches, or 10 1/3 feet (9 1/2- × -13). The finished widths for main stairs vary with the style of the installation, but 3 to 4 feet is common.

Stringer Layout

The stringers are laid out according to the number and size of the treads and risers. First, you need to determine the length of the stringer, which is cal-

culated from the Pythagorean theorem ($A^2 + B^2 = C^2$) discussed earlier. In the previous example, the rise is 108 inches and the run is 124 inches:

$$108^2 = 11,664$$
$$124^2 = 15,376$$
$$11,664 + 15,376 = 27,040$$

The square root of 27,040 is approximately 165 inches, or 13 3/4 feet. This means that you will need a 14-foot-long board for the stringer, usually a 2 × 12.

Next, cut a piece of straight lumber to the same measurement that you calculated between floors, in this case 108 inches. Set a pair of large dividers to the calculated riser height, which in this example is 7.7 inches. Starting at one end of the board, use the dividers to lay off 14 risers of approximately 7.7 inches each. If the last space you lay off is not equal to all the others, adjust the dividers accordingly and try it again. Continue this procedure until the board has been divided into 14 equal parts. Measure the setting of the dividers at this point, which will be the exact height of the risers you'll use in the layout.

Select a straight No. 1 grade 2 × 12, 14 feet long. It should be as free of knots, splits, and other defects as possible. Set it out on a pair of sawhorses or other supports to make it easy and convenient to work on. Hold a framing square against the top edge of the stringer so that the height of the riser is shown on the tongue, and the width of the tread is shown on the blade. Draw a line along the outside edge of the square to get the layout of the first tread and riser. Move the square to where the tread line meets the edge, and repeat the procedure. Continue along the board in this manner until you have laid out all of the treads and risers.

To speed this procedure and increase the accuracy, place a short board along the edge of the stringer, underneath the square. (See Fig. 21-14.) Be certain the tread and riser numbers are exactly on the edge of the stringer. When the square is aligned, clamp it to the board. This setup will allow you to rapidly move the square to each riser location while maintaining the same setting.

Finally, you will need to reduce the height of the bottom riser by an amount equal to the thickness of the material you'll be using for the treads. (See Fig. 21-13.) This reduction is to compensate for the tread thickness and make the first step come out equal with the last.

Using a handsaw or circular saw, carefully cut out the stringer. Using this stringer as a pattern, mark and cut two more to the same size. These three stringers will make up the stair carriage.

Trimming the Stairs

You will install the stairway parts after you have finished installing the drywall in the stairwell. Cut and install the finished stringer, usually a 1 × 10 or 1 × 12, along both walls if the stairway is fully enclosed. Then attach the rough stringers to the finished stringers, and to the first and second floor. Install the third rough stringer between the other two, and fasten it to the two floors. (See Fig. 21-15.) A variation is to install the rough stringers directly against the wall, then finish off with a notched stringer. (See Fig. 21-16.) The layout of the notched stringer is the opposite of the rough stringer, and one can serve as a pattern for the other.

When the rough and finished stringers are in place, rip the riser material to width. Cut each piece for a snug fit, and install them so that the top of

Fig. 21-14. Using a board clamped to a framing square to duplicate the tread and riser cutouts.

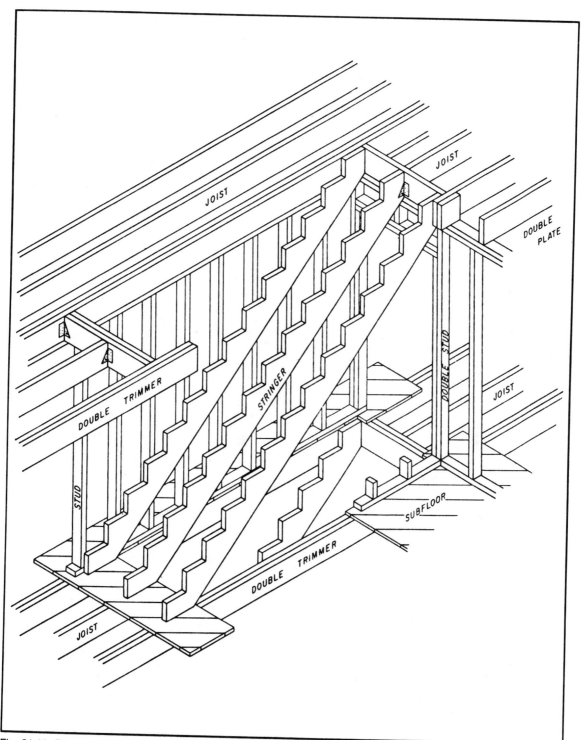

Fig. 21-15. Rough stringers installed and ready for trimming out (Courtesy of National Forest Products Association).

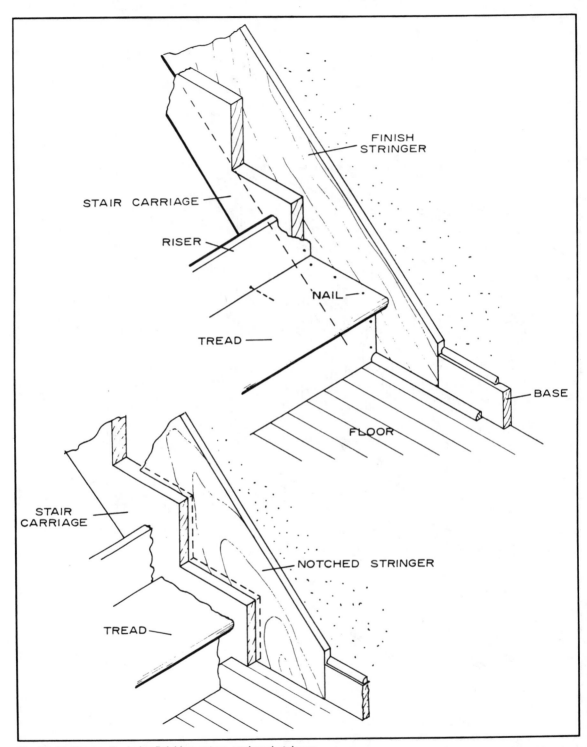

Fig. 21-16. Two methods for finishing out an enclosed stairway.

the riser is exactly flush with the top of the stringer notch. Cut and install the treads after the risers, again concentrating on a clean fit between the finished stringers and a good line against the riser.

The material you select for the treads and risers depends on whether the stairs will be carpeted. If they will be, then 3/4-inch plywood will work fine. (See Fig. 21-17.) Use an A-C grade with the A side exposed, and secure it with glue and 6d or 8d nails, or screws. If the stairs are to be left exposed, select a clear hardwood for both the treads and the risers. Oak is a common choice because of its beauty and durability. Attach the pieces with glue and finish nails.

Several companies manufacture balusters, handrails, and other related stair parts and accessories (Fig. 21-18). Secure a catalog from your lumberyard, and select the appropriate style and size of parts for your particular application. They will come individually wrapped and with all the necessary hardware for assembly. Follow the manufacturer's instructions carefully.

CABINETS

If your addition includes a new kitchen or bathroom or you are planning built-in bookcases or other storage, you will need to select and order your cabinets well in advance of the trim-out stage. Whether they are custom or modular, expect a 2- to 6-week time span before they are delivered.

To install modular cabinets, double-check the layout established when the plans were prepared

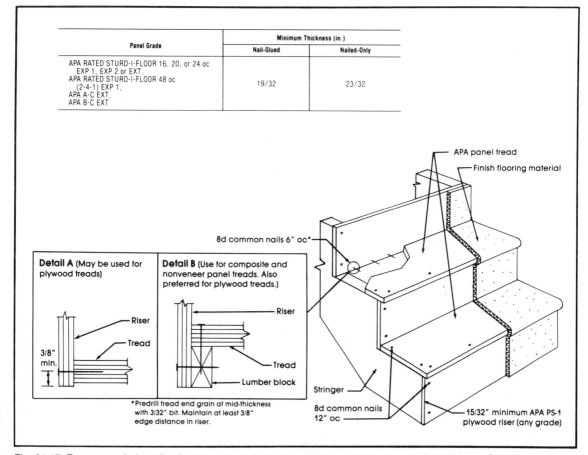

Panel Grade	Minimum Thickness (in.)	
	Nail-Glued	Nailed-Only
APA RATED STURD-I-FLOOR 16, 20, or 24 oc EXP 1, EXP 2 or EXT, APA RATED STURD-I-FLOOR 48 oc (2-4-1) EXP 1, APA A-C EXT, APA B-C EXT	19/32	23/32

Fig. 21-17. Recommended application procedures for the use of plywood for stair threads and risers (Courtesy of American Plywood Association).

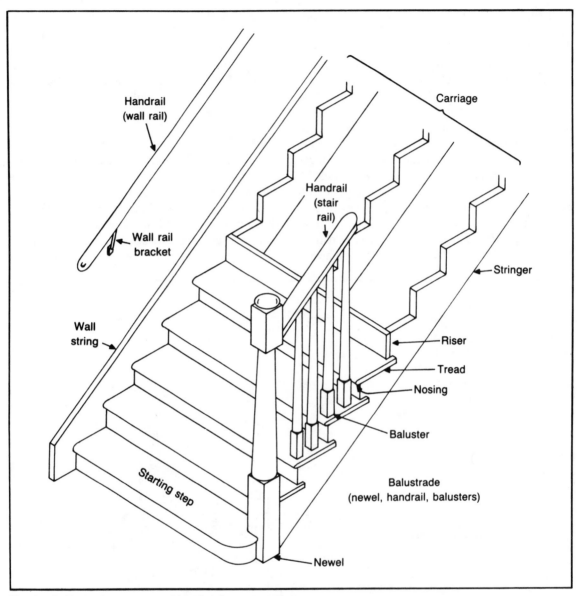

Fig. 21-18. The various parts used for trimming out a stairway.

against the cabinets you were shipped. The actual installation begins with the wall cabinets, starting from one corner and working out.

Wall Cabinets. If the wall cabinets do not go all the way up to the ceiling, or to a soffit, you'll first need to mark the wall where the cabinet tops will be. Nail a long, straight board to the wall at this point, making sure it's level.

Have a helper place the first cabinet in the corner, sliding it up the wall until it meets the ceiling or the board. Check it for plumb and level (final leveling will come later). Locate the upper nailing strip, which is the board inside the cabinet, against the back at the very top. Drill through the nailing strip into the studs, then attach the cabinet loosely to the wall with screws. Use 3- or 3 1/2-inch drywall screws or another type of flathead screws, and a screw gun if possible. You might wish to remove the cabinet doors for easier access.

Set the next cabinet in place beside the first, and visually align the face frames. Again, loosely screw the cabinet to the wall, just enough to hold it. Be certain the screws are hitting the studs. Using bar clamps or C-clamps, align and clamp the adjacent face frames of the two cabinets together.

Carefully drill through the edge of the face frame of one cabinet into the face frame edge of the other cabinet. Countersink the hole with a countersink bit, then screw the face frames together. Place one screw near the top and the bottom, then one every 12 inches.

With your helper again supporting the cabinets, check for both plumb and level in several areas. Working with two cabinets at once makes it easier to level them accurately. Using thin, tapered wooden shims, shim between the cabinet and the walls or ceiling as necessary. Be sure to check the cabinet against both walls of the corner.

When the two cabinets are plumb and level, finish driving the screws. Double-check with the level to be certain that the screws didn't rack the cabinet.

Proceed around the room with the rest of the upper cabinets. Plumb and level each one, shimming as necessary, and screw them to the walls and to each other. If necessary, you can rip filler strips of matching wood to width and place them between the face frames, adjusting the width of the overall cabinet run to fit the length of the wall. Screw through the bottom nailing strip also, then replace the doors and adjust them for fit and appearance.

Base Cabinets. For the base cabinets, again start from a corner. Screw the first two cabinets together and set them in place. Shim between the cabinets and the wall and floor until they are plumb and level, then screw through the backs into the wall studs. Use filler strips as necessary. Continue in this manner, screwing the cabinets to each other and to the walls, until all the base cabinets on one wall are done.

Working out from the same corner, begin the adjacent run. Screw the cabinets to the wall and to each other, plumbing and leveling as you go. Next, check to see if the two cabinet runs form a 90-degree corner, using a 3:4:5 measurement. If not, loosen the wall screws and adjust the shims to "open" or "close" the corner, pulling the runs closer together or farther apart as necessary. For U-shaped kitchens, it's easiest if you install the run along the base wall of the U first, then square both side runs to the base run.

When all of the base cabinets are in, lay a long, straight board across any two adjacent runs. Set a level on the board, and check that the two runs are level to each other as they proceed around the room. Check in several places, and adjust the shims as necessary. Finally, tighten all the screws, adjust the doors, and cut off any exposed shims. Finish off the job with matching moldings as desired.

Other Cabinets. Many manufacturers of modular kitchen cabinets also offer bath cabinets. In addition, various bookcases and storage cabinets are available. They can be an attractive alternative to more expensive custom cabinets, and can finish a room by giving it a "built-in" look. These cabinets should be carefully plumbed, leveled, and attached in the same way as kitchen cabinets.

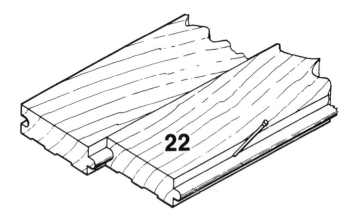

Painting, Decorating, and Flooring

The possibilities for the interior finish are many, and your final choices will depend in large part on how the addition is to tie into the existing house. Some additions, a sun porch for example, can be an integral yet separate part of the house, with exterior lines and finish that blend in with the existing house and an interior that sets the room completely apart. Other areas, such as an enlarged living and dining area, need to become one with existing rooms in order to look right. For them, you might need to completely refinish the interior of the existing rooms at the same time you trim out the addition in order to get just the right look and feel.

COLORS AND PATTERNS

When you are shopping for all of your interior finish needs, pay particular attention to those styles and colors that blend well with the mood you're trying to create. (See Fig. 22-1.) Heavy moldings, dark woods, and other dark colors in paint, wallpaper, and tile all will tend to close a room in, and also can make a room more intimate and cozy. These colors might work well for areas that appear overly large or feel too open. Light colors and smaller moldings and trim can combine to open up a small room, and impart a more spacious and airy feeling. They also tend to make a low ceiling seem higher.

In rooms that tend to become overly hot, such as kitchens or west or south bedrooms, stick with cool colors such as light blues and greens. They will make the room feel cooler and more inviting in warm weather. The opposite is true for reds and yellows, which can warm up a cool room. Vertical stripes in wallpaper, or vertical lines in wall paneling, tend to make a room appear taller and the ceiling seem higher. Horizontal strips and lines make a room feel wider, and can be a big help in rooms with overly tall ceilings.

Consider selecting a "look" for the entire house, and carry it over into each room. This option gives the home a coordinated look, and goes a long way toward making the addition blend in. For example, if you like a casual, country look, you might try warm wood tones in natural or lightly

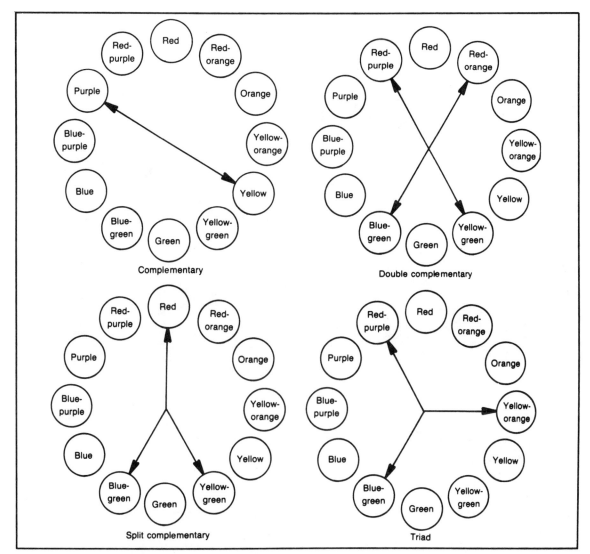

Fig. 22-1. A color wheel can be used to compare and coordinate colors.

stained pine and fir, accented with cheerful wall-papers and draperies. Slender painted moldings and foil wall coverings can blend well with a contemporary look, and dark paneling and stained ceiling moldings against heavily textured white walls might be just the thing for a Mediterranean look.

Many suppliers of paint, wallpaper, carpet, draperies, and other interior finish materials have interior designers on staff that can help you with your decisions. Quite often their services are free,

or they might charge a moderate fee that is credited toward purchases you make at that store. Above all, don't be afraid to experiment a little. A little imagination and the right materials can make a world of difference in a drab room.

PAINTING

Paint is still the most popular of all the wallcoverings, both for interior and exterior use. (See Fig. 22-2.) It is relatively inexpensive, easy to apply, and

Fig. 22-2. Using paint color chips can help with decorating decisions (Courtesy of National Paint & Coatings Association).

easy to change when you are redecorating. The keys to a good paint job are quality paint, the right tools, and proper surface preparation.

Choosing a Paint

There is a bewildering selection of paint on the market, with different grades of quality, degrees of gloss, resin types, coverage, and recommended applications. Following are some of the basic things you should know in order to make the proper choice.

Quality. Paint is one area where you shouldn't skimp on quality. A bargain paint is usually thin, with poor hiding power, and might require additional coats to get a good finish. If you need to apply a second coat to get the same finish you could have gotten with one coat of quality paint, then you certain did not get a bargain.

Price is usually a fairly good indicator of a paint's quality. You will find that most of the major brands are priced competitively, and that any

one of them will give you a good paint job. Some stores carry a *house brand,* which is a paint that has been produced by a major manufacturer but that carries a private label. These paints often can be a good value, as long as you can be assured by the dealer of who made it and what the guarantee is. Most dealers will let you return what you've bought, including a partial gallon, if you tried it and were totally dissatisfied.

Many manufacturers offer stock colors, which are premixed at the factory. These are usually $1 to $3 less per gallon then custom-mixed colors, and offer the advantage of an exact color match if you need to buy more. You also can return unused gallons to the store if you bought too much, which you can't do with custom colors.

Most paint stores will custom-match paint colors also. This service can be a real advantage if the paint on your house is still in good condition, and all you want to do is paint the addition to match. Bring in a sample of the color, either from an old

328

can of paint, or by removing something from the house that's been painted.

Gloss. There are four levels of gloss in a finished paint surface. The same additives, called *extenders,* that give a paint its abrasion resistance also control the amount of gloss, so the more gloss a paint has, the easier it is to wash and the more resistant it is to damage.

Flat paint has virtually no gloss to it at all, and is a common choice for interior walls in most living areas, where a high degree of shine on the painted surfaces is not desirable and constant cleaning is not necessary. *Satin* and *semigloss* finishes have some degree of shine, with semigloss being the glossier of the two. These finishes are often used in kitchens and bathrooms for their easier cleaning, and for trim and woodwork where some gloss adds a nice finished appearance. *Gloss* paint is used primarily on appliances, machinery, outdoor furniture, and other applications requiring high wear and cleaning properties.

Resin Types. *Water base* and *oil base* are terms you will hear quite often. They refer to the makeup of the liquid portion of the paint, called the *vehicle,* which allows the paint's pigments to flow onto the surface.

Latex resins, which are water based, are the most popular type today. They are easy to work with, require no thinning, and can be cleaned quickly and easily with only soap and water. Flat and semigloss latex will work fine for most of your wall and ceiling painting needs. Latex semigloss does not level out as well as the oil-based compounds, however, and tends to show brush marks. Acrylic resin, which is durable and resistant to ultraviolet light, often is blended with latex to improve the paint's overall quality, particularly for exterior use.

Alkyd resin, an alcohol and acid blend, is the most common of the oil-based paints in use today, and is a big improvement over the oil bases of the past. Alkyd paints are easy to use, level well, and are a very good choice for doors, trim, and other areas where a very smooth finish with no brush marks is desired. Cleanup is with paint thinner.

Two special-purpose resins are *epoxy* and *ure-thane,* both of which are hard and durable, and offer excellent weather, chemical, and abrasion resistance. They are somewhat harder to work with than other types of paint, and require special solvents for cleanup. They are used primarily in masonry paint, and in factory-applied enamels.

Coverage. Coverage is based on square feet per gallon, and is listed on the label. A number of factors affect how much area a gallon of paint will cover. The coverage listed on the label usually reflects this situation by listing a square footage range, achieved under certain conditions.

For most flat paints, 200 to 400 square feet is common, with the surface porosity being the major factor. New materials, such as drywall and wood, tend to absorb paint, and so the coverage is less than that over a previously painted surface. Your best bet is to figure up how many square feet you need to cover, then discuss the existing conditions with the people at the paint store. They are familiar with how their product will act under certain conditions, and can give you a better idea of the expected coverage than the label will.

PAINTING EQUIPMENT

Good painting equipment, like any other tool, can make a big difference in how easily the paint goes on and how good the finished product is. Good brushes, properly cared for, will last through years of paint jobs.

Paintbrushes

When you are selecting a brush, you will have a choice between natural and synthetic bristles. Natural bristles are somewhat softer and are a good choice for oil-based paints and varnishes. They should not be used with latex paint because the bristles do not react well to the water in the latex formula. Synthetic bristles are used with latex paint, and also will work well for most oil-based applications, making a good-quality synthetic bristle brush the best choice for your all-around painting needs.

The bristles should have a number of small split ends, which hold more paint and enable it to flow easier. Tug gently on the bristles to see that they are firmly anchored in the handle. One of the annoying tendencies of bargain brushes is to leave loose bristles in the paint job. Also, the handle should be comfortable in your hand and the brush should not feel heavy. A comfortable feel is an important consideration in a paintbrush, and should not be overlooked.

Two sizes should be sufficient for most of your needs: a 1 1/2- or 2-inch brush with an angled end for trim, and a 2 1/2- or 3-inch straight-cut brush for cut-in and most other work. You can add smaller and larger brushes as the need arises.

Paint Rollers

For most interior walls and ceilings, and certain exterior applications, a paint roller is the common choice. It applies the paint quickly to a large area, and rolls it out uniformly and smoothly.

You will need a paint tray, which is a formed sheet-metal pan with a reservoir at one end where the paint is held, and an inclined surface where the roller is coated and excess paint is removed. You also will need a roller handle, of which 9 inch is the most common, and one or more roller covers, which slip onto the end of the roller handle. You sometimes can buy these components prepackaged at a lower price, but the roller cover is often of low quality and might not be appropriate for your application. A handy option is a threaded extensions pole, which you screw into the roller handle to enable you to paint ceilings and floors more easily. Be sure that whatever roller handle you buy is threaded for use with an extension pole.

Select a good-quality roller cover that is compatible with the paint you're using and the type of surface you'll be painting. Low-nap covers are for smooth surfaces; medium-nap covers are for slightly rough and textured surfaces, and will work for most of your painting needs; and long-nap covers are for very rough surfaces, such as stone. Carpet-napped roller covers are available for creating a stipple texture in freshly applied paint, and slit-foam covers are used for painting acoustical tile and sprayed acoustic ceilings. Narrow rollers and rollers that are cut on an angle are also available for painting trim, corners, and confined areas.

These are a matter of preference, and you may find that a brush works just as well in these areas.

Spray Equipment

For large areas, especially outside, a paint sprayer might be worth considering. There are two basic types—air and airless—and you can purchase or rent them in a variety of sizes.

Air-powered sprayers have been around for years, and are still widely used to apply factory enamels on appliances and automobiles, and to spray lacquer and other finishes. The paint is placed in a cup attached to the spray head, and is forced out the nozzle with air supplied by a compressor. They provide an excellent finish. For residential use, however, they tend to be a little difficult to regulate properly, and overspray can be a problem. Also, some types of air sprayers will not work well with latex paint.

A better choice is the airless sprayer (Fig. 22-3), which has gained tremendous popularity in recent years for residential use. The airless sprayer uses a high-pressure piston assembly that atomizes the paint and forces it out the spray nozzle without hav-

Fig. 22-3. An airless paint sprayer, available from most rental yards.

ing to mix it with a stream of air. They are very simple to use and offer very good control over the spray pattern, thus allowing you to paint quite close to windows and other objects with a minimum of overspray. They draw paint directly out of the can, so constant refilling of the cup is eliminated—a real plus when you are spraying large areas.

SURFACE PREPARATION

The importance of preparing the surface correctly cannot be overstressed. The primary cause of failure in a finished coat of paint is dirt, moisture, or other problems with the underlying surface to which the paint was applied. The paint sticks to the dirt rather than a solid surface, and so tends to flake away easily.

Dirty interior walls, particularly kitchen walls which might be coated with a light layer of grease, should be washed down with a solution of trisodium phosphate (TSP) and water. TSP and other wall-cleaning chemicals are available wherever you buy your paint. Follow the manufacturer's instructions for proper use.

For exterior walls, a pressure washer works great. Pressure washers are available in both gas- and electric-powered models, and can be rented by the day or the half day. They have an inlet for direct connection to a garden hose, and a high-pressure outlet for connection to an adjustable, trigger-operated nozzle. A wide spray from the nozzle will wash most of the fine dirt and cobwebs off the walls, while the narrowest, strongest stream will chip off loose paint.

Vary the spray pattern and pressure as needed, and wash down the entire exterior. Pay particular attention to the underside of the soffits, and to the corners and edges around doors and windows where dirt accumulates. In most cases, a minor amount of hand-scraping is all that's necessary after you've finished with the pressure washer, and you'll be assured of a clean surface that will make painting much easier and help the finished paint job last a lot longer. Allow the walls to dry for at least 24 hours before you paint them.

For the cleanest, most professional finished ap-

pearance, you should remove everything from the room that you don't want painted, if at all possible. Such things includes curtain rods, switch and receptacle plates, door knobs, cabinet handles, and towel racks. Removing them takes only a few minutes with a screwdriver, and you'll more than gain that time back from faster and easier painting. Cutting in around all these objects is tedious and time consuming, and getting even a little paint on them can make the entire job look sloppy.

Objects that cannot be removed but that are not to be painted should be worked around carefully. You might wish to mask these surfaces off with masking tape and paper, or protect them with drywall blade or other shield as you paint next to them. Do not paint electrical outlets and switches! Paint seeping into any electrical devices can be both dangerous and destructive to the device, and the resulting paint job looks very amateurish.

When painting around windows, some painters carefully apply masking tape to the glass to keep a clean line between the glass and the surface being painted. Other painters simply paint down onto the glass, then scrape the excess off with a single-edged razor blade as soon as it has dried. This method has the advantage of creating a paint film seal between the glass and the frame, which helps prevent air from entering, but you run the risk of permanently scratching the glass. If you use masking tape, remove the tape from the glass as soon as you are done painting. Peeling the tape off after the paint has dried on it also might pull some of the paint off.

Fill in small holes and other imperfections in the surface before you begin to paint. A premixed spackling compound (Fig. 22-4) is the easiest to use; if you're using it outside, be sure it's approved and intended for exterior use. For larger holes and to level out imperfections, use a powdered synthetic filler, such as Fixall.

Around the outside of the house, caulk up cracks around windows, doors, wood joints, flashings, and other areas. Take your time and fill all gaps and cracks you find. The finished job will look better, the paint and the underlying surface will last longer, and you'll reduce drafts into the house. Re-

Fig. 22-4. Using a premixed spackling compound to seal small holes prior to painting (Courtesy of National Paint & Coatings Association).

fer to Chapter 18 for a complete listing of caulks and sealants.

APPLYING THE PAINT

For interior painting with a roller, the common procedure is to first cut-in the room with a brush. This is simply a matter of painting all the areas that the roller won't be able to reach, such as corners, along baseboards, and around windows, doors, and light fixtures.

Fill the reservoir in the paint tray about half full with paint, and dip the roller partly into it. Roll it out over the inclined portion of the tray to coat the entire roller cover. Initially, you might need to dip and roll it a couple of times to get the cover evenly coated. The roller should not be so full of paint that it drips.

Use the roller to apply paint to about a 3-foot-square area at a time, beginning with one corner of the ceiling (Fig. 22-5). Roll as close to the corners

as possible, since the roller leaves a different texture then a brush, and you want to hide the difference as much as possible. Work the roller in several different directions to thoroughly cover the area, using light strokes, then work out in one direction when the roller is partially empty. Keep the roller wet with paint. Don't try to press down on the roller and wring out all the paint; this can actually pull paint back off the surface and leave it splotchy and uneven.

Overlap each previously painted area to cover the overlap marks, and plan on painting the entire ceiling at one time. When the ceiling is done, do one wall at a time, starting from the top and working toward the floor.

The trim should be the last thing you paint, after the walls and ceiling are done. Use an angled trim brush, and work slowly in one direction. Dip the brush into the can just enough to wet approximately half the bristles. Tap the brush gently against the inside of the can to remove the excess paint. Dragging the bristles across the lip of the can will separate them and remove too much paint. The end of the brush should be wet but not dripping.

Work the brush with gentle, even strokes, reducing the pressure on it as you finish each stroke. To paint cleanly along an edge, the brush should push a small amount of paint ahead of it. Allow this leading edge of wet paint to form the line, not the actual bristles. Always keep the brush wet, and overlap each new section onto the old one, paying particular attention to blending the sections together.

You should paint doors in a set sequence for best results. With panel doors, paint the individual panels first, starting from the top. Next, paint each of the stiles and rails between the panels, then paint the top and bottom rails, and finally the two long side stiles. Always paint with the grain for the best appearance.

For spraying, latex or oil-based paints can be pumped directly from their containers. Thicker paints might require a little bit of thinning. To paint with an airless sprayer, simply place the screened pickup tube in a 5-gallon bucket of paint (if you're using single gallons, it's best to pour them into a clean 5-gallon bucket), activate the unit, then turn the priming knob. When paint comes out the overflow tube, the sprayer is primed. Shut off the priming knob, and you're ready to paint. A trigger on the spray handle controls the spray nozzle, and a knob on the motor unit regulates the spray pressure, increasing or decreasing it as needed.

Use masking tape and paper or plastic sheeting to cover windows and other areas you don't intend to spray. Do not use newspaper, since the moisture in the paint can cause the ink to run.

Use the bucket lid to keep the top of the bucket covered as much as possible. This keeps debris out of the paint, and helps prevent a skin from forming on top. Check the bucket periodically, and re-

Fig. 22-5. Using a paint roller to cover large areas of a wall quickly (Courtesy of National Paint & Coatings Association).

move any skin that might have formed to keep it from clogging the paint pickup screen.

Do not hold the nozzle too close to the wall, and keep it moving at all times while spraying. Remember that these units pump the paint out very quickly, and staying in one place too long will cause runs. Move the sprayer parallel with the surface to apply an even coating. Do not move the sprayer in an arc, since this leaves the area at the beginning and the end of the arc without much paint.

When you are done spraying, check the wall carefully for runs or areas that have been lightly coated, and touch these up with a brush. It might be necessary to touch up around fixtures and openings, also. If there is overspray on any trim, allow it to dry before you apply the trim color.

One important safeguard when you are using an airless sprayer: Do not allow your hands or any other exposed area of skin to come in contact with the spray! This type of spray equipment pushes the paint out under tremendous pressure, and actually can inject paint through your skin and into your body, causing serious injury. If any paint appears to have penetrated your skin, do not treat it as a simple cut. Seek medical attention immediately.

PAINT CLEANUP

When you are finished with any type of painting, clean up your tools right away. Scrape excess paint off brushes by pulling them across a straightedge, such as a putty knife. Rinse them thoroughly in the proper cleaning solvent, changing liquid as necessary when it becomes dirty. For latex paints, you can clean the brush under warm running water with a little mild detergent. Comb the bristles out, let the brush dry, then replace it in its original wrapping or in stiff paper. Store brushes by hanging them from the handle or laying them flat; propping them up on their bristles can cause permanent deformation.

Drain excess paint out of the paint tray, and rinse it clean to prevent paint from building up. Disposable plastic tray liners are also available, and greatly simplify the cleanup chores. Scrape or squeeze off excess paint from the roller cover, then remove the cover from the handle and rinse off the handle. Wash and rinse the roller cover in paint thinner or warm, soapy water, then run your hand down it several times to squeeze out the excess water.

To clean spray equipment, first wash off all external paint from the nozzle, hose, and paint pickup screen. Place the pickup in clean thinner or water and activate the pump. Turn the primer knob to flush paint out of the overflow, and let it run in this position for a minute. Close the priming valve, and activate the gun to flush the rest of the paint from the system. Repeat this procedure once or twice with clean water, spraying into an empty bucket, until the discharge from the sprayer is clear. Some manufacturers recommend running a light oil or solvent through the system to keep the internal parts of the machine from rusting. Follow the manufacturer's recommendations or the instructions from the rental yard.

Using a brush or a rag, wipe excess paint from the lip of the paint cans. Place the lid on the can, cover it with a rag, and press down firmly to seat the lid. Tap the lid with a hammer to completely seal it to the can. Finally, use a large felt-tip marker to clearly label the can as to what area of the house it was used for, thus making future touch-up work a lot easier.

WALLPAPER

Wallpapering has the reputation of being a messy, frustrating job that's best left to the professionals, but that's not necessarily true. The key elements for a successful job are the right tools, a correctly prepared wall, and patience.

Wall paper comes in two basic forms: dry, which must be coated with paste before hanging; and prepasted, which only needs to be soaked in water. To avoid possible color variations between rolls, buy enough paper at one time to cover the entire area, and double-check the dye-lot numbers on the packages. Most stores will allow you to return unused, unopened rolls. Installation instructions are almost always packaged with the rolls, and you should read them over carefully for any tips or restrictions that the manufacturer offers for that particular type of paper.

Wallpaper is priced and specified by the single roll, which, regardless of width or length, always contains 36 square feet of paper. Depending on the pattern match and how many small, wasted pieces are left off the end of each roll, you can figure on having about 30 square feet of usable paper per roll. (See Table 22-1.) Paper is often sold in double rolls, which contain 72 square feet. Bring your wall-height and exact square-footage needs to the wallpaper store with you. Your dealer will help you determine how much paper you'll need, based on the pattern repeat for that particular style.

For dry paper, the type and quantity of paste will vary with the type of wallpaper. Follow the recommendations of your dealer to select the right one for your job. For prepasted paper, buy a small amount of compatible paste or wallpaper-repair adhesive to repair any loose spots.

You will need the following basic tools: a paste brush or short-nap paint roller for applying paste to dry paper, or a water trough for prepasted paper; a smoothing brush; a seam roller; a clean bucket; scissors; a chalk line or level; a 12-inch taping knife or similar straightedge; sponges; and a utility knife and spare blades, or several single-edged razor blades. You will also need a work table, which can be simply a piece of plywood, about 3 × 6 feet, set over sawhorses and covered with a plastic sheet.

If your walls are already papered and the existing paper is solid, you usually can paper over it. Sand down the old seams to prevent them from showing through the new paper, and repair any loose or torn spots. Test some of the new adhesive on one small spot to see if it will loosen the old paper. If it does, the old paper will need to come off.

If the paper is already loose, you often can remove it by grasping it at the bottom and slowly peeling it upward, one small section at a time. If necessary, you might need to soak the paper to get it to come loose. You can use a small tank-type garden sprayer for this, or you can rent a wallpaper steamer. You can add liquid wallpaper remover to the water or steam if you desire. As each section of paper is moistened, scrape it off with a 6-inch drywall knife, then move on to a new section. Take care not to gouge the underlying wall surface.

For pained walls, patch any holes and remove any peeling paint, then wash the walls down with TSP or a strong detergent. You will need to sand down glossy walls with medium-grit sandpaper to give the wallpaper adhesive something to grip to.

New drywall is an extremely porous material, and should be painted first in order to seal it. Most

Table 22-1. Wallpaper Coverage Chart.

TOTAL WALL LENGTH, IN FEET	SINGLE ROLLS NEEDED	TOTAL WALL LENGTH, IN FEET	SINGLE ROLLS NEEDED
1-3	1	49-52	14
4-7	2	53-56	15
8-11	3	57-60	16
12-15	4	61-63	17
16-18	5	64-67	18
19-22	6	68-71	19
23-26	7	72-75	20
27-30	8	76-78	21
31-33	9	79-82	22
34-37	10	83-86	23
38-41	11	87-90	24
42-45	12	91-93	25
46-48	13	94-97	26

Deduct 1 single roll for every 2 average size windows or doors.
   For rooms with 8-foot-high ceilings based on a single roll of 36 square feet, yielding 30 square feet with waste allowance.

manufacturers recommend an oil-base sealer.

Using *wall sizing,* although not always necessary, is a good habit to get into for any kind of wall surface. Sizing is a special compound that seals and coats the wall, making it more compatible with the wallpaper paste, and allowing the paper to "slip" over the wall surface for easier positioning. Sizing comes as a powder for mixing with clean water, following the package directions. You can apply it with a brush, but for large areas it's easiest to apply it with a paint roller.

As with painting, remove all the wall plates, curtain rods, towel bars, and other items. Set up your work table in a convenient spot, and cover it with a sheet of plastic.

Select your starting point, which might be a corner, a doorway, a fireplace, or other long, vertical break. If you are papering the entire room, bear in mind that by the time you have returned to the starting point, the pattern probably won't match exactly. For this reason, you should start and end at a fairly unobtrusive spot.

Measure out from the starting point a distance that is 1/2 inch less than the width of the paper. Using a chalk line attached to a plumb bob, or a long level, mark a plumb line at this point. It's impor-

tant that you take care to establish this first line as plumb as possible, to prevent the paper from starting to "lean" as you work your way around the room. If you intend to paper the ceiling, measure in from one long wall 1/2 inch less than the width of the paper, and mark the ceiling. Place another mark at the other end of the ceiling, and snap a chalk line between the two marks.

Cut the first piece of paper 4 inches longer than the height of the wall. For dry paper, lay the strip face down on the table and use the pasting brush or paint roller to apply an even coating of paste from the top of the strip to the middle, leaving a 1-inch strip at the top unpasted. Fold the top half to the middle, paste side to paste side. Paste the bottom half, and fold the bottom to the middle. Do not crease the folds.

Prepasted paper must be soaked in water to activate the adhesive. After you have the piece to length, loosely reroll it with the back side out. Place the water tray on the floor at the end of the table, and fill it half full with lukewarm water. Place the roll of paper into the water so that it will unroll with the pattern side facing the table. Rotate it to wet it completely, and leave it in the water about 15 seconds, or as the instructions recommend.

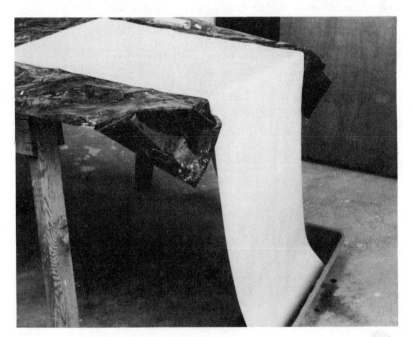

Fig. 22-6. Unroll the paper onto the work table, paste side up.

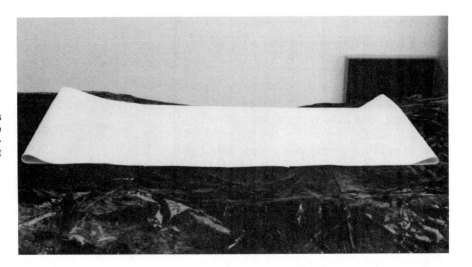

Fig. 22-7. Fold both ends up to the middle, paste side to paste side, for easier handling. Do not crease the folds.

Slowly unroll it out of the tray and drape it pattern side down on the table (Fig. 22-6). Check it as you unroll it to be sure the entire back is wet. Use a small sprayer to moisten any dry areas. Fold each end to the center, pasted sides facing, and let the piece sit to activate the adhesive (Fig. 22-7).

Drape the folded paper over your arm and carry it to the wall. Hold the strip by the top edge, and unfold the top half. Line up the edge with the plumb line, allowing a 2-inch overlap at the ceiling, and use the smoothing brush or a damp sponge to gently work the air from the center to the edges. Unfold the bottom half and smooth it into place. The important thing is to smooth out the big bubbles with the brush or sponge; the smaller ones will disappear as the paper dries. If the paper is not hanging straight, peel it away from the wall and reposition it, rather than trying to move it with the brush or sponge. Use the seam roller to gently flatten out the edges, unless the manufacturer instructs otherwise.

To trim the paper against a corner, ceiling, or baseboard, work the paper gently into the corner with a 12-inch drywall taping knife or other similar straightedge (Fig. 22-8). Work carefully, pushing gently with your fingers also, to avoid tearing the paper or shifting it away from the plumb line. Using the straightedge as a guide, cut the paper off with a sharp razor blade. Razor blades dull quite quickly when they are used to cut wallpaper, and

nothing is worse for the paper than trying to cut with a dull blade. Change blades as often as necessary, usually every three to four cuts.

Keep a sponge and a bucket of clean water handy at all times. After each cut, rinse any excess paste off your hands and tools, and also off the ceil-

Fig. 22-8. Using a 12-inch drywall blade as a guide, trim the paper off in the corners with a razor blade. Change blades often.

ing, walls, and trim. Wipe off the plastic on the work table after each piece also, to avoid getting paste on the face of the next piece.

Cut the next strip to length, matching the pattern and allowing a 2-inch overlap at the top and bottom. Abut the second strip to the first without overlapping, carefully matching the pattern, and smooth the strip into place. Sponge the paper with clean water to remove any excess glue. After about 10 minutes, use the seam roller to roll the entire length of the first seam, then sponge it clean.

Proceed along the wall in this manner, papering over the outlets and switches, also. At each outlet, make an X cut from corner to corner of the electrical box (Fig. 22-9) then cut out around the edges (Fig. 22-10). For immovable objects, smooth the paper down to the top of the object, then make an X cut across its center. Gradually enlarge the X as you smooth out the paper to all sides, then trim carefully around all four edges.

At windows and doors, roughly cut out the opening area, leaving about a 2-inch excess. Make a diagonal cut at the corners to allow the paper to smooth down around the window or door frame, then trim it exactly to size as you did at the corners, using the taping knife as a guide. Paper the small areas above and below the opening to keep the pattern going correctly, then continue to paper around the room in one direction.

If the window does not have jambs and casings and the paper is to extend into the window open-

Fig. 22-10. Trim around the box with a razor blade to remove the excess paper.

ing, you will need to trim the paper so that it is long enough to reach all the way into the window. Carefully make a 45-degree cut at the corner, and wrap the paper into the opening. You will need to cut two small pieces, matching the pattern, in order to fill in the corner.

As you approach each inside corner, measure from the last installed strip to the corner in several places, then cut a strip 1/2 inch wider than the widest measurement. Install the strip, allowing the excess to lap onto the next wall. Use the chalk line to mark a vertical line on the new wall, then work the next strip from this line back into the corner, matching the pattern. This slight overlap in the corner is virtually unnoticeable, and it will hide the corner if the paper ever shrinks.

As a nice professional touch, consider taking the time to paper the switch and receptacle plates, which is not as difficult as it seems. First, clean the plate in warm soapy water, dry it, and replace it over the outlet. Cut a large square of dry scrap paper, and hold it over the plate, carefully aligning the pattern. With a sharp pencil, make a tiny dot on (not through) the paper at each corner of the plate, then remove the paper and the plate.

Using the dots as a guide, trim the paper about 1 inch larger than the size of the plate. Wet or paste the paper, place it face down on the table, and set the plate on it. Align the corner dots, and smooth the paper onto the plate. Wrap the paper around

Fig. 22-9. Paper directly over receptacles, then cut an X over them and smooth out the paper.

the edges of the plate and onto the back, cutting a small square out of each corner so the corners will lay down without bunching up. After the paper has dried, cut out the openings in the plate with a sharp blade. Use a sharp pencil to carefully open the screw holes, then replace the plate.

CERAMIC WALL TILE

Another wallcovering option worth considering, and one that has also moved into the realm of the do-it-yourselfer in recent years, is ceramic tile. Tile, and also masonry veneers (Fig. 22-11) is easy to install with the right adhesives, and can add a very elegant touch to any room.

Fig. 22-11. Gluing a masonry veneer around a fireplace (Courtesy of Durabond Division of USG Industries, Inc., a wholly owned subsidiary of USG Corporation).

You will need a solid surface underlying the tile, such as drywall, most smooth wood surfaces, or special tile-backing panels such as Durabond (Fig. 22-12). Be certain the wallcovering material is firmly attached to the underlying framing. Seal porous materials such as drywall and plywood according to the instructions on the can of adhesive.

Using a piece of tile as a guide (Fig. 22-13), determine how far off the floor, or the bathtub or shower pan, the first course of tile will extend. With a board and a level, mark a level line on the wall at this point (Fig. 22-14).

Following the manufacturer's instructions, apply the proper adhesive to the wall with a notched trowel (Fig. 22-15), covering one small section of the wall at a time. Press the first row of tiles into the adhesive, aligning them with the level line. Continue to glue and tile the wall in sections, carefully aligning the tiles to each other (Fig. 22-16). Use a small tile cutter to cut fill pieces as necessary (Fig. 22-17).

When the wall is finished and the adhesive has dried, grout the tile with a compatible grouting material. Use a rubber float (Fig. 22-18) or a small squeegee and work both horizontally and diagonally across the tiles. As the grout begins to dry, wipe up the excess with a damp sponge (Fig. 22-19). Wring the sponge out often in a bucket of water, and change the water as often as necessary.

After about 24 hours, go over the tile again with a clean, damp sponge to remove the haze (Fig. 22-20), then shine it with a dry cloth. If directed by the manufacturer, apply a silicone compound to the tile to seal the grout against moisture.

STAINING

Depending on the look and style of your home's interior, you might wish to stain the doors and trim instead of painting them. Stain lets the true beauty of the wood's grain show through, and can enhance the warmth of a room considerably.

If you intend to stain the trim, it's easiest to do it all before it's installed. Lay the trim pieces out on sawhorses or boxes, and apply the stain with a paintbrush or disposable foam brush. (See Fig. 22-21.) Foam brushes work quite well for this

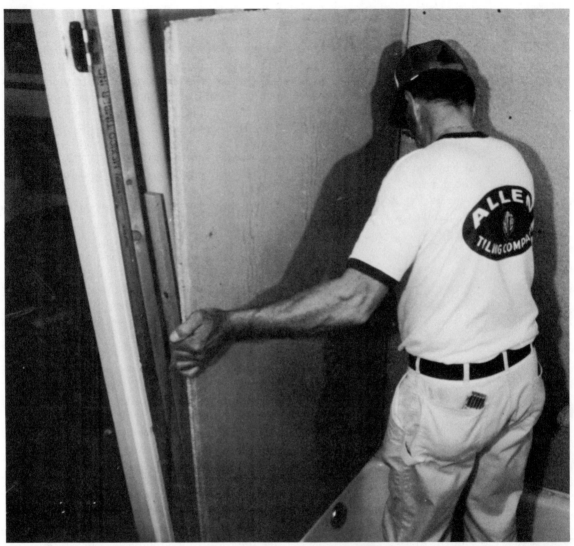

Fig. 22-12. Installing a tile backer board around a bathtub to provide a solid base for the ceramic tile (Courtesy of Dura-bond Division of USG Industries, Inc., a wholly owned subsidiary of USG Corporation).

procedure. They leave no brush marks or loose bristles, and they're inexpensive enough to simply throw away after you're done. You can stain pre-hung door units in this manner before installation, also.

Most of the stains on the market today are known generically as wiping stains and are usually oil based. You can apply them by brush. Simply wipe off the excess with a clean, lint-free rag, leaving a uniform color. You can apply additional coats as desired to deepen the color.

Wait to install the trim until everything else in the room is done. Doing so will simplify the installation of wallpaper, and also allow you to apply paint more quickly, without fear of splattering the stained moldings.

FLOOR UNDERLAYMENT

Before you install finish floor-covering materials,

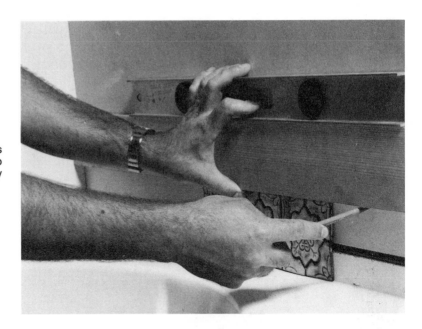

Fig. 22-13. Using a piece of tile as a guide, mark the height off the top of the tub for the first row (Courtesy of ColorTile).

you should install an underlayment material. (See Fig. 22-22.) An underlayment ensures a clean, smooth surface for the flooring to bond to, and is especially important with linoleum and floor tiles. (See Table 22-2.)

The most common choice for underlayment is 3/8-inch particleboard. Leave about a 1/32- to 1/16-inch gap between the sheets to allow for possible expansion. A matchbook cover makes a handy spacer for this situation. Stagger the joints between the sheets so that four corners do not come together in the same place, and nail the sheets down securely

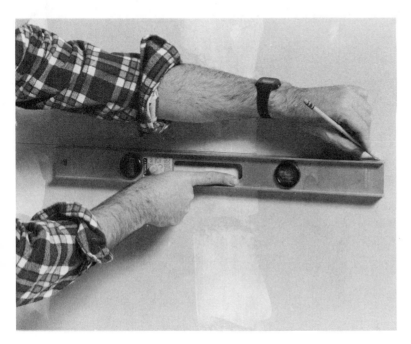

Fig. 22-14. Use a level to extend the marks and create a level line to work to (Courtesy of ColorTile).

Fig. 22-15. Applying wall adhesive with a notched trowel (Courtesy of ColorTile).

Fig. 22-16. Carefully place and align the tiles, taking care that they remain straight (Courtesy of ColorTile).

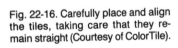

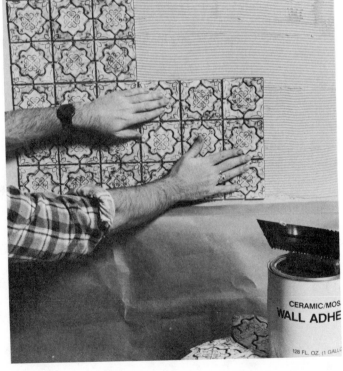

Fig. 22-17. Using a small tile cutter to cut fill pieces (Courtesy of ColorTile).

with ring nails on 6-inch center.

CERAMIC TILE

Ceramic floor tile makes a beautiful, durable floor covering, and it's not difficult to install, even for the beginner. Many of the materials on the market today are geared toward the do-it-yourselfer, and there is a huge selection of tile colors, patterns, sizes, and shapes available. Sizes range from 1 inch

Fig. 22-18. After the adhesive is dry, use a rubber float to apply the grout (Courtesy of ColorTile).

Fig. 22-19. Wipe off the excess grout as it begins to dry (Courtesy of ColorTile).

Fig. 22-20. When the grout has dried, wipe off the haze and polish the tile (Courtesy of ColorTile).

square, or less, up to 12 inches square. Generally speaking, tiles smaller than 4 inches square will be prespaced and bound together on a mesh backing for easier installation.

Tiles are also available glazed or unglazed. The glazing, a clear, factory-baked finish, seals the tile to make it harder. It also provides a smooth, slightly glossy finish that is easier to clean, but is somewhat slippery when wet. Also, be certain that the tile you buy is floor tile. Some of the tiles on the market

Fig. 22-21. Prestain moldings and trim prior to installation for a neater job. Note the small foam brush being used to apply the stain.

APA Plywood Underlayment[e]

Plywood Grades[a] and Species Group	Application	Minimum Plywood Thickness (in.)	Fastener Size and Type	Fastener Spacing (in.)[b]	
				Panel Edges	Intermediate
Groups 1, 2, 3, 4, 5 APA UNDERLAYMENT INT (with interior or exterior glue) APA UNDERLAYMENT EXT APA C-C Plugged EXT	Over smooth subfloor	1/4	18 ga. staples or 3d ring-shank nails[c] [d]	3	6 each way
	Over lumber subfloor or other uneven surfaces.	11/32	16 ga. staples[c]	3	6 each way
			3d ring-shank nails [d]	6	8 each way
Same grades as above, but Group 1 only.	Over lumber floor up to 4" wide. Face grain must be perpendicular to boards.	1/4	18 ga. staples or 3d ring-shank nails[c] [d]	3	6 each way

(a) When 19/32 inch or thicker underlayment is desired, APA RATED STURD-I-FLOOR may be specified. In areas to be finished with thin floor coverings such as tile, linoleum or vinyl, specify Underlayment, C-C Plugged or STURD-I-FLOOR with fully sanded face.

(b) If green framing is used, space fasteners so they do not penetrate framing.

(c) Use 16 ga. staples for 11/32 inch and thicker plywood. Crown width 3/8 inch for 16 ga. .

3/16 inch for 18 ga. staples, length sufficient to penetrate completely through, or at least 5/8 inch into, subflooring.

(d) Use 3d ring-shank nails also for panels up to 1/2 inch and 4d ring-shank nails for thicker panels up to 3/4 inch.

(e) For underlayment recommendations under ceramic tile, refer to Table 12.

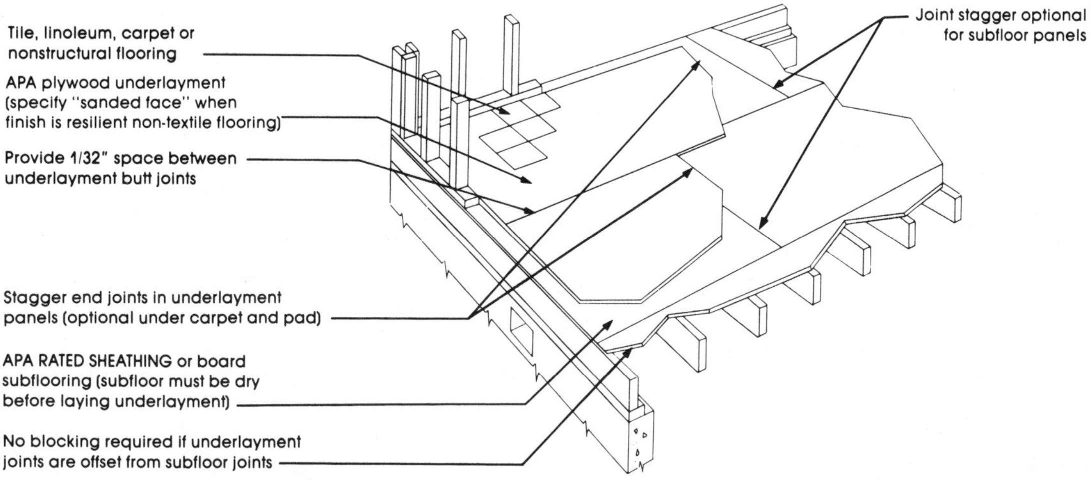

Tile, linoleum, carpet or nonstructural flooring

APA plywood underlayment (specify "sanded face" when finish is resilient non-textile flooring)

Provide 1/32" space between underlayment butt joints

Stagger end joints in underlayment panels (optional under carpet and pad)

APA RATED SHEATHING or board subflooring (subfloor must be dry before laying underlayment)

No blocking required if underlayment joints are offset from subfloor joints

Joint stagger optional for subfloor panels

Fig. 22-22. Recommendations for the installation of plywood underlayment (Courtesy of American Plywood Association).

are intended for wall or countertop use, and will not withstand the constant traffic and abuse that a floor receives. (See the section on Ceramic Tile earlier in this chapter.)

Figure the square footage of the area to be tiled, then add about 10 percent for waste. In addition to the tile, your basic shopping list will include mastic, grout, a notched trowel, a squeegee or rubber float, rubber gloves, sponges and rags, and a bucket. You also will need a tile cutter, which you can rent or borrow from the tile dealer.

Ceramic tile can be installed over almost any solid, level surface, including concrete, wood, linoleum, and most types of floor tile. Your tile dealer can supply you with the proper type of mas-

tic for the tile you're using and the material you're tiling. For a concrete floor, be certain that the concrete has cured completely. For new wood, a primer is usually recommended to seal the wood first, preventing moisture in the mastic from being absorbed too quickly and weakening the bond.

Prepare the floor by first removing all baseboards, edge moldings, floor registers, and other obstructions. If the existing linoleum or wood flooring is sound, simply rough it up with coarse sandpaper. Sweep and vacuum the floor thoroughly.

All floor tiles, ceramic or otherwise, must be carefully laid out in relation to the size and shape of the room. This layout step is very important in achieving a pleasing and symmetrical look in the

Table 22-2. Plywood and Adhesive Recommendations for Ceramic Tile Flooring.

(Based on ANSI Standard A108 and recommendations of the Tile Council of America)

Joist Spacing (in.)	Minimum Panel Thickness (in.)		Tile Installation
	Subfloor[a]	Underlayment[b]	
Residential			
16	15/32	(d)	"Dry-Set" mortar; or latex – Portland Cement mortar
16	19/32	—	Cement mortar (3/4" – 1-1/4")
16	19/32	11/32	Organic adhesive
16	19/32	15/32[e]	Epoxy mortar
16	19/32 T&G[c][e]	—	Epoxy mortar
Commercial			
16	15/32	(d)	"Dry-Set" mortar; or latex – Portland Cement mortar
16	19/32	—	Cement mortar (3/4" – 1-1/4")
16	19/32	19/32[c][e]	Epoxy mortar

(a) APA RATED SHEATHING with subfloor Span Rating of 16" oc (15/32" panel) or 20" oc (19/32" panel), except as noted.
(b) APA Underlayment or sanded Exterior grade, except as noted.
(c) APA RATED STURD-I-FLOOR with 20" oc Span Rating.
(d) Bond glass mesh mortar units to subfloor with latex – Portland Cement mortar, prior to spreading mortar for setting ceramic tile.
(e) Leave 1/4" space at panel ends and edges; trim panels as necessary to maintain end spacing and panel support on framing. Fill joints with epoxy mortar when it is spread for setting tile. With single-layer residential floors, use solid lumber blocking or framing under all panel end and edge joints (including T&G joints).
(f) See Table 6, 9, 10 or 11, as applicable, for panel fastening recommendations.

(Courtesy of the American Plywood Association)

finished floor. (See Figs. 22-23 and 22-24.) You'll usually want the tile to run straight out from whichever is the main entrance into the room. Determine the center point of the wall containing the main doorway, and the wall opposite it. Snap a chalk line between these two points, establishing your main layout line. Mark the center of this line, and snap a second line perpendicular to it, using the 3:4:5 method.

Working out from these lines, set out several tiles, without adhesive, until you reach the wall. If the piece that remains at the wall is less than half the width of a tile, you'll want to change the layout. Simply shift the tiles so that they start out centered over the room's centerlines instead of abutting their edges to it.

Prepare the mastic according to the manufacturer's instructions. Start at a back wall, in line with the center layout line, and cover an area of about 6 square feet. Use a notched trowel recommended for the tile and mastic you're installing, leaving even rows of mastic as you spread it (Fig. 22-25). Press the tiles firmly down into the mastic, but try not to slide them. Remove excess mastic from the tile edges and tops as you go along.

As you install the tiles, you will need to maintain an even spacing between them, ranging from 1/8 to 3/8 inch, depending on the size of the tile and personal preference. The easiest method for maintaining this spacing is to use precut plastic spacers (Fig. 22-26), which are available at most tile dealers. The spacers fit between the tiles at the corners, automatically spacing them. If the tile is thick enough, you can leave the spacers in place, and later cover them with grout. If they protrude above the top of the tile, you will need to remove them as the tile begins to set up.

Use a tile cutter to create the smaller pieces needed to fill in along the walls. Measure and mark the tile, then use the wheel on the cutter to score

Fig. 22-23. Checking the clearance of a piece of tile under a sliding glass door sill.

the tile's surface. Press down with the cutter's handle, and the tile will snap along the scored line. If curves or irregular shapes are needed, mark the tile, then score along the marked line with a standard glass cutter. Use tile nippers to "nibble" away the unwanted tile (Fig. 22-27). An alternate method is to use a saber saw equipped with a carbide grit-edged blade.

Fig. 22-24. Laying out the tile to check its appearance and alignment in the room.

Fig. 22-25. The floor adhesive is applied with a heavily notched trowel, different from the type used for wall adhesive.

Let the mastic dry from 10 to 48 hours, depending on the manufacturer's recommendations, then begin grouting. Mix the grout as instructed on the package, working it to a smooth texture about the consistency of pudding. Use a rubber float or squeegee to work the grout diagonally across the joints (Fig. 22-28), filling the spaces and leaving a thin layer on the tile surface. After about 10 minutes,

Fig. 22-26. Spacing the tiles uniformly is greatly simplified with the use of plastic spacers.

Fig. 22-27. A hand cutter, left, and tile nippers are used for irregular shapes and notches (Courtesy of ColorTile).

go back over the area with a wet sponge, again working diagonally over the tile in straight lines, to remove most of the grout on the surface. Rinse the sponge frequently in clean water. Wait another

10 minutes, then wipe again, this time using a gentle, circular motion. Use your finger to rub grout into any small gaps you discover.

After 1 or 2 days, you'll notice a dull haze on

Fig. 22-28. A rubber float is used to apply the grout, working diagonally across the joints.

the tile. Use a soft cloth and a circular rubbing motion to remove the haze, buffing the tile to a shine. Finally, seal the grout with a liquid silicone sealer formulated for tile. Sealing will improve the grout's water resistance and keep it looking new. Repeat this procedure about once a year.

FLOOR TILE

There are several other types of floor tile on the market, including vinyl asbestos (VA), vinyl, cork and hardwood. They are all installed in essentially the same manner. The only difference is the type of adhesive used. Some types of tile have a self-adhesive back, and you only need to remove the protective backing paper and press the tile into place (Fig. 22-29).

The layout and installation (Fig. 22-30) of floor tile is exactly the same as for ceramic tile. The only difference is that the tiles are abutted tightly to each other, with no grouting. Cutting is done with scissors or a utility knife, for most types of tile (Fig. 22-31) or with a fine-toothed saw for wood tiles.

LINOLEUM

Linoleum and other types of large sheet materials, called sheet goods, are considerably more difficult to install, although some types are now being geared toward the do-it-yourselfer. (See Fig. 22-32.) Because the sheets are awkward to handle, exact fitting becomes more difficult. Most professionals make a paper pattern first, by laying overlapping sheets of paper on the floor and abutting them to

Fig. 22-29. Self-adhesive floor tiles are installed simply by removing the protective paper backing. Note the layout lines penciled on the floor (Courtesy of Armstrong World Industries, Inc.).

Fig. 22-30. Place the tiles along the layout lines first, carefully aligning them before pressing them down (Courtesy of Armstrong World Industries, Inc.).

Fig. 22-31. Cuts on this type of tile are easily made with a pair of scissors (Courtesy of Armstrong World Industries, Inc.).

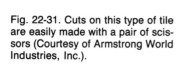

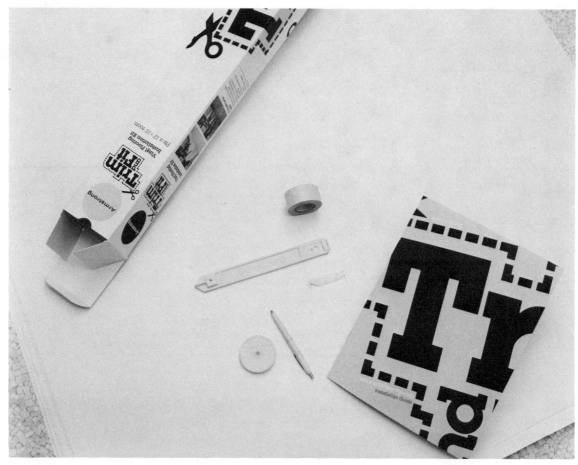

Fig. 22-32. A do-it-yourself installation kit for vinyl sheet flooring (Courtesy of Armstrong World Industries, Inc.).

the walls, cabinets, and other obstacles. (See Fig. 22-33.) Make all necessary cutouts on the paper, and securely tape the sheets together to make a full-size pattern.

Working on a large, flat area, such as the garage floor, lay out the sheet material and place the pattern on top of it. Trace carefully around the pattern (Fig. 22-34). Using a straightedge as a guide, cut the material with a utility knife or special linoleum knife (Fig. 22-35). The sheet is usually worked on from the back side, because it's easier to see and cut without the pattern. Remember to invert the pattern also.

Roll up the sheet and carry it into the house. You might need a helper for this step. Unroll the sheet carefully and work it into position (Fig. 22-36),

doing any necessary trimming as you go.

When the fit is right, roll back one end for several feet and apply the adhesive. Press the sheet firmly into the adhesive, working out any air bubbles with your hands. Roll the rest of the sheet up onto the already glued portion, glue the rest of the floor, and unroll the sheet back into position. Use a weighted roller, which can be rented, to completely roll the floor and remove any air bubbles.

HARDWOOD FLOORING

Hardwood flooring is traditionally installed in narrow, random-length strips, usually with tongue-and-groove edges. For best appearance, it should be installed before any of the baseboards are in place.

352

Fig. 22-33. Use the guide disk to mark the paper pattern, following the contours of the room layout (Courtesy of Armstrong World Industries, Inc.).

Fig. 22-34. Guided by the straight-edge, trace the paper pattern onto the vinyl (Courtesy of Armstrong World Industries, Inc.).

Fig. 22-35. Then cut out the sheet along the pattern lines (Courtesy of Armstrong World Industries, Inc.).

Fig. 22-36. After cutting, roll the sheet out in the room, trim it as necessary, and glue it down (Courtesy of Armstrong World Industries, Inc.).

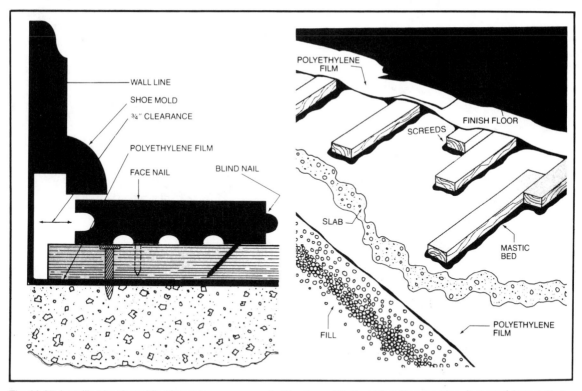

Fig. 22-37. Installing hardwood flooring strips over concrete (Courtesy of National Oak Flooring Manufacturers' Association).

Purchase the flooring a week or so before its scheduled installation and place in the room so it can become acclimated to the temperature and humidity. If you are laying over concrete, you can put down the flooring with adhesive, or you can install wood furring strips first (Fig. 22-37).

Begin the installation along one wall with a long strip, leaving a 1/4-inch gap along the wall (Fig. 22-38). Face-nail the first and last pieces; blind-nail all the others diagonally through the tongue (Fig. 22-39). Lay out several rows of flooring before you install them (Fig. 22-40), so that you can arrive at a desirable pattern of lengths and joints. Avoid installing the boards so that too many of the joints line up.

Using a piece of scrap flooring to protect the tongue, tap the boards tightly against each other and nail them in place. Abut the ends and keep these joints tight also. As you reach the end of each row, carefully measure the fill piece and cut it with a fine-toothed saw. Leaving a 1/4-inch gap at the

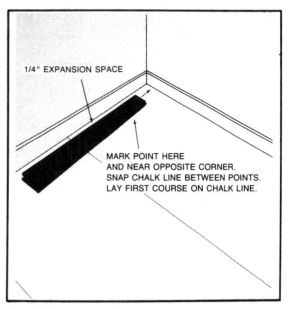

Fig. 22-38. Install the first strip with a 1/4-inch expansion space along the wall (Courtesy of National Oak Flooring Manufacturers' Association).

355

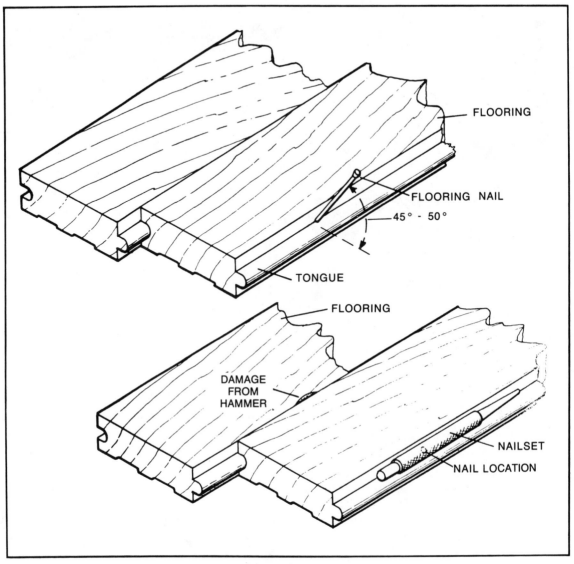

FLOORING

FLOORING NAIL

45° - 50°

TONGUE

FLOORING

DAMAGE
FROM
HAMMER

NAILSET

NAIL LOCATION

Fig. 22-39. Install the strips by blind-nailing through the tongue.

walls to make the fitting easier. This gap will be covered later by the baseboards.

When you encounter doorways and other obstacles, make a paper or cardboard pattern of the necessary cuts. Trim the pattern until you have a good fit, then use the pattern as a guide for laying out and cutting the flooring.

When all of the flooring is in place, use a commercial, drum-type sander to sand the entire floor. Sand it once with a coarse-grit paper to even out

the flooring, then with a medium or fine grit to get a smooth finish. Always sand with the grain to avoid scratching the wood. Finish off the edges against the walls with an electric pad sander, or by hand. Thoroughly sweep and vacuum the floor at least twice to remove the sanding dust, then apply a coat of stain, if desired. Finish off the installation with one or two coats of clear polyurethane floor finish, following the manufacturer's instructions, then install the baseboards.

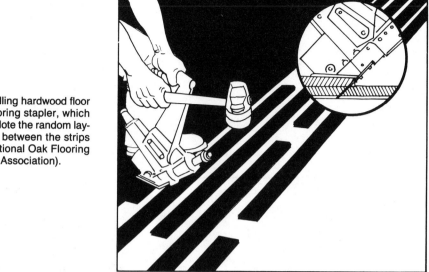

Fig. 22-40. Installing hardwood floor strips with a flooring stapler, which can be rented. Note the random layout of the joints between the strips (Courtesy of National Oak Flooring Manufacturers' Association).

WALL-TO-WALL CARPETING

Wall-to-wall carpeting is one installation best left to the professionals. The amount of money you will save by doing it yourself, considering your expenditures for tool rentals and special supplies, is negligible, and your finished product probably won't live up to what you'll get from an experienced installer. If you want to lay the carpet yourself, however, use the following instructions.

Wall-to-wall carpeting requires the installation of a tack strip around the perimeter of all the walls, then cut the carpet roughly to size for each room. Use a special device called a *carpet stretcher* to stretch the carpet along one wall, adhering it to the strip. Then stretch out the carpet into the room in several directions. Proper stretching is essential to prevent wrinkles and distortion in the carpet.

After stretching, trim off the carpet along the walls, and tuck down the cut edge alongside the strip, giving the edges a finished appearance. Seam the carpet in doorways, and as needed in large rooms, by first carefully trimming the edges perfectly straight and abutting the pieces together. Lay a heat-sensitive tape beneath the joint, and use a special flat iron to melt the glue on the tape. As you move the iron, press down the carpet into the hot adhesive to make the joint. You can rent carpet stretchers, seaming irons, and other carpet-laying tools at most larger rental yards.

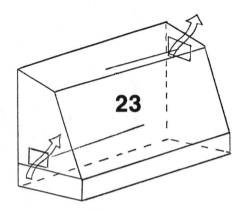

Sunspaces, Greenhouses, and Sun Porches

One type of addition that is rapidly growing in popularity is the sunspace. These rooms, designed specifically to capture the sun for heat, plants, or aesthetics, are treated a little differently than conventional additions. Because of their design, with a large amount of glass concentrated in one area, they are somewhat more difficult to blend in with the architecture of the existing house.

On the exterior, every attempt should be made to match roof lines, siding material, window and door frames, and other visible features, as much as the design allows. Inside, the sunspace is treated as a separate room that can be closed off from the rest of the house when not in use. In most cases, one or more doors provide the only connection between the house and the room. This is an important consideration, because nighttime heat loss though the large amount of glazing actually can rob heat from the house if the space is not closed off.

In this respect, the sunspace is somewhat easier to construct than a conventional room addition, since the number of transitions and connections are reduced, and the interior finish work can contrast completely with the interior of the rest of the house.

The term sunspace has become somewhat of a generic term, encompassing three different types of rooms that serve different purposes:

☐ *Sunspace.* A sunspace is actually a room that is designed to capture solar radiation from the sun, store it, and release it to the house in the form of heat. Ducts or fans are used to connect the room with the rest of the house, bringing in heat as temperatures in the sunspace become high enough. There is normally a wide range of temperatures that occur in the space, making them unsuitable in many instances for plant growth or comfortable living space.

☐ *Greenhouse.* A greenhouse is a somewhat modified version of a sunspace, designed to provide a warm environment for plant growth rather than as a heat source for the house, although it might have some use in that capacity also. The glazing area is increased to provide more natural light, and the mass is increased to limit the temperature swings, which would be harmful to

358

the plants. A greenhouse provides a more comfortable living space, although some people might find the relatively high levels of humidity produced by the plants to be uncomfortable.

☐ *Sun Porch.* The third type of rom is the sun porch, which is designed solely around livability. Glazing is often placed more for appearance and to encompass a wide view of the outdoors than it is for true solar gain, and storage mass is less than that for a greenhouse. This type of room usually will produce enough heat to keep itself at a comfortable temperature, providing a cozy spot on a winter day, but it will not produce enough to warm any adjacent spaces. The temperature usually are sufficient to extend the normal growing season for plants, but not for year-around plant production.

Because of all the glazing, there are some definite energy conservation measures that must be incorporated into the design and construction of any of these types of rooms. All of the glass should be double glazed, with some type of movable insulation, such as insulated draperies or blinds or removable foam insulation blocks, to minimize both nighttime heat loss and unwanted heat gain during the summer. Wall insulation should be at least R-11, and R-19 is preferred. Concrete slabs should be insulated to at least R-5, and the roof must be R-19 or better.

All of the rooms are, of course, still additions to the house, and as such need to meet minimum setback requirements and comply with other local codes and ordinances. If the sunspace is attached to a bedroom in such a way that it reduces or eliminates the emergency egress from that bedroom, you will need to place an exterior door or operable glazing in the sunspace to meet the fire safety codes. Check with your building department for exact requirements.

ORIENTATION

In the winter, the sun remains low in the southern sky. (See Fig. 23-1.) For this reason, sunspaces must be oriented to face south, so that maximum advantage can be taken of the winter sunlight. You

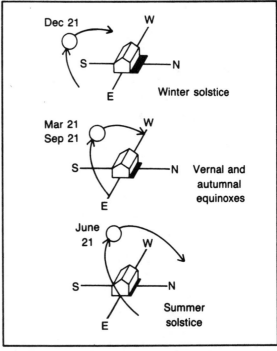

Fig. 23-1. The sun's yearly path in the sky. During the winter, it appears low in the southern sky.

will need a small pocket compass to check if your intended building site has the correct orientation. You also will need to know the *declination* for your area, which is the deviation between magnetic south and true south. You can obtain this information by calling your local airport.

Stand where the addition is to be built and face south, holding the compass in the palm of your hand. With the needle pointed toward magnetic south, orient yourself to face true south by adjusting your position to match the declination (Fig. 23-2). If the glazing on the sunspace will face within 30 degrees east or west of true south, then the orientation should be fine. If it won't, you will need to redesign or reorient the room until it falls within this range.

You also will need to check if solar access is adequate. A sun locator, which is a simple device that lets you estimate how much winter sunlight will strike the glazing, usually can be borrowed from your county extension office, or sometimes can be rented from local building designers. A sim-

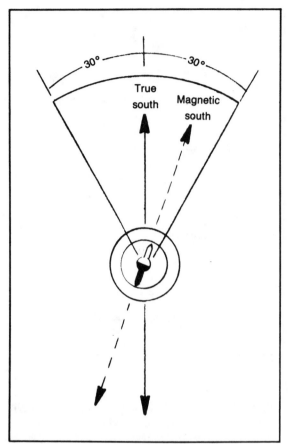

Fig. 23-2. Using a hand compass, adjusted for declination, to determine the orientation of the sunspace.

ple but effective do-it-yourself version of the sun locator can be found in the February, 1975, issue of *Popular Science* magazine.

Using the locator, determine what trees, buildings, or other obstacles might block the sunlight from the glazing. Remember that deciduous trees, although appearing as an obstacle in the summer, will lose their leaves and become less of a problem during the winter. For optimum effectiveness, the glazing should be unshaded during the months of November through February for at least 5 hours daily between 9 A.M. and 3 P.M.

VENTING

Venting must be incorporated into the room in order to allow heat to enter the house during the win-

ter, and to allow unwanted heat to escape to the outside during the summer. Venting can be accomplished through natural air movement, which is quiet and uses no energy but might not be reliable at all times; or through powered vents, which are sized to provide for all the room's ventilating needs, but which require electrical hookups and might be objectionably noisy.

When you are shopping for a fan, be certain it has good, airtight shutters or louvers, which will prevent heat loss through it when it's not in use. Also check the manufacturer's ratings for the noise level, or better yet, see if the salesperson has a sample he can plug in and let you hear.

Winter Venting

Winter venting is used to bring heat from the room into the house during the winter. In many sunspace additions, this venting is no more than the doors and windows that connect the addition to the house. One problem with this type of venting is that the doors and windows require constant monitoring by the occupants so they are closed at the right times. Also, if the sunspace has a high ceiling, much of the heat will collect up there, above the level of the doors and windows.

The alternative is a thermostatically controlled fan set in the wall between the addition and the house. This placement will ensure that the fan will come on only when sufficient heat is available to add to the main house. Control is automatic, whether you are in the house or not.

The fan should be installed at the high point of the wall, and should have airtight dampers or shutters to prevent loss from the house to the sunspace at night. Size the fan to provide 2 to 3 cubic feet of air per minute (CFM) per square foot of glazing, and set the thermostat at 80 to 85 degrees Fahrenheit.

Summer Venting

Summer venting is used to rid the sunspace of unwanted heat in the summer, so that it does not adversely affect the house. (See Fig. 23-3.) For natural ventilation, the easiest solution is to determine

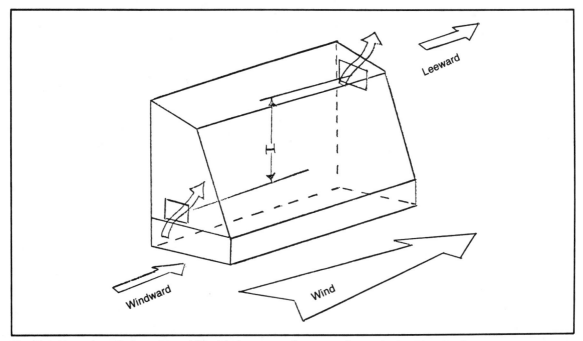

Fig. 23-3. Natural ventilation achieved through the proper placement of vents in the sidewalls (Courtesy of the Oregon State University Energy Extension Service).

the direction of the prevailing winds, then to place a screened vent low on the windward side, and one high on the leeward side. The total vent area should equal 1/6 to 1/5 of the total floor area of the addition.

If you desire, you can use fan-forced ventilation. The fan should have the capacity to exhaust the total volume of air in the space at least 8 times per hour. For example, if the sunspace was 8 feet × 12 feet with a 7-foot ceiling, it would contain 672 cubic feet of air (8 feet × 12 feet × 7 feet). You would need a fan capable of moving that volume of air out of the space 8 times each hour. The fan

would need to have a capacity of 5,376 cubic feet per hour (672 cubic feet × 8 air changes), or about 90 CFM (5,376 cubic feet per hour ÷ 60 minutes). For a greenhouse, the fan should be sized as much as 50 percent to 100 percent larger, because of the high levels of humidity that it must control.

SUNSPACE DESIGN

There are three basic designs for attached sunspaces: roofed, lean-to, and semi lean-to. (See Fig. 23-4.) Each design has some advantages and dis-

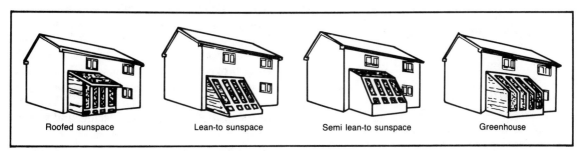

Roofed sunspace   Lean-to sunspace   Semi lean-to sunspace   Greenhouse

Fig. 23-4. Common sunspace and greenhouse configurations (Courtesy of The Oregon State University Energy Extension Service).

advantages that must be weighed.

☐ *Roofed.* A roofed sunspace uses very conventional construction details in the wall (Fig. 23-5) and roof (Fig. 23-6) framing, and uses vertical glass. (See Fig. 23-7.) Whether you are building it yourself or having it built, the construction is quite straightforward. The solid roof allows good insulation to be incorporated, and the vertical glazing is easy to shade. You can incorporate overhang into the roof lines to shade the glass against the high summer sun. This type of room also offers good headroom throughout, and the end walls provide enough room for an exit door, if needed. The only real disadvantage is that natural light is minimized by the solid roof and vertical glazing. You can compensate for this problem to some degree by using light interiors.

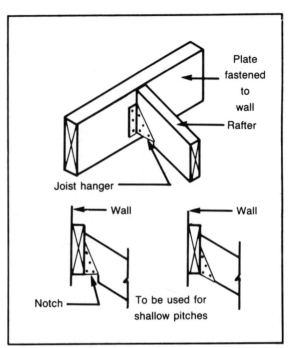

Fig. 23-6. Details of the attachments of the angled rafters to the house (Courtesy of The Oregon State University Energy Extension Service).

☐ *Lean-To.* A lean-to sunspace uses a simple design and few materials, so it is usually the cheapest to build. It provides a good amount of winter sunlight, and might be the most effective design for pure heat production. However, it has limited headroom for much of the space, and might not offer enough wall area for an exit door. The glazing is harder to fit and make leakproof, and the architectural style is difficult to blend into the existing house.

☐ *Semi Lean-To.* A semi lean-to sunspace is actually a combination of the other two styles, with angled glazing and a shortened roof. It also combines some of their advantages and disadvantages, depending on the design. The headroom is improved over the lean-to, as is the sidewall access, and the roof allows better insulation and some summer shading. The angled glass is still difficult to install, seal, and shade, and will require more cleaning than vertical glass. Again, this type of design might not fit well with the style of the existing house.

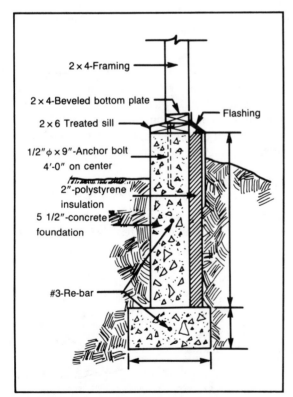

Fig. 23-5. Footing and foundation details for a sunspace. Note the exterior insulation (Courtesy of The Oregon State University Energy Extension Service).

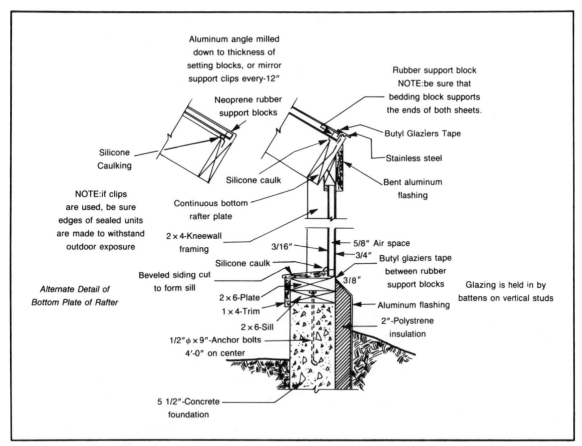

Fig. 23-7. Glazing details (Courtesy of The Oregon State University Energy Extension Service).

SUNSPACE MASS

Storage mass serves two purposes in a sunspace: it absorbs heat to prevent the space from overheating, thus minimizing the temperature swings, and it stores that heat so it can be used when the sun is not shining, whether at night or on cloudy days.

The two most common forms of solar storage mass are water and masonry, both of which will store a large amount of heat in relation to their mass. Whatever type of mass you will be using, at least part of it must be exposed to direct sunlight to really be effective. Ideally, at least half of the mass area should be exposed to the direct sunlight for at least half of the day.

You can store water in metal drums, plastic tubes, or any other container. To optimize the effectiveness of the storage, cover the containers in dark colors, such as black, dark blue, or dark green. For heat production only, provide approximately 1/2 to 1 gallon of water for each square foot of glazing.

Masonry should be medium- to high-density materials such as concrete, stone, bricks, or blocks. It can take the form of a concrete slab floor, a brick or stone back wall, or any other convenient design. Provide approximately 2/3 of a cubic foot of masonry for each square foot of glass.

GREENHOUSE DESIGN

A greenhouse makes use of both vertical and angled glazing in order to allow the maximum amount of sunlight to enter, which encourages plant growth. (See Fig. 23-4.) Headroom is good throughout al-

363

most the entire room, and the sidewalls are adequate for a door or worktable. Greenhouses usually can be constructed to blend in nicely with the existing house, and provide an interesting architectural detail.

The difficulty with constructing a greenhouse comes primarily from the joint between the vertical and angled glass. This is a difficult detail to handle correctly, and is often prone to air and water leakage. In addition, the angled overhead glazing is difficult to cover against nighttime heat loss, and summer shading is also difficult. The roof glazing must be cleaned regularly, and the large amount of glass and sophisticated joinery make cleaning it rather costly and difficult project for the do-it-yourselfer.

Several manufacturers offer complete greenhouse kits, which might be an alternative that's well worth considering. They are available in a wide range of sizes and designs to fit just about any configuration and area you're likely to encounter. Although they're definitely on the expensive side, they do solve the problem of joining all the glazing into a leakproof structure. Also, several of these types of greenhouses have built-in tracks to which screens or shades can be attached, greatly simplifying the problems of covering the overhead glazing.

GREENHOUSE MASS

For a greenhouse, where growing plants is the primary concern, the mass requirements are different from those of a heat-producing sunspace. For water storage, you'll want to provide about 3 gallons per square foot of glazing. For masonry, plan on 1 to 2 cubic feet per square foot of glass.

SUN PORCHES

You can design a sun porch to strike a happy medium between a sunspace and a greenhouse, or you simply can design it as a pleasant, warm, brightly sunny room. Many people construct this type of an addition to house a hot tub, spa, or indoor swimming pool, or just as a place for casual lawn furniture and hanging plants.

The design can take any form you desire, although a shed-roofed structure with vertical glazing is the most common. This type of design offers simple construction, good headroom, high insulation, and easy summer and nighttime shading. Take care to blend the exterior lines and materials with the existing house, so that the addition takes on the look of a planned extension of the home, not a tacked-on afterthought. You can match the interior to the existing house, but most people choose to decorate it in a completely different style. Warm, natural woods and brick or ceramic tile floors are a particularly pleasing combination.

SUN-PORCH MASS

You can incorporate storage mass into a sun porch as desired to minimize temperature swings. The ideal mass for this type of room would be 1 to 2 gallons of water or 2/3 to 1 cubic foot of masonry per square foot of south glazing.

A SIMPLE SUN PORCH

This project offers a simple, easy-to-build sun porch that blends in nicely with the existing lines of the house. (See Fig. 23-8.) The shed roof is an extension of the existing roof line, and the fully insulated floor is incorporated right into the home's existing deck (Fig. 23-9). Vertical glazing, matched to the home's existing windows, is provided on three sides, with operable windows on two opposing walls to take advantage of the prevailing summer breezes. Two wood-frame, double-glass skylights are incorporated into the roof to provide lots of natural light and to give the room a real feeling of being part of the outdoors. Factory-installed retractable shades over the skylights provide summer shading and nighttime heat-loss protection, as do adjustable blinds on the windows.

This small addition leads directly off the home's master bedroom, and with a table, chairs, and lush plants provides a warm, cozy place to enjoy the outdoor scenery on a snowy winter morning. The addition is attached directly to the existing house walls with no cutting or transitions, and access is through the existing sliding patio door. A new wood door in the addition, glazed with double glass, provides

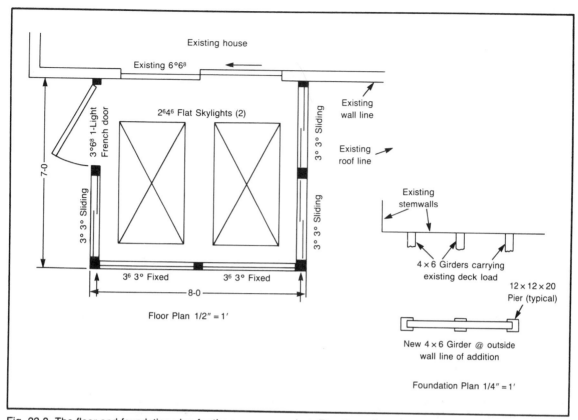

Existing house

Existing 6°6⁸

Existing wall line

2⁶4⁶ Flat Skylights (2)

3°6⁸ 1-Light French door

3° 3° Sliding

Existing roof line

3° 3° Sliding

3° 3° Sliding

7-0

3⁶ 3° Fixed   3⁶ 3° Fixed

8-0

Floor Plan 1/2″ = 1′

Existing stemwalls

4 × 6 Girders carrying existing deck load

12 × 12 × 20 Pier (typical)

New 4 × 6 Girder @ outside wall line of addition

Foundation Plan 1/4″ = 1′

Fig. 23-8. The floor and foundation plan for the sunspace project. The dimensions can be adjusted to any desired size.

Fig. 23-9. The addition is constructed directly on the existing deck.

an emergency exit from the bedroom.

The interior walls and ceiling are covered with stained 3/8-inch-thick 1- × -4 tongue-and-groove cedar strips. Clear cedar is used for the window and door trim, the skylight enclosures, and the baseboards. The existing exterior siding on the wall between the house and the addition was left in place and covered with matching cedar strips, and new cedar trim was used around the existing sliding glass door. A floor of 8-inch-square ceramic tiles completes the warm, inviting interior.

Framing the Floor

Begin by laying out the outside perimeter of the room on the existing decking boards (Fig. 23-10). Square each of the sidewalls off the house wall using the 3:4:5 method (Fig. 23-11), and measure between the walls at several points to be certain they're parallel. Lay off the back wall parallel to the house wall. Using a circular saw, carefully cut along the layout lines and remove the existing decking (Fig. 23-12). Be very careful walking on the cut edges of the decking until the floor framing is finished and new supports are installed.

Because the back wall of the addition will support the load of the new roof rafters, you must provide a bearing foundation. Using the deck cutout as a guide, plumb down to the ground at each corner, and then on 5-foot centers along the entire back wall. Excavate a 12-inch-square hole to a depth of 20 inches, or as required for the frost line in your area. Fill the holes with concrete, and allow them to set up for at least 48 hours.

Attach a 4- × -6 joist hanger to the existing deck ledger in line with each of the sidewalls (Fig. 23-13). Measuring from one side, install 2- × -6 hangers on 24-inch centers between the two 4- × -6 hangers. If the existing deck girders fall on one of the center locations, you can use them as part of the new floor system. If they don't fall on one of these locations, ignore them and maintain the 24-inch spacing.

Measure the distance from the ledger or the outside of the back wall, and cut two 4 × 6s and as many 2 × 6s as necessary to that length. Cut an additional 4 × 6 so it the same length as the width of the addition. This piece will serve as a girder to support the ends of the floor joists.

Set one end of each of the floor joists into the joist hangers, letting the other end sit on the ground

Fig. 23-10. Using strings or strips of plywood, lay out the walls of the room.

366

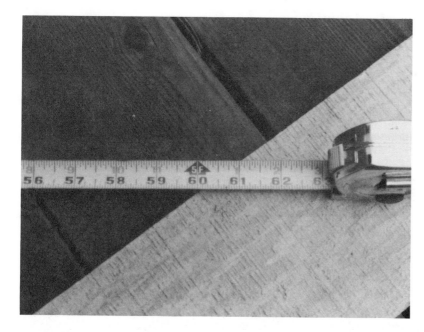

Fig. 23-11. Use the 3:4:5 method to check the wall layout for square.

under the back wall. Slip the 4-×-6 girder under the ends of the joists and center it so that it's parallel with the house wall and directly under the deck cutout.

Center a small automotive scissor jack under the girder, setting it on a block of wood (Fig. 23-14). Activate the jack to raise the girder and the ends of the joists until the tops of the joists are level with the underside of the decking. Using a hammer, tap the ends of the joists to be certain they're seated

Fig. 23-12. Using a circular saw, cut through the deck boards along the layout lines.

Fig. 23-13. Use joist hangers to secure the new joists to the existing ledger.

completely in the joists hangers. Adjust the joists so that the two outside ones are in line with the deck cutout, directly under the location where the new walls will be erected. The ends should be on 24-inch centers to match the ends in the joist hangers. Cut blocks of pressure-treated 4- × -4 lumber and place them between the girder and the concrete piers

Fig. 23-14. Using a small automotive jack, lift the main girder up under the joists.

Fig. 23-15. Place pressure-treated posts under the girder, and remove the jack.

(Fig. 23-15). The blocks should fit snugly, and be toenailed to the girder with 8d nails.

When everything is correctly in place, nail the joists to the girder and to the joist hangers, then release the jack. Finish the underfloor framing by nailing a 2 × 6 to the outside face of the two outside joists, to act as supports for the cut ends of the decking. Space the ends of the decking uniformly, and nail them to the supports with 16d galvanized nails. You might need to predrill to prevent the ends of the decking from splitting.

Insulating and Enclosing the Floor

You now will want to insulate the floor and seal it off from above and from underneath. First, install 2- × -6 blocking between the ends of the joists, and caulk around the blocks to completely seal them. Then close off the underside of the floor using 3/8-inch CDX plywood. Be sure that all the seams, both edge and end, fall over solid blocking. Add additional blocking as necessary. None of the insulation should be accessible through the seams in the plywood.

Using 24-inch R-19 fiberglass blanket insulation with the vapor barrier up, insulate between the joists. Apply a bead of construction adhesive to the tops of the joists, and install 3/4-inch CDX plywood perpendicular to the joists as subflooring. Use 8d nails to securely nail the plywood in place. At this point, the plywood should be 3/4 inch below the level of the decking.

Framing the Walls and Roof

Before you can frame the walls, you will need to determine their exact height, which is based on a projected line of the existing rafters. To establish this line, clamp a board to the underside of one of the existing rafters, carefully aligning the bottom of the board to the bottom of the rafter. Measure out horizontally from the house the inside length of the addition, and mark this point on the bottom edge of the board.

You will need to measure the ends of the existing rafters to determine how deep the bird's-mouth was cut. Transfer this measurement to the board at the level of the mark you just made, and draw in the bird's-mouth. Now measure up vertically from the subfloor to the level cut of the bird's-mouth. This measurement will be the exact wall height.

You will be using a single bottom plate and two top plates, so subtract 4 1/2 inches from the wall height measurement to determine the length of the studs. Cut and lay out the plates as described in Chapter 10, and cut the necessary number of studs and trimmers. Assemble the walls. Apply a bead of caulking to the subfloor around the perimeter, and stand the walls onto the caulking.

Nail the sidewalls to the end walls, and check that everything is square and plumb. Nail temporary braces to the deck as necessary to hold everything in place. Nail down through the bottom plates directly into the joists. Plumb the walls where they connect to the house, and nail through the last wall stud into the existing siding.

Cut the new rafters from lumber of the same dimensions as the existing rafters, so that both the top and the bottom will line up. With the assistance of a helper, hold a new rafter up against one of the existing ones, in line with the outside corner of the plates. Using the top of the plate as a guide, mark the bird's-mouth cut on the new rafter. Cut out the bird's mouth, make a plumb and level cut on the end of the rafter to match what's existing, and set the rafter in place to check the fit. If everything is correct, use the new rafter as a pattern to cut out the rest of the rafters.

In some cases, extending the new rafters out past the wall the same distance as the existing ones might make them too low, and create a situation where someone walking by on the deck could hit his head. In this case, extend the rafter tails over the outside of the plate by a distance equal to the thickness of the siding material.

Install the new rafters by nailing or bolting them to the ends of the existing rafters (Fig. 23-16). Match the spacing at the wall plate, and toenail them to the plates with 8d nails. For the skylights, determine the rough-opening size from the manufacturer's specifications, and box in the openings between the joists accordingly. Space the openings equally from side to side, and center them from front to back.

Frame up from the top of the plates to the outside rafters (Fig. 23-17), completing the gable end on each side of the addition. It might be necessary to step the framing up over the door opening, but the interior and exterior siding will hide this transition (Fig. 23-18). Install the fascia board and the two barge rafters, again matching or at least complementing what's existing. The fascia board should overlap the ends of the two barge rafters. Finally, sheathe the roof, using 1/2-inch CDX except where the underside will show; there use 1/2-inch CC plugged and sanded.

Roofing and Siding

Patch in the roofing using the same material that the existing house uses. (See Fig. 23-19.) Work up to the skylight openings (Fig. 23-20), and install and flash the skylights as per the manufacturer's instructions. (See Fig. 23-21.) Continue roofing until you reach the old roofing, and make the necessary tie-ins, as described in Chapter 12. (See Fig. 23-22.) Caulk the skylight flashing as necessary.

Fig. 23-16. Attach the new rafters directly to existing rafter tails.

Using 15-pound felt, enclose the framing from the outside. Remember to work from the bottom up, and overlap each subsequent sheet by at least 2 inches. Install the new windows and door as described in Chapter 13. Caulk behind the window flanges before you install them.

Fig. 23-17. Details of the gable end framing, barge rafter, and fascia.

Fig. 23-18. Step up the sidewall framing over the rough opening for the doorway.

Select an exterior siding material that matches the existing material as closely as possible. Stain the siding and the trim material before installation. Scribe the first piece of siding to match up against the house, making sure it is plumb. Start from the house and work out to cover each of the sidewalls, then side the back wall. Trim around the windows and doors with material that matches to the exist-

Fig. 23-19. Install new roofing, selected to match the existing, over plywood sheathing.

Fig. 23-20. Attach the skylights to the sheathing with L brackets.

ing, especially in size. Cut the corner joints in the same style that was used on the rest of the house.

Use a matching trim material to trim the area where the addition meets the deck (Fig. 23-23). The trim hides the cut edge of the decking, and makes it easier to get a good airtight seal around the outside of the siding. Use a good-quality caulking, and seal the joints where the siding meets the house,

Fig. 23-21. Use step flashings along the sides of the skylights.

Fig. 23-22. Carefully blend in the new roofing with the existing shingles.

where the trim meets the siding and deck, and around the windows and door.

Finishing the Interior

In order to bring the flooring up to the proper level, install sheets of 3/8-inch CC plugged and sanded plywood. Run the sheets perpendicular to the direction of the subflooring to provide a smooth, clean surface for the flooring, and to bring the level up to 3/8 inch below the sliding glass door. This last 3/8 inch is the thickness of the floor tile, which

Fig. 23-23. Use a trim piece of 1- x -2 cedar where the walls join the deck.

will bring the finished flooring level with the door.

Prestain the interior siding boards and any material you'll be using for trim. Starting at the back wall, begin installing the boards, working up to where the ceiling meets the existing house wall. Leave a 1/8-inch gap between the first board and the back wall, which will be covered by the wall boards. Use 5d or 6d finish nails, and drive them diagonally through the tongue.

Cover the back wall next. Scribe the first board so it meets snugly against the ceiling, then work down toward the floor. Leave a 1/2-inch gap between the bottom of the last board and the plywood floor so the tile can fit under it.

Apply the boards to the two sidewalls next, keeping the joints between the boards in line with the joints on the back wall. Do the existing house wall last. If the boards have been correctly and carefully installed, the lines of the joints should run uninterrupted around the room at the same level.

Construct two boxes of clear cedar to finish off the inside of the skylight openings. Rip the box material so that it is equal to the distance from the inside of the skylight frame to the finished surface of the ceiling. Shim the boxes into position so that they are square, and secure them to the framing with finish nails. Using the same methods and materials, box the inside of each of the window openings, also.

Trim out the interior with 1- x -3 clear cedar. Apply the trim around all of the windows, the new door, the sliding glass door, and the skylights. Leave the baseboards off until the flooring is finished.

Lay out and install the ceramic tile as described in Chapter 22. Start from the back wall and work toward the sliding glass door. Cut the tiles as necessary at the sidewalls, and slip the cut edges under the paneling boards. Let the tile dry 24 hours, then apply the grout. After the grouting is dry, wipe down the floor and install the baseboards, again using 1- x -3 clear cedar to match the rest of the trim.

Joining	Nailing Method	Nails		
		Num-ber	Size	Placement
Header to joist	End-nail	3	16d	
Joist to sill or girder	Toenail	2	10d or	
		3	8d	
Header and stringer joist to sill	Toenail		10d	16 in. on center
Bridging to joist	Toenail each end	2	8d	
Ledger strip to beam, 2 in. thick		3	16d	At each joist
Subfloor, boards:				
1 by 6 in. and smaller		2	8d	To each joist
1 by 8 in.		3	8d	To each joist
Subfloor, plywood:				
At edges			8d	6 in. on center
At intermediate joists			8d 8	
Subfloor (2 by 6 in., T&G) to joist or girder	Blind-nail (casing) and face-nail	2	16d	
Soleplate to stud, horizontal assembly	End-nail	2	16d	At each stud
Top plate to stud	End-nail	2	16d	
Stud to soleplate	Toenail	4	8d	
Soleplate to joist or blocking	Face-nail		16d	16 in. on center
Doubled studs	Face-nail, stagger		10d	16 in. on center
End stud of intersecting wall to exterior wall stud	Face-nail		16d	16 in. on center
Upper top plate to lower top plate	Face-nail		16d	16 in. on center
Upper top plate, laps and intersections	Face-nail	2	16d	
Continuous header, two pieces, each edge			12d	12 in. on center
Ceiling joist to top wall plates	Toenail	3	8d	
Ceiling joist laps at partition	Face-nail	4	16d	
Rafter to top plate	Toenail	2	8d	
Rafter to ceiling joist	Face-nail	5	10d	
Rafter to valley or hip rafter	Toenail	3	10d	
Ridge board to rafter	End-nail	3	10d	
Rafter to rafter through ridge board	Toenail	4	8d	
	Edge-nail	1	10d	
Collar beam to rafter:				
2 in. member	Face-nail	2	12d	
1 in. member	Face-nail	3	8d	
1-in. diagonal let-in brace to each stud and plate (4 nails at top)		2	8d	
Built-up corner studs:				
Studs to blocking	Face-nail	2	10d	Each side
Intersecting stud to corner studs	Face-nail		16d	12 in. on center
Built-up girders and beams, three or more members	Face-nail		20d 32	
Wall sheathing:				
1 by 8 in. or less, horizontal	Face-nail	2	8d	At each stud
1 by 6 in. or greater, diagonal	Face-nail	3	8d	At each stud
Wall sheathing, vertically applied plywood:				
3/8 in. and less thick	Face-nail		6d	6 in. edge
1/2 in. and over thick	Face-nail		8d	12 in. intermediate
Wall sheathing, vertically applied fiberboard:				
1/2 in. thick	Face-nail			1 1/2 in. roofing nail)
				3 in. edge and
25/32 in. thick	Face-nail			1

Joining	Nailing Method	Nails		
		Num-ber	Size	Placement
Roof sheathing, boards, 4-, 6-, 8-in. width	Face-nail	2	8d	At each rafter
Roof sheathing, plywood:				
3/8 in. and less thick	Face-nail		6d	
1/2 in. and over thick	Face-nail		8d 6	

Product	Description	Nominal Size		Dressed Dimensions		
				Thicknesses and Widths In.		
		Thickness In.	Width In.	Surfaced Dry	Surfaced Unseasoned	Lengths Ft.
DIMENSION	S4S . . . . Other surface combinations are available. See "Abbreviations" below.	2 3 4	2 3 4 5 6 8 10 12 Over 12	1$^1/_2$ 2$^1/_2$ 3$^1/_2$ 4$^1/_2$ 5$^1/_2$ 7$^1/_4$ 9$^1/_4$ 11$^1/_4$ Off $^3/_4$	1$^9/_{16}$ 2$^9/_{16}$ 3$^9/_{16}$ 4$^5/_8$ 5$^5/_8$ 7$^1/_2$ 9$^1/_2$ 11$^1/_2$ Off $^1/_2$	6' and longer in multiples of 1'
SCAFFOLD PLANK	Rough Full Sawn or S4S . . . . (Usually shipped unseasoned)	1$^1/_4$ & Thicker	8 and Wider	If Dressed refer to "DIMENSION" sizes.		6' and longer in multiples of 1'
TIMBERS	Rough or S4S . . . . (Shipped unseasoned)	5 and Larger		Thickness In. Width In. $^1/_2$ Off Nominal (S4S) See 3.20 of WWPA Grading Rules for Rough.		6' and longer in multiples of 1'

Product	Description	Nominal Size		Dressed Dimensions (Dry)		
		Thickness In.	Width In.	Thickness In.	Face Width In.	Lengths Ft.
DECKING	2" (Single T&G)	2	5 6 8 10 12	1$^1/_2$	4 5 6$^3/_4$ 8$^3/_4$ 10$^3/_4$	6' and longer in multiples of 1'
	3" and 4" (Double T&G)	3 4	6	2$^1/_2$ 3$^1/_2$	5$^1/_4$	
FLOORING	(D&M), (S2S & CM)	$^3/_8$ $^1/_2$ $^5/_8$ 1 1$^1/_4$ 1$^1/_2$	2 3 4 5 6	$^5/_{16}$ $^7/_{16}$ $^9/_{16}$ $^3/_4$ 1 1$^1/_4$	1$^1/_8$ 2$^1/_8$ 3$^1/_8$ 4$^1/_8$ 5$^1/_8$	4' and longer in multiples of 1'
CEILING AND PARTITION	(S2S & CM)	$^3/_8$ $^1/_2$ $^5/_8$ $^3/_4$	3 4 5 6	$^5/_{16}$ $^7/_{16}$ $^9/_{16}$ $^{11}/_{16}$	2$^1/_8$ 3$^1/_8$ 4$^1/_8$ 5$^1/_8$	4' and longer in multiples of 1'
FACTORY AND SHOP LUMBER	S2S	1 (4/4) 1$^1/_4$ (5/4) 1$^1/_2$ (6/4) 1$^3/_4$ (7/4) 2 (8/4) 2$^1/_2$ (10/4) 3 (12/4) 4 (16/4)	5 and wider except (4" and wider in 4/4 No. 1 Shop and 4/4 No. 2 Shop)	$^3/_4$ (4/4) 1$^5/_{32}$ (5/4) 1$^{13}/_{32}$ (6/4) 1$^{19}/_{32}$ (7/4) 1$^{13}/_{16}$ (8/4) 2$^3/_8$ (10/4) 2$^3/_4$ (12/4) 3$^3/_4$ (16/4)	Usually sold random width	4' and longer in multiples of 1'

ABBREVIATIONS

Abbreviated descriptions appearing in the size table are explained below.
S1S—Surfaced one side.
S2S—Surfaced two sides.

S4S—Surfaced four sides.
S1S1E—Surfaced one side, one edge.
S1S2E—Surfaced one side, two edges.
CM—Center matched.

D&M—Dressed and matched.
T&G—Tongue and grooved.
Rough Full Sawn—Unsurfaced lumber cut to full specified size.

(Courtesy of Western Wood Products Association)

Product	Description	Nominal Size		Dry Dressed Dimensions		
		Thickness In.	Width In.	Thickness In.	Width In.	Lengths Ft.
SELECTS AND COMMONS	S1S, S2S, S4S, S1S1E, S1S2E	4/4 5/4 6/4 7/4 8/4 9/4 10/4 11/4 12/4 16/4	2 3 4 5 6 7 8 and wider	$3/4$ $1 5/32$ $1 13/32$ $1 19/32$ $1 13/16$ $2 3/32$ $2 3/8$ $2 9/16$ $2 3/4$ $3 3/4$	$1 1/2$ $2 1/2$ $3 1/2$ $4 1/2$ $5 1/2$ $6 1/2$ $3/4$ Off nominal	6' and longer in multiples of 1' except Douglas Fir and Larch Selects shall be 4' and longer with 3% of 4' and 5' permitted.
FINISH AND BOARDS	S1S, S2S, S4S, S1S1E, S1S2E Only these sizes apply to Alternate Board Grades	$3/8$ $1/2$ $5/8$ $3/4$ 1 $1 1/4$ $1 1/2$ $1 3/4$ 2 $2 1/2$ 3 $3 1/2$ 4	2 3 4 5 6 7 8 and wider	$5/16$ $7/16$ $9/16$ $5/8$ $3/4$ 1 $1 1/4$ $1 3/8$ $1 1/2$ 2 $2 1/2$ 3 $3 1/2$	$1 1/2$ $2 1/2$ $3 1/2$ $4 1/2$ $5 1/2$ $6 1/2$ $3/4$ Off nominal	3' and longer. In Superior grade, 3% of 3' and 4' and 7% of 5' and 6' are permitted. In Prime Grade, 20% of 3' to 6' is permitted.
RUSTIC AND DROP SIDING	(D&M) . . . . If $3/8$'' or $1/2$'' T&G specified, same over-all widths apply. (Shiplapped, $3/8$'' or $1/2$'' lap).	1	6 8 10 12	$23/32$	$5 3/8$ $7 1/8$ $9 1/8$ $11 1/8$	4' and longer in multiples of 1'
PANELING AND SIDING	T&G or Shiplap	1	6 8 10 12	$23/32$	$5 7/16$ $7 1/8$ $9 1/8$ $11 1/8$	4' and longer in multiples of 1'
CEILING AND PARTITION	T&G.	$5/8$ 1	4 6	$9/16$ $23/32$	$3 3/8$ $5 3/8$	4' and longer in multiples of 1'
BEVEL SIDING	Bevel or Bungalow Siding . . . . . . Western Red Cedar Bevel Siding available in $1/2$'' $5/8$'' $3/4$'' nominal thickness. Corresponding thick edge is $15/32$'' $9/16$'' and $3/4$'' Widths for 8'' and wider, $1/2$'' off nominal	$1/2$ $3/4$	4 5 6 8 10 12	$15/32$ butt, $3/16$ tip $3/4$ butt, $3/16$ tip	$3 1/2$ $4 1/2$ $5 1/2$ $7 1/4$ $9 1/4$ $11 1/4$	3' and longer in multiples of 1' 3' and longer in multiples of 1'

				Surfaced		Surfaced		
				Dry	Green	Dry	Green	
STRESS-RATED BOARDS	S1S, S2S, S4S, S1S1E, S1S2E	1 $1 1/4$ $1 1/2$	2 3 4 5 6 7 8 and Wider	$3/4$ 1 $1 1/4$	$25/32$ $1 1/32$ $1 9/32$	$1 1/2$ $2 1/2$ $3 1/2$ $4 1/2$ $5 1/2$ $6 1/2$ Off $3/4$	$1 9/16$ $2 9/16$ $3 9/16$ $4 5/8$ $5 5/8$ $6 5/8$ Off $1/2$	6' and longer in multiples of 1'

MINIMUM ROUGH SIZES. Thickness and Widths, Dry or Unseasoned, All Lumber
80% of the pieces in a shipment shall be at least $1/8$'' thicker than the standard surfaced size, the remaining 20% at least $3/32$'' thicker than the surfaced size. Widths shall be at least $1/8$'' wider than standard surfaced widths.

When specified to be full sawn, lumber may not be manufactured to a size less than the size specified.

NOMINAL SIZE OF PIECE	BOARD FEET CONTENT WHEN LENGTH IN FEET EQUALS											
	2	4	6	8	10	12	14	16	18	20	22	24
1 x 2	1/3	2/3	1	1 1/3	1 2/3	2	2 1/3	2 2/3	3	3 1/3	3 2/3	4
1 x 3	1/2	1	1 1/2	2	2 1/2	3	3 1/2	4	4 1/2	5	5 1/2	6
1 x 4	2/3	1 1/3	2	2 2/3	3 1/3	4	4 2/3	5 1/3	6	6 2/3	7 1/3	8
1 x 6	1	2	3	4	5	6	7	8	9	10	11	12
1 x 8	1 1/3	2 2/3	4	5 1/3	6 2/3	8	9 1/3	10 2/3	12	13 1/3	14 2/3	16
1 x 10	1 2/3	3 1/3	5	6 2/3	8 1/3	10	11 2/3	13 1/3	15	16 2/3	18 1/3	20
1 x 12	2	4	6	8	10	12	14	16	18	20	22	24
2 x 2	2/3	1 1/3	2	2 2/3	3 1/3	4	4 2/3	5 1/3	6	6 2/3	7 1/3	8
2 x 3	1	2	3	4	5	6	7	8	9	10	11	12
2 x 4	1 1/3	2 2/3	4	5 1/3	6 2/3	8	9 1/3	10 2/3	12	13 1/3	14 2/3	16
2 x 6	2	4	6	8	10	12	14	16	18	20	22	24
2 x 8	2 2/3	5 1/3	8	10 2/3	13 1/3	16	18 2/3	21 1/3	24	26 2/3	29 1/3	32
2 x 10	3 1/3	6 2/3	10	13 1/3	16 2/3	20	23 1/3	26 2/3	30	33 1/3	36 2/3	40
2 x 12	4	8	12	16	20	24	28	32	36	40	44	48
2 x 14	4 2/3	9 1/3	14	18 2/3	23 1/3	28	32 2/3	37 1/3	42	46 2/3	51 1/3	56
3 x 4	2	4	6	8	10	12	14	16	18	20	22	24
3 x 6	3	6	9	12	15	18	21	24	27	30	33	36
3 x 8	4	8	12	16	20	24	28	32	36	40	44	48
3 x 10	5	10	15	20	25	30	35	40	45	50	55	60
3 x 12	6	12	18	24	30	36	42	48	54	60	66	72
3 x 14	7	14	21	28	35	42	49	56	63	70	77	84
3 x 16	8	16	24	32	40	48	56	64	72	80	88	96
4 x 4	2 2/3	5 1/3	8	10 2/3	13 1/3	16	18 2/3	21 1/3	24	26 2/3	29 1/3	32
4 x 6	4	8	12	16	20	24	28	32	36	40	44	48
4 x 8	5 1/3	10 2/3	16	21 1/3	26 2/3	32	37 1/3	42 2/3	48	53 1/3	58 2/3	64
4 x 10	6 2/3	13 1/3	20	26 2/3	33 1/3	40	46 2/3	53 1/3	60	66 2/3	73 1/3	80
4 x 12	8	16	24	32	40	48	56	64	72	80	88	96
4 x 14	9 1/3	18 2/3	28	37 1/3	46 2/3	56	65 1/3	74 2/3	84	93 1/3	102 2/3	112
4 x 16	10 2/3	21 1/3	32	42 2/3	53 1/3	64	74 2/3	85 1/3	96	106 2/3	117 1/3	128
6 x 6	6	12	18	24	30	36	42	48	54	60	66	72
6 x 8	8	16	24	32	40	48	56	64	72	80	88	96
6 x 10	10	20	30	40	50	60	70	80	90	100	110	120
6 x 12	12	24	36	48	60	72	84	96	108	120	132	144
6 x 14	14	28	42	56	70	84	98	112	126	140	154	168
6 x 16	16	32	48	64	80	96	112	128	144	160	176	192
6 x 18	18	36	54	72	90	108	126	144	162	180	198	216
6 x 20	20	40	60	80	100	120	140	160	180	200	220	240
6 x 22	22	44	66	88	110	132	154	176	198	220	242	264
6 x 24	24	48	72	96	120	144	168	192	216	240	264	288
8 x 8	10 2/3	21 1/3	32	42 2/3	53 1/3	64	74 2/3	85 1/3	96	106 2/3	117 1/3	128
8 x 10	13 1/3	26 2/3	40	53 1/3	66 2/3	80	93 1/3	106 2/3	120	133 1/3	146 2/3	160
8 x 12	16	32	48	64	80	96	112	128	144	160	176	192
8 x 14	18 2/3	37 1/3	56	74 2/3	93 1/3	112	130 2/3	149 1/3	168	186 2/3	205 1/3	224
8 x 16	21 1/3	42 2/3	64	85 1/3	106 2/3	128	149 1/3	170 2/3	192	213 1/3	234 2/3	256
8 x 18	24	48	72	96	120	144	168	192	216	240	264	288
8 x 20	26 2/3	53 1/3	80	106 2/3	133 1/3	160	186 2/3	213 1/3	240	266 2/3	293 1/3	320
8 x 22	29 1/3	58 2/3	88	117 1/3	146 2/3	176	205 1/3	234 2/3	264	293 1/3	322 2/3	352
8 x 24	32	64	96	128	160	192	224	256	288	320	352	384
10 x 10	16 2/3	33 1/3	50	66 2/3	83 1/3	100	116 2/3	133 1/3	150	166 2/3	183 1/3	200
10 x 12	20	40	60	80	100	120	140	160	180	200	220	240
10 x 14	23 1/3	46 2/3	70	93 1/3	116 2/3	140	163 1/3	186 2/3	210	233 1/3	256 2/3	280
10 x 16	26 2/3	53 1/3	80	106 2/3	133 1/3	160	186 2/3	213 1/3	240	266 2/3	293 1/3	320
10 x 18	30	60	90	120	150	180	210	240	270	300	330	360
10 x 20	33 1/3	66 2/3	100	133 1/3	166 2/3	200	233 1/3	266 2/3	300	333 1/3	366 2/3	400
10 x 22	36 2/3	73 1/3	110	146 2/3	183 1/3	220	256 2/3	293 1/3	330	366 2/3	403 1/3	440
10 x 24	40	80	120	160	200	240	280	320	360	400	440	480

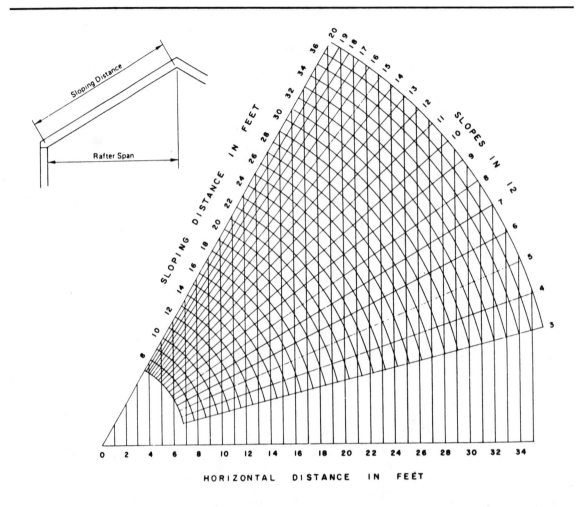

HORIZONTAL   DISTANCE   IN   FEÉT

To use the diagram select the known horizontal distance and follow the vertical line to its intersection with the radial line of the specified slope, then proceed along the arc to read the sloping distance. In some cases it may be desirable to interpolate between the one foot separations. The diagram also may be used to find the horizontal distance corresponding to a given sloping distance or to find the slope when the horizontal distances are known.

Example: With a roof slope of 8 in 12 and a horizontal distance of 20 feet the sloping distance may be read as 24 feet.

(Courtesy of the National Forest Products Association, Washington, DC)

Air
Heat Flow Up:

Air film (still air, inside wall)	0.61
3/4″ space	0.77
3 1/2″ space	0.84

Heat Flow Down:

Air film (still air, inside wall)	0.92
3/4″ space	1.02
3 1/2″ space	1.22

Heat Flow Horizontal:

Air film (still air, inside wall)	0.68
3/4″ space	0.94
3 1/2″ space	0.91
Outside air film, 7.5 mph wind	0.25
Outside air film, 15 mph wind	0.17

Building Boards

Asbestos cement board, per inch	0.25
Asbestos cement board, 1/4″	0.07
Drywall, 3/8″	0.32
Drywall, 1/2″	0.45
Insulating board, 1/2″ drop-in ceiling tiles	1.25
Insulating board, 1/2″ sheathing	1.32
Hardboard, tempered, per inch	1.00
Particleboard, medium density, per inch	1.06
Particleboard, 5/8″ underlayment	0.82
Plywood, per inch	1.25
Plywood, 1/4″	0.31
Plywood, 3/8″	0.47
Plywood, 1/2″	0.63
Wood sheathing, plywood or wood panels, 3/4″	0.98

Flooring

Asphalt tile, 3/16″	0.04
Carpet and fiber pad	2.08
Carpet and rubber pad	1.23
Ceramic tile, 1/4″	0.04
Cork tile, 0/88	
Linoleum	0.08
Hardwood strips, 5/8″	0.68

Masonry

Brick, per inch	0.20
Cement mortar, per inch	0.20
Concrete, per inch	0.08
Concrete blocks, 8″	1.00
Gypsum plaster, perlite aggregate, per inch	0.67
Gypsum plaster, sand aggregate, per inch	0.18
Limestone or sandstone, per inch	0.08
Pumic blocks, 8″	2.00
Stucco, per inch	0.20

Paper

Felt building paper	0.06
Felt flooring paper	0.06

Roofing

Asbestos-cement shingles	0.21
Asphalt roll roofing	0.15
Asphalt shingles	0.44
Built-up roofing, 3/8″	0.33
Slate shingles, 1/2″	0.05

Wood shingles	0.94
Siding	
Aluminum or steel, hollow back	0.61
Asbestos-cement shingles	0.21
Asbestos roll	0.15
Wood, bevel siding, 1/2" × 8", lapped	0.81
Wood, bevel siding, 3/4" × 10", lapped	1.05
Wood, drop siding, 1" × 8"	0.79
Wood, plywood, 3/8"	0.59
Wood siding shingles, 7 1/2" exposure	0.87
Thermal Insulation	
Batts:	
Fiberglass, per inch	3.20
Mineral wool, per inch	3.50
Loose Fill:	
Cellulose, per inch	3.70
Fiberglass, per inch	2.20
Mineral wool	3.00
Perlite, expanded, per inch	2.70
Vermiculite, expanded, per inch	2.20
Wood shavings, per inch	2.20
Rigid:	
Polystyrene, expanded bead board, per inch	3.57
Polystyrene, extruded board, per inch	5.26
Polyurethane foam, per inch	6.25
Urea-formaldehyde foam, per inch	4.17
Wall Sections	
Standard frame wall, insulated	14.29
Standard frame wall, uninsulated	4.35
Windows	
Architectural glass	0.10
Double glass window, 1/4" air space	1.59
Double glass window, 1/2" air space	1.75
Single glass window	0.91
Single glass window, with storm, 1" to 4" air space	1.82
Wood	
Hardwood, per inch	0.91
Softwood, per inch	1.25
Softwood, 1 1/2"	1.89
Softwood, 3 1/2"	4.35

Grit Number	O Series Number	Abrasive Properties
600	—	Super Fine
500	—	Super Fine
400	10/0	Super Fine
360	—	Super Fine
320	9/0	Super Fine
280	8/0	Very Fine
240	7/0	Very Fine
220*	6/0	Very Fine

*(Grit usually supplied when paper is simply called "very fine")

180	5/0	Fine
150*	4/0	Fine

*(Grit usually supplied when paper is simply called "fine")

120	3/0	Medium
100*	2/0	Medium

*(Grit usually supplied when paper is simply called "medium")

80	1/0	Medium
60*	1/2	Coarse

*(Grit usually supplied when paper is simply called "coarse")

50	1	Coarse
40	1 1/2	Coarse
36	2	Very Coarse
30	2 1/2	Very Coarse
24	3	Very Coarse

Index

tile,
  ceramic floor, 343
  ceramic wall, 339
  vinyl asbestos floor, 350
tile roofing, 160
timber connectors, 57
tongue-and-groove wood siding, 205
tools, 59
top chords, 146
top flange hanger, 58
top plate, 113
transit, 85
trap, 225
trap seal, 225
trimmers, 105, 113
trusses,
  floor, 109
  roof, 146

U

underfloor framing, 100
underlayment, 161

V

vapor barriers, 92, 271
variances, 36
vent baffle, 276
vent flashing, 169
vent pipes, 227
ventilation,
  attic, 152

roof, 152
vinyl asbestos floor tile, 350
volt, 237

W

wall cabinets, 324
wall forms, 86
wall framing, 113
  assembly of, 118
  bay and bow window, 197
  blocking of, 122
  bracing for, 120
  components of, 113
  corners and intersections in, 115
  cost estimation for, 30
  doubling top plates in, 122
  erecting the wall during, 119
  insulation in, 278
  layout of, 116
  lumber sizes for, 114
  openings in, 115
  partition walls, 122
  plate layout of, 118
  platform, 113
  stud spacing in, 115
  techniques in, 115
wall-to-wall carpeting, 357
wallpaper, 334
waste lines, 225
water lines, 229
watt, 237

weight-bearing wall, 65
whole-house fans, 266
windows
  casing and trim for, 314
  energy-efficient, 194
  finishes used on, 192
  installation of, 195
  materials used in, 192
  multiple glazing in, 195
  recycling, 64
  styles of, 190
wiring, 239, 247
wood shingles, 159
  flashing for, 176
  hips and ridges in, 176
  installation of, 172
  valleys in, 175
wood stoves, 261, 265
wooden siding
  installation of, 205
  styles of, 203
  transitions in, 207
  types of, 205
woodworking, 307

Y

yard lumber, 52

Z

zone cooling and heating, 260
zoning variance, 37

Edited by Suzanne L. Cheatle

Other Bestsellers From TAB

☐ **HOME PLUMBING MADE EASY: AN ILLUSTRATED MANUAL—James L. Kittle**

Here, in one heavily illustrated, easy-to-follow volume, is all the how-to-do-it information needed to perform almost any home plumbing job, including both water and waste disposal systems. And what makes this guide superior to so many other plumbing books is the fact that it's written by a professional plumber with many years of practical working experience. That means plenty of hands-on instruction, meaningful advice, practical safety tips, and emphasis on getting the job done as easily and professionally as possible! Whether you want to learn something about household plumbing so you can save time and money next time a problem occurs, or you're thinking of making major plumbing or septic additions or repairs to your home, this completely up-to-date sourcebook is the right place to start! 272 pp., 250 illus., 7" × 10".

Paper $14.95   **Hard $24.95**
Book No. 2797

☐ **THE BUILDING PLAN BOOK: Complete Plans for 21 Affordable Homes—Ernie Bryant**

Here, in one impressive, well-illustrated volume, are complete building plans for a total of 21 custom-designed homes offering a full range of styles and features—efficiency dwellings, ranches, capes, two-story homes, split-levels, even duplexes. It's a collection of practical, good looking home designs that not only offer comfort, convenience, and charm but can be built at a reasonable cost. 352 pp., 316 illus., 8 1/2" × 11".

Paper $14.95   **Hard $24.95**
Book No. 2714

☐ **79 FURNITURE PROJECTS FOR EVERY ROOM—Percy W. Blandford**

Just imagine your entire home filled with beautiful, handcrafted furniture! Elegant chairs, tables, and sofas, a hand-finished corner cupboard, luxurious beds and chests, and more! With the hands-on instructions and step-by-step project plans included here, you'll be able to build beautiful furniture for any room . . . or every room in your home . . . at a fraction of the store-bought cost! 384 pp., 292 illus., 7" × 10".

Paper $16.95   **Hard $24.95**
Book No. 2704

☐ **101 PROJECTS, PLANS AND IDEAS FOR THE HIGH-TECH HOUSEHOLD—Julie Knott and Dave Prochnow**

If you're looking for decorative effects, you'll be impressed with the number of projects that have been included. Electronics hobbyists will be amazed at the array of projects included here—all of them with clear building instructions, schematics, and construction drawings. And you'll find exciting ways to use a microcomputer as a key decorative element in your high-tech atmosphere. 357 pp., 176 illus., 7" × 10".

Paper $16.95   **Book No. 2642**

☐ **33 *USEFUL* PROJECTS FOR THE WOODWORKER—*School Shop Magazine***

A wealth of information for beginning and advanced hobbyists . . . tools, techniques, and dozens of exciting projects. Here's a handbook that deserves a permanent spot on every woodworker's tool bench. Packed with show-how illustrations and material lists, this invaluable guide provides you with a wide variety of useful, and fun-to-make woodworking projects: a spice rack, a wall clock, a plant stand, a cutting board, a wooden chest, a magazine rack, a serving cart, a child's playhouse, and more! 160 pp., 280 illus., 7" × 10".

Paper $12.95   **Hard $19.95**
Book No. 2783

☐ **THE COMPLETE BOOK OF BATHROOMS—Judy and Dan Ramsey and Charles Self**

Simple redecorating tricks . . . remodeling advice . . . plumbing techniques . . . it's all here. Find literally hundreds of photographs, drawings, and floorplans to help you decide exactly what kind of remodeling project you'd like to undertake; plus, step-by-step directions for accomplishing your remodeling goals. It's all designed to save you time and money on your bathroom renovations! 368 pp., 474 illus., 7" × 10".

Paper $15.95   **Book No. 2708**

☐ **ROOFING THE RIGHT WAY—A Step-by-Step Guide for the Homeowner—Steven Bolt**

If you're faced with having to replace your roof because of hidden leaks, torn or missing shingles, or simply worn roofing that makes your whole house look shabby and run down . . . don't assume that you'll have to take out another mortgage to pay for the project. The fact is, *almost anyone can install a new or replacement roof easily and at amazingly low cost compared with professional contractor prices!* All the professional techniques and step-by-step guidance you'll need is here in this complete new roofing manual written by an experienced roofing contractor. 192 pp., 217 illus., 7" × 10.

Paper $11.95   **Hard $19.95**
Book No. 2667

☐ **68 FAMILY HANDYMAN® WOOD PROJECTS**

Here are 66 practical, imaginative, and decorative projects . . . literally something for every home and every woodworking skill level from novice to advanced cabinetmaker! You'll find complete step-by-step plans for room dividers, a free-standing corner bench, china/book cabinets, coffee tables, desk and storage units, a built-in sewing center, even your own Shaker furniture reproductions! 210 pp., 306 illus., 7" × 10".

Paper $14.95   **Book No. 2632**

Other Bestsellers From TAB